Communications
in Computer and Information Science 3

Joaquim Filipe   Helder Coelhas
Monica Saramago (Eds.)

E-business and Telecommunication Networks

Second International Conference, ICETE 2005
Reading, UK, October 3-7, 2005
Selected Papers

Volume Editors

Joaquim Filipe
Helder Coelhas
Monica Saramago
INSTICC
Av. D. Manuel I, 27A - 2. Esq.
2910-595 Setúbal, Portugal
E-mail: j.filipe@est.ips.pt
{helder,monica}@insticc.org

Library of Congress Control Number: 2007938213

CR Subject Classification (1998): K.4.4, D.4.6, C.2

ISSN 1865-0929

ISBN 978-3-540-75992-8 Springer Berlin Heidelberg New York

Springer is a part of Springer Science+Business Media

springer.com

© Springer-Verlag Berlin Heidelberg 2007

Typesetting: Camera-ready by author, data conversion by Scientific Publishing Services, Chennai, India
Printed on acid-free paper   SPIN: 12179596   06/3180   5 4 3 2 1 0

Preface

This book contains the best papers of the Second *International Conference on E-business and Telecommunication Networks (ICETE)*, which was held, in 2005, at the Microsoft Research Centre - Reading, in the UK. The conference was organized by INSTICC (*Institute for Systems and Technologies of Information, Communication and Control*) in collaboration with the University of Westminster/WITRC, UK.

ICETE reflects a continuing effort to increase the exchange of expertise among professionals who work in the fields of e-business and telecommunication networks, including aspects related to security, wireless systems, signal processing, and all sorts of applications, who are bringing new services and technologies into the lives of ordinary consumers. The major goal of this conference was thus to bring together researchers and developers from academia and industry working in areas related to e-business to stimulate a debate with a special focus on telecommunication networks.

Four simultaneous tracks were held, covering different aspects, namely: *"Global Communication Information Systems and Services"*, *"Security and Reliability in Information Systems and Networks"*, *"Wireless Communication Systems and Networks"* and *"Multimedia Signal Processing"*. Each of these tracks appealed to a global audience of engineers, scientists, business people and policy experts, interested in the research topics of ICETE. All tracks focused on specific topics of research and real world applications and relied on contributions from industry, with different solutions for end-user applications and enabling technologies, in a diversity of communication environments. The papers accepted and presented at the conference demonstrated a number of new and innovative solutions for e-business and telecommunication networks, showing that the technical problems in both fields are challenging and worthwhile.

The conference received 151 paper submissions in total, with contributions from 38 different countries, from all continents, which really shows the global dimension of the conference. To evaluate each submission, a double blind paper evaluation method was used: each paper was reviewed by at least two internationally known experts from our Program Committee. In the end, 85 papers were selected for oral presentation and publication in the proceedings, corresponding to a 56% acceptance ratio. Then, a short list including only the very best and most significant papers was selected to appear in this book.

We hope that you will find these papers interesting and that they will prove a helpful reference in the future for all those who need to address the areas of e-business and telecommunication networks.

June 2007   Joaquim Filipe

Conference Committees

Conference Chair

Joaquim Filipe, Polytechnic Institute of Setúbal / INSTICC, Portugal

Organizing Committee

Paulo Brito, INSTICC, Portugal
Helder Coelhas, INSTICC, Portugal
Bruno Encarnação, INSTICC, Portugal
Vitor Pedrosa, INSTICC, Portugal
Mónica Saramago, INSTICC, Portugal

Program Committee

Arup Acharya, USA
Ralf Ackermann, Germany
Rui Aguiar, Portugal
Khalid Al-Begain, UK
Colin Allison, UK
Salah Al-Sharhan, Kuwait
Jörn Altmann, Germany
Abbes Amira, UK
Lachlan Andrew, Australia
Nirwan Ansari, USA
Pedro Assunção, Portugal
Hakim Badis, France
Nicholas Bambos, USA
Balbir Barn, UK
Anthony Bedford, Australia
Giampaolo Bella, Italy
Luis Bernardo, Portugal
Fernando Boavida, Portugal
David Bonyuet, USA
Mohammed Boulmalf, UAE

Raouf Boutaba, Canada
Rahmat Budiarto, Malaysia
Ryszard S. Choraś, Poland
Roy Campbell, USA
Xiaojun Cao, USA
Vito Cappellini, Italy
Mihaela Cardei, USA
Claudio Casetti, Italy
Erdal Cayirci, Turkey
Surendar Chandra, USA
Chung-Kuo Chang, USA
Lap-Pui Chau, Singapore
Chang Wen Chen, USA
Xiaodong Chen, UK
Soumaya Cherkaoui, Canada
Kwok Wai Cheung, China
Tibor Cinkler, Hungary
Rodney Clarke, UK
Alexander Clemm, USA
Reuven Cohen, Israel

Rui Valadas, Portugal
Bartel Van de Walle, The Netherlands
Cesar Vargas-Rosales, Mexico
Emmanouel (Manos) Varvarigos,
    Greece
Enrique Vazquez, Spain
Aníbal Figueiras-Vidal, Spain
Yu Wang, USA
Hans Weghorn, Germany
Robert Weigel, Germany
Susanne Wetzel, USA
Erik Wilde, Switzerland
Andreas Wombacher,
    The Netherlands
Kainam Thomas Wong, Canada
Hongyi Wu, USA

Jim Wu, Australia
Chunsheng Xin, USA
Alec Yasinsac, USA
Bulent Yener, USA
Boon Sain Yeo, Singapore
Qinghe Yin, Singapore
Hee Yong Youn, Republic of Korea
Chan Yu, USA
Weider Yu, USA
Soe-Tsyr Yuan, Taiwan
Lisandro Zambenedetti Granville,
    Brazil
Gergely Zaruba, USA
Ty Znati, USA
Alf Zugenmaier, UK

Invited Speakers

Mohammad S. Obaidat, Monmouth University, NJ, USA
Yin-Leng Theng, Nanyang Technological University, Singapore
David Wood, Symbian, UK
Susanne Wetzel, Stevens Institute of Technology, USA
Mark d'Inverno, University of Westminster, UK
Paulo T. de Sousa, European Commission, Belgium
Rohit Dhamankar, Manager of Security Research, USA

Table of Contents

Part III: Wireless Communication Systems and Networks

Part IV: Multimedia Signal Processing

Part I

Global Communication Information Systems and Services

Sharing Service Resource Information for Application Integration in a Virtual Enterprise – Modeling the Communication Protocol for Exchanging Service Resource Information

Hiroshi Yamada and Akira Kawaguchi

NTT Service Integration Laboratories, 9-11, Midori-Cho, 3-Chome, Musashino-Shi,
Tokyo, 180-8585, Japan
yamada.hiroshi@lab.ntt.co.jp, akira.kawaguchi@lab.ntt.co.jp

Abstract. Grid computing and web service technologies enable us to use networked resources in a coordinated manner. An integrated service is made of individual services running on coordinated resources. In order to achieve such coordinated services autonomously, the initiator of a coordinated service needs to know detailed service resource information. This information ranges from static attributes like the IP address of the application server to highly dynamic ones like the CPU load. The most famous wide-area service discovery mechanism based on names is DNS. Its hierarchical tree organization and caching methods take advantage of the static information managed. However, in order to integrate business applications in a virtual enterprise, we need a discovery mechanism to search for the optimal resources based on the given a set of criteria (search keys). In this paper, we propose a communication protocol for exchanging service resource information among wide-area systems. We introduce the concept of the service domain that consists of service providers managed under the same management policy. This concept of the service domain is similar to that for autonomous systems (ASs). In each service domain, the service information provider manages the service resource information of service providers that exist in this service domain. The service resource information provider exchanges this information with other service resource information providers that belong to the different service domains. We also verified the protocol's behavior and effectiveness using a simulation model developed for proposed protocol.

Keywords: Resource sharing, Protocol modeling, Business integration, EAI, Grid computing, Web service.

1 Introduction

Integrated services using grid and web service technologies are increasing. Using these technologies, we can orchestrate several business applications and share more resources in the network autonomously. In an enterprise or a virtual enterprise, EAI (enterprise application integration) tools are used to integrate several applications and

J. Filipe et al. (Eds.): ICETE 2005, CCIS 3, pp. 3–14, 2007.

resources in the enterprise network. This service architecture needs to define mechanisms for creating, naming, and discovering transient service instances. In addition, it also needs to provide location transparency and multiple protocols for binding a service instance. That is the initiator of the integrated service or resource-sharing service has to be able to answer questions such as: "which server is the target application with the name "A" running on", "which server has sufficient CPU power to deal with our request", and "which server has the lighted load?.""

In the above architecture, the information service should be designed to support the initial discovery and ongoing monitoring of the existence and characteristics of resources, services, computations, and other things. Hereafter, we call these characteristics service resource information (SRI). Some SRI may be static and long-lived while other service information may be highly dynamic. For example, computation specifications like CPU power, operating system name, and memory size are static SRI, but the CPU load of the application server is highly dynamic SRI.

The most successful and famous wide-area service resource discovery mechanism is the domain name service (DNS). This is based on server names. Its hierarchical tree-like organization and caching methods take advantage of rather static information like names. However in grid computing and web service environments, the initiator of the integrated services requires specific sets of service information attributes, for example, the application name, and required operating system in order to provide the optimum service quality. The scheduling policy engine can calculate and determine the appropriate set of required service resources using the SRI obtained by the discovery mechanism. In particular, dynamic service resource information like CPU load is one of the important parameters. Unlike the discovery mechanism using static service resource information, the search mechanism using dynamic SRI can benefit from a certain degree of approximation. For example, such a discovery mechanism can search for the server whose CPU load is less than 30% or idle disk space is larger than 6MB.

This paper is organized as follows. Related work about discovery of SRI is summarized in Section 2. Several concepts that define the architecture for systematically exchanging SRI are introduced in Section 3. Using a simulation model developed for the proposed protocol (Yamada, 2004), we verify the protocol's behavior and effectiveness in a case study in Section 4. Section 5 summarizes the proposed protocol and mentions further studies.

2   Related Work – Discovery of Sri

SRI discovery mechanisms based on static resource attribute like a file name are discussed in P2P computing environments. In P2P computing, SRI is used to search for the server location. There are various searching mechanisms. For example, Gnutella (Gnutella) uses flooding method. Freenet (Clarke et al, 2000) uses a combination of informed request forwarding and file replication methods. These discovery methods are based on static SRI.

The decentralized resource discovery method in the grid environment is discussed in (Iamnitchi et al, 2001). The basic framework of this discovery mechanism is the request-forwarding mechanism. In this framework, one or two SRI providers are considered and the provider server is called a peer or node. A virtual organization has one or two nodes. Each node can store service resource information and provide service information about one or more resources. The initiator of the coordinated service sends a request to the node. The node responds with the matching service resource description if it has the requested service information. Otherwise, the node forwards the SRI request to other nodes. If a node can respond to the request, it directly answers the initiator. This framework needs a membership protocol. Each node should know the other nodes to which it forwards requests when it cannot respond.

In Web services, UDDI (Universal Description, Discovery, and Integration) (UDDI) is the information provider. The service provider registers the service information including the XML code (WSDL (Web services description language (WSDL)) access the service provider. The requester first accesses UDDI and learns how to access the target service provider. A quantitative study of the information service is the starting point.

The grid information service architecture was proposed in (Czajowski et al, 2001). It consists of two components: highly distributed service information providers and specialized aggregation directory service providers. The information provider deals with dynamic information about grid resources and the aggregate directory service provider deals with static information. The information provider sends a registration message to the aggregate directory. Communication among different aggregate directory providers and among different information providers is not explicitly considered. The service information flow follows a tree structure.

One example of a resource information service is the network weather service (NWS) (Wolski, 1997). In this service, several sensors are implemented in nodes or links in the network and they monitor resource consumption. The collected sensory data is sent to the central database. The data is analyzed by several statistical methods. The central database corresponds to the information provider.

In the discovery mechanism proposed in this paper, the service resource information providers exchange SRI each other. We also regard the SRI provider as the nodes in (Iamnitchi et al, 2001). We introduce the concept of the service domain like that in autonomous systems (ASs) in BGP (border gateway protocol). A virtual enterprise has several service domains. The application service providers are managed in one service domain. The SRI provider stores the static and dynamic SRI of all service providers in the service domain. The SRI provider establishes connections between neighboring SRI providers in different service domains. The initiator of a coordinated service sends a request to the SRI provider. Because the service information provider exchanges the SRI with other SRI providers, it can responds to the request. The exchange of SRI is similar to the exchange of NLRI (Network Layer Reachability Information) in BGP.

3 Architecture Model

3.1 Overview

In this paper, we consider three players: SRI provider, service provider, and requester (the initiator of the coordinated service). The service provider is the server that provides the application services, for example, processing the requester's computation or providing the files. The SRI provider is the server that manages the SRI of the service providers and exchanges the service resource information about the managing service providers with other service resource information providers. The requester asks the service resource information provider, obtains the service resource information, and decides which server it should access based on the obtained service information and the scheduling rule, and finally accesses the service provider where the target application service is running.

In grid computing, two protocols are used: grid information protocol (GRIP) and grid registration protocol (GRRP) (Czajowski et al, 2001). GRIP is a protocol for looking up SRI and discovering the appropriate server. The requester uses it. GRRP is a protocol for sending the service information from the service provider to the SRI provider.

In (Czajowski et al, 2001), the following architecture is considered. This architecture has information providers and aggregate directory service providers. The service resource information provider manages the SRI about several service providers. The aggregation directory service providers communicate with the SRI provider and manage the aggregated service information. The requester can ask either provider. In this architecture, communication among different information providers and among the aggregate directory service providers is not explicitly considered.

In this paper, we consider the architecture shown in Figure 1. The SRI providers manage the SRI about all service providers in the service domain and communicate with other SRI providers in order to exchange the SRI that each service provider manages. The requester can access a nearby SRI provider and ask for a SRI of the

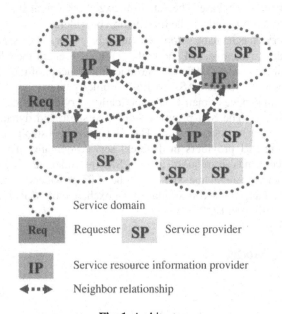

Fig. 1. Architecture

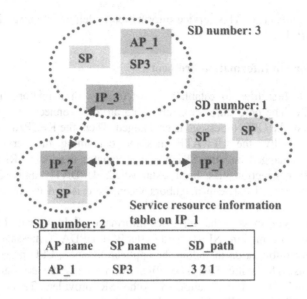

Fig. 2. SD_path

service provider that can provide the application service that the requester desires. Let us call the communication protocol between the SRI providers service domain information protocol (SDP).

Here we introduce the concept of the service domain (SD), like that in anonymous systems (ASs) in BGP, which is defined as a group of service providers. The information provider is the representative of the service domain. A unique number is assigned to the service domain. Let us call it the service domain number. The SRI provider communicates with all the service providers. The service provider registers the SRI and reports the current load status (a dynamic resource attribute) in order to update the registered SRI. If the service provider stops providing the registered service, a request to discard the SRI is sent to the SRI provider. The SRI provider also communicates with the other SRI providers to exchange SRI with them. Let us call a peer for exchanging service information a neighbor.

SDP can control and modify service resource information and associated attributes. For example, if the service resource information provider requires that a neighboring SRI provider does not forward the received SRI to any other information providers, then SDP stops it being forwarded.

This mechanism is similar to the control scheme in BGP. In BGP, the device manager can configure the route map in order to control the forwarding route information. Because the scheme for exchanging SRI is based on BGP, SDP can also control the SRI. SDP creates and maintains the SRI base (SIB) in the SRI provider. When this SRI provider receives an update message from a neighboring SRI provider, it updates its SIB table. Figure 2 shows an example. SD_path is included as one of the associated path attributes. This shows the service domain numbers for delivering the registered service resource information. For example, an application called "AP_1" is running on service provider "SP3". This SRI is created in the SRI provider with service domain number 3. This service information is delivered via service domains 3, 2, and 1 to "IP_1".

3.2 Service Domain Information Protocol

Like BGP, SDP first tries to establish connections with neighbors listed in the configuration file. The procedure for establishing an SDP connection is the same as that in BGP. First, the OPEN message is exchanged. Then, the KEEPALIVE message is exchanged. Finally, the UPDATE message containing the service resource information is exchanged and the SRI provider updates the local SRI base (SIB). Once the SDP connection has been established, UPDATE and KEEPALIVE messages are exchanged between neighbors when there is and is not, respectively, new SRI.

The SDP UPDATE message has a service information field instead of the network layer reachability information (NLRI) field in the BGP UPDATE message. This field stores the service information including the application name, CPU power level, and CPU load status. The static SRI is configured in SDP. The configured SRI is exchanged through the SDP connection with other SRI providers. This mechanism is the same as the NLRI in BGP. On the other hand, dynamic SRI is also exchanged. When the CPU load status in the service provider is changed, the service provider reports the current SRI that needs to be updated. This SRI is set in the service information field in the SDP UPDATE message and is exchanged among neighbors. In BGP, the network route information redistributed from interior gateway protocol (IGP, e.g., OSPF and IGRP) is dynamically set in the NLRI field in the BGP UPDATE message. The neighbors that receive the SDP UPDATE message also update their SIB and send the updated service resource information to their neighbors.

The path attributes are also considered in SDP protocol like in BGP. They are used to select the appropriate SRI among multiple entries in SIB. These entries have the same information about the application name and server names and IP address but they have different path attributes. In the current version of the developed simulation SDP model, the following are considered as SDP path attributes: origin, SD path, community, and local preference. Here, the origin means how to obtain the service information and has two values: "DFP" or "ESDP". "DFP" means that the SRI is obtained from the service provider by the registration protocol or is statically configured in the SRI provider. "ESDP" means that the SRI is obtained from another SRI provider. The SD path means the set of SD numbers of the service domain along which the SDP UPDATE message traverses from the original information provider to this information provider. The local preference means the preference of the original SRI provider. The SRI selection rule is defined as follows in the current version. First, path attributes preferences are compared. The SRI entry that has the larger preference value is selected. Second, if the preference values are the same, the lengths of the SD path attributes are compared. The SRI entry with its shorter SD path is selected. If the SD path lengths are also the same, the values of the origin are compared. Here, we select the SRI entry with "DFP" rather than that with "ESDP". If the SRI entries have the same values for the above condition, finally, we compare the identifiers of the advertising SRI providers. The SRI providers have unique identifiers. In this model, the largest value among the IP addresses of the interfaces is assigned as the SRI provider identifier. The SRI entry that is advertised by the highest SRI provider identifier is selected. We can consider several alternative rules for selecting the SRI entries. And the path attribute can be modified in the SRI provider when the SRI provider exchanges service resource information with neighbors as in BGP protocol. A sophisticated scheme for controlling the path attributes is for further study.

4 Case Study

In order to verify and analyze the protocol behavior and effectiveness, we developed a simulation model of proposed protocol by OPNET (Yamada, 2004). Using this simulation model, we considered the following virtual enterprise system.

4.1 Network Model

In this case study scenario, three companies that have their own networks decide to make a virtual enterprise, as shown in Figure 3. The core network is created and these

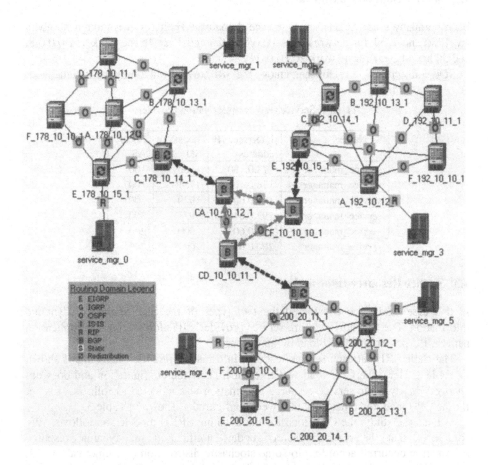

Fig. 3. Case study network

companies' networks are connected to the core network. The routing architecture is as follows. The OSPF routing protocol with each different tag number is running on each company's network. In the core network, OSPF routing protocol is also running. Each company's network has a different AS number. The AS numbers of networks 178.0.0.0/8, 192.0.0.0/8, and 200.0.0.0/8, are 100, 300, and 200, respectively. In the edge routers of each network, BGP protocol is configured. Exterior BGP (EBGP) connections are established between the edge routes in each network and the core network. The Interior BGP connections are fully meshed among edge routers in the core network. The redistribution command is configured in the edge routers of each company's network. The outside routes obtained by BGP protocol are redistributed into ones by OSPF routing protocol and the routes in the company's network are also redistributed into ones by BGP protocol. Synchronization is off in the BGP configuration. The SRI and router node are connected by RIP protocol. In order that each is reachable from others, redistribution is also done in the router. The SRI provider is located for each service domain as in the following table.

4.2 Service Domain Configuration

Each company's network has two service domains. Their service domain numbers are 1780 and 1781 for network 178.0.0.0/8, 1920 and 1921 for network 192.0.0.0/8, and 2000 and 2001 for network 200.0.0.0/8.

SDP connections are established among the SRI providers in a fully meshed manner.

Table 1. Service resource information provider

Name	Interface IP address	Local SD	Local AS
service_manager_0	178.0.100.2	1780	100
service_manager_1	178.0.101.2	1781	100
service_manager_2	192.0.60.2	1920	300
service_manager_3	192.0.61.2	1921	300
service_manager_4	200.0.60.2	2000	200
service_manager_5	200.0.61.2	2001	200

4.3 Service Resource Information

In this case study, we considered the two types of the SRI: static and dynamic information. The SRI attributes are service provider's IP address, running application name, CPU power, and CPU load in this scenario.

The static SRI that each service resource information provider maintains is shown in Table 2. Here, the CPU load was fixed at time of the configuration and does not change. The dynamic service resource information was modeled as follows. Except for the CPU load, the other attributes were configured as shown in Table 3.

In this case study, the CPU load for the dynamic SRI is modeled as follows. We considered that the service resource update notification for dynamic resource information occurred according to some stochastic distribution (in numerical results, we considered the Poisson process). In order to determine the CPU load at the epoch of the update notification, we also configured the upper and lower bounds. If the outcome of the uniform distribution was less than the lower bound, the CPU load was low (L). If it was larger than the upper bound, the CPU load was high (H). Otherwise the CPU load was medium (M). If the CPU level changed from the previous level, an update message was created and exchanged among other SRI providers.

Table 2. Static service resource information entry

Server IP address (manager #)	Running application names	CPU power/ load
178.0.120.10(0)	ap_1, ap_2, ap_3, ap_4	H/H
178.0.121.20(0)	ap_4, ap_6	M/M
178.0.102.10(1)	ap_1	L/L
178.0.103.10(1)	ap_2, ap_3	H/M
192.0.110.10(2)	ap_7, ap_8, ap_10	M/H
192.0.111.11(2)	ap_2	H/L
192.0.112.10(2)	ap_3, ap_8, ap_9	H/M
192.0.140.10(3)	ap_1	L/L
192.0.141.20(3)	ap_7, ap_8	H/M
192.0.142.10(3)	ap_3, ap_5	M/H
200.0.90.10(4)	ap_1, ap_4, ap_6, ap_8	H/H
200.0.91.20(4)	ap_4	L/L
200.0.80.10(5)	ap_2, ap_11, ap_12	H/L
200.0.81.10(5)	ap_5, ap_13	L/M

Table 3. Dynamic service resource information entry

Server IP address (manager #)	Running application names	CPU power
178.0.126.1(0)	ap_31, ap_32	M
178.0.127.11(0)	ap_33, ap_35	H
178.0.128.20(0)	ap_34	L
178.0.129.22(0)	ap_36	M
178.0.52.10(1)	ap_41	L
178.0.53.10(1)	ap_42	H
178.0.54.20(1)	ap_43	H
192.0.130.10(2)	ap_57, ap_58, ap_59	M
192.0.131.11(2)	ap_52	H
192.0.132.10(2)	ap_53, ap_58, ap_59	H
192.0.150.10(3)	ap_61	L
192.0.151.20(3)	ap_67, ap_31	H
192.0.152.10(3)	ap_32, ap_35	M
200.0.95.10(4)	ap_41, ap_34, ap_53, ap_58	H
200.0.96.20(4)	ap_61	L
200.0.85.10(5)	ap_57, ap_32, ap_58	H
200.0.86.10(5)	ap_59, ap_43	L

4.4 Exchanging the Service Resource Information

In the simulation experiment, we considered the following scenarios. Here, we set the mean value of the update notification interval is 15 and 30. The lower and upper bound were set to 0.3 and 0.6, respectively.

Here, we focused on the SRI table maintained in service_manager_0. Table 4 shows the part of the SRI in the service_manager_0. We focused on the entries of ap_3. This resource information was statically configured in the SRI provider. Because these entries were statically configured, their CPU load attributes did not change. There were four entries. The service provider is selected among these four entries based on the selection rule.

Next, table 5 shows part of the table at 300, 400 and 800. Here we focused on the entries of application, ap_32. There were three entries for ap_32 in these tables. This application was dynamically registered in the SRI provider, so, the CPU load attribute of these entries varied. If the policy for selecting the service provider was that a lower CPU load and higher CPU power were the best, then at 300, the requester selected 178.0.126.1. At 400, the requester selected 200.0.85.10. And at 800, if the requester's policy gave priority to the CPU power, then 200.0.85.10 was selected. Of course, we can consider the various selection policies.

Table 4. Service resource information table (We focus on ap_3.)

IP address	CPU power	CPU load	Source protocol	SD path
192.0.112.10	H	M	ESDP	1920
192.0.142.10	M	H	ESDP	1921
178.0.103.10	H	M	ESDP	1781
178.0.120.10	H	H	SDP	-

Table 5. Service resource information table (We focus on ap_32.)

At 300 seconds

IP address	CPU power	CPU load	Source protocol	SD path
192.0.152.10	M	M	ESDP	1921
200.0.85.10	H	H	ESDP	2001
178.0.126.1	M	L	SDP	-

At 400 seconds

IP address	CPU power	CPU load	Source protocol	SD path
192.0.152.10	M	H	ESDP	1921
200.0.85.10	H	L	ESDP	2001
178.0.126.1	M	H	SDP	-

At 800 seconds

IP address	CPU power	CPU load	Source protocol	SD path
192.0.152.10	M	H	ESDP	1921
200.0.85.10	H	H	ESDP	2001
178.0.126.1	M	M	SDP	-

Let us consider the case where the SRI provider with the service domain 2001 wants to reject access from requesters in outside networks. Then, this service resource provider sends an update message in which the CPU load attribute in server 200.0.85.10 is set to "H". So, the other SRI provider receives the message and set the CPU load attribute to "high". Therefore, the requesters in an outside network can never access server 200.0.85.10. Using this service information discovery mechanism, the manager of the virtual enterprise system can configure the strategic policy to block the access.

4.5 Update Traffic

Figure 4 shows the sent traffic generated by this protocol from the service_manager_0 in this case study scenario. When we set the mean value of the update notification interval to 15, the generated traffic was larger than that when the mean was 30. When the lower and upper bounds were set to 0.2 and 0.9, that is when the frequency of CPU load status changes was low, the generated traffic was the smallest. The update traffic generated by this SDP protocol depended on the registered SRI, update notification frequency, number of the neighbors, and strategic policy.

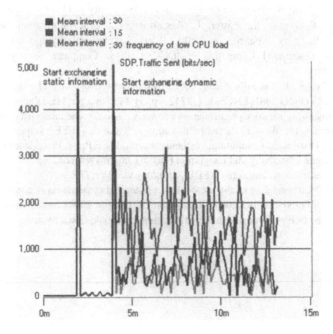

Fig. 4. Traffic sent from service_mgr_0

5 Conclusion

In order to coordinate several applications and share service resources autonomously, a service that provides SRI is important in grid computing and Web service environments. This paper presented a communication protocol for exchanging SRI among wide-area systems and showed its behaviour using a simulation model. This communication protocol is based on BGP. In future, we will expand its attributes and introduce several strategic policies for exchanging SRI. We plan to extend the protocol that exchanges SRI among IP peers in a further study. To reduce the number of SDP sessions, hierarchical architecture and functions are useful for dealing with the scalability issue. In the BGP, the route reflector mechanism reduces the number of iBGP sessions and enables us to make a scalable network. We plan to expand our proposed SRI exchanging protocol, which has the same mechanism as the route reflector in the BGP. The created SRI table is used to determine which server is appropriate for the request. We will develop a simulation model that autonomously simulates the application integration according to the business process. We will develop modeling to evaluate service performance when this protocol is applied to the application orchestration system.

References

Gunutella protocol specification, http://www.clip2.com/articles.html

Clarke, I., Sandberg, O., Wiley, B., Hong, T.: A distributed anonymous information storage and retrieval system. In: Workshop on Design Issues in Anonymity and Underservability (2000)

Czajowski, K., Fitzgerald, S., Foster, I., Kesselrnan, C.: Grid Information Services for Distributed Resource Sharing. In: 10th IEEE International Symposium on High-Performance Distributed Computing (HPDC-10), IEEE Computer Society Press, Los Alamitos (2001)

Iamnitchi, A., Foster, I.: On fully decentralized resource discovery in grid environments. In: Lee, C.A. (ed.) GRID 2001. LNCS, vol. 2242, pp. 51–62. Springer, Heidelberg (2001)

Wolski, R.: Forecasting network performance to support dynamic scheduling using the network weather service. In: Wolski, R. (ed.) Proceedings of the 6th IEEE symposium on High Performance Distributed Computing, Portland, Oregon, IEEE Press, Los Alamitos (1997)

Universal description discovery and integration (UDDI), http://www.uddi.org

Web Services Description Language (WSDL), http://www.w3.org/TR/wdsl

Yamada, H.: OPNET modeling of the protocol to register and circulate service information. In: Proceedings of OPNETWORK2004, Washington DC (August 2004), htpp:// www.opnet.com

William, P.: Cisco BGP-4 command and configuration handbook, Cisco Systems (2001)

Advertising Via Mobile Terminals – Delivering Context Sensitive and Personalized Advertising While Guaranteeing Privacy

Rebecca Bulander[1], Michael Decker[1], Gunther Schiefer[1], and Bernhard Kölmel[2]

[1] Insitute AIFB, University of Karlsruhe, Englerstr. 11,76128 Karlsruhe, Germany
{bulander,decker,schiefer}@aifb.uni-karlsruhe.de
[2] CAS Software AG,Wilhelm-Schickard-Str. 10-12, 76131 Karlsruhe, Germany
bernhard.koelmel@cas.de

Abstract. Mobile terminals like cellular phones and PDAs are a promising target platform for mobile advertising: The devices are widely spread, are able to present interactive multimedia content and offer as almost permanently carried along personal communication devices a high degree of reachability. But particular because of the latter feature it is important to pay great attention to privacy aspects and avoidance of spam-messages when designing an application for mobile advertising. Furthermore the limited user interface of mobile devices is a special challenge. The following article describes the solution approach for mobile advertising developed within the project MoMa, which was funded by the Federal Ministry of Economics and Labour of Germany (BMWA). MoMa enables highly personalized and context sensitive mobile advertising while guaranteeing data protection. To achieve this we have to distinguish public and private context information.

Keywords: Mobile Advertising, context sensitivity, data protection.

1 Introduction

Advertising is defined as the non personal presentation of ideas, product and services whereas someone has to pay (Kotler & Bliemel, 1992). Mobile or wireless[1] advertising uses mobile terminals likes cellular phones and PDAs.

There are a couple of reasons why mobile terminals are an interesting target for advertising:

- There are quite a lot of them: In Germany there are more than 64 million cellular phones, a number that exceeds that of fixed line telephones. The average penetration rate of mobile phones in Western Europe is about 83 percent (RegTP, 2004), estimates for the worldwide number of cellular

---

[1] Most authors use „wireless" and „mobile" as synonyms which is strictly considered incorrect since wireless and mobile are orthogonal concepts (Wang, 2003). "Mobile advertising" can also denote advertising on a mobile surface (e.g. bus, aeroplane, train), but we don't use the term that way.

J. Filipe et al. (Eds.): ICETE 2005, CCIS 3, pp. 15–25, 2007.
© Springer-Verlag Berlin Heidelberg 2007

phones are far beyond one billion according to the International Telecommunication Union (ITU).

- Mobile terminals are devices for personal communication, so people carry such devices with them most of the day which leads to a high reachability of up to 14 hours a day (Sokolov, 2004). Conventional advertising can reach its audience only in certain timespans and situations (e.g. TV commercials reach people when they are sitting in their living room after work, newspaper ads are usually read at breakfast time), but mobile advertising can reach people almost anywhere and anytime.
- Since each mobile terminal can be addressed individually it is possible to realise target-oriented and personalized advertising. Most conventional advertising methods inevitably reach people not interested in the advertised product or service.
- Mobile devices enable interaction. When one receives an ad on his mobile terminal he can immediately request further information or forward it to friends.
- In the future most mobile devices will be capable of presenting multimedia-content, e.g. little images, movies or music sequences. This is important if logos and jingles associated with a certain brand have to be presented.
- The emerging mobile networks of the third generation (e.g. UMTS) will provide enormous bandwidths, so that until nowadays unthinkable mobile services will be possible.

However there are also some serious challenges to mention when talking about mobile advertising:

- Because of the permanently increasing portion of spam-mail on the internet — statistics state values far beyond 50 % (MessageLabs, 2004) — there is the concern of this trend spilling over to mobile networks. A survey recently conducted "[...] indicates that more than 8 in 10 mobile phone users surveyed have received unsolicited messages and are more likely to change their operator than their mobile number to fight the problem [...]" (International Telecommunication Union, 2005). Spam-messages in mobile networks are a much more critical problem, since mobile terminals have relatively limited resources (bandwidth, memory for storage of messages, computation power).
- The user of a mobile advertising application will only provide personal data (e.g. age, marital status, fields of interest) if data protection is warranted. Especially when location based services are able to track the position of users this causes concerns about privacy (Barkhuss & Dey, 2003).
- Usability: Because of their small size mobile terminals have a limited user interface, like small displays or no full-blown keyboard. Thus a mobile application should demand as few user entries as possible. But the small display can be also considered as advantage: only the text of the advertisement will be displayed, nothing else will distract the user.
- Expenses of mobile data transmission: today the usage of mobile data communication is still very expensive (e.g. about one Euro for 1 Mbyte data traffic when using GPRS or UMTS, 0.20 Euro for sending a SMS or 0.40 Euro

for a MMS). This hinders many people from using mobile devices for internet research on products and services. Again nobody wants to pay for advertisement, so the advertiser should pay for the data transportation.

Within the project „Mobile Marketing (MoMa)" we developed a system for mobile advertising which takes all of the mentioned problems into account and makes highly personalized advertising possible while guaranteeing data protection.

The rest of this article is organized as follows: the second chapter deals with related work. In chapter three we describe the functionality, architecture and business model of the MoMa-system. Afterwards we discuss the different types of context information in chapter four, before a summary in the last chapter is given.

2 Related Work

2.1 Mobile Advertising

The high potential of mobile advertising along with its specific opportunities and challenges is widely accepted in literature, see Barnes (2002), Tähtinen & Salo (2004) or Yunos, Gao & Shim (2003) for example. The latter article also discusses the business models for mobile advertising by vendors like Vindigo, SkyGo and AvantGo.

Today's most common form of mobile advertising is the delivery of ads via SMS (Barwise & Strong, 2002), e.g. misteradgood.com by MindMatics. SMS is very popular – in Germany approximately 20 billion SMS were sent in 2003 (RegTP, 2003) – but the length of the text is limited to 160 characters and images can't be shown, so it shouldn't be the only used channel in a marketing campaign (Dickinger et al., 2004).

Other more academic approaches for mobile advertising are the distribution of advertisement using multi-hop ad-hoc networks (Straub & Heinemann, 2004, Ratsimor, 2003) or location aware advertising using Bluetooth positioning (Aalto et al, 2004). There is also the idea of advertising using wearable computing (Randell & Muller, 2000).

Some systems even provide a monetary incentive to the consumers for receiving advertisement like the above mentioned misteradgood or the one described by de Reyck & Degraeve (2003).

A very important concept in mobile advertising due to the experience with spam-e-mails is permission marketing (Godin, 1999): consumers will only receive ads after they have explicitly opted-in and they can opt-out anytime. Because a consumer has to know a firm before he can opt-in it might be necessary to advertise for a mobile advertising campaign, see the three case studies in Bauer et al. (2005) for example.

2.2 Context Sensitive Mobile Applications

The term context with regard to mobile applications was introduced by Schilit, Adams & Want (1994) and means a set of information to describe the current situation of an user. A context sensitive application makes use of this information to adapt to the needs of the user. For mobile applications this is especially important, since the terminals have a limited interface to the user.

The most often cited example of context sensitive applications are location based services (LBS): Depending on the current position the user is provided with information concerning his environment, e.g. a tourist guide with comments about the sights in the surrounding area (Cheverst, 2000). Technically this location context could be detected using a GPS-receiver or the position of the used base station (cell-ID).

But there are far more kinds of context information than just location, see Schmidt, Beigl & Gellersen (1999) or chapter four of this article for example.

Other kinds of thinkable context sensitive services depend on profile information. These profiles can be retrieved with explicit support by the user (active profiling) or when analysing earlier sessions (passive profiling). Active profiling could be implemented using a questionnaire, passive profiling could apply data mining methods. Active profiling means some work for the end user but is completely transparent to him. Moreover not all relevant information can be retrieved with the needed accuracy using passive profiling, e.g. the age of a person.

2.3 Empirical Results

Based on a survey (N=1028) Bauer et al. (2004) tried to figure out the factors important for consumer-acceptance of mobile advertising. Their results indicate that the personal attitude is important for the user acceptance of mobile advertising campaigns. This attitude is mainly influenced by the perceived entertaining and informative utility of adverts, further also by social norms. "Knowledge concerning mobile communication" and "attitude towards advertising" didn't show a strong effect.

Another survey conducted by Bauer et al. (2005) was aimed at executives responsible for marketing (N=101). More than one half already had experience with mobile advertising campaigns, over 50 % of those who didn't intended to use the mobile channel for advertising in the future. As most important advantages "direct contact to customers" (87 %), "ubiquity" (87 %), "innovation" (74 %), "interactivity" (67 %) and "viral effects" (38 %) were considered. As disadvantages "high effort for implementation" (59 %), "limited creativity" (56 %), "untrustworthy" (43 %), "target group can't be reached" (11 %) and "lack of consumer acceptance" (8 %) were mentioned.

An often cited empirical study in the field of mobile advertising is the one conducted by Barwise & Strong (2002): one thousand people aged 16-30 were chosen randomly and received SMS-adverts during a trial which lasted for 6 weeks. The results are very encouraging: 80 % of the test persons didn't delete the adverts before reading them, 74 % read at least three quarters of them, 77 % read them immediately after reception. Some adverts included competitions which generated an average response rate of 13 %. There was even a competition where 41 % of those who responded did so within the first minute. Surprisingly 17 % of test persons forwarded one or more text adverts to a third party, which wasn't intended by the research design. Another result is that respondents felt that receiving three text messages a day was "about right".

3 Description of the MoMa-System

3.1 Overview

The basic principle of the MoMa-system is illustrated in figure 1: The end users create orders according to a given catalogue whereas the client software automatically queries needed context parameters. The catalogue (see figure 2 for a screenshot) is a hierarchical ordered set of possible product and service-offers which are described by appropriate attributes: on the uppermost level we may have "travelling", "sport & fitness" or "gastronomy" for example, whereas the latter could subsume categories like "pubs", "restaurants" or "catering services". Each category is specified by certain

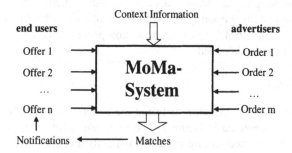

Fig. 1. Basic principle of the MoMa-system

Fig. 2. Screenshot of client application on Symbian OS (catalogue view)

attributes, in the gastronomy example this could be "price level" and "style". When creating an order the client application will automatically fill in appropriate context parameters, e.g. "location" and "weather": the gastronomy facility shouldn't be too far away from the current location of the user and beer gardens shouldn't be recommended if it's raining.

On the other side the advertisers put offers into the MoMa-System. These offers are also formulated according to the catalogue. When the system detects a pair of a matching order and offer the end user is notified. Then he can decide if he wants to contact the advertiser to call upon the offer, but this is beyond the scope of the MoMa-system.

The end user only gets advertising messages when he explicitly wants to be informed about orders matching certain criterions. He is anonymous with regard to the advertisers as long as he doesn't decide to contact them. The later described architecture of the system supports the employment of a trust third-party as mediator between end users and MoMa, so even transaction-pseudonymity with regard to the operator of MoMa can be achieved.

3.2 Business Model

The flows of money and information between the different roles within the business model of MoMa are depicted in figure 3. The roles are: advertiser, MoMa-operator, context-provider, mobile network operator, trusted party and end user.

For the end user MoMa is free, he only has to pay his network provider for the transferred data when he submits an order to the system. Since the data volume generated when sending one order is less than 1 Kbyte, these costs are almost negligible. On the other side the advertisers only have to pay for actual contacts. The price for one contact depends on the used category of the catalogue, for example one contact of the category "real estate" may be more expensive than a "lunch break"-contact. If the number of "lunch break"-offers should explode, the price for that category could be adjusted. The price for one contact has at least to cover the communication-costs for the notification of the end user.

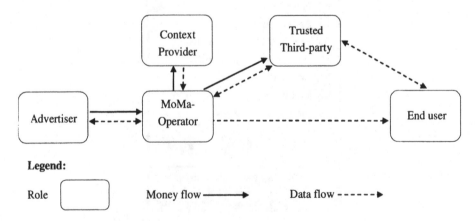

Fig. 3. Money and data flows of the MoMa-business model

Another source of revenue for the MoMa-operator is providing statistical analyses about what kind of products and services the users of the MoMa-system are interested in. The MoMa-operator has to pay for the services of the trustworthy party and the context-providers.

When introducing a system like MoMa there is the well known "hen-and-egg"-problem of how to obtain the critical mass of advertisers and end users: without a certain number of advertisers there won't be enough interesting offers but without offers MoMa isn't interesting for end users. However without many end users MoMa isn't interesting for advertisers. To overcome this problem there is the possibility of automatically putting offers from well-established eCommerce-platforms into the system without charging the operators of those platforms. Since many of them offer a webservice-interface this can be achieved without much effort.

3.3 Architecture and Technical Details

Each end user of the MoMa-system (see figure 4) has an unique user-id and at least one general and one notification profile. The general profile contains information concerning the user which could be relevant for the creation of an order, e.g. age, family status, fields of interest. A notification profile describes how (SMS/MMS, e-mail, text-to-speech, etc) an user wants to be notified when an offer matching one of his orders is found; this notification mode can depend on the current time, e.g. text-to-speech-calls to phone number A from 9 a.m. till 16 p.m. and to phone-number B from 16 p.m. till 20 p.m., send e-mail-message else. The instances of both kinds of profiles can be stored on a server of the anonymization service, so they can be used on different terminals of an user. Only the notification profiles have to be readable for the anonymization service, the general profiles can be encrypted in a way only the user can decrypt them.

For the creation of an order X the user chooses one of his general and notification profile each and specifies what he desires using the categories and attributes of the catalogue. In doing so, single attribute values will be looked up automatically in the chosen general profile respective the available private context parameters if applicable. Please note: the order X itself contains no declaration about the identity or end addresses of the user. The user-ID, the index of the chosen notification profile and a randomly generated bit string are put together and encrypted[2], the resulting cipher text be denoted with C. The pair {X, C} is sent to the anonymizer which forwards it to the core system. This loop way ensures the MoMa-operator cannot retrieve the IP- or MSISDN-address of the order's originator. Should a private context parameter change while an order is active (e.g. new location of user) the updated X' along with the old C will be send to the core server, where the old order X can be looked up by C and be replaced with X'.

The advertiser defines his offer Y using the catalogue and transmits it to the MoMa-Server directly. Furthermore he deposits different templates for notifications of end users on the publishing & rendering-server.

---

[2] For the architecture it doesn't matter if a symmetric or asymmetric encryption algorithm is used. Symmetric encryption is favourable in terms of the needed computation power (which may be limited on a mobile device), but requires a secure channel for the initial exchange of the key.

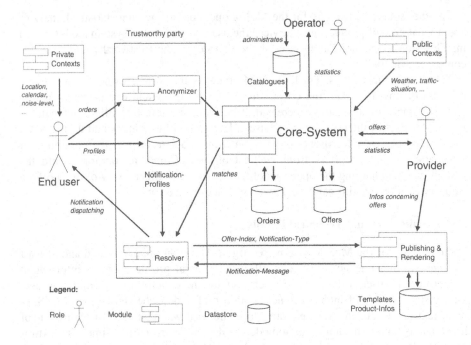

Fig. 4. Architecture of the MoMa-system

Triggered by events like new/updated orders and offers or changed public context parameters the MoMa-server tries to find matching pairs of orders and offers. For each match {{X, C}, Y} found C along with the ID of Y will be sent to the resolver-component of the trustworthy party. Here C is decrypted so the notification profile can be looked up to request the needed notification from the publishing-server. This message will be dispatched to the given end address.

If there is already a matching offer in the database, the users immediately gets an answer, so we could consider this as pull-advertisement; if the matching order enters the system after the offer, the notification of the user is a push-advertisement. Using context information we can amend the orders in a "smart" way, so MoMa can be denoted as *combined smart push & pull approach*.

The advertisers don't have access to the personal data of the end users, in particular they can't find out about the end addresses to send unsolicited messages and have no physical access to components of the system where addresses are stored. Even the operator of MoMa only sees the cipher text C. This ciphertext C is different for each order, even if two orders have the same user ID and use the same notification profile, because of the random information included. Thus C can be considered as transaction pseudonym, which is the most secure level of pseudonymity (Pfitzmann & Köhntopp, 2000)[3].

---

[3] Transaction pseudonyms are more secure than other kinds of pseudonyms (relation or role pseudonyms, personal pseudonyms), since it is less likely that the identity (or end address) of the user behind a pseudonym is revealed.

4 Different Classes of Context Information

The anonymization of the orders requires the distinction between public and private context information (see columns c_{i1}, c_{i2} in table 1):

- Private context parameters are retrieved by the mobile terminal and its sensors or the mobile terminal is at least involved. Thus private context parameters can't be retrieved anonymously but they can be processed anonymously. Examples: position, background noise level, temperature, calendar, available technical resources like display size or speed of CPU.
- Public context information can be retrieved without knowledge about the identity of the respective user. Examples: weather, traffic jams, rates at the stock exchange.

For the reasonable processing of some parameters of the public context it might be necessary to know about certain private context parameters, e.g. the weather in a given city is a public context parameter, but one has to know the location of the user to look up the weather in the right city.

Furthermore context parameters can be characterised by different degrees of variability (rows c_{1j}, c_{2j}, c_{3j} in table 1):

- Static context parameters have never or very seldom to be updated. Examples: gender or mother-tongue.
- Semistatic context parameters changes have to be updated but not very often (several weeks or years). Examples: age, family status.
- Dynamical context parameters change often or even permanently. Example: current location of a user, surrounding noise level.

Table 1. Different classes of context

Context dimension c_{ij} (examples)	public c_{i1}	private c_{i2}
c_{1j} Static	c_{11} (currency, timestamp format, frequency of radio access network)	c_{12} (gender, date of birth)
c_{2j} Semistatic	c_{21} (season, bathing season)	c_{22} (salary, job, number of kids)
c_{3j} Dynamic	c_{31} (weather, traffic situation, delayed train)	c_{32} (location, display size, surrounding noise level)

When combining these two classification schemes we obtain the six classes shown in table 1. Based upon these six classes we can give statements how to retrieve the respective context parameters:

- Public static context parameters (c_{11}) will be determined via configuration when installing a MoMa-System.
- Public semistatic context parameters (c_{21}) will be set manually by the MoMa-operator or derived from rules depending on the date if applicable.
- Public dynamic context parameters (c_{31}) will be queried by the MoMa-operator from special context providers.
- Private static and semistatic parameters (c_{12}, c_{22}) have to be determined using active profiling. According to their definition these parameters change never or very seldom so it isn't much work for the end user to keep them up to date.
- The parameters of the private dynamic context (c_{32}) have to be determined for each order by the mobile terminal of the end user.

5 Summary

The presented system in this article enables context sensitive mobile advertising while guaranteeing a high level of privacy. To achieve this, the distinction of private and public context parameters is necessary. An end user will only receive personalized offers when he defines orders so there is no danger of spamming. The costs for the transmission of the ads are covered by the MoMa-operator respective the advertisers. Since mobile terminals have a limited user interface the MoMa-client-application is designed in a context sensitive manner to assist the end user. There are also different kinds of profiles to support the usability.

The industry-partners of the MoMa-consortium plan to utilize the results of the project within the scope of the Soccer World Championship 2006.

References

Aalto, L., Göthlin, N., Korhonenm, J., Ojala, T.: Bluetooth and WAP Push based location-aware mobile advertising system. In: MobiSYS 2004, Boston, USA, ACM Press, New York (2004)

Bauer, H.H., Reichardt, T., Neuman, M.M.: Bestimmungsfaktoren der Konsumentenakzeptanz von Mobile Marketing in Deutschland – Eine empirische Untersuchung (in German). Institut für Marktorientierte Unternehmensführung (IMU), Universität Mannheim (2004)

Bauer, H.H, Lippert, I., Reichardt, T., Neumann, N.N.: Effective Mobile Marketing – Eine empirische Untersuchung (in German). Institut für Marktorientierte Unternehmensführung (IMU), Universität Mannheim (2005)

Barkhuss, L., Dey, A.: Location-Based Services for Mobile Telephony: a study of users' privacy concerns. In: INTERACT 2003, 9th IFIP TC13 International Conference on Human-Computer Interaction (2003)

Barnes, S.: Wireless digital advertising: nature and implications. International journal of advertising 21, 399–420 (2002)

Barwise, P., Strong, C.: Permission-based mobile advertising. Journal of interactive Marketing 16(1) (2002)

Cheverst, K.: Providing Tailored (Context-Aware) Information to City Visitors. In: Proc. of the conference on Adaptive Hyper-media and Adaptive Webbased Systems, Trento (2000)

Dickinger, A., Haghirian, P., Murphy, J., Scharl, A.: An investigation and conceptual model of SMS marketing. In: Proceedings of the 37th Hawaii international conference on system sciences 2004, IEEE Computer Society Press, Los Alamitos (2004)

Godin, S.: Permission Marketing: Turning strangers into friends, and friends into customers. Simon and Schuster (1999)

International Telecommunication Union (ITU), First empirical global spam study indicates more than 80 percent of mobile phone users receive spam. (2005), http://www.mobilespam.org

Kotler, P., Bliemel, F.: Marketing Management. Poeschel, Stuttgart (1992)

MessageLabs, Intelligence Annual Email Security Report 2004 (2004)

Pfitzmann, A., Köhntopp, M.: Anonymity, unobservability, and pseudonymity: A proposal for terminology. In: Federrath, H. (ed.) Designing Privacy Enhancing Technologies. LNCS, vol. 2009, pp. 1–9. Springer, Heidelberg (2001)

Randell, C., Muller, H.: The Shopping Jacket: Wearable Computing for the Consumer. Personal Technologies 4(4), Springer, London (2000)

Ratsimor, O., Finin, T., Joshi, A., Yesha, Y.: eNcentive: A framework for intelligent marketing in mobile peer-to-peer environments. In: Proceedings of the 5th international conference on electronic commerce, Pittsburgh, Pennsylvania, ACM Press, New York

RegTP, Jahresbericht 2003 – Marktdaten der Regulierungsbehörde für Telekommunikation und Post. German Regulatory authority of telecommunication and postal system (2003)

de Reyck, B., Degraeve, Z.: Broadcast scheduling for mobile advertising. Operations Research 51(4) (2003)

Schilit, B.N., Adams, N.I., Want, R.: Context-Aware Computing Applications. In: Proceedings of the IEEE Workshop on Mobile Computing Systems and Applications, Santa Cruz, CA, IEEE Computer Society Press, Los Alamitos (1994)

Schmidt, A., Beigl, M., Gellersen, H.-W.: There is more to context than location. Computer and Graphics 23(6) (1999)

Straub, T., Heinemann, A.: An anonymous bonus point system for mobile commerce based on word-of-mouth recommendations. In: Proc. of the 2004 ACM symposium on Applied computing, Nicosia, Cyprus, ACM Press, New York (2004)

Sokolov, D.: Rabattstreifen per SMS. Spiegel Online, 20.10.2004 (2004)

Tähtinen, J., Salo, J.: Special features of mobile advertising and their utilization. In: Proceedings of the 33rd EMAC conference, Murcia, Spain. European Marketing Academy (2004)

Yunos, H., Gao, J., Shim, S.: Wireless advertising's challenges and opportunities. IEEE Computer 36(5) (2003)

Wang, Z.: An agent based integrated service platform for wireless and mobile environments. Shaker (2003)

On Digital Cash-Like Payment Systems

Daniel A. Nagy

Queen's University, Dept. of Math. and Stats.
Jeffrey Hall, Kingston, ON, K7L 3N6, Canada
nagydani@mast.queensu.ca

Abstract. In present paper a novel approach to on-line payment is presented that tackles some issues of digital cash that have, in the author's opinion, contributed to the fact that despite the availability of the technology for more than a decade, it has not achieved even a fraction of the anticipated popularity. The basic assumptions and requirements for such a system are revisited, clear (economic) objectives are formulated and cryptographic techniques to achieve them are proposed.

Keywords: online payment systems, digital cash, security, cryptography.

1 Introduction

Chaum *et al.* begin their seminal paper (D. Chaum, 1988) with the observation that the use of credit cards is an act of faith on the part of all concerned, exposing all parties to fraud. Indeed, almost two decades later, the credit card business is still plagued by all these problems and credit card fraud has become a major obstacle to the normal development of electronic commerce, but digital cash-like payment systems similar to those proposed (and implemented) by D. Chaum have never become viable competitors, let alone replacements for credit cards or paper-based cash.

One of the reasons, in the author's opinion, is that payment systems based on similar schemes lack some key characteristics of paper-based cash, rendering them economically infeasible. Let us quickly enumerate the most important properties of cash:

1. "Money doesn't smell." Cash payments are – potentially – *anonymous* and untraceable by third parties (including the issuer).
2. Cash payments are final. After the fact, the paying party has no means to reverse the payment. We call this property of cash transactions *irreversibility*.
3. Cash payments are *peer-to-peer*. There is no distinction between merchants and customers; anyone can pay anyone. In particular, anybody can receive cash payments without contracts with third parties.
4. Cash allows for "acts of faith" or *naïve transactions*. Those who are not familiar with all the anti-forgery measures of a particular banknote or do not have the necessary equipment to verify them, can still transact with cash relying on the fact that what they do not verify is nonetheless verifiable in principle.
5. The amount of cash issued by the issuing authority is public information that can be verified through an auditing process.

J. Filipe et al. (Eds.): ICETE 2005, CCIS 3, pp. 26–38, 2007.

The payment system proposed in (D. Chaum, 1988) focuses on the first characteristic while partially or totally lacking all the others. The same holds, to some extent, for all existing cash-like digital payment systems based on untraceable blind signatures (Brands, 1993a; Brands, 1993b; A. Lysyanskaya, 1998), rendering them unpractical.

In his invited paper to Scientific American (Chaum, 1992), D. Chaum eloquently argues the importance of untraceability, so there is no need to repeat it here. It is worth noting, however, that while coins are truly untraceable in practice, paper-cash with its unique serial numbers is not. Yet, it does not seem to hamper its wide acceptance, because the anonymity of the transactions provides for sufficient privacy. The importance of the other four characteristics lies in the economics behind cash:

Irreversibility removes an important transaction cost, namely that of potential reversal. An insurance against reversal has to be built into the price of services offered in exchange for reversible payment. Anonymity is a necessary, but not sufficient component of irreversibility. The payment system proposed in (D. Chaum, 1988) sacrifices irreversibility in order to allow for off-line transactions, assuming that communication with the issuing authority is more expensive than communication between the transacting parties or complex computations. At the time of writing, this might have been the case, but today, when the infrastructure for low-bandwidth communication (such as short text messages, http queries, etc.) is ubiquitous, the benefits of off-line transactions are clearly inferior to those of irreversible transactions.

The *peer-to-peer* nature of a payment system also removes a significant cost; if a contract with a third party is necessary to receive payments, it is very likely that this third party will charge for its service. This raises the entry barrier for sellers and thus narrows the assortment of goods and services available in exchange for the payment that is not peer-to-peer, reducing its liquidity. In addition to this, merchant contracts unnecessarily expose sellers to the provider of the payment service; their income becomes known. It is important to emphasize that by peer-to-peer payment I do not imply that there are no servers or other centralized entities involved; it merely means that there is no distinction between sellers and buyers, merchants and customers. Anyone can pay anyone.

Naïve transactions help reducing the costs of distributing the tools (hardware and software) used for transactions. Contrarily to the assumptions of (D. Chaum, 1988), computation is far less ubiquitous than communication. While everyone with a cellular or a touch-tone telephone, a web-browser or email client in its readily available, out-of-box configuration is able to transmit short messages (up to a few hundred bits), performing complex calculations involving strong asymmetric cryptography requires additional tools which not everyone possesses or can afford to run. The fact that it is impossible to transact without performing complex calculations in real time is a far more serious obstacle than the need to contact the issuer for each transaction. It also undermines the trust in the system, as the the failure of the equipment used for storing and transacting with such "cash" (a very serious problem with (Brands, 1993b)) can cause unlimited damage, that cannot be mitigated. The fact that low-tech, naïve transactions are possible (and, in fact, quite common) with cash, greatly contributes to its acceptance and popularity. It is important to stress that no-one is *forced* to transact naïvely, and always has a choice of performing extra verification and discover attempts at cheating. Just as one always has the option of verifying one or more security features of a banknote before accepting it.

The *transparent governance* of the issuer is perhaps the most important reason to trust it. If the issuer is able to issue digital money without anybody noticing, its credit-worthiness cannot be established and the incentive to hyper-inflate (overborrowing by irresponsible emission) is enormous. While the information about the distribution and the holders of cash is private, its total amount should be public and verifiable. The lack of transparency of emission, in the author's opinion, is among the primary reasons for the failure of digital cash-like payment systems in the market.

In the rest of the paper, we develop a set of protocols that provide for all of the above characteristics of a digital payment system under certain model assumptions. The proposed system resembles the one proposed by Jakobbson (Jakobsson, 1999) in that it can be regarded as one with disposable anonymous accounts. Such disposable anonymous account based systems have achieved greater acceptance in the market (most notably WebMoney at `http://wmtransfer.com`) than those based on untraceable transfers between accounts tied to identity, but the current implementations either do not provide sufficient security for high-value transactions or impose too high overhead costs on low-value ones. The system outlined in this paper permits the users to choose the appropriate security measures that they deem appropriate for the given transaction. This is our principal contribution.

2 Preliminaries

In the proposed system, the issuer I maintains a public record of transactions, consisting of a chronologically ordered sequence of digitally signed statements S_i, where $i = 1, 2, 3, \ldots$ is called the *serial number* of the statement. The serial number can be unambiguously inferred from S_i. Digitally signed means that anybody can verify using only publicly available information in a computationally inexpensive way that S_i originates form I. Public-key signature schemes such as those described in (R. L. Rivest, 1978; Elgamal, 1985; NIST, 1991) can provide for such functionality in practice, together with some public key distribution protocol. These implementation details lie outside of the scope of this paper.

After some S_n has been published, it can be verified by anyone that for all $i \in \mathbb{N}^+$ such that $i < n$, S_i has also been (previously) published and that different statements do not share the same serial number. The structure of the statements is the following: $S_i = (i, I, V_i, C_i, N_i, \Sigma_i)$ where $\Sigma_i = \sigma_I(i, I, V_i, C_i, N_i)$ is the digital signature unique to the rest of S_i and I. Each statement implies the promise of issuer I to pay V_i units of value to anyone who first responds to cryptographic challenge C_i (which requires the possession of some secret D_i). N_i is the request message resulting in issuing S_i that may be the response to some earlier C_j (where $j < i$). Note that in a practical implementation the promise can be explicitly stated as an additional piece of information within S_i, signed together with the rest.

The request message N_i can be one of the following five kinds:

1. $\mathcal{E}$: emission request. In this case $N_i = (\mathcal{E}, C_i, V_i, \Omega_i)$ where C_i is a new challenge, V_i is the value of newly issued currency and $\Omega_i = \sigma_J(\mathcal{E}, C_i, V_i)$ is the digital

signature unique to the rest of N_i and J – an authorized individual. After receiving N_i, the issuer verifies Ω_i and the fact that C_i has never been used before. If the request is accepted, a new statement $S_i = (i, I, V_i, C_i, N_i, \Sigma_i)$ is issued where i is just the next available serial number at the time of receiving the request.

2. $\mathcal{X}$: exchange request. In this case $N_i = (\mathcal{X}, j, C_i, R_j)$ where $j < i$, C_i is a new challenge and R_j is the additional information making N_i a valid response to C_j – an older challenge. After receiving N_i, the issuer verifies whether or not it constitutes the first valid response to C_j, and if it does and C_i has never been used before, the new statement $S_i = (i, I, V_j, C_i, N_i, \Sigma_i)$ is issued. The fact of issuing S_i "invalidates" S_j in that future responses to C_j can be rejected by pointing to N_i inside S_i; a previous response.

3. $\mathcal{M}$: merge request. In this case $N_i = (\mathcal{M}, j, k, R_j)$ where $j, k < i$, R_j is the additional information making N_i a valid response to C_j – an older challenge. After receiving N_i, the issuer verifies whether or not it constitutes the first valid response to C_j, and if it does and S_k is a pending promise in that it has not been fulfilled or superseded answering an earlier request, the new statement $S_i = (i, I, V_j + V_k, C_k, N_i, \Sigma_i)$ is issued. The fact of issuing S_i fulfills the promise of S_j and supersedes the promise of S_k thus "invalidating" both of those.

4. $\mathcal{S}$: split request. In this case $N_i = (\mathcal{S}, j, C_i, V_i, C_{i+1}, R_j)$ where $j < i$, C_i and C_{i+1} are new challenges, $V_i < V_j$ and R_j is the additional information making N_i a valid response to C_j – an older challenge. After receiving N_i, the issuer verifies whether or not it constitutes the first valid response to C_j, and if it does and C_i and C_{i+1} have never been used before and $V_i < V_j$ then two new statements are issued: $S_i = (i, I, V_i, C_i, N_i, \Sigma_i)$ and $S_{i+1}(i + 1, I, V_j - V_i, C_{i+1}, N_i, \Sigma_{i+1})$. The fact of issuing S_i or S_{i+1} "invalidates" S_j by fulfilling its promise. Note that S_i and S_{i+1} can be reconstructed from one another by I, thus the issuing of the two can be regarded as an atomic operation.

5. $\mathcal{I}$: invalidation request. In this case $N_i = (\mathcal{I}, j, \Omega_i', R_j)$ where $j < i$ and R_j is the additional information making N_i a valid response to C_j – an older challenge and $\Omega_i' = \sigma_J(\mathcal{I}, j)$ is the digital signature of J – an authorized individual. After receiving N_i, the issuer verifies Ω_i' and whether or not N_i constitutes the first valid response to C_j, and if it does, the new statement $S_i(i, I, 0, C_j, N_i, \Sigma_i)$ is issued effectively invalidating S_j and removing the amount V_j from circulation. N_i constitutes a proof that the promise of S_j has been fulfilled (outside the payment system).

Since all S_i statements are public, anyone can verify that they follow the above specification. Most importantly that the ones with $\mathcal{X}$, $\mathcal{M}$ and $\mathcal{S}$ requests make and fulfill promises of equal values. The amount of issued currency can be calculated as follows:

$$V = \sum_{i:N_i \in \mathcal{E}} V_i - \sum_{i:N_i \in \mathcal{I}} V_{j(N_i)}$$

that is the summary value of emission requests minus the summary value of invalidation requests. The ability of the issuer to live up to its outstanding promises can be verified through traditional auditing.

3 Transaction Protocols

A party in possession of D_i is said to be the holder of the (public) promise embodied in S_i, unless that promise has already been fulfilled or superseded. Thus, it is the set of D_i secrets that constitute the title to certain value. The physical means of storing these secrets does not really matter as long as it permits the owner to protect the secrecy and to retrieve when necessary. Because of this, anybody can hold such a currency who is able to store and retrieve small amounts of information, allowing for the third property of cash discussed in section 1. The "act of faith" mentioned in conjunction with the fourth property of cash is in this case believing that some D_i indeed corresponds to C_i from S_i which is indeed a statement issued by the issuer.

In order to transact securely, the following capabilities can be required:

1. Sending short messages to the issuer in a reliable fashion and access to the public records with the issuer's public statements.
2. Verifying the digital signature of the issuer.
3. Generating random pairs of challenges C and corresponding secrets D required for a valid response.
4. Generating R_i for a valid response to some C_i once in possession of the corresponding D_i.
5. An established digital identity with the capability of sending signed messages in a secure fashion.

3.1 Fund Transfer Without Receipt

In this scenario Alice (A) wants to transfer some V amount of funds to Bob (B), but does not need a proof for some third party that Bob has received the funds; all she needs is to make sure that nobody else but Bob receives the payment and she knows that it has happened. For doing so, Alice only needs to possess some $\mathbf{D}_k = \{D_{k1}, D_{k2}, \ldots\}$ set of secrets so that $\sum_{j \in k(\mathbf{D}_k)} V_j \geq V$ that is she needs to have enough funds.

1. A assembles a set $\mathbf{D}_m = \{D_{m1}, D_{m2} \ldots\}$ of secrets such that $\sum_{j \in \{m(\mathbf{D}_m)\}} V_j = V$ and a set $\mathbf{J}_m$ of corresponding serial numbers. If $\mathbf{D}_k$ has a suitable subset, then she can use that. If not, she selects a subset $\mathbf{D}_n \subset \mathbf{D}_k$ (with a corresponding serial number set $\mathbf{J}_n$) and an additional secret $D_x \in \mathbf{D}_k \setminus \mathbf{D}_n$ such that $\sum_{j \in n(\mathbf{D}_n)} V_j < V$ and $\sum_{j \in n(\mathbf{D}_n)} V_j + V_x > V$. Then she generates two new challenge-secret pairs (C_y, D_y) and (C_z, D_z), and sends the message $N = (\mathcal{S}, x, C_y, V - \sum_{j \in \{n(D_n)\}} V_j, C_z, R_x)$ to I. At this point, $\mathbf{D}_m := \mathbf{D}_n \cup \{D_x\}$ and $\mathbf{J}_m = \mathbf{J}_n \cup \{i\}$ where i is the serial number of the statement that I published in response to N.
2. A sends $\mathbf{D}_m = \{D_{m1}, D_{m2}, \ldots\}$ and $\mathbf{J}_m = \{j_{m1}, j_{m2}, \ldots\}$ to B.
3. B generates a set of new challenge-secret pairs $\{(C_{b1}, D_{b1}), (C_{b2}, D_{b2}), \ldots\}$ with the same cardinality as $\mathbf{D}_m$ and $\mathbf{J}_m$. Then, for each $D_k \in \mathbf{D}_m$ he sends the following message to I: $N_k = (\mathcal{X}, j_{mk}, C_{bk}, R_k)$ where R_k is calculated from D_k and the rest of N_k. His set $\mathbf{D}_b = \{D_{b1}, D_{b2}, \ldots\}$ becomes a value worth V at this point. Using further $\mathcal{S}$ and $\mathcal{M}$ messages, he can rearrange it in any way he wants.

4. A can verify that the transaction has been completed by verifying that all the promises embodied in $\{S_j : j \in \mathbf{J}_m\}$ have been fulfilled. If she is convinced that the message to B has not been intercepted, she can be also convinced that B took possession of the transfered funds. However, she has no means of proving this to a third party.

The above described transaction is in direct analogy with cash transfers: first A selected an appropriate amount of cash from her wallet (possibly splitting a large denomination at the bank to make sure she has exact change), then handed it over to B, who exchanged all the received cash with the bank (so that A doesn't know the serial numbers of his banknotes).

This protocol is perfectly suitable for low-value purchases (e.g. micropayment), as the computational and communicational requirements on A's part are minimal. For example, if A has to pay for viewing a webpage, and she has "exact change", that is she possesses some D_x, such that the corresponding S_x is a valid promise of the required value, all she has to do is to enter D_x (and x, if it cannot be retrieved) when the website asks for payment.

Note, furthermore, that the transaction is initiated by the sender, thus anybody can be paid in this fashion; the naïve recipient can make an "act of faith" (believing that the honest sender "forgot" the secrets that have been transfered) and use the received secrets as payment without exchanging them with the issuer.

3.2 Fund Transfer with Receipt

For high-value transactions, the protocol described in 3.1 is unsuitable, because the recipient can deny the receiving of funds without legal or reputational consequences, as the sender has no means to prove it to a third party. In the scenario described in this section, Alice (A) wants to buy something expensive (worth V) from Bob (B).

1. B generates a challenge-secret pair (C, D) and sends the signed invoice $Y = (V, C, X, \Theta)$ to A, where X is the identifier of the service that A wants to buy from B and $\Theta = \sigma_B(V, C, X)$ is the digital signature of the invoice by B. Y constitutes a promise by B that upon receiving V amount of funds in a way accessible to the holder of the secret corresponding to C he will perform X.
2. A verifies Θ and if it is correct, she assembles $\mathbf{D}_m$ as in 3.1 and sends a sequence of messages to I. The first message is $N_{m1} = (\mathcal{X}, j_{m1}, C, R_{m1})$ where R_{m1} is calculated from D_{m1} and the rest of N_{m1}. Let i_{mk} denote the serial number of the statement published by I in response to N_{mk}. N_{m1} is followed by a sequence of $N_{mk} = (\mathcal{M}, j_{mk}, i_{m(k-1)}, R_{mk})$ for $k = 2, 3, \ldots$.
3. At this point A is in possession of a conclusive proof that she has fulfilled her side of the contract: the pair $P_X = (Y, i_{mk})$. The private invoice Y is signed by B certifying his offer, while the public statement $S_{i_{mk}}$ signed by I certifies that the corresponding payment has been made. The two are linked by the equalities of $V_{i_{mk}} = V$ and $C_{i_{mk}} = C$. A sends P_X to B.
4. B extracts V, C and Θ from the received P_X, verifies Θ, downloads $S_{i_{mk}}$ from the public records, verifies $\Sigma_{i_{mk}}$ and checks whether $V_{i_{mk}} = V$ and $C_{i_{mk}} = C$. If everything matches, he performs X.

In case of dispute, A can show P_X to the judge at which point it is up to B to prove that X has been performed.

4 Attacks and Vulnerabilities

The security of the proposed payment system depends on the nature of the used cryptographic challenges; the actual objects behind C_i, D_i and R_i and the way the various messages are transfered between the various participants. Even without defining these, it is clear that the untraceability hinges on the fact that the users of the payment system are not identified when sending the messages (those denoted by N_i) to the issuer. This is weak anonymity and in this respect the proposed system is inferior to the ones based on blind signatures. However, it is not inferior to paper-based cash and prevents the issuer from knowing the turnover of the individual users, which the system described in (D. Chaum, 1988) does not.

It is also very important to emphasize that the costs of protecting oneself against fraud should not exceed the transaction value. Since on-line payment systems are often used for micropayment, it is important that it can be performed with minimum effort and tools, even at the cost of exposing oneself to fraud by a highly sophisticated attacker. As long as the attack costs significantly more than the transaction value, the payment system can be considered secure enough.

In this section, some attack and fraud scenarios are investigated.

4.1 Theft

Successful theft is defined as follows: attacker (T) manages to make I issue a public statement S_t so that $V_t > 0$ and D_t corresponding to C_t in known to T, even though T has not previously owned any secret corresponding to the challenges on the already published statements.

By definition, I issues public statements with $V_i > 0$ only upon accepting $\mathcal{E}$, $\mathcal{X}$, $\mathcal{M}$ and $\mathcal{S}$ messages. Thus, T needs to forge one of these.

The acceptance of $\mathcal{E}$ messages depends on the validity of Ω_i. If the signature function σ is secure, then forging the signature for an $\mathcal{E}$ message with a newly generated C_i is infeasible. Previous valid $\mathcal{E}$ messages cannot be reused, because C_i has to be new. Intercepting and modifying a valid $\mathcal{E}$ message is similarly computationally infeasible, if σ is secure.

$\mathcal{X}$, $\mathcal{M}$ and $\mathcal{S}$ messages are accepted if they constitute a valid response to some earlier challenge C_j. One way of forging such a message is by guessing the secret that corresponds to one of the valid challenges. Let us assume that there is some maximal reasonable complexity for the challenge and the probability of finding a corresponding secret by random guess to such a challenge is p. Note that the secret is not assumed to be unique to the challenge. If there are n valid challenges, the probability of guessing one is $1 - (1 - p)^n$ which if $p \ll n^{-1}$ is approximately pn. If T has the resources for trying m secrets, the probability of one of them corresponding to a valid challenge equals $1 - (1 - p)^{nm}$ which if $p \ll m^{-1}n^{-1}$ is approximately pnm. If this number is comfortably low, the system is secure against brute-force attacks. However, since it is the users who generate the challenge-secret pairs, I cannot protect them against poorly chosen (low-entropy) secrets; having a weak random source leaves one vulnerable to theft.

Another way of forging $\mathcal{X}$, $\mathcal{M}$ or $\mathcal{S}$ messages is by extracting a suitable secret from public information or intercepted communication. In the public records, T can find a large number of challenge-response pairs and this number is growing as the system is being used. Thus, it is instrumental for the security of the system that challenges and responses are uncorrelated.

Secrets are being communicated directly in the protocol described in 3.1. Hence, if T is able to intercept and decode the messages that payers send to recipients in this protocol, he is able to use them before the recipient. Therefore, it is important that the secrecy of the communication between the users is well protected in this protocol. Otherwise the payer is vulnerable to theft during the period of time when A has already sent the message to B but B hasn't yet sent the messages to I. Naïve recipients who do not exchange the received secrets immediately are vulnerable not only to fraud by the payer but also to theft if the communication has been intercepted. Naïve payers using open channels of communication are vulnerable to theft for a short period of time, which for micropayments can be a manageable risk worth taking, if using a secure channel is overly expensive.

In both protocols described in 3.1 and 3.2, one of the parties sends messages to I. If such a message (N_i) can be intercepted and decoded by T before it reaches I, much depends on the nature of the cryptographic challenge. In general, R_i is the function of some D_j and the rest of N_i. If it is feasible to compute (or guess with a high probability) D_j from N_i or some R_i' so that substituting C_i with C_i' (generated by T) and R_i with R_i' results in a valid response to C_j before the message reaches I, then the parties are vulnerable to theft. If it is not feasible to forge R_i without knowing D_j or to alter the message so that N_i' remains a valid response to C_j then the parties are not vulnerable to theft in this way, even if the communication with I can be intercepted, decoded and tampered with.

4.2   User Fraud

User fraud is intentional deception of a user of the payment system by another user assuming that the issuer issues public statements only as described in 2. There are two meaningful deceptions within a payment system: the paying party (A) fraudulently claims that a payment has been made or the receiving party (B) fraudulently claims that a payment has not been received.

There are two distinct issues with fraud: whether or not the other party can detect it and whether or not it can be proven to a third party. Naïve users can be defrauded in many ways. The present analysis is restricted to participants that perform all the necessary verifications in order to avoid being deceived.

In case of receiptless fund transfer as described in 3.1, fraudulent claims (of both kinds) cannot be proven to a third party, as none of the messages used in the transaction can be linked to the involved parties. However, A and B know exactly what has happened. Thus, this protocol is suitable only for transactions where one can afford the loss of one payment to establish the dishonesty of the other party.

The protocol described in 3.2 offers much better protection against fraud for both users. In order to claim a payment, A must produce P_X. A valid P_X, where $i(P_X)$ and $Y(P_X)$ are such that $C(S_i) = C(Y)$, cannot be produced without actually transferring the right amount of funds into B's exclusive possession, assuming that Y (which is signed by B) cannot be forged and some other Y' does not offer the same service X. It is instrumental that X is unique to each transaction. In order for A to be able to verify the uniqueness of X, X may incorporate a signed order of the service from A. P_X is a conclusive proof of the payment, disproving the fraudulent claim of B that the payment has not been made. The proof of rendering service X depends on the service and is not part of the payment system.

The vulnerability of users to fraud by one another does not depend on how the cryptographic challenges are implemented, as long as it is computationally infeasible to respond to the challenge without knowing the corresponding secret.

4.3 Issuer Fraud

By issuing digital currency, I is essentially borrowing from all holders. In this framework, fraud can be interpreted as misrepresenting one's creditworthiness. The public sequence $S_1, S_2, \ldots, S_i$ is essentially I's credit history. There are two kinds of meaningful deceptions when it comes to credit: borrowing more or defaulting on (parts of) existing debt without leaving a trace in the credit history. Since in the proposed system the act of borrowing (issuing) is the same as the act of publishing it (Grigg, 2004), the first kind of fraud is impossible by definition.

Thus, we can define successful issuer fraud as failure to respond to user messages as defined in 2. It is important to emphasize that the defrauded party is *not* the one who has sent the message that has not been appropriately processed but all the holders of I's "currency". Before going into more detailed analysis, it is worth noting that the messages do not contain information regarding their origin, thus if I attempts fraud, it can never be sure that it is not a spot-check by an auditor or the law enforcement. Thus, there are strong incentives not to commit fraud when dealing with anonymous customers.

The first important observation is that I can ignore the received messages; pretend as if they have not been received. It is the information carrier service that can provide various facilities to prevent this from happening without a trace, but most carriers do not provide them.

Secondly, the issuer can obviously do anything to a message that an attacker described in section 4.1 can. Thus, all the vulnerabilities mentioned there apply; theft can be perpetrated by I under the same conditions. The only difference is that I can operate with $\mathcal{I}$ requests as well.

If the cryptographic challenge is implemented in such a way that a valid response does not divulge the secret or allow for altered valid responses (see also 4.1), the customer (A) can accuse I by publishing the message (N) that has been supposedly ignored by I. Of course, it has no immediate consequences for I, as A could not have transfered the message previously, but after N has been published, I can disprove the accusation of fraud by processing N.

5   Suitable Cryptographic Challenges

In this section, some cryptographic challenge implementation are proposed and their advantages and disadvantages explained. Since it is the legitimate holder of the value who picks the corresponding challenge, it is possible to implement more challenges and let the users decide which ones they deem appropriate for protecting their wealth and privacy.

This list is by no means comprehensive. New kinds of challenge-response pairs are being developed, fulfilling various requirements resulting from different assumptions about the capabilities of the paying and the receiving party.

5.1   Message Digest (Hash) Function

Challenge: $C = h(D)$, an element from the range of the hash function
Secret: D, a random element from the domain of the hash function
Response: $R = D$ same as the secret. Valid if $h(R) = C$.

In this case, the challenge is the cryptographic hash (e. g. the SHA1[1](NIST, 1995)) of the secret, which is chosen randomly from a large enough pool, so that the probability of guessing it is sufficiently low. The valid response to the challenge is simply a message including the secret itself.

The advantages of this implementation are the following: It is very simple and computationally undemanding, offering good protection with relatively short secrets (e.g. 200 bits), that can be transfered using very narrow channels (e.g. speech, barcodes, typing, etc.). It is easy to compute the challenge corresponding to the secret, which in turn can be used as the key of the public statement database. Hence, it is not necessary to store the index of the corresponding statement together with the secret.

The disadvantage is that the response reveals the secret, thus leaving the payer vulnerable to theft, when communicating with the issuer over an insecure channel.

5.2   Public Key Signature

Challenge: $C = K$, a public signature key
Secret: $D = K'$, the private pair of K
Response: $R = \sigma_K(N')$, the digital signature of the message.

In this case, the challenge is a public signature key (e.g. an RSA or a DSA public key (NIST, 1991; R. L. Rivest, 1978)) and the secret is its private pair. The two are selected randomly by the customer from a large enough pool, so that the probability of guessing is sufficiently low. The valid response is a message with a valid digital signature.

---

[1] At the time of writing, the collision attack against SHA1 by Wang *et al.* was not known. However, even a successful collision attack against the hash function used in this implementation (and the ones below) does not allow, to the author's best knowledge, for attacks against the proposed payment system, as long as finding pre-images for a given hash value is infeasible, so even in the light of recent developments, it is safe to use SHA1 for this purpose. Nevertheless, it may be wise to consider alternatives. Collision attacks against the hash function used as part of the σ function (from Section 2) can be more worrisome.

The advantages are the following: The secret is not revealed by the response, thus the ownership can be proved without disclosure. It is secure against theft even if the communication channel is insecure. It is secure against theft by the issuer.

Disadvantages: The secret is too long to be transfered though low-capacity channels or to be recorded quickly using low-tech means (e.g. scribbled down on a piece of paper). The transactions are computationally costly. In particular, generating a secure random key-pair takes minutes even on a modern computer. Elliptic Curve Cryptography (ECC) promises to alleviate these problems to some extent by providing equivalent security with shorter keys.

Note that it is possible to use a blinding scheme compatible with this type of challenge to break traceablity. The real difficulty in this case is preserving the accountability of the issuer. A scheme similar to the one proposed in (M. Stadler, 1995) could be utilized as a disincentive for the issuer to issue unbacked "coins".

5.3   Public-Key Signature and Message Digest

Challenge: $C = h(K)$, the one-way hash of the public signature key
Secret: $D = (K, K')$, a public/private key pair
Response: $R = (\sigma_K(N'), K)$, a digital signature and the corresponding public key

This modification of the previous scheme allows for seamless integration with the scheme described in 5.1, as the challenge has the same format. Thus, the same system can easily provide for both kinds of challenges. The advantages and the disadvantages are the same as those in 5.2.

An additional advantage is that the public key is not available for cryptanalysis by an attacker until too late. Since the key has to be used only once for generating exactly one signature, it can be substantially weaker than the one required for the previous case, allowing for a decrease in the required computational power on the user side even with traditional asymmetric cryptography.

5.4   Public-Key Signature and Symmetric-Key Block Cipher

Challenge: $C = (K, \rho_D(K'))$, a public signature key and the encrypted version of its
    private pair
Secret: D, a randomly chosen symmetric key for the block cipher ρ.
Response: $R = \sigma_K(N')$, the digital signature of the message

In this case, the challenge consists of a public signature key and its private counterpart encrypted using a symmetric-key block cipher ρ (e.g.). The secret D is the symmetric key needed to decrypt the private key K'. The valid response is the same as in 5.2.

The advantage of this challenge over the one described in 5.2 is that the secret is short and thus can be transfered and stored easily using low-tech means, similarly to 5.1. However, the challenge cannot be deduced from the secret, thus one needs to record the index of the corresponding public statement as well.

5.5 Message Digest, Public-Key Signature and Block Cipher

Challenge: $C = (h(D), K, \rho_D(K'))$, a hash of the secret, a public key and the encrypted version of its private pair
Secret: D, a randomly chosen symmetric key for the block cipher ρ.
Response: $R = \sigma_K(N')$ or $R = D$, the digital signature of the message or the secret itself

In this case, the challenges described in sections 5.1 and 5.4 are used in conjunction, so that a valid response to either one is accepted. The corresponding secret is the same.

The advantages of this approach include all the advantages of the two methods, with the exception of computational simplicity offered by 5.1; generating a random challenge is still difficult.

It is up to the individual customers to chose which part of the challenge they use, depending on the available facilities and security requirements.

6 Conclusions

The proposed digital payment system is more similar to cash than the existing digital payment solutions. It offers reasonable measures to protect the privacy of the users and to guarantee the transparency of the issuer's operations. With an appropriate business model, where the provider of the technical part of the issuing service is independent of the financial providers and serves more than one of the latter, the issuer has sufficient incentives not to exploit the vulnerability described in 4.3, even if the implementation of the cryptographic challenge allowed for it. This parallels the case of the issuing bank and the printing service responsible for printing the banknotes.

The author believes that an implementation of such a system would stand a better chance on the market than the existing alternatives, none of which has lived up to the expectations, precisely because it matches paper-based cash more closely in its most important properties.

Open-source implementations of the necessary software are being actively developed as parts of the ePoint project. For details, please see `http://sf.net/projects/epoint`

References

Lysyanskaya, A.Z.R.: Group blind digital signatures: A scalable solution to electronic cash. In: Hirschfeld, R. (ed.) FC 1998. LNCS, vol. 1465, p. 184. Springer, Heidelberg (1998)
Brands, S.: An efficient off-line electronic cash system based on the representation problem. Technical Report CS-R9323, CWI (1993a)
Brands, S.: Untraceable on-line electronic cash in wallets with observers. In: Brickell, E.F. (ed.) CRYPTO 1992. LNCS, vol. 740, pp. 302–318. Springer, Heidelberg (1993)
Chaum, D.: Achieving electronic privacy. Scientific American, 96–101 (1992)
Chaum, D., Fiat, A.: Untraceable electronic cash. In: Goldwasser, S. (ed.) CRYPTO 1988. LNCS, vol. 403, pp. 319–327. Springer, Heidelberg (1990)

Elgamal, T.: A public-key cryptosystem and a signature scheme based on discrete logarithms. IEEE Transactions on Information Theory IT-31, 469–472 (1985)

Grigg, I.: The ricardian contract. In: Proceedings of IEEE Workshop on Electronic Contracting July 6, pp. 25–31. IEEE Computer Society Press, Los Alamitos (2004)

Jakobsson, M.: Mini-cash: A minimalistic approach to e-commerce. In: Imai, H., Zheng, Y. (eds.) PKC 1999. LNCS, vol. 1560, pp. 122–135. Springer, Heidelberg (1999)

Stadler, M.J.-M., Piveteau, J.C.: Fair blind signatures. In: Guillou, L.C., Quisquater, J.-J. (eds.) EUROCRYPT 1995. LNCS, vol. 921, pp. 209–210. Springer, Heidelberg (1995)

NIST Proposed federal information processing standard for digital signature standard (dss). Federal Register 56, 42980–42982 (1991)

NIST Secure hash standard. FIPS 180-1 (1995)

Rivest, R.L., Shamir, A.L.A.: A method for obtaining digital signatures and public-key cryptosystem. Communications of the ACM 21, 120–126 (1978)

In-Depth Analysis of Selected Topics Related to the Quality Assessment of E-Commerce Systems

Antonia Stefani[1], Dimitris Stavrinoudis[1], and Michalis Xenos[1,2]

[1] School of Sciences & Technology,Hellenic Open University,23 Sachtouri Str, Patras, Greece
`stefani@eap.gr,stavrino@eap.gr,xenos@eap.gr`
[2] Research Academic Computer Technology Institute, 61 Riga Feraiou Str, Patras, Greece

Abstract. This paper provides an in-depth analysis of selected important topics related to the quality assessment of e-commerce systems. It briefly introduces to the reader a quality assessment model based on Bayesian Networks and presents in detail the practical application of this model, highlighting practical issues related to the involvement of human subjects, conflict resolution, and calibration of the measurement instruments. Furthermore, the paper presents the application process of the model for the quality assessment of various e-commerce systems; it also discusses in detail how particular features (data) of the assessed e-commerce systems can be identified and, using the described automated assessment process, lead to higher abstraction information (desiderata) regarding the quality of the assessed e-commerce systems.

Keywords: E-commerce Systems, Quality Assessment, Bayesian Networks.

1 Introduction

In the past few years, a large number of e-commerce systems have been developed. To ensure the production of high quality e-commerce systems, it is important for developers to be able to assess the quality of such systems. The latter is inevitably linked with the receivers' perception of quality. It must be noted that e-commerce systems differ from other web applications in that a basic condition of their success is the total involvement of the end-user at almost every stage of the purchasing process (Henfridsson & Holmstrom, 2003), which is not the case with other web applications. The growth that Business to Consumer (B2C) e-commerce systems have experienced in the past few years has given rise to the problem of identification of those factors that determine end-user acceptance of such systems (Chen et al., 2004).

The work presented in this paper is based on a Bayesian Network model (Stefani et al., 2003). The attributes of this model are quality characteristics. Quality assessments using this model can take the form of either a probability value for the abstract 'quality', or a vector of values for each quality characteristic. To be able to interpret this vector of values in a way that provides conclusions about e-commerce systems' quality, one should have collected and analyzed a significant volume of data that will aid in calibrating the measurement scales. This is what this paper focuses on: the presentation of the process used to conduct the quality assessment. Moreover, to help

J. Filipe et al. (Eds.): ICETE 2005, CCIS 3, pp. 39–48, 2007.

make the discussion clearer, this paper presents and explains selected practical cases, serving as examples, related to the process of quality assessment.

This paper is structured in five sections. After this brief introduction, section 2 presents related work. Section 3 presents the model and describes the process used for quality assessment of e-commerce systems. Then, section 4, presents practical cases of quality assessment, used to explain the application of the model and how its results can lead to higher abstraction conclusions. Finally, section 5 summarizes the main conclusions of the paper.

2   Related Work

A number of approaches towards assessing the quality of e-commerce systems focus on the technological aspects of such systems, thus providing a technology-oriented view of quality (Zwass, 1996; Elfriede & Rashka, 2001). Other approaches assess the quality of e-commerce systems as perceived by the end-user, but focusing mainly on the usability of such systems. Such approaches use software evaluation methods such as inspection (Nielsen, 1994) and inquiry methods (Shaw & DeLone, 2002) in order to record end-users' perception of usability. Studies on e-commerce systems quality also focus on more specific quality characteristics such as issues that warrant successful transactions (Bidgoli, 2002), maximize the perceived trustworthiness (Egger, 2001; Slyke et al., 2004), or ensure e-commerce systems reliability (Elfriede & Rashka, 2001).

Although, all the above factors are affecting the quality of e-commerce systems and are prerequisites for their success, they are not the only ones that relate to e-commerce systems quality. In order to model e-commerce systems quality, a global approach, such as the one discussed in this paper, is required combining all factors affecting quality.

Some related works are using questionnaires to detect users' opinions, the data from which are statistically analyzed in order to lead in values measuring quality characteristics such as usability (Sauro & Kindlund, 2005). This is a common practice, since users' opinion is very important for the assessment of e-commerce systems (Julian & Standing, 2003), as well as the active involvement of users into the evaluation process (Henfridsson & Holmstrom, 2003; Chen et al., 2004).

The work presented in this paper, differs from questionnaire-based surveys in that it uses a process aiming to limit subjectivity and frequent errors in similar surveys. Furthermore, thanks to the nature of the used model, the assessment process can be used forwards and backwards, i.e. during the quality design phase for setting the quality goals of an e-commerce system.

3   The Model Application Process

In order to assess the quality of e-commerce systems as perceived by the end-users, one must focus on the user oriented quality characteristics of ISO 9126 (ISO/IEC 9126, 2001), which are functionality, usability, reliability and efficiency, and their sub-characteristics. The model used in this process is based on Bayesian Networks, which are a special category of graphic models where nodes represent variables and the directed arrows the relations between them. In this case, the model's nodes are the above mentioned quality characteristics as well as e-commerce characteristics that are connected to the appropriate quality characteristics, forming a number of relations between them. For each node of this model the dependent probabilities that describe the relations between the variables is determined.

The model can be used both forwards and backwards. In the forward use, the user inserts evidence to the nodes of the e-commerce characteristics, which have only two possible states: 'yes' and 'no'. In this way, the model estimates the system's quality providing the probabilities for the possible states of the nodes that represent the quality characteristics and the overall quality. The backward use of the model provides assessments regarding the child nodes (e.g. nodes of e-commerce characteristics) when the value of a parent node (e.g. node of 'quality' characteristic) is defined. Since the purpose of this paper is to present the process followed for assessing the quality of already existing e-commerce systems, we focus mainly on the forward use of the model.

This process, which is also represented in figure 1, consists of 4 different steps: a) the assignment of an e-commerce system to two evaluators and the filling of an appropriate evaluation sheet by them, b) the examination of the identity between the two evaluation sheets, c) the forward use of the model and d) the classification of the e-commerce system. These steps are described more analytically hereinafter.

The most important benefit of applying this model is the fact that it provides an easy and non-subjective way to rank an e-commerce system according not only to the overall quality, but to each quality characteristic as well. The limitation of the subjectivity while evaluating such a system is achieved because of the values of the possible states of the nodes that represent the e-commerce characteristics in the model. In other words, the evaluators are asked to determine the existence, or not, of these specific characteristics answered in the evaluation sheet by a simple yes or no. Although the contribution of the evaluators to the assessment of the quality of e-commerce systems is trivial and non-subjective, the first step of the process is to assign this task to two evaluators. In this way, possible errors while filling the evaluation sheet, mainly because of careless mistakes or because of the possibility of misunderstanding a question of the sheet, are avoided. It must also be stressed that the evaluators chosen for this process must be experts. This does not necessarily indicate that they should be experienced in judging or estimating the quality of a software product. But they should be expert users of such e-commerce systems and they should also be aware of the used terminology. Besides, they examine these systems only from their customer's viewpoint.

The evaluation sheet is in the form of a simple questionnaire, where the possible answers of each question are only two: 'yes' or 'no'. Although the aspects that it is concerned with are trivial, the questions must be clearly stated, and in some cases more specifically commented on, in order to avoid any misinterpretation by the evaluators. The evaluation sheet is then delivered to the evaluators either electronically or by hard copy. The questions on this sheet are stated as follows, so that they can be answered by a simple 'yes' or 'no':

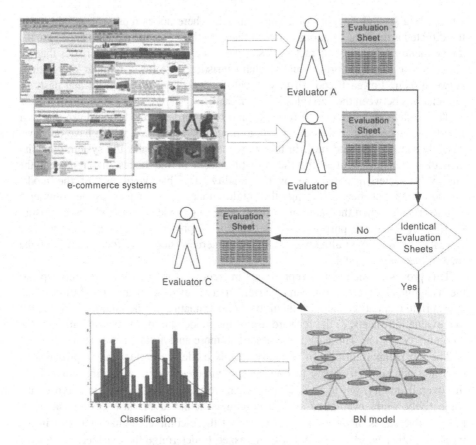

Fig. 1. The model application process

"Does the e-commerce system provide frequently asked questions (FAQs) to the user?",

"Is there a shopping cart available to the users in the e-commerce system?",

"Can the user sort automatically the results of a search by various parameters (e.g. order by price, order by manufacturer, alphabetical order, etc.)?".

The questionnaire is structured in such a way, in order to be clear to the evaluators which questions concern each quality factor. Furthermore, the sequence of the questions is in tune with the most possible sequence of actions that a user of the e-commerce system will follow when he visits the site and has a transaction with it.

The second step of the process is the examination of the answers given by the evaluators. The two evaluation sheets must be identical, since their questions are quite trivial and with obvious answers. However, because of possible mistakes while filling them, as mentioned above, a third evaluator is needed in this process. His role is to provide conflict resolution in such cases. Of course, these possible differences are easy to be solved by the first two evaluators if this is possible for them in terms of time and place. But, if this is not possible, then a third person must determine the appropriate answer when a difference between the evaluation sheets appears. The

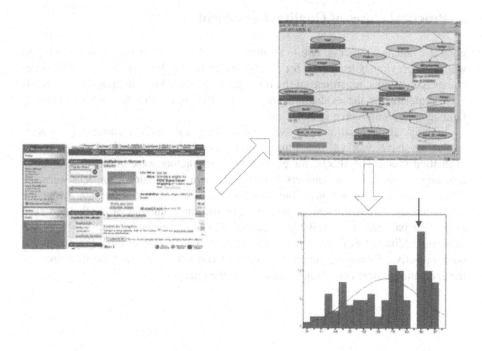

Fig. 2. Case of attractiveness

purpose of the third evaluator is also to eliminate the subjectivity if this appears in cases of significant differences between the opinions of the first two evaluators.

Having a fixed and correct evaluation sheet, the model can be used to assess the quality of the e-commerce system. In the next step of the process the answers of the sheet are inserted into the model as evidence to the nodes of the e-commerce characteristics, which are the leaf nodes of the Bayesian Network. Thus, by the forward use of the model, the corresponding probability values of all the parent nodes can be estimated automatically, since all the Node Probability Tables have already been specified. In this way, one can easily gather the provided results not only for the overall quality of the system, but also for all the quality characteristics and sub-characteristics used in the model.

The provided results from the model cannot be directly exploitable to determine the quality of the system. In fact, they are probability values of the possible states of the nodes. For example, a result of 0.88 for the usability node does not imply directly the level of the usability of the system. Thus, in the final step of the process the classification of the system for each quality characteristic and sub-characteristic is specified. This classification can be found by the means of the scale calibration table and the accompanying histograms that has been presented in (Stefani et al., 2004). In this way, using the boundaries and the scales of the probability values of the model, one is able to determine the specific category (good, average or poor) in which the e-commerce system belongs according to each quality characteristic. In other words, he can identify the cluster to which each quality characteristic belongs and detect the possible drawbacks of the system.

4 Practical Cases of Quality Assessment

For the evaluation process, two evaluators for each e-commerce system are selected who have previously used (e.g. for purchasing an item online) at least two distinct e-commerce systems, regardless of the time spent on them. This shopping experience is a pre-requisite for the evaluation process, because it ensures that the evaluator is familiar with e-commerce systems' use.

Initially an evaluation pair was established for each e-commerce system. Evaluators have worked individually and answered with 'yes' or 'no' on the evaluation sheet. The sheets, for every pair of evaluators were checked in order to find any conflicts in the answers between the two evaluators. Conflicts were the different answers that we have found on the evaluation sheets. Less than 5% of the evaluation sheets have revealed conflicts; the maximum number of conflicts of each evaluation pair was two, and the questions that have presented conflicts were the same for additional evaluation pairs. Therefore it is logical to assume the results are quite objective. Reasoning for the existence of conflicts was either the time spent at the evaluation process or misunderstanding of the questions.

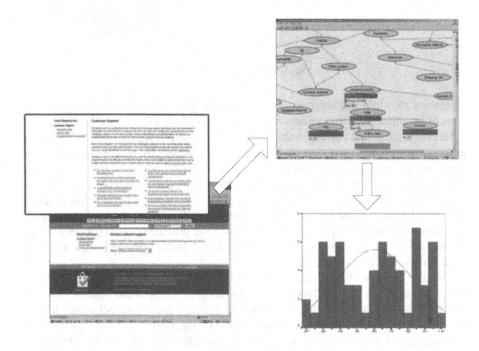

Fig. 3. Case of understandability

For example, the evaluators were addressed to examine if the e-commerce system provides video applications for the presentation of the product. The first evaluator answered 'no', because he had not found video application in the categories of Video and DVD at the e-commerce system, but the second evaluator had found video application at the CD category of the same e-commerce system and answered 'yes'.

In order to avoid these kind of conflicts, we asked the evaluators to use the ten most popular products of the e-commerce system or the products that the system sells at its home page. Additionally we asked the evaluators to proceed in a check out process in order to have a complete shopping experience.

In an ongoing process we have detected all the questions that presented conflict on the evaluation sheet and have edited them. Finally a third evaluator has been used in order to reduce the impact of the human factor. The third evaluator individually has provided answers for the questions that still presented conflicts and as a result of this process we had evaluation sheets with no subjectivity, because two evaluators agreed individually for a 'yes' or 'no'. So we have the final evaluation sheet for each e-commerce system that was used at the next step of the evaluation process. The answers for each final evaluation sheet were used as evidence in respect of the child node of the model's tool. Hereinafter we present three practical cases extracted from the quality assessment process of several e-commerce systems. In these cases we present the evaluators' answers for the evaluation sheets' criteria and also we present, in an anonymous representation, the functions and services which each e-commerce system offers.

4.1 First Case

For example, the evaluators were asked to examine the presentation of the products at each e-commerce system. The e-commerce system usually presents a product by text description where its properties are described; so each evaluator can have a description for products' characteristics and also information for cost and availability. Complementary e-commerce systems offer photographs, audio, video, graphics and 3-D representation of each product.

Figure 2 shows evaluators' evidence about the product's presentation. For image, and additional images in greater size, audio, and video samples the evaluators have answered 'yes'.

The probability value for the parent node titled 'Visualization', which refers to the visual representation of the product, is 0.88 and the value for product presentation by text and images is 0.94. Finally the probability value for the quality characteristic of Attractiveness is 0.89 and the meaning of these probability values can be explained using the scale calibration from our previous work (Stefani et al., 2004). Figure 2 presents the histogram for Attractiveness. This e-commerce system is characterized as 'Good' but the value of Attractiveness is on the boundaries between 'Good' and 'Average', meaning that the e-commerce system needs improvement at Graphics, 3-D representation, and animation.

4.2 Second Case

At the evaluation process each evaluator used Help functions that each e-commerce system supports. As Help functions we have defined the existence of FAQ (Frequently Asked Questions), contact capability via e-mail, or fax and online help. Figure 3 presents the help evaluation of an e-commerce system. The Understandability of the system as it is perceived by the customer is presented by the probability value 0.93. That means this e-commerce system belongs at Category A of the model's scale calibration, also the probability value for Usability is 0.87 which means that belongs also at category A.

4.3 Third Case

Another category of questions on the evaluation sheet is related to the search function of the e-commerce system. Usually the search function appears as a form where the evaluator can insert words as keywords for a question. In advance the evaluator can use the search function by defining the products' categories and limits for price in order to have more accurate results. The evaluator could search by keyword but the system did not provide advanced methods. The tool defines the search engine of the e-commerce system as good by the probability value of 0.62. This result means that the search engine of the e-commerce system usually provides correct results according to evaluators' keywords. That is the most common search option at e-commerce systems, but the same system by not providing advanced methods of searching does not offer a completely operable searching function.

According to operability the same e-commerce system offers informative features as compare features for products, and cross selling mechanism for complementary products, but the e-commerce system provides notification services by e-mail to the frequent customers. Finally the e-commerce system offers metaphors like shopping cart but not shopping list where the customer could save his/her shopping preferences. Figure 4 presents these values and the total operability of the e-commerce system, which is 0.55.

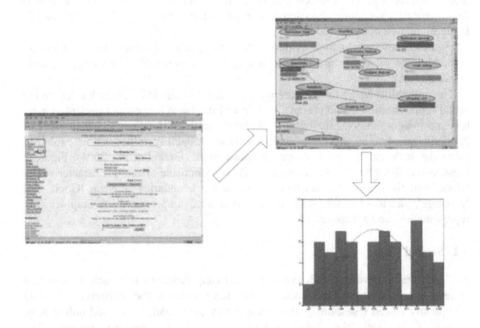

Fig. 4. Case of operability

In another case it is obvious that the absence of search functions that are extremely helpful at the purchasing process reflect the total quality of the system. The evaluator desired to view the search history of his/her searches in order to proceed with the results, and to have alternative ordering options, but the system offers none of these search options. On this evidence the model reveals that the absence of these options indicates search from this source is poor.

5 Conclusions

This paper presents a measurement process for the quality of e-commerce systems. This process uses a model based on a Bayesian Networks and consists of different steps, which are described analytically. The process has been applied in different e-commerce systems and cases of their results are also presented. Expert evaluators were asked to rank e-commerce systems by filling an appropriate evaluation sheet and by determining the existence or not of specific e-commerce characteristics in them. This sheet was formed in such a way in order to minimize subjectivity while evaluating such a system. Moreover, the process itself provides a way to eliminate any possible conflict between the evaluators' opinions.

Having a fixed evaluation sheet of an e-commerce system and by applying the Bayesian Network model the probability values of the overall quality and the quality characteristics can be assessed. Furthermore, by the means of the appropriate boundaries and scale calibration tables, the classification of the system for each quality characteristic and sub-characteristic can be specified.

The model can be used both forwards and backwards. Although the presented process is based on the forward use of the model as a summative evaluation of e-commerce systems, future work includes the application of the model during the design phase of an e-commerce system. In other words, it includes the formative evaluation of such systems. Moreover, the process of using the model should be refined dynamically, due to the continuous evolution and enhancement of the e-commerce systems and the appearance of new characteristics and functions provided by them.

References

Bidgoli, H.: Electronic Commerce Principles and Practice. Academic Press, San Diego (2002)

Chen, L., Gillenson, M., Sherrell, D.: Consumer Acceptance of Virtual Stores: A Theoretical Model and Critical Success Factors for Virtual Stores. The DATA BASE for Advances in Information Systems 35(2) (2004)

Egger, F.: Affective Design of E-Commerce User Interfaces: How to Maximise Perceived Trustworthiness. In: Egger, F. (ed.) International Conference on Affective Human Factors Design, Asean Academic, London (2001)

Elfriede, D., Rashka, J.: Quality Web Systems, Performance, Security, and Usability. Addison – Wesley, New York (2001)

Henfridsson, O., Holmstrom, H.: Developing E-commerce in Internetworked Organizations: A Case of Customer Involvement Throughout the Computer Gaming Value Chain. The DATA BASE for the Advances in Information Systems, 33(4) (2003)

ISO/IEC 9126, Software Product Evaluation – Quality Characteristics and Guidelines for the User. International Organization for Standardization, Geneva (2001)

Julian, T., Standing, C.: The value of User Participation in the E-Commerce Systems Development. Informing and IT Education Conference, Pori, Finland (2003)

Nielsen, J.: Designing Web Usability: The Practice of Simplicity. New Riders Publishing, Indianapolis. Indiana (2000)

Sauro, J., Kindlund, E.: A Method to Standardize Usability Metrics Into a Single Score. CHI 2005 Methods and Usability, Portland, Oregon, USA (2005)

Shaw, N., DeLone, W.: Sources of Dissatisfaction in End-User Support : An Empirical Study. The DATA BASE for Advances in Information Systems, 33(2) (2002)

Slyke, C., Belanger, F., Comunale, C.: Factors Influencing the Adoption of Web – Based Shopping: The Impact of Trust. The DATA BASE for Advances in Information Systems, 35(2)

Stefani, A., Xenos, M., Stavrinoudis, D.: Modeling E-Commerce Systems' Quality with Belief Networks. In: VECIMS, IEEE International Conference on Virtual Environments, Human-Computer Interfaces and Measurement Systems, IEEE, Los Alamitos (2003)

Stefani, A., Stavrinoudis, D., Xenos, M.: Experimental Based Tool Calibration used for Assessing the Quality of E-Commerce Systems. In: ICETE2004, 1st IEEE International Conference on E-Business and Telecommunication Networks, Portugal, IEEE Computer Society Press, Los Alamitos (2004)

Zwass, V.: Structure and macro-level impacts of electronic commerce: from technological infrastructure to electronic marketplaces. International Journal of Electronic Commerce, 1 (1996)

A Novel Real-Time Self-similar Traffic Detector/Filter to Improve the Reliability of a TCP Based End-to-End Client/Server Interaction Path for Shorter Roundtrip Time

Wilfred W.K. Lin[1], Allan K.Y. Wong[1], Richard S.L. Wu[1], and Tharam S. Dillon[2]

[1] Department of Computing, The Hong Kong Polytechnic University, Hung Hom, Kowloon,
Hong Kong S.A.R.
cswklin@comp.polyu.edu.hk, csalwong@comp.polyu.edu.hk,
csslwu@comp.polyu.edu.hk
[2] Faculty of Information Technology, University of Technology Sydney, Broadway, Sydney,
Australia
tharam@it.uts.edu.au

Abstract. The *self-similarity* (S^2) *filter* is proposed for real-time applications. It can be used independently or as an extra component for the *enhanced* RTPD (*real-time traffic pattern detector*) or E-RTPD. The S^2 *filter* basis is the "*asymptotically second-order self-similarity*" concept (alternatively called *statistical* $2^{nd} OSS$ or $S2^{nd} OSS$) for stationary time series. The focus is the IAT (inter-arrival times) traffic. The filter is original because similar approaches are not found in the literature for detecting self-similar traffic patterns on the fly. Different experiments confirm that with help form the S^2 *filter* the FLC (*Fuzzy Logic Controller*) dynamic buffer size tuner control more accurately. As a result the FLC improves the reliability of the client/server interaction path leading to shorter roundtrip time (RTT).

Keywords: Real-time traffic pattern detection (RTPD), stationary, asymptotically second-order self-similarity, CAB, Gaussian property, fractal.

1 Introduction

It is hard to harness the roundtrip time (RTT) of an end-to-end client/server interaction path over a TCP channel in time-critical applications. The problem is the heterogeneity and sheer size of the Internet. If the path error probability for retransmissions is ρ, the *average number of trials* (ANT) for successful transmission is

$$\sum_{j=1}^{\infty} j[\rho^{j-1}(1-\rho)] \approx \lim_{j\to\infty} \frac{1}{(1-\rho)}$$

The value ρ encapsulates different faults and errors, and one of them is caused by buffer overflow along the end-to-end interaction path. There are two levels of buffer overflows: a) system/router level that includes all activities inside the TCP channel, and b) user level that involves the buffer at the receiving end. Methods to prevent

J. Filipe et al. (Eds.): ICETE 2005, CCIS 3, pp. 49–61, 2007.
© Springer-Verlag Berlin Heidelberg 2007

network congestion that causes router buffer overflow include *active queue management* (AQM) (Braden, 1998). One effective approach to eliminate user-level buffer overflow to improve the end-to-end path reliability is *dynamic buffer size tuning* (Wong, 2002). The accuracy and stability of the tuning process, however, are affected by the Internet traffic patterns in terms of messages' inter-arrival times (IAT). To resolve this problem the previous *real-time traffic pattern detector* (RTPD) (Lin, 2004) was proposed. With the detected results the dynamic buffer size tuners can mitigate/nullify the ill effects by traffic on system stability and performance in a dynamic fashion. The RTPD, however, does not detect self-similar traffic, and this leads to the proposal of the *self-similarity* (S^2) *filter* in this paper. Inclusion of the S^2 *filter* into RTPD created the *enhanced* RTPD (E-RTPD). It will be demonstrated later how E-RTPD helps the Fuzzy Logic Controller (Lin, 2004B) self-tune better on the fly to gain more accurate and smoother user-level dynamic buffer size tuning and shorter RTT as a result.

The Internet involves many different client/server interaction protocols (Lewandowski, 1998), and its traffic follows the power law (Medina, 2000). Over time the traffic in any part of the Internet may change suddenly, for example, from LRD (*long-range dependence*) to SRD (*short-range dependence*) or vice versa (Willinger, 2003). Using the Hurst (H) effect (i.e. H_{ss} (Taqqu, 2003)) as the yardstick then $0.5 < H < 1$ is for LRD and $0 < H \leq 0.5$ for SRD. If $X^m = \{X_l^m : l \geq 1\}$ is a time series aggregate of size m in a stochastic process X, its *autocorrelation function* (ACF) (*correleogram*) is $r^m(l) = \sum_{l=1}^{N} r^m$, where r^m is the autocorrelation of X^m and l for the aggregate level. The ACF of LRD traffic is non-summable (i.e. $\sum_{l=1}^{N \to \infty} r^m \approx \infty$), but it is summable for SRD (i.e. $\sum_{l=1}^{N \to \infty} r^m < \infty$).

It is impractical to monitor the overwhelming number of network parameters in the Internet to harness the client/server RTT. A practical approach is to treat the Internet as a *"black box"* and measure the end-to-end RTT to interpret the channel behavior. This is the IEPM (*Internet End-to-End Performance Measurement* (Cottrel, 1999)) approach. Any sudden changes in the IAT traffic pattern affect the performance of applications running on the Internet. The traffic's ill effect on the FLC stability and accuracy (Lin, 2004) is an example. Figure 1 shows how the *mean deviations* (MD) from the FLC steady-state reference due to traffic changes in one deployment. Traffic *self-similarity* (or *self-affinity*) consistently produces the largest deviations compared to heavy-tailed and Markovian traffic. Two objects are geometrically similar if one is derived from another by linear scaling, rotation or translation. The GP% (gradient percentage) in Figure 1 is a derivative (D) control parameter in FLC. For the same GP value different traffic patterns produce different MD values. The reconfigurable version of the FLC uses the RTPD to detect a traffic pattern on the fly and utilizes the result to neutralize traffic ill effects by choosing the correct GP value accordingly (Lin, 2004). The RTPD differentiates LRD from SRD and identifies heavy-tailed traffic, but it does not detect self-similar patterns. Combining the previous RTPD

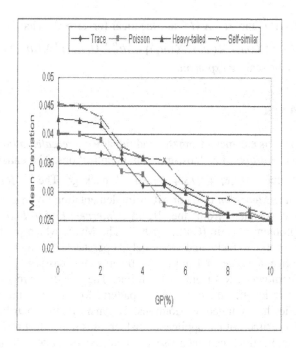

Fig. 1. Internet traffic impact on FLC accuracy

model with the *self-similarity* (S^2) *filter* (or simply S^2 *filter*) creates the *enhanced* RTPD (E-RTPD), which has the capability to identify self-similarity and compute its *dimension* (D). If an object is geometrically, recursively split into similar pieces, then at the Kth iteration step the total measure of the object is "*product of the number of similar pieces and* O^D ". The parameter O is the splitting *resolution* or *reduction*. The *Cantor Set* is an example in which a line segment of interval [0,1] is drawn as the first step (i.e. $K = 0$). This line is then manipulated by the subsequent steps: a) divide the line into three equal portions (i.e. *resolution* is $\dfrac{1}{3}$) and remove the middle portion (i.e. $K = 1$), b) remove the middle portions from the remaining two (i.e. $K = 2$), and c) repeat the last step *ad infinitum*. The Kth iteration produces 2^K similar line segments of length $s = (\dfrac{1}{3})^K$ each. The *Cantor Set's* self-similarity dimension is defined by the formula $D_s = 2^K * (\dfrac{1}{3})^K$ or alternatively

$$D_s = [\dfrac{(K \log(2))}{(K \log(3))}] \approx 0.63$$

An object is fractal if its D value is non-integer. Different non-converging dimension definitions exist, the *Cantor Set* provides only a conceptual basis. A stochastic process $X(t)$ is H_{ss}, self-similar and fractal, provided that its two finite-dimensional distributions , $X(at)$ and $a^H X(t)$ are identical for $a > 0$. That is, the following expression holds: $\{X(at_1), X(at_2)...X(at_n)\} \equiv \{a^H X(t_1),...a^H X(at_n)\}$; $\equiv$ means equality and H is the scaling *exponent*.

2 Related Work

The previous RTPD is enhanced from the traditional R/S (*rescaled adjusted statistics*) approach for *non-real-time* (i.e. "post-mortem") applications. The enhanced R/S (i.e. E-R/S) is a real-time "$M^3 RT + R/S + filtration$" package. The $M^3 RT$ element is a *micro Convergence Algorithm* (CA) or MCA implementation (Wong, 2001). The CA is the technique adopted from the IEPM (*Internet End-to-End Performance Measurement*) problem domain (Cottrel, 1999). The MCA, which predicts the mean of a traffic waveform quickly and accurately, operates as a logical object to be invoked for service anytime and anywhere by message passing. It helps the R/S mechanism differentiates SRD from LRD on-line. The *filtration* process activates an appropriate filter to identify the exact traffic pattern; for example, the *modified QQ-plot filter* identifies heavy-tailed distributions. The main RTPD contribution is that it can be a part of any time-critical application, which uses it to detect traffic patterns on the fly. These applications can then use the detected result to self-tune for better system performance (Lin, 2004). Similar to its R/S predecessor, the E-R/S calculates the Hurst (H) parameter/value but on-line. The $0.5 < H < 1$ range means LRD traffic (e.g. heavy-tailed and self-similar traces) and $0 < H \leq 0.5$ for SRD (short-range dependence, e.g. Markovian traffic) (Molnar, 1999).
The traditional R/S is defined by

$$R/S = \frac{\max\{W_i : i = 1,2,....,k\} - \min\{W_i : i = 1,2,...,k\}}{\sqrt{\mathrm{var}(X)}}$$

The parameter W_i is computed as

$$W_i = \sum_{m=1}^{i} (X_m - \overline{X})$$

for i=1,2,...k, where $\overline{X}$ is the mean of. $\overline{X} = \frac{1}{k} \sum_{i=1}^{k} X_i$.

The best value for k is usually found by trial and error, and this becomes the drawback because R/S accuracy and speed depend on k. The R/S ratio is the rescaled range of the stochastic process X over a time interval k, $\{X_i : i = 1,2,...k\}$. A useful R/S feature is the log-log of $R/S \approx (k/2)^H$, which yields the H value.

The CA operation, which is derived from the *Central Limit Theorem*, is summarized by the equations: (2.1) and (2.2). The estimated mean M_i in the ith prediction cycle is based on the fixed F (*flush limit*) number of data samples. The cycle time therefore depends on the interval for collecting the F samples. It was confirmed previously that M_i has the fastest convergence for F=14 (Wong, 2001). Other parameters include: a) M_{i-1} is the feedback of the last predicted mean to the current M_i prediction cycle, b) m_j^i is the jth data item sampled in the current i^{th} M_i cycle, $j = 1,2,3,....,(F-1)$, and c) M_0 is the first data sample when the MCA had started running. In the E-R/S, M_i replaces $\overline{X}$ to yield .

$$W_i = \sum_{m=1}^{i}(X_m - M_i)$$

This replacement makes the E-R/S more suitable for real-time applications because the number of data items (e.g. IAT) to calculate W_i becomes predictable (i.e. $F = 14$). In real-life applications $\overline{X} = \frac{1}{k}\sum_{i=1}^{k}X_i$ will need much longer computation time than M_i for two reasons: a) k is usually larger than F, and b) the IAT among X_i could be so large that the product of "k and average IAT" means a significant time delay. In an E-RTPD implementation the E-/RS, M^3RT and filter modules are running in parallel. The E-RTPD execution time depends on the E-R/S module, which has the longest execution. The *Intel's VTune Performance Analyzer* (Intel VTune, 2002) records from the Java RTPD prototype the following average execution times in clock cycles: 981 for E-R/S, 250 for M^3RT, and 520 for the *modified QQ-plot filter*. The novel s^2 *filter* provides RTPD with the additional capability to quickly detect self-similar traffic on the fly.

$$M_i = \frac{M_{i-1} + \sum_{j=1}^{j=F-1}m_j^i}{F}\,..........\,(2.1);$$

$$M_0 = m_{j=0}^{i=1}\,..........\,(2.2); i \geq 1$$

3 The Self-similarity Filter

LRD traffic has at two basic components: heavy-tailed and self-similar. The proposed *self-similarity* (S^2) *filter* differentiates heavy-tailed IAT patterns from self-similar ones. Self-similarity in many fractal point processes results from heavy-tailed distributions, for example, FRP (*Fractal Renewal Process*) inter-arrival times. The heavy-tailed property, however, is not a necessary condition for self-similarity because at least the FSNDPP (*Fractal-Shot-Noise-Driven Poisson Process*) does not have heavy-tailed property. The S^2 *filter* basis is the *"asymptotically second-order self-similarity"* concept, or simply called *statistical* $2^{nd}OSS$ or $S2^{nd}OSS$, which associates with a sufficiently large *aggregate level* or *lag l* in a stochastic process X. For an aggregate $X^m = \{X_l^m : l \geq 1\}$ of size m in X, $S2^{nd}OSS$ for $m \to \infty$

means that the associated *autocorrelation function* (ACF), namely $r^m(l)$ (for X^m) is proportional to $l^{-(2-2H)}$. $S2^{nd} OSS$ is LRD for its ACF is non-summable, as indicated by .

$$r^m(l) = \sum_{l-1}^{\infty} r^m = \infty$$

The condition of "$r^m(l) \propto l^{-(2-2H)}$ for $m \to \infty$" is mathematically equivalent to the *slowly decaying variance property*. That is, the variance of the mean of sample size m decays more slowly than m. This phenomenon is represented by the expression: $Var(X^m) \propto m^{-\beta}$. For a stationary $2^{nd} OSS$ process X and $0.5 < H < 1$ the value of $\beta = 2 - 2H$ should apply. Equations (3.1) and (3.2) summarize the $S2^{nd} OSS$ property and they hold for the weaker condition in equation (3.3). The *slowly decaying variance* property is clear if a log-log plot is produced for equation (3.1). As shown by equation (3.4), $\log(Var(X))$ is a constant, $\log(Var(X^m))$ versus $\log(m)$ yields a straight line with slope $-\beta$. The H value can then be calculated by the

$$H = 1 - (\beta/2)$$

formula. The S^2 *filter* finds β for X^m on the fly. The $Var(X^m)$ calculation uses the mean value $E(X^m)$ estimated by the $M^3 RT$ process. $E(X^m)$ is

$$m^{-1} \sum_{n=(l-1)m+1}^{lm} X_n$$

conceptually, and the key for the S^2 *filter* operation is to choose a sufficiently large m, which is the multiples (i.e. C) of $F = 14$ to virtually satisfy $m \to \infty$; $m = C*F$ for estimating β. The detected result is available at the Ag time point. In Figure 2 for example, the β result for aggregate 2 is available at the point of $Ag = 2$.

$$Var(X^m) = \frac{1}{m^{(2-2H)}} Var(X) \dots\dots\dots\dots\dots\dots\dots\dots(3.1)$$

$$r^m(l) = r(k) \dots\dots\dots\dots\dots\dots\dots\dots\dots\dots\dots(3.2)$$

$$\lim_{m \to \infty} r^m(l) = r(k) \dots\dots\dots\dots\dots\dots\dots\dots\dots(3.3)$$

$$\log(Var(X^m)) = \log(Var(X)) - \beta \log(m) \dots\dots\dots\dots\dots\dots(3.4)$$

The process in the S^2 *filter* to calculate β is the "*continuous aggregate based (CAB)*" method. The CAB evaluates if an aggregate is stationary by checking its Gaussian property or "Gaussianity" (Arvotham, 2001) by the *kurtosis* and *skewness* metrics. A symmetrical normal distribution has perfect Gaussianity indicated by *kurtosis* = 3 and *skewness* = 0. Statistically measured *kurtosis* and *skewness* values are rarely perfect, and reasonable limits can be used to indicate the presence of a bell curve, which belongs to the exponential family of independent stationary increments. The S^2 *filter* follows the CAB procedure and finds β by linear regression, and the quality of which can be judged by the *coefficient of determination* or R^2 between 0 and 1 (Jain, 1992). Higher R^2 implies better quality for the linear regression. By the predefined threshold Th_{R^2} (e.g. 0.85 or 85%) the S^2 *filter* can reject a hypothesis of self-similarity in X^m for $R^2 < Th_{R^2}$. The CAB operation in Figure 2 works with the aggregates $X^m_{Ag=l}$ in a stochastic process X along the time axis. Assuming: a) P1, P2, and P3 are the log-log plots for three successive aggregates based on equation (3.4), b) these plots yield different β values: β_1 for P1 with $R^2 = 0.82$, β_2 for P2 with $R^2 = 0.98$, and β_3 for P3 with $R^2 = 0.95$, c) $Ag = l$ is the aggregate level, and d) $Th_{R^2} = 0.9$, then both P2 and P3 confirms self-similar traffic but not P1 (for $R^2 < Th_{R^2}$). If P2 and P3 yield very different β values, their H values by

$$H = 1 - (\beta/2)$$

indicate different dimensions or D. The D value may change over time due to various factors, for example, the ON/OFF situations in the network (Willinger, 2003). A changing D or H is a sign of non-linearity in the stochastic process being examined. A D/H correlation will be demonstrated, but the focal discussion of how H or D could affect system stability will be left out.

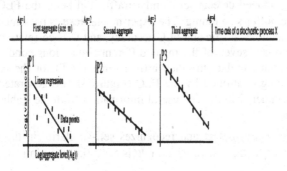

Fig. 2. The "*aggregate based* (AB)" approach

Skewness is represented by $\dfrac{\sum_{i=1}^{N}\left(x_{i-\bar{x}}\right)^3}{(m-1)\,sd^3}$,

where $\bar{x}$ and sd are the measured mean and standard deviation respectively for the aggregate of m samples. It measures the symmetry of a bell-shape aggregate distribution. A positive value indicates that the bell curve skews right and the right tail is heavier than the left one. *Kurtosis* is represented by

$$\frac{\sum_{i=1}^{N}(x_i-\overline{x})^4}{(m-1)\,sd^4},$$

and its value decides whether the bell curve is *peaked* (for positive value) or *flat* (or negative value) compared to the normal distribution with *kurtosis* = 3 and *skewness* = 0.

4 Experimental Results

The S^2 *filter* was verified by simulations based on the CAB approach. The experiments were conducted on the stable Aglets mobile agent platform, which is designed for Internet applications. The Aglets makes the experimental results scalable for the open Internet. The setup for the experiments is shown in Figure 3, in which the driver and server are both aglets (agile applets). The driver picks a known waveform or a pre-collected IAT trace that may embeds different traffic patterns over time. The pick simulates the IAT among the requests that enter the server queue. The FLC dynamic buffer size tuner is the test-bed for the S^2 *filter*. It adjusts the buffer size on the fly by leveraging the current queue length, buffer length, and detected traffic pattern. The traffic pattern(s) that drives the IAT is also recorded by the E-RTPD that has included the S^2 *filter*. This helps matching the FLC control behavior with the specific traffic pattern. The VTune measures the E-RTPD's average execution time so that its contribution to time-critical applications on the Internet can be evaluated. Experiments with different IAT traffic patterns were carried out. The results conclude that the S^2 *filter* indeed detects self-similar traffic and helps the FLC deliver more accurate dynamic buffer size tuning. The experimental results presented here include: self-similarity detections, traffic and FLC accuracy, and D/H correlation.

Table 1 summarizes seven of the many different simulations conducted. The self-similar traces, which simulate the inter-arrival times (IAT) for the request into the server's buffer being controlled by the FLC (Figure 3), are generated by using the Kramer's tool (Kramer, 2002). The useful information from the Table 1 summary is listed as follows:

The S^2 *filter* always detect and recognizes self-similarity in the IAT traffic as long as the network loading or utilization ψ is 50% (i.e. 0.5 simulated by the same tool) or less.

ψ is proportional to the self-similarity dimension (explained later with Figure 9). For $\psi > 0.4$ the traffic self-similarity scales differently as indicated Figure 5 and 6. Our analysis indicates that this is possibly the beginning of non-linear scaling or a sign of possible multifractal traffic. Both Figure 5 and 6 work with $Th_{R^2} = 0.9$.

The scaling exponent H (Hurst effect) changes with ψ, which is inversely proportional to the IAT length that is the "*reduction/resolution*" in light of traffic. For

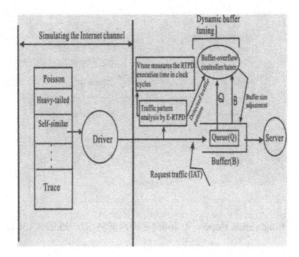

Fig. 3. Setup for the S^2 *filter* experiments

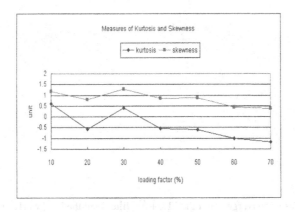

Fig. 4. Kurtosis and skewness measurements

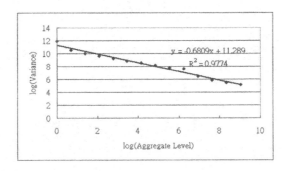

Fig. 5. S^2 filter yields slope = -0.6809(β = 0.6809), R^2= 97.74% for ψ = 0.2

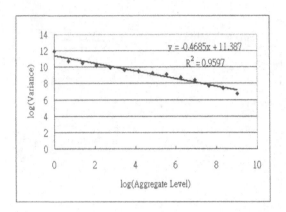

Fig. 6. S^2 filter yields slope = -0.4685($\beta = 0.4685$), R²= 95.97% for $\psi = 0.5$

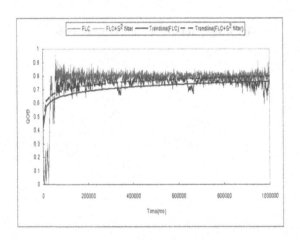

Fig. 7. Faster convergence of the FLC+ S^2 filter than the FLC working alone

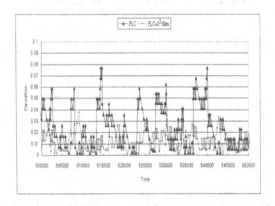

Fig. 8. Less MD deviation by FLC+ S^2 than the FLC alone

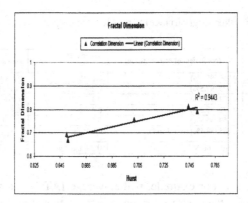

Fig. 9. D/H correlation for Table 1

$\psi \leq 0.4$ the scaling is basically the same (i.e. a *monofractal* sign). The β value in every case (row) in Table 1 is the average of several aggregates for the same stochastic process X.

The kurtosis and skewness are different for the different self-similar traces. Nevertheless they always indicate the presence of a bell curve.

The kurtosis and skewness values for each case (row) in Table 1 are plotted for comparison (Figure 4). These values are obviously affected by the loading. When the loading is high (e.g. 60% and 70%) the bell curve tends to skew less but still to the right. Meanwhile the bell curve tends to get flatter. Comparatively the skewness of the bell curves for the seven simulation cases in Table 1 are less than a Weibull ($gamma = 1.5$) distribution, which is relatively more peaked ($kurtosis \approx 4.5$). The trend-lines in Figure 7 for the IAT traffic trace in Figure 5 shows that the " $FLC + S^2$ *filter*" combination converges much faster to given steady state than the FLC working alone. With help from the S^2 *filter* the FLC adjusts the GP value for the derivative (D) control element on the fly according to the currently detected self-similarity. As a result it produces less MD than the FLC working alone (Figure 8). In the experiments the *FD3* tool (Sarraille, 2004), which confirms if an image (e.g. a time series generated by the Kramer's tool) is really fractal and measures its dimension D, was used. The purpose is to evaluate the D/H correlations (Peitgen, 2004). This correlation for Table 1 is plotted and shown in Figure 9. It shows that if D changes suddenly, H also rescales accordingly to indicate possible traffic nonlinearity. In contrast, if H scales linearly, it is a sign of *monfractal* traffic. The *intrinsic* average S^2 *filter* execution time as observed from all the experiments is 1455 clock cycles as measured by the *Intel's VTune Performance Analyzer*. It is intrinsic because it works with immediately available data (without any actual IAT delay) in a trace. For a platform of 100 mega hertz the corresponding physical time is $1455 /(100*10^6)$ or 14.55 micro seconds. In real-life applications the S^2 *filter* has to collect enough IAT samples on the fly before computing β. This sampling latency can be significant, and therefore the success of S^2 *filter* application depends of choosing size m for the

Table 1. S^2 filter'(log(variance) versus log (aggregate level) to find β

β	$H = (1 - \beta/2)$	R^2 (coefficient of determination)	loading ψ	kurtosis	skewness
0.6583	0.671	0.956 (95.6%)	0.1 (10%)	0.597045	1.180861
0.6809	0.660	0.975 (97.5%)	0.2	-0.56218	0.798282
0.6425	0.679	0.977 (97.7%)	0.3	0.40215	1.277175
0.6473	0.677	0.972 (97.2%)	0.4	-0.53386	0.861215
0.4685	0.766	0.959 (95.9%)	0.5	-0.58417	0.892037
0.3762	0.812	0.885 (88.5%) (less than Th_{R^2})	0.6 (rejected)	-1.01033	0.446756
0.1978	0.901	0.605 (60.5%)	0.7 (rejected)	-1.16043	0.388599

X^m aggregate correctly. For example, if the average IAT is one second, $m = 1000$ means 1000 seconds. On the contrary for the same size m and mean IAT of 1 ms, the physical time is only one second. Therefore, the m value for the S^2 *filter* Java prototype is a variable rather than a chosen constant, and the user/tester should fix the time span T instead of collecting the fixed m samples on the fly. That is, the number of samples (i.e. m) in an aggregate within T depends on the IAT; shorter IAT delays yield a larger m. Then, the S^2 *filter* works adaptively with the m value decided by the IAT for the *"timed aggregate"* based on the chosen T.

5 Conclusions

The novel *self-similarity* (S^2) *filter* is proposed for real-time applications. It is based on the *"asymptotically second-order self-similarity"* concept (alternatively called *statistical* $2^{nd} OSS$ or $S2^{nd} OSS$) for stationary time series. As a component in the *enhanced* RTPD or E-RTPD it helps the FLC dynamic buffer tuner yield more accurate control by detecting self-similarity in the IAT traffic. This means improved reliability for the client/server interaction path and shorter roundtrip time. The S^2 *filter* is original because there is no previous examples in the literature that can detect self-similarity in a time series on the fly. The next step in the research is to perfect the CAB approach by enabling it to determine the range of aggregate size m that can produce accurate traffic detection but without any unnecessary and significant latency in the process.

Acknowledgements

The authors thank the Hong Kong PolyU and the Department of Computing for funding the RTPD research with grants APG51 and HJZ91.

References

Arvotham, S., Riedi, R., Barabniuk, R.: Connection-Level Analysis and Modeling of Network Traffic. In: Proc. of the IEEE/ACM Internet Measurement Workshop (2001)
Braden, B., et al.: Recommendation on Queue Management and Congestion Avoidance in the Internet, RFC2309 (April 1998)

Cottrel, L., Zekauskas, M., Uijterwaal, H., McGregor, T.: Comparison of Some Internet Active End-to-End Performance Measurement Projects Intel's VTune Performance Analyzer (1999), http://www.slac.stanford.edu/comp/net/wan-mon/iepm-cf.html, http://www.slac.stanford.edu/ comp/net/wan-mon/iepm-cf.html

Jain, R.: The Art of Computer Systems Performance Analysis – Techniques for Experimental Design, Measurement, Simulation, and Modeling. Wiley, Chichester (1992)

Kramer, Generator of Self-Similar Network Traffic, http://wwwcsif.cs.ucdavis.edu/~kramer/code/trf_gen1.html

Lewandowski, S.M.: Frameworks for Component-based Client/Server Computing. ACM Computing Surveys 30(1), 3–27 (1998)

Lin, W.W.K., Wong, A.K.Y., Dillon, T.S.: A Novel Real-Time Traffic Pattern Detector for Internet Applications. In: Proc. of the Australasian Telecommunication Networks and Applications Conference, Sydney, Australia (ATNAC'04), pp. 224–227 (2004)

Lin, W.W.K., Wong, A.K.Y., Dillon, T.S.: A Novel Adaptive Fuzzy Logic Controller (A-FLC) to Reduce Retransmission and Service Roundtrip Time for Logical TCP Channels over the Internet. In: Proc. of the EU2004 Conference, Japan, pp. 942–951 (2004)

Medina, A., Matta, I., Byers, J.: On the Origin of Power Laws in Internet Topologies. ACM SIGCOMM 30(2), 18–28 (2000)

Lin, W.W.K., Wong, A.K.Y., Dillon, T.S.: A Novel Fuzzy-PID Dynamic Buffer Tuning Model to Eliminate Overflow and Shorten the End-to-End Roundtrip Time for TCP Channels. In: Cao, J., Yang, L.T., Guo, M., Lau, F. (eds.) ISPA 2004. LNCS, vol. 3358, pp. 783–787. Springer, Heidelberg (2004), http://www.springerlink.com/index/VF155CH38XFLLB4H

Molnar, S., Dang, T.D., Vidacs, A.: Heavy-Tailedness, Long-Range Dependence and Self-Similarity in Data Traffic. In: Proc. of the 7th Int'l Conference on Telecommunication Systems, Modelling and Analysis, Nashville, USA, pp. 18–21 (1999)

Peitgen, H.O., Jurgens, H., Saupe, D.: Chaos and Fractals. New Frontiers of Science, 2nd edn., p. 686. Springer, Heidelberg (2004)

Sarraille, J., DiFalco, P.: FD3, http://life.bio.sunysb.edu/morph/fd3.html

Taqqu, M.S.: Fractional Brownian Motion and Long-Range Dependence. In: Doukhan, P., et al. (eds.) Theory and Applications of Long-Range Dependence, Birkhäuser, pp. 5–38 (2003)

Willinger, W., Paxson, V., Hiedi, R.H., Taqqu, M.S.: Long-Range Dependence and Data Network Traffic. In: Doukhan, P., et al. (eds.) Theory and Applications of Long-Range Dependence, Birkhäuser, pp. 373–408 (2003)

Wong, A.K.Y., Wong, J.H.C.: A Convergence Algorithm for Enhancing the Performance of Distributed Applications Running on Sizeable Networks. The International Journal of Computer Systems, Science & Engineering 16(4), 229–236 (2001)

Wong, A.K.Y., Lin, W.W.K., Ip, M.T.W., Dillon, T.S.: Genetic Algorithm and PID Control Together for Dynamic Anticipative Marginal Buffer Management: An Effective Approach to Enhance Dependability and Performance for Distributed Mobile Object-Based Real-time Computing over the Internet. Journal of Parallel and Distributed Computing (JPDC) 62, 1433–1453 (2002)

Strategies for Service Composition in P2P Networks

Jan Gerke[1], Peter Reichl[2], and Burkhard Stiller[3]

[1] Swiss Federal Institute of Technology ETH Zurich, Computer Engineering and Networks Lab
TIK Gloriastrasse 35, CH-8092 Zurich, Switzerland
gerke@tik.ee.ethz.ch
[2] Telecommunications Research Center FTW Vienna
Donau City Strasse 1, A-1220 Vienna, Austria
reichl@ftw.at
[3] University of Zurich, Department of Informatics IFI and ETH Zrich, TIK
Winterthurerstrasse 190, CH-8057 Zurich, Switzerland
stiller@ifi.unizh.ch

Abstract. Recently, the advance of service-oriented architectures and peer-to-peer networks has lead to the creation of service-oriented peer-to-peer networks, which enable a distributed and decentralized services market. Apart from the usage of single services, this market supports the merging of services into new services, a process called service composition. However, it is argued that for the time being this process can only be carried out by specialized peers, called service composers. This paper describes the new market created by these service composers, and models mathematically building blocks required for such a service composition. A general algorithm for service composition developed can be used independently of solutions for semantic difficulties and interface adaption problems of service composition. In a scenario for buying a distributed computing service, simulated strategies are evaluated according to their scalability and the market welfare they create.

Keywords: Service Composition, Peer-to-Peer Network, Service-oriented Architecture.

1 Introduction

In recent years the development of distributed systems especially the Internet has been influenced heavily by two paradigms: Service-orientation and peer-to-peer (P2P) (A. Oram (Editor), 2001). The benefit of service-oriented architectures (SOA) is their support of loose coupling of software components, *i.e.*, providing a high degree of interoperability and reuse (He, 2003) by standardizing a small set of ubiquitous and self-descriptive interfaces, *e.g.*, the standardization of web services (World Wide Web Consortium, 2004) by the world wide web consortium, and its implementations like .NET (Microsoft Developer Network, 2004). Additionally, P2P file sharing systems like BitTorrent have proven to be scalable content distribution networks (Izal et al., 2004). This scalability is achieved by the distributed nature of P2P networks. Rather than using centralized server infrastructure, they rely on distributed hosts, the peers, and their self-organization abilities. Lately, P2P networks have also

J. Filipe et al. (Eds.): ICETE 2005, CCIS 3, pp. 62–77, 2007.

been put to commercial use. For instance, Blizzard uses the BitTorrent technology to distribute program updates to their customer base of several hundred thousands, thus reducing the need for a centralized server infrastructure (Blizzard Corporation, 2005).

In order to combine the benefits of the two paradigms and to achieve a decentralized platform for loosely coupled software components, an architecture of a service-oriented middleware was proposed by (Gerke et al., 2003). In order to implement this architecture, (Gerke and Stiller, 2005) presented a JXTA-based middleware. This middleware enables a fully distributed service market, in which peers provide services to other peers. This middleware supports this market by providing mechanisms to search within the underlying distributed P2P network for services, to negotiate the terms of service usage, and finally to charge for service usage. The market itself offers low entrance hurdles, as any Internet host can enter the market by running this middleware implementation.

In addition to the usage of a single service by a single peer, the middleware-enabled service market makes it possible to combine services into new value-added services. This process, called service composition, allows for the maximum benefit from service reusability when creating new services. Thus, new services can be deployed much quicker and the expert knowledge of service developers can be used in new services.

Service composition consists of two main sub problems: (a) understanding what functionality is provided by services and (b) understanding how services communicate through their interfaces. The first problem has been tackled through the development of semantic service descriptions (Hendler et al., 2002), as well as through the application of artificial intelligence (Carman et al., 2003). The second problem is addressed mainly through interface description languages like WSDL (Web Services Descriptions Working Group, 2005). Other interface standards like CORBA do not offer the self-description capabilities of web services, thus reducing the reusability of software components.

The highest benefit from service composition would be achieved, if it could be carried out by any peer in a completely automated manner, at high speed, and costs approaching zero. However, both sub problems described above have not yet been completely solved. Therefore, for the time being, service composition can only be carried out by specialized peers, called service composers at a certain cost.

Therefore, this paper investigates composition strategies for service composers, while abstracting from the detailed technique used. To this end, a general algorithm for service composition is defined and its evaluation is performed in a scenario, where computing power is bought from various peers. Thus, general influences of parameters onto this algorithm are evaluated, and the welfare a service composer can create is defined. The overall goal is to find a strategy for service composition, which scales well while creating high welfare for service consumers and service composers. How this welfare is distributed fairly between the two is out of the scope of this paper, but will addressed elsewhere with the help of public auctions (Varian, 2003).

The remainder of this paper is structured as follows. Section 2 gives an overview of the distributed service market and the underlying P2P architecture. Section 3 contains definitions of services, their properties and descriptions. Section 4 introduces the general service composition algorithm proposed. While Section 5 presents the evaluation of this algorithm with different parameters, Section 6 concludes the work and gives an overview over future work.

2   P2P Service Market

Before investigating service composition, it is necessary to describe the environment in which it takes place. Thus, the underlying service-oriented P2P network and roles being part of the system are outlined. Additionally, the service market enabled by the underlying P2P network and the markets for composed services are discussed.

2.1   Underlying Technology

The P2P network is not a physical network, but is built on top of the Internet (A. Oram (Editor), 2001). This implies that peers are Internet hosts and links of the P2P network are end-to-end (e2e) connections through the Internet between such hosts. Thus, the set of hosts taking part in the P2P network and the e2e connections between them form an overlay network on top of the Internet, consisting of peers and links. In turn, the notion of terms like 'link' or 'neighbor' is different in the Internet and in the overlay network. It is assumed that connections provide an e2e quality of service guarantees when required by services, regardless of the technology used to provide these guarantees, e.g., IntServ or DiffServ.

Every peer inside the network can provide and request services to and from other peers. The term service is defined as functionality which is offered by a peer to other peers, and which can be accessed through input and output interfaces. Services are described through documents called *service descriptions*, including service functionality and interfaces, but also characteristics such as terms of usage, e.g., prices and methods of payment. Services can be used by *applications*, which are programs running on peers which are not provided as services themselves and offer user interfaces.

A peer providing a service to another peer is acting as a *service provider*, while a peer which is using a service from another peer is acting as a *service consumer*. A single peer can take over both roles successively or even at the same time, if he provides a set of services to a set of peers and uses a set of other services from another set of peers. The service usage is always initiated by the service consumer, thus a service provider can not supply unrequested services to consumers or even demand payment for services delivered in such a fashion. Due to the dynamic nature of P2P networks, the duration of a service usage is restricted, i.e., it is not possible to rely on the availability of a certain service for weeks or months.

Service usage follows a one-to-one relationship between service consumer and provider, i.e., neither do several service consumers use the same service instance, nor do several service providers together provide a service to a consumer directly. Several service consumers can still use the same service at the same time, but several service instances are created by the service provider and service usage takes place independently. Furthermore, service providers can use services from other service providers, in order to provide a new value-added service to a service consumer. This process of combining services is called *service composition*. A peer carrying out this process is said to play the role of a *service composer*. There is no direct relation between additional service providers and the service consumer. Examples of such service usages are shown in Figure 1.

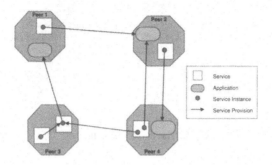

Fig. 1. The use model (Gerke and Stiller, 2005)

2.2   Market Model

The service market consists of the peers which offer services and use them, without composing new services on demand. This service market is assumed to be a global market with low entrance barriers, due to its open P2P nature. This market is characterized through perfect competition between its participants since the number of market participants is large. Therefore, if a peer was offering a service for a price much higher than his own costs, another peer would offer the same service at a lower price. Thus, prices for services are set by the market itself through competition, service prices are given and not negotiable. Service providers do not have to price their services. Either they are able to offer a service for the market price or they do not offer the service at all.

However, the market model is clearly different when service composition is considered. Service composition is a complex process. Therefore, it is assume that only a small number of peers decide to take on the role of service composer. Each of them carries out his own variant of service composition, using his own business secrets. Service composers act as brokers between service consumers and service providers. They take part in the service market as buyers and in the composed service market as sellers, as shown in Figure 2.

Because of the high specialization required, only a small number of overall peers will act as service composer. Therefore, the market for composed services will not have perfect competition but will be dominated by an oligopoly of service composers. In fact, there is a separate market for every new composed service. It is created whenever a service consumer contacts an oligopoly of service composers with the request to compose a new service. Thus, pricing is an important issue in the composed services market, as a price has to be found for a previously inexistent service. Table 1 covers key properties of these two markets.

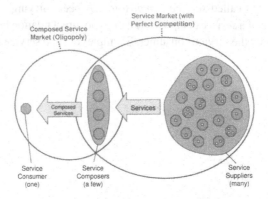

Fig. 2. The two markets model

Table 1. Comparison of the Two Markets

	Service Market	Composed Service Market
No. of Sellers	Many	Some
No. of Buyers	Many	One
Market Form	Perfect competition	Oligopoly
Traded Good	Services	Composed Services
Persistence	Constant	Created by request
Prices	Set by market	Pricing required

3   Service Properties

Due to the market-based view and discussion above, goods traded need a formal definition. Therefore, services must be described by specifying their properties as well as the implications of these properties are explained.

(American Heritage Dictionaries (Editor), 2000) defines a service as *an act or a variety of work done for others, especially for pay*. In the scope of this paper, this definition is applied only to the envisioned technical system and its participants (the peers). Thus, a service is a piece of software or a software component operated by one of the systems participants. It fulfills one or several tasks on behalf of another participant of the system, thus carrying out work for him, for which he is paid.

Every service S has properties $S' = (S'_1, ..., S'_n), n \in \mathbf{N}$ which describe the characteristics of the service (Dumas et al., 2001), especially the task which is carried out by the service. These properties may include parameters and information from four different groups:

- Functionality: A formal description of what the service should do (if specified by the service consumer) or what it can do (if specified by the service provider)
- Quality: A list of QoS parameters which describe with which quality the service should be provided (if specified by the service consumer) or can be provided (if specified by the service provider). All parameters can have fixed values or can be described with value ranges.
- Cost: A tariff (Reichl and Stiller, 2001) used to charge the consumption of the service (if specified by the service provider, the actual cost is calculated by applying the tariff to the functionality and quality properties measured during the service delivery) or the willingness-to-pay function (if specified by the service consumer) which describes how much the consumer is willing to pay for a service depending on its functionality and quality parameters.
- Others: Who is providing/requesting the service.

Based on these definitions and explanations of services and their properties the following formalized approach is taken.

Service properties are specified in service descriptions, where every property S'_x consists of a formal *property description* S''_x and a *property range* $S^*_x = [\underline{S'_x}, \overline{S'_x}]$. The property description describes the meaning of properties according to a common semantic standard shared by all peers (Hendler et al., 2002). The property range describes the degree of fulfillment of this property in numerical values. Metrics generating these values are part of the property description.

Two property descriptions *match* when they are semantically equal according to the common semantic standard. Thus, a property A'_x is said to *fulfill* another property B'_y, if and only if, A''_x matches B''_x and their property ranges overlap, i.e., $\underline{B'_x} \leq \underline{A'_x} \leq \overline{B'_x}$ or $\underline{B'_x} \leq \overline{A'_x} \leq \overline{B'_x}$. Analogously, a property A'_x is said to *exactly fulfill* another property B'_y, if and only if, A''_x matches B''_x and $\underline{A'_x} = \underline{B'_x}$ and $\overline{A'_x} = \overline{B'_x}$.

Then, a service S with properties $S' = (S'_1, ..., S'_n), n \in \mathbf{N}$ is said to *implement* a service description D with properties $D' = (D'_1, ..., D'_m), m \in \mathbf{N}$, if and only if, all its properties fulfill the properties specified in the service description, i.e., $n = m$ and $\forall i \in [1, n] : S'_i$ fulfills D'_i. Analogously, a service S with properties $S' = (S'_1, ..., S'_n), n \in \mathbf{N}$ is said to *exactly implement* a service description D with properties $D' = (D'_1, ..., D'_m), m \in \mathbf{N}$, if and only if, $n = m$ and $\forall i \in [1, n] : S'_i$ exactly fulfills D'_i. Thus, a service S is called an *(exact) implementation* of a service description D, if and only if, S (exactly) implements D. Vice versa, a service description D is said to *(exactly) describe* a service S, if and only if, S (exactly) implements D. It is assumed that exact service descriptions exist and have been published within the P2P network for all services offered by peers acting as service providers. Of course, service descriptions can exist without corresponding implementations.

Even if a consumer specifies fixed property values in a service description, an infinite number of different services can implement his service description. Thus, a *service class* is defined as a set of services which has specific common properties. Let $S = \{S_1, ..., S_n\}, n \in \mathbf{N}$ be the set containing all services and let D be a service description with properties $D' = (D'_1, ..., D'_m), m \in \mathbf{N}$. Then, $\hat{D}$ is called a service class for a service description D, if and only if, $\widehat{D} = \{S_x | S_x \text{ implements } D\}, S_x \in S$. All services which have these properties are called *members* of the service class. Let C be the service class for a service description D. Then, a service S is called a *member* of C, if and only if, S implements D. Thus, every implementation of a service description is a member of the service class created by the description. Furthermore, every service description automatically creates a service class, though this class does not need to have any members.

4   Service Composition

From the service composers point of view, the service composition process starts when he receives a service description from a service consumer. The service consumer does not have to state fixed service properties within this description, but can make use of property ranges as defined in Section 3.

After receiving the consumers service description, the composer searches the P2P network for member services of the service class described by this description. If he can not find such a service, he starts composing the service by combining other services. In order to do this, he must obtain or create a building plan (Gerke, 2004), which describes how to achieve the properties of the original service class by combining members from other service classes. Generally, a building plan describes how members of a specific service class can be combined with members of other specific service classes to create a new composed service. In particular, it describes properties of the composed service and how these properties relate to the properties of its component services. This process is supported by the mapping m in such a way that if D is a service with properties $D^{'}$, then B is called a building plan for D, if and only if, B contains service descriptions $\{D_1, ..., D_n\}, n \in (N)$ and a mapping $m : D_1^{'} \times ... \times D_n^{'} \rightarrow D^{'}$ which describes the relation between properties of component services (*i.e.*, specific services fulfilling the service descriptions) on the properties of the composed service (*i.e.*, the service created by composing the component service as also described in the building plan).

When the composer has obtained one or several building plans for the service class described by the consumers service description, he searches the P2P network for implementations of the service classes described within them. If he is unable to find any of these service classes, he recursively creates building plans for this service class. Thus, he creates a service dependency graph, as shown in Figure 3.

The original service class (described by the consumers service description) is the root of this tree. Several ways to implement this service (one implementation and two building plans) are connected to the root node via an or node, while service classes are connected to the building plan via and nodes. Composed services can be found by traversing the tree from its root node. At each or node exactly one link must be chosen for traversal, while at each and node all links have to be traversed. A sub tree found by applying this algorithm models a composed service when only services form this trees leaves. Such a tree is called a *cover* of the original service dependency tree and is also shown in Figure 3. The algorithm does rate the quality of a composed service in any way. Building plans only ensure that every composed service fulfills the consumers initial service description (*i.e.*, the functionality is the same and all properties overlap with described properties).

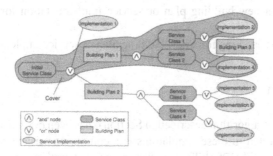

Fig. 3. An example service dependence tree

The following pseudo code defined a recursive algorithm to build a service dependence tree.

```
buildDependenceTree(ServDescr SC) {
   while (ServDescr SI =
   searchNewServiceImplementation (SC)
   != nil) {
      buildDependenceTree (SI);
      SC.addChild (SI);
   }
   while (BuildingPlan BP =
   searchNewBuildingPlan (SC) != nil) {
      for (int i=0; i <
      BP.getChildren().length; i++)
         buildDependenceTree
         (BP.getChildren()[i];
       SC.addChild (BP);
   }
}
```

In order to achieve this presentation, slightly simplified, the following assumptions have been made:

- The classes ServiceDescription and BuildingPlan are tree nodes.
- The and and or nodes are neglected. All children of a ServiceDescription are inherently connected via an or node and all children of a BuildingPlan are inherently connected via an and node.
- Each new BuildingPlan already comes with ServiceClass children (instead of connecting them by hand according to service descriptions).

The algorithm describes a general way to build service dependence trees. By using it, any kind of service dependence tree can be created. The decision about what tree is created is made by the two functions searchNewServiceImplementation and searchNewBuildingPlan. These methods include individual secrets of each service composer, namely:

- How to find a new building plan or service implementation for a given service description.
- When to stop searching for a new building plan or service implementation.

5   Evaluation

The general service algorithm described in Section 4 has been evaluated by simulations. The service requested in these simulations is a computing service with a computing power measured in GFLOPS (billions of floating point operations per second). Different strategies for when to stop searching for more building plans are evaluated. The criteria for evaluation is the achieved average welfare $W(S)$ of a composed service S. The welfare of a composed service depends on the utility $U(S)$ the consumer receives from the service, the cost of the service $C(S)$, and the cost for composing the service $B(S)$ in such a way that $W(S) = U(S) - C(S) - B(S)$ holds. The cost of the composed service is equal to the sum of the costs of the services needed to create it. *I.e.*, let $S_1...S_i, i \in [1, m]$ be the services used to create the composed service S, then $C(S) = \sum_{i=1}^{m} C(S_i)$.

5.1   General Assumptions

The simulations make the following assumptions:

- The code to be executed with the computing power can be parallelized to a granularity of 1 GFLOPS, which is also the smallest amount which can be bought as a single service.
- The parallelization incurs no extra effort. Especially, no additional synchronization or signalling overhead must be taken into account.
- Any amount of required GFLOPS can be bought directly as a service implementation from at least one service provider. This assumption is reasonable due to the perfect competition existing in the service market.
- For any amount of GFLOPS five building plans exist, which describe how to obtain the GFLOPS by buying two GFLOPS shares instead. This assumption is not stringent, as there are not many differences between finding a bad building plan and finding none at all. Plans describe 0.9/0.1 (worst), 0.8/0.2, 0.7/0.3, 0.6/0.4 and 0.5/0.5 (best) ratios of the original amount of GFLOPS.
- The cost of finding a new building plan or finding out that no more building plan exist is fixed and is equal to . However, it is also assumed that the service composer has no previous knowledge of the cost, *i.e.*, only after every search for building plan does he know what this search did cost.
- The cost of finding service implementations is negligible, as this functionality is provided by the service search of the underlying P2P network. Thus, let n be the number of searched building plans, then $B(S) = n \cdot Z$.
- The utility function of the service consumer is increasing monotonously and it is convex, based on the amount of GFLOPS received. Thus, additional utility created by additional amounts of GFLOPS decreases monotonously.

- Since there is perfect competition in the service market, all service providers use a similar cost function. This cost function is increasing monotonously and it is concave, based on the amount of GFLOPS received. Thus, the cost of additional GFLOPS is monotonously increasing.
- Properties are fixed. This means, that the service consumer does not specify a range of GFLOPS, but rather a precise amount of GFLOPS. Since building plans define exact ratios for their two respective component services, the amount of GFLOPS in service classes and service implementations also becomes fixed.

5.2 Simulation Setup

The service composition algorithm was implemented in Java and executed with different search strategies and parameters. Simulations were carried out on a PC with 512 MB memory and a 1.8 GHz CPU. For all settings, the average welfare was calculated as the average over 100 simulation runs. In all simulations the amount of the requested computing power has been set to 1024 GFLOPS. The cost function used in those simulations is $C(x) = \frac{x^2}{10000}$, the utility function is $U(x) = \log x \cdot 10$ (x being the number of GFLOPS), as shown in Figure 4.

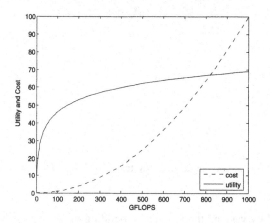

Fig. 4. Utility and cost functions

5.3 Balanced Search

The algorithm used to build the service dependence tree is constructed from the root as a balanced tree. This means that for every service class in the tree the same amount of searches for building plans is carried out until the previously defined search depth is reached. Figure 5 depicts the welfare for different costs of finding building plans, when building plans are only searched once, *i.e.*, no recursion takes place (strategy #1). Vice versa, Figure 6 depicts the welfare for different costs of finding building plans, when recursion takes place until a certain tree depth is reached. At all steps only a single building plan is searched (strategy #2).

Both strategies produce good results for the average cost for searching building plans of 3. Thus, this cost was chosen for strategy #3, which investigated, whether the welfare

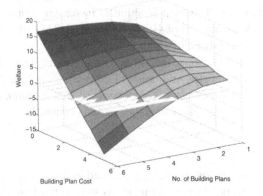

Fig. 5. Welfare for different numbers of building plan searches and different building plan costs

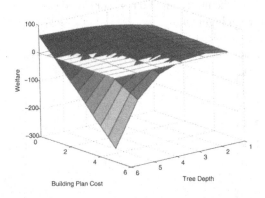

Fig. 6. Welfare for different service dependency tree depths and different building plan search costs

could be increased by varying the number of building plans searched at every step, as well as the tree depth. However, the results depicted in Figure 7 clearly show, that the increased benefit achieved by building a wide and deep service dependency tree is by far outweighed by the increased cost for building this tree. In order to optimize the welfare, more sophisticated heuristics for influencing the trees width and depth are required.

5.4 Search Until Welfare Decreases

In order to avoid search cost explosions (cf. Figure 7), the service composition algorithm was extended with strategy #4: The service dependency tree is built recursively without a predefined search depth. The recursion is stopped when the previous search for a building plan has created less additional benefit than the search cost, *i.e.*, the welfare decreased.

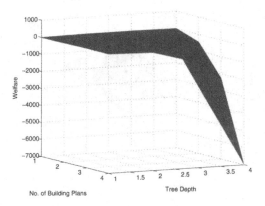

Fig. 7. Average welfare for different numbers of building plan searches and different service dependency tree depths, with fixed building plan cost of 3

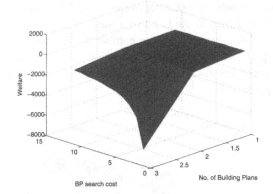

Fig. 8. Average welfare for different numbers of building plan searches and building plan search costs, using the local welfare decrease heuristic

Strategy #4 is clearly not optimal, as the next search for a building plan could still provide a higher benefit. However, results depicted in Figure 8 clearly show that this strategy makes the algorithm resistant against high building plan search costs. Still, the algorithm produces bad results for higher numbers of building plans searched.

5.5 Tree Width Decreases with Increasing Tree Depth

Strategy #5 makes the following extension to the previous one: If the search continues (*i.e.*, the last search step produced additional welfare), the number of building plans searched will be decreased by one in comparison to the previous search step. This strategy outperforms the previous one in all cases except one: When initially only a single building plan is searched the tree depth will only be 1 and the resulting welfare will be equal to the welfare as depicted in Figure 9 for the search of a single building plan.

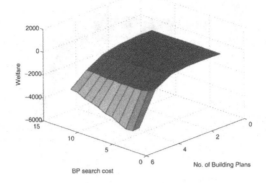

Fig. 9. Average welfare for strategy #5

5.6 Tree Width Decreasing with Welfare Decrease

Finally, strategy #6 computes the number of building plans depending on the size of the additional welfare created in the last search step. The welfare divided by the cost for searching the building plan equals the number of building plans to be searched next. This strategy performs worse than the previous one for higher numbers of initially searched building plans, but always creates higher welfare for a maximum number of searched building plans of 1.

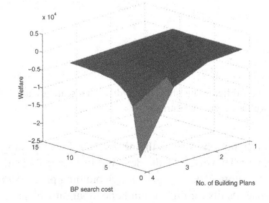

Fig. 10. Average welfare for strategy #6

5.7 Discussion

The set of strategies show a number of different heuristics. However, measuring scalability requires to count the number of searches for building plans carried out, which have been omitted in detail for space reasons, but they are part of the calculated welfare in the form of the cost for building the service dependence tree. Thus, the depicted welfare functions clearly show the influence of bad scalability in the rapid drops of welfare due to a high number of searches for building plans.

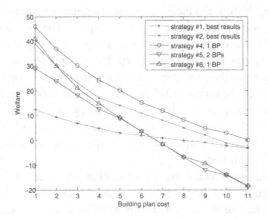

Fig. 11. Comparison of optimal sub-strategies

On one hand, simulation results show that all strategies produce bad results when building a wide service dependence tree, *i.e.*, when searching for several building plans for a single service class. On the other hand, results indicate that controlling the depth of the tree, *i.e.*, deciding when to stop the recursion, can be handled very well by strategies. For each of theses strategies an optimal sub-strategy exists. Strategy #4 and #6, produce their highest welfare when at each algorithm step a single building plan at the most is searched. Strategy #5, produces its highest welfare when initially searching for two building plans. Welfare of these sub strategies are compared in Figure 11. It can be clearly seen, that strategy #4 outperforms all other strategies. Furthermore, it produces higher welfare than the theoretical hulls of strategies #1 and #2, which were created by manually selecting the best sub strategy for each building plan search cost. Thus, for any building plan search cost investigated the described sub strategy #4 is the best choice. Furthermore, the results depicted in Figure 11 indicate that for high building plan search costs strategy #4 produces the same welfare as the hulls of strategy #1 and #2. This is logical, since for high building plan search costs no profit can be made, in which case all three strategies will stop after a single search for a building plan.

6 Summary

Different strategies for service composition in P2P networks have been investigated. Based on the distributed and decentralized service market together with its underlying P2P network, the service market model was extended by the composed service market. Driven by models of all building blocks for the service composition process the generic service composition algorithm was specified, resulting in service dependence trees. Different strategies for building this tree were developed and evaluated in simulations of composing a distributed computing service.

Such strategies for building the service dependence tree can differ in the width of the tree (*i.e.*, how many building plans are searched for each service class) and the depth of the tree (*i.e.*, when to stop the recursion of the tree building algorithm). Those results show that extending the tree and the width at the same time quickly leads to a dropping welfare of several orders of magnitude. However, improved heuristically strategies control the width and depth of the tree. All strategies proved to be very sensitive to the number of building plans searched at each step. Not a single heuristic was able to produce a high (or even positive) welfare, when a larger number of building plans could be searched for. In fact, these results indicate that at the most two building plans should be searched for within any service class. If those strategies were used in this way, they produced positive welfare for most of the investigated spectrum of building plan search costs. One strategy produced positive welfare for the whole spectrum, and continually outperformed all other strategies.

Thus, it has been shown that service composition can be economically successful, when a generic algorithm is used with the proposed strategies and a small number of building plans searched for at each step. Future work includes the development of public auctions for composed services, thus enabling the service consumer to publish his utility function, which in turn enables the maximization of the welfare of the composed service market.

This work has been partially performed in the EU-projects MMAPPS and DAIDA-LOS, and the Austrian Kplus competence center programme.

References

Oram, A. (ed.): Peer-to-Peer: Harnessing the Power of Disruptive Technologies. O'Reilly (2001)

American Heritage Dictionaries (Editor): The American Heritage Dictionary of the English Language, 4th edn. Houghton Mifflin (2000)

Blizzard Corporation, Blizzard Downloader F.A.Q. (2005),
http://www.worldofwarcraft.com/info/faq/blizzarddownloader.html

Carman, M., Serafini, L., Traverso, P.: Web service composition as planning. In: ICAPS 2003 Workshop on Planning for Web Services, Trento, Italy (2003)

Dumas, M., O'Sullivan, J., Heravizadeh, M., ter Hofstede, A., Edmond, D.: Towards a semantic framework for service description. In: IFIP Conference on Database Semantics, Hong Kong, China (2001)

Gerke, J.: Service composition in peer-to-peer systems. In: Proceedings of the Dagstuhl Seminar on Peer-to-Peer Systems and Applications, Dagstuhl, Germany (2004)

Gerke, J., Hausheer, D., Mischke, J., Stiller, B.: An architecture for a serviceoriented peer-to-peer system (sopps). In: Praxis der Informationsverarbeitung und Kommunikation (PIK), 2 (2003)

Gerke, J., Stiller, B.: A service-oriented peer-to-peer middleware. In: Müller, P., Grotzhein, R., Schmitt, J.B. (eds.) Kommunikation in Verteilten Systemen (KiVS) 2005, Informatik Aktuell. Springer, Heidelberg (2005)

He, H.: What is Service-Oriented Architecture. In: O'Reilly webservices.xml.com (2003),
http://webservices.xml.com/pub/a/ws/2003/09/30/soa.html

Hendler, J., Berners-Lee, T., Miller, E.: Integrating applications on the semantic web. Journal of the Institute of Electrical Engineers of Japan 122(10) (2002)

Izal, M., Urvoy-Keller, G., Biersack, E., Felber, P., Hamra, A.A., Garces-Erice, L.: Dissecting bittorrent: Five months in a torrent's lifetime. In: Passive and Active Measurements (PAM), Antibes Juan-les-Pins, France (2004)

Microsoft Developer Network, NET Framework Product Overview (2004),
  http://msdn.microsoft.com/netframework/technologyinfo/
  overview/
Reichl, P., Stiller, B.: Nil nove sub sole? why internet tariff schemes look like as they do. In: 4th
  Internet Economics Workshop (IEW'01), Berlin, Germany (2001)
Varian, H.: Intermediate Microeconomics: A Modern Approach. W.W. & Company, Norton
  (2003)
Web Services Descriptions Working Group, Web Services Description Language (WSDL) Version 2.0. (2005), http://www.w3.org/2002/ws/desc
World Wide Web Consortium, Web Services Activity Statement (2004),
  http://www.w3c.org/2002/ws/Activity

End to End Adaptation for the Web: Matching Content to Client Connections

Kristoffer Getchell, Martin Bateman, Colin Allison, and Alan Miller

School of Computer Science, The University of St Andrews, St Andrews, Fife, Scotland
{kg,mb,ca,alan}@dcs.st-andrews.ac.uk

Abstract. The size and heterogeneity of the Internet means that the bandwidth available for a particular download may range from many megabits per second to a few kilobits. Yet Web Servers today provide a one size fits all service and consequently the delay experienced by users accessing the same Web Page may range from a few milliseconds to minutes. This paper presents a framework for making Web Servers aware of the Quality of Service that is likely to be available for a user session, by utilizing measurements of past traffic conditions. The Web Server adapts the fidelity of content delivered to users in order to control the delay experienced and thereby optimize the browsing experience. Where high bandwidth connectivity and low congestion exist high fidelity content will be delivered, where the connectivity is low bandwidth or the path congested lower fidelity content will be served and delay controlled.

Keywords: Internet, monitoring, quality of service, adaptation, media, perception.

1 Introduction

Access bandwidths now range from a few kilobits per second through a mobile phone up to gigabits per second through Local Area Networks. Despite the bandwidth at the core of the Internet increasing, many bottlenecks continue to exist within the system; even users with high bandwidth connectivity may experience significant delays when engaging in network communication. At present the Internet largely relies upon the congestion control mechanisms embedded in TCP (Jacobson 1988) to prevent congestion collapse (Jain and Ramakrishnan 1988), which would render it unusable, yet applications are in a strong position to know how best to react to the onset of congestion (Floyd, Jacobson et al. 1997). If an application was made congestion aware it could directly control the amount of data sent. If congestion was high it could reduce the absolute number of bytes transmitted as well as the rate at which they were sent.

This paper addresses two questions: How is it possible for an application to become aware of network conditions and, given this awareness, how can a system be designed to allow application led adaptation to occur. A framework, which consists of three components, is proposed. A Network Monitor provides a Server with measurements of the Quality of Service (QoS) that the network is providing. A Network Aware Web Server handles the dynamic decisions required in order to

J. Filipe et al. (Eds.): ICETE 2005, CCIS 3, pp. 78–90, 2007.

determine the optimal version of a site to send to a connecting client and a Content Adaptation Tool allows content providers to generate, from a single high quality site, versions that are appropriate for different connection types.

From the user perspective a number of factors contribute to the perceived QoS offered, with both the speed of presentation and the quality of resources being important. A fast loading, simple Web Site is not necessarily going to be considered to be high quality by all users, and neither is a slow loading, highly detailed one (Bouch and Sasse 1999; Bouch, Kuchinsky et al. 2000; Bouch and Sasse 2000). From the content provider's perspective, a trade-off must be met whereby a balance between the speed at which resources can be provided to the target audience and the quality of the resources provided is achieved. Currently this trade-off is managed offline with content providers producing Web Sites which will be viewable within reasonable periods of time by the majority of Internet users. Those Internet users with connections slower than the speeds accounted for during the development of a site will be left with a poor browsing experience, whilst those with faster connections could have been supplied with pages of a higher fidelity. As the diversity of connection technologies continues to expand, this disparity is set to grow yet further.

By considering the QoS offered to the browsing client by the network, an adaptation framework would afford content providers the ability to focus on producing the highest quality resources, without having to consider the limitations that slow network links may cause. Lower fidelity resources can then be generated automatically using adaptation tools.

This paper continues with a discussion of related work in section 2 which leads to a discussion of the QoS issues of relevance to this work. Section 4 describes the framework used to allow the Network Aware Server to modify its behaviour as described in section 5. An evaluation of the framework thus far is provided in section 6, with section 7 concluding and drawing the paper to a close.

2 Related Work

Numerous studies have advocated the adaptation of content delivery in response to the load placed upon a Web Server (Barnett 2002; Pradhan and Claypool 2002). A similar approach to content adaptation as advocated in (Barnett 2002; Pradhan and Claypool 2002) is adopted by our work. However unlike (Barnett 2002; Pradhan and Claypool 2002) we address the case where the total load on the server is manageable but specific users are receiving a poor service because of network congestion or connectivity issues.

With the expansion of the e-commerce sector, the ways in which people interact with online vendors is of great importance to business sectors. (Bhatti, Bouch et al. 2000) discuss the issues surrounding user tolerance, with regards to the levels of service offered, reiterating the importance of user perceptions. Through experimenttation the level of user satisfaction is tested, with the results showing that if a user is provided with some feedback relatively quickly, they are generally satisfied to wait for extended periods while the remainder of their request is fulfilled.

Taking the concept of adaptation to mobile devices, (Abdelzaber and Bhatti 1999; Shaha, Desai et al. 2001) discuss the issues surrounding the need to augment our traditional understanding of QoS in order to make the best use of this new wave of access device. Existing services designed for PC delivery are not well suited to PDAs. Owing to the poor quality of PDA delivered content it is hardly surprising that the mobile device users are often left frustrated and alienated. Media adaptation techniques, however, may help by allowing mobile users to more readily gain access to the QoS adapted versions of a particular resource.

3 Quality of Service Issues

In this section the characteristics of QoS as perceived by users and as observed on the network are discussed, along with the ways in which an application may be able to adapt media. The aim of this work is to provide mechanisms that can maximise the QoS perceived by users for a given set of network conditions. In order to do so it is necessary first to establish metrics for both the user perceived and network observed QoS.

3.1 User Perceived Quality of Service

There is no single mapping between network level metrics and the way in which a user perceives the QoS being offered. Here we identify three factors that contribute to whether a user perceives a Web Browsing session as satisfying or not.

1. **Fidelity:** The quality of data sent to clients is vitally important – if the technical quality is too low (i.e. videos are blurry, sound is skewed, images are fuzzy and too small etc) then the user will perceive poor resource quality. However if the technical quality is too high (i.e. videos and sounds are jumpy because there are delays in getting data to the client, images are too large to fit on screen etc) then the user will again perceive poor quality.
2. **Delay and Feedback:** When a user is interacting with a Web Site, they require feedback for their actions. If it takes 20 minutes to load each page on a site, then the length of time required in order to supply feedback to the user (i.e. the next page they asked for) would be considered excessive and so user-perceived quality will be deemed as low. However if the pages load too quickly, then it is possible that the user will not recognise the true speeds – delays of anything under 30ms are almost unnoticed by users and as such resources should not be wasted trying to reduce delays below 50ms or so (Abdelzaber and Bhatti 1999).
3. **Consistency:** If there is consistency of presentation within a session the user will perceive a higher QoS during their browsing session (Bouch and Sasse 2000).

By controlling the fidelity of data it is possible to control the delay that users experience. Thus for a known set of network conditions it is possible to trade off fidelity for delay with the aim of maximising user satisfaction. However this presupposes knowledge about the state of the network.

3.2 Network Quality of Service

QoS is usually quantified at the network level. At this level there are two challenges; how to discover the QoS that is being experienced by traffic and how to communicate this information in a timely and useful way to the application.

1. **Round Trip Time:** The length of time to send a packet to a remote host and back to originator. In general, the lower this value the better – links with a high RTT appear sluggish and unresponsive. However most users will not notice delays around the 10s or possibly 100s of ms range (Abdelzaber and Bhatti 1999).
2. **Jitter:** The variation in the RTT measurements recorded. Low jitter is better as it indicates a more stable and therefore more predictable link. Jitter is important for interactive, real-time or streaming applications. The amount of jitter defines the buffer size required for playback.
3. **Bandwidth:** The amount of data that is transferred per unit time. Together with RTT this impacts on the delay experienced by a client. To use an analogy with water distribution; RTT is the length of the pipe and bandwidth the width.
4. **Packet Loss:** The proportion of packets lost on a link in a given time period. Lower loss values are better and indicate a more efficient use of a link: Lost packets are wasteful as the network resource used to send the lost packet is wasted and further wastage is introduced as a duplicate packet has to be sent.

The approach adopted in this work is to alter the fidelity of media in response to feedback on the level of network congestion, thereby achieving the appropriate trade off between technical quality and delay. Consistency of presentation is achieved by setting the fidelity at the start of a user session. In the absence of sharp and prolonged changes in network QoS, a consistent fidelity will be presented throughout a session.

3.3 Adaptability of Media

When considering the types of media available within Web Pages, they can broadly be categorised into one of several categories, some of which may be adjusted to account for the QoS that a connecting client is receiving, and some which may not. Table 1 provides an overview of the type of resources and the level of QoS adaptation that can be applied to them:

Table 1. QoS Adaptability of Media

Media Type	QoS Adjustable?
Plain text – HTML, TXT, PDF etc.	Limited
Graphics – GIF, JPG, TIFF etc.	Yes
Video – AVI, MPEG, DIVX etc.	Yes
Streaming Media	Yes
Active Content - Flash, Java etc.	Limited

Document: The document type limits the transformations that can be performed on a given document. Transformations can be made converting Word documents into PDF, which will reduce the file size but also reduce the usability of the document since they are no longer editable. For still lower quality the PDF can be turned into an HTML page. A smarter extraction mechanism can be envisioned which not only extracts the text but also the images. HTML down to plain text is a simple transformation but can result in a large loss of information, such as images, media files and the links relating to other documents. A better solution is to apply a filtering mechanism to the HTML mark-up removing items such as embedded scripting and cascading style sheet information. Additional mark-up within the HTML could also be used to provide QoS hints.

Graphics: Images, with the exception of photographs, could be described as SVG files and then rendered to a lower quality for inclusion in the final Web Sites. SVG is a vector based image format which, when rendered into the more traditional image formats (PNG, GIF etc), will give a better quality of image than if a GIF was reduced in quality. This is because GIF to GIF transcoding has to deal with encoding artefacts from the original GIF image whereas an SVG to GIF transformation does not.

Downloadable Media: Downloadable media, files that are downloaded wholly to the local machine before playback commences, can be adjusted in the temporal and spatial domains for lower file size. Other aspects of the media can be altered such as the encoding CODEC, perhaps choosing a lossy CODEC with a high compression rate over a CODEC with a lower rate of compression but less lossy output.

Streaming Media: Streaming media files that are played back whilst still downloading to the client machines have an extra complication as retransmission of lost packets is not possible due to timeliness constraints imposed by instantaneous playback. The choice of packet repair technique is therefore of vital importance as it can have a large influence on the experienced QoS.

Active Content: Active content proves difficult to adapt since there is a programmatic element to the resource. Embedded media within the active content may be transformed as in the case of graphical or downloadable objects. Other than this a static image of the first frame of the object could be generated but it is unlikely that this will be of more than marginal use.

4 System Framework

There are three main components to the framework: a Network Monitor, a Network Aware Server or Servers and Content Adaptation Tools. Figure 1 illustrates the Network Monitor positioned so that it is able to monitor all incoming and outgoing traffic, with the resulting QoS data being distributed into a Quality of Service Multicast Zone, where all interested servers can then receive it. The Network Monitor uses online passive monitoring techniques (Mogul 1990; Mogul 1992) to discover the QoS that flows are receiving. Passive monitoring is used in preference to active probes for two reasons. Firstly, no extra wide area traffic is generated which

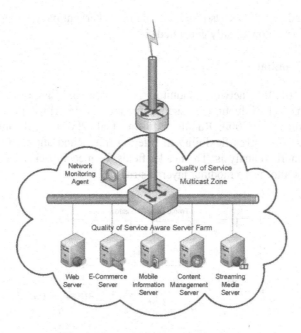

Fig. 1. Network Monitor Positioning

could adversely impact upon the client traffic. Secondly, by extracting measurements from observed traffic there will be the most data for the locations where there is the most traffic. Consequently, predictions of expected network conditions will be more accurate for those locations that use the service the most. Within this framework it is possible to have several different Network Aware Servers, providing a variety of services to connecting clients, each receiving their QoS information from a single Network Monitoring Agent: A large server farm is not required to have a dedicated Network Monitoring Agent for each server in operation.

The Network Aware Web Server provides the same content that a "standard" Web Server would. It is an important constraint of this architecture that the Server be able to make QoS decisions automatically. The user is not being asked to continually give feedback on QoS but is able instead to concentrate on the content. A second important requirement is that client browsers should not need to be aware that they are interacting with a Network Aware Server. Consequently, the Server can and does work with the existing browser base. The Server supplies different versions of content depending on the QoS characteristics of a link. It does not do this by transforming the content on the fly as this would take up valuable processing power and introduce extra latency. Instead the Server chooses between different versions of a Web Site that are held on backing store.

Although it is possible for Web developers to supply different Web Sites for different connection qualities, if this was the only option, the extra work would probably be a disincentive to using the system. A tool suite has been developed which takes as input a single high quality Web Site and converts it into a number of versions appropriate for different link qualities. This submission process takes place only once and is automated. The tools also facilitate human intervention in order to allow the optimisation of an automatically generated site.

4.1 Network Monitor

The structure of the network monitor is shown in figure 2. The design, implementation, and evaluation of such a monitor is described in more detail in (Ruddle, Allison et al. 2000; Ruddle, Allison et al. 2002). TCPDump is used to capture packets. This gives flexibility in filtering traffic and allows trace files to be made for post-mortem analysis. The header fields from each packet are passed to the monitor. The monitor has a modular layered structure.

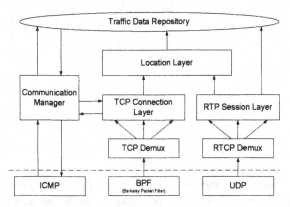

Fig. 2. Network Monitor Structure

The Location Information Server (LIS) extracts congestion information from Transport Control Protocol (TCP) data streams and feeds this information back to end points, The TCP-LIS is located on the WAN/LAN Interface, and uses passive monitoring of TCP traffic to obtain network level information such as congestion events and RTTs. Information extraction occurs within a connection layer where per connection state is maintained. Each reading is then passed to a location layer where statistics are maintained on a per location basis.

At the connection layer state is maintained for all open connections. As each packet arrives a hash table look up is done. This locates the state for the connection that the packet belongs to. Both TCP Macro state, which controls the set up and closure of connections, and Micro state, which controls the flow of data, are monitored. Packet loss is detected, by the observation of duplicate acknowledgements, or by the observation of a repeat packet. RTTs are measured by observing the delay between the receipt of an acknowledgement and the observation of the packet that generated the acknowledgement. Only one RTT measurement is attempted per window of data. When a connection finishes all state associated with that connection is reclaimed.

When events occur such as a packet being observed, a loss being discovered or the RTT being measured these are communicated to the Location Layer. The Location Layer maintains state for aggregates of IP addresses where a Location is defined as an aggregation of hosts to which traffic is likely to experience similar network conditions. State maintained for each location includes the proportion of packets lost, the RTT and the maximum bandwidth observed.

The observation of SYN packets allows new connection requests to be detected and predictions of likely network conditions for that connection to be communicated to the local host in a timely fashion. These predictions are contained within a Location Information Packet. Extensions to the LIS, which support the sharing of congestion information between TCP and Real Time Protocol (RTP) traffic, have been designed (Miller 2002).

4.2 Network Aware Web Server

A list of Quality of Service Aware media types was defined above. Here it is necessary to actually decide how to dynamically choose which quality version to send to a given client. In order to facilitate this decision mechanism, an integrated, modular framework into which Network Aware Servers can be plugged has been developed and is illustrated in Figure 3. A packaging system has been adopted which has seen the components in the systems separated into a number of distinct areas:

1. **Server Realm** – this package contains the server functionality and interfaces directly with the connecting clients, fulfilling their requests as appropriate.
2. **QoS Realm** – this package is responsible for gathering, and providing to the Server Realm, all available QoS information concerning currently active connections.
3. **DataStore Realm** – this is a utility package used by both the Server and QoS Realms and provides the functionality to quickly store and retrieve data on an as-required basis. Within this category there are several implementations of DataStores, both managed and unmanaged, that are customised to specific needs, whatever they may be.

This packaging of components simplifies code management and helps to make clear the lines of responsibility within the system. For example any server related operations are managed within the Server Realm whereas any QoS or Data Storage operations are managed within the QoS and DataStore Realms respectively.

Once the QoS information has been received by an interested Network Aware Server, it is then equipped to deal with a connecting client in the most suitable way. The flow of information through the proof-of-concept Network Aware Web Server is summarised in Figure 3 above. Owing to the unreliable transmission of QoS data into the framework, safeguards have been implemented to ensure the correct operation of the system in the absence of required QoS information. As Figure 4 shows, if QoS information is lacking, the framework reverts to "standard" operation, serving the non-QoS adapted version of the requested resource.

Assuming access to the required QoS information is possible, the framework implements only marginal changes to the model implemented in "standard" Web Servers, with the Connection Handler speaking to the Link Evaluation Mechanism and then the Content Provisioning Mechanism before returning the most appropriate resource to the requesting client. It is at this stage that indirection is used to send to a client the most suitable resource (based on the quality of the client link). At present

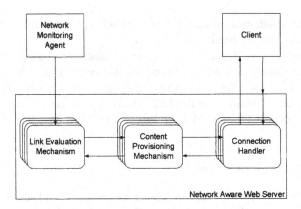

Fig. 3. Network Aware Web Server Architecture

the framework has been developed to support five distinct quality levels – this is done in order to provide distinct sets into which various links can be graded and thus reduce the possible problems caused by a slightly erroneous quality classification – there is less likelihood that small errors will cause a change in grading and so we protect the perceived user quality by reducing unnecessary quality reclassifications, therefore ensuring a more consistent session presentation.

The steady state behaviour of TCP provides a benchmark against which the behaviour of other congestion control schemes have been judged (Mahdavi and Floyd 1997; Floyd 2001). The steady state behaviour of TCP is given by the following equation (Mathis, Semke et al. 1997) where MSS is the maximum segment size on a link, C is a known constant, RTT is the round trip time and P is the probability of loss. Estimates of RTT and P are provided by the LIS, MSS for a connection is known and C is a known constant.

$$T = \frac{MSS * C}{RTT * \sqrt{P}} \tag{1}$$

If the data flow is application limited low levels of loss may suggest an available bandwidth in excess of the actual physical bandwidth. This can be accounted for by measuring the actual bandwidth utilisation and setting the estimated available bandwidth to the minimum of that estimated from congestion feedback and actual utilisation.

The bandwidth category that a connection request falls into (Q) is then given by:

$$Q = \min\left(\left[T = \frac{MSS \times C}{RTT \times \sqrt{P}}\right], \max(B)\right) \tag{2}$$

In this way the expected available bandwidth for a destination can be calculated based on past measurements. The result may not correspond to the actual access bandwidth, but may rather correspond to the share of bandwidth available on the bottleneck link. Having established the bandwidth available to a destination the server can then choose the appropriate version of the site to transmit.

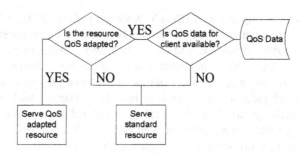

Fig. 4. QoS Decision Mechanism

The system makes use of the concept of a human session in meeting the consistency requirement. The aim is to provide a consistent fidelity through the lifetime of a session. Here we define a human session as an amount of time spanning a series of requests during which a user might alternate between assimilating the information within a page and downloading new pages. For example a user receives Page 1 from a site and spends 10 minutes reading it, he then proceeds to request Page 2; ideally we want to ensure that the quality of Page 2 is similar to the quality of the Page 1 that has already been received – this will ensure continuity throughout the browsing session. In this situation the Human Session timeout should not be set to anything below 10 minutes. During a session all pages should aim to be served from the same QoS adapted version of the site.

Regardless of any Human Session periods that attempt to give a unified feel to the browsing experience, changes in the QoS readings are tracked during a session. If an initial link quality evaluation is found to be consistently lacking then it may be necessary that remedial action is undertaken, resulting in the link quality being re-graded, in order to provide the most suitable browsing experience to the connecting client. However such a decision should not be taken lightly and cannot be based solely on one, or possibly a handful of bad readings, instead historical data should be considered, with the weight attached to historical data diminishing over time as the data becomes more and more out of date. In order to achieve this data smoothing an Exponentially Weighted Moving Average (EWMA) is used. It also deals with the ageing of historical data, something that the arithmetic mean cannot do.

5   Resource Mapping

There are perceptual limitations to the quality of media that is worth transmitting. For example there is little point in transmitting a picture with a resolution greater than that of the display. There is also little point in encoding a video file at more than 25 frames per second, with around 12 to 15 fps being the lowest point where motion is still perceived without jerkiness. When considering the delay associated with the transfer of resources, we must take care to ensure that the user is provided with feedback as quickly as possible; at tens of milliseconds delays become perceivable. Whilst at seconds delays impact negatively upon user perceived quality. Pages downloading in times exceeding tens of seconds have a serious impact on user perception, with people believing that the site is of low quality and thus highly likely to abandon their browsing sessions (Bouch, Kuchinsky et al. 2000). For each page there should be a maximum delay of ten seconds between the user request being made and the page being fully displayed. Unfortunately differing processing capabilities on client machines mean that this is an almost impossible target to achieve since we have no indication of how long a given page will take to render on each client device.

The approach adopted in this paper is to provide a series of tools which, when given a single high quality Web Site and a meta-level description, are able to transform the single site into a number of Web Sites which are suitable for a range of bandwidths. The transformation happens once offline and creates a series of Web Sites that are aligned for the quality levels chosen. With this approach we avoid the situation of having to re-encode media files on the fly which could add an unacceptable amount of delay to loading the Web Page. There are two issues that need to be addressed. Firstly, extra storage space is required for multiple versions of the Web Site. As storage is cheap and given that the amount used does not negatively impact on the user perceived QoS this is a reasonable cost to pay. Secondly, a method for the handling of dynamic content is needed. The use of a Meta Interface Model (MIM) would allow the customisation of the dynamic content along similar lines to static content. Little extra delay would be introduced since all the images and media would have already been encoded and it would only be customisation of the textual components (HTML, scripting, CSS etc) which would need to be done dynamically, templates could be generated in advance along with the static content.

Aligning the Web Sites with the bandwidths for common access technologies provides the choice of target bandwidths. We choose the following bands; mobile phones (at 0-10 Kbit/sec), modems (10 – 56 Kbit/sec), ISDN (56 – 150 Kbit), broadband 150 Kbit/sec – 1.5 Mbit/sec) and finally local area network (1.5 Mbit/sec and above).

6 Evaluation

The predictive powers of the network monitoring agent has been evaluated using live Internet experiments, between hosts in the US, the UK, Spain, Germany and Eastern Europe. Figure 5 shows the predicted verses the actual levels of congestion

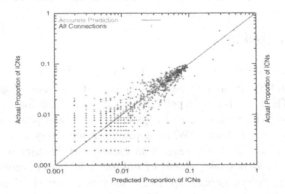

Fig. 5. Predicted vs. Actual Congestion

experienced. The metric used is the proportion of Implicit Congestion Notifications (ICNs). Packet loss is taken as an implicit indication of congestion. Yet in a single congestion event several packets may be lost, consequently in these experiments only the first packet loss in a window of packets is taken as an ICN.

It is of interest that on links experiencing high levels of congestion the accuracy of prediction increases. Furthermore it was found that the correlation between prediction and result remained high for periods of time in excess of 20 minutes. These results suggest that it is possible to use the measurement of past traffic to predict the network conditions that are likely to be experienced by future traffic. Consequently the approach adopted here is valid.

7 Conclusion

We have presented the design, implementation and evaluation of a framework for making the Web Quality of Service Aware. The approach adopted is to use passive monitoring of transport level headers to make predictions about the QoS that is expected to be experienced by a particular location. A mechanism for translating a single high fidelity Web Site into a set of Web Sites that are appropriate for different bandwidths has been outlined. When a user session starts the Web Server uses QoS information to determine which bandwidth is appropriate. It then serves up Web Pages from the appropriate Web Site. This approach allows Web designers to leverage the increasing bandwidth many clients have available without producing Web Pages that are inaccessible to others.

References

Abdelzaber, T., Bhatti, N.: Web Server QoS Management by Adaptive Content Delivery. In: International Workshop on Quality of Service, London (1999)

Barnett, C.M.: Adaptive Content Web Serving (2002) Retrieved June 20, 2005, from http://zoo.cs.yale.edu/classes/cs490/01- 02b/barnett.casey.cmb68/paper.htm

Bhatti, N., Bouch, A., et al.: Integrating User- Perceived Quality into Web Server Design. In: 9th International World Wide Web Conference, Amsterdam (2000)

Bouch, A., Kuchinsky, A., et al.: Quality is in the Eye of the Beholder: Meeting Users' Requirements for Internet Quality of Service. In: CHI 2000 (2000)

Bouch, A., Sasse, M.A.: Network Quality of Service: What do users need? In: 4th International Distributed Conference, Madrid (1999)

Bouch, A., Sasse, M.A.: The Case for Predictable Media Quality in Networked Multimedia Applications. In: MMCN 2000, San Jose, CA (2000)

Floyd, S.: Less Conservative Congestion Control (2001)

Floyd, S., Jacobson, V., et al.: A reliable multicast framework for light-weight sessions and application level framing. IEEE/ACM Transactions on Networking 5(6), 784–803 (1997)

Jacobson, V.: Congestion Control and Avoidance. ACM Computer Communications Review 4(18), 314–329 (1988)

Jain, R., Ramakrishnan, K.K.: Congestion Avoidance in Computer Networks with a Connectionless Network Layer: Concepts, Goals and Methodology. In: IEEE Computer Networking Symposium, IEEE, Washington D.C (1988)

Mahdavi, J., Floyd, S.: TCP-Friendly Unicast Rate-Based Flow Control. Technical note sent to the end2end-interest mailing list (1997) http://www.psc.edu/networking/papers/tcp_friendly.html

Mathis, M., Semke, J., et al.: The Macroscopic Behavior of the Congestion Avoidance Algorithm. Computer Communications Review 27(3) (1997)

Miller, A.: Best Effort Measurement Based Congestion Control. Department of Computer Science. University of Glasgow, Glasgow (2002)

Mogul, J.C.: Efficient use of Workstations for Passive Monitoring of Local Area Networks. ACM SIGCOMM 20(4), 253–263 (1990)

Mogul, J.C.: Observing TCP Dynamics in Real Networks. ACM SIGCOMM 22(4), 305–317 (1992)

Pradhan, R., Claypool, M.: Adaptive Multimedia Content Delivery for Scalable Web Servers. International Network Conference, Plymouth (2002)

Ruddle, A., Allison, C., et al.: A Location Information Server for the Internet. In: IEEE International Conference on Computer Communications and Networks, IEEE, Las Vegas, NV (2000)

Ruddle, A., Allison, C., et al.: A Measurement Based Approach to TCP Congestion Control. European Transactions on Telecommunications 13(1), 53–64 (2002)

Shaha, N., Desai, A., et al.: Multimedia Content Adaptation for QoS Management over Heterogeneous Networks. In: International Conference on Internet Computing, Las Vegas, NV (2001)

Part II

Security and Reliability in Information Systems and Networks

Voice Biometrics Within the Family: Trust, Privacy and Personalisation

Delphine Charlet[1] and Victor Peral Lecha[2]

[1] France Telecom
2 avenue Pierre Marzin, 22307 Lannion Cedex, France
delphine.charlet@francetelecom.com
[2] France Telecom
Building 10, Chiswick Business Park, 566 Chiswick High Road, London W4 5XS,
United-Kingdom
victor.perallecha@francetelecom.com

Abstract. Driven by an increasing need for personalising and protecting access to voice services, the France Telecom R&D speaker recognition system has been used as a framework for experimenting with voices in a family context. With the aim of evaluating this task, 33 families were recruited. Particular attention was given to 2 main scenarios: a name-based and a common sentence-based scenario. In each case, members of the family pronounce their complete name or a common sentence respectively. Moreover, this paper presents a database collection and first experiments for family voices.

The results of this preliminary study show the particular difficulties of speaker recognition within the family, depending on the scenario, the genre and age of the speaker, and the physiological nature of the impersonation.

Keywords: Voice biometrics, speaker recognition, privacy, trust, personalisation, family voices evaluation.

1 Introduction

Privacy within a family is a sensible subject: each member of a family may require some privacy, but achieving privacy protection through traditional means (such as pin code) may be resented by the other members of the family. Indeed, traditional privacy protection is based on "what you know" information, thus, to be effective, it needs to be hidden from the others. So the use of traditional authentication password or PIN is inadequate with the global feeling of mutual trust that often exists within the family. Hence, speaker recognition appears to be an interesting way for privacy protection since it is based on "what-you-are" and not on "what-you-hide". On the other hand, the genetic links that exist between parents and children as well as the same cultural and geographical contexts they share may hamper speaker recognition, as it is pointed by (van Leeuwen, 2003). Moreover, children constitute a difficult target for speech recognition in general (Wilpon and Jacobsen, 1996).

As far as we know, no published study has been done on this subject. Thus, for the purpose of this preliminary study we collected a database of family voices in order to perform technological evaluation of the performances of speaker recognition in the context of family voices.

J. Filipe et al. (Eds.): ICETE 2005, CCIS 3, pp. 93–100, 2007.

2 Application Design

We have defined a standard application to evaluate the feasability to personalise home telecoms services for each member of a family, based on voice recognition. It has been decided that personalisation should be done through an explicit step of identification/authentication. Thus, if this step is explicit, it has to be as short as possible. These ergonomic considerations lead us to two technological choices:

- Identification and authentication performed on the same acoustical utterance.
- Text-dependent speaker recognition: as it achieves acceptable performances for short utterances (less than 2 seconds).

Two scenarios were defined, depending on the content of the utterance pronounced by the speaker.

2.1 Name-Based Scenario

In this scenario, the user pronounces his/her first and last name to be identified and authenticated. The main characteristics of such an application are:

- It is easy to recall.
- It is usually rather short.
- It enables deliberate impostor attempts: e.g. a mother can claim to be her daughter.

As for each member of the family, the phonetic content of the voiceprint is different, the identification process is performed on both the voice and the phonetic context, although there is no explicit name recognition process. Thus it can be expected that the identification error rate will be negligeable. On the other hand, as the authentication is performed on a short utterance (e.g. 4 syllables), the authentication performances are expected to be rather poor.

2.2 Common Sentence-Based Scenario

In this scenario, the user pronounces a sentence, which is common to all the members of the family. The main characteristics of such an application, compared to the name-based scenario are:

- It is less easy to recall: the sentence should be prompted to the user, if he does not remember.
- The length of the sentence may be longer than a simple name.
- It prevents deliberate impostor attempts: e.g. a mother can not claim to be her daughter.

As for each member of the family the phonetic content of the voiceprint is the same, the identification process is performed only on the voice. Thus it can be expected that the identification error rate will be higher than in the context of name-based recognition. On the other hand, as the authentication is performed on a longer sentence (10 syllables), the authentication performances are expected to be better than those of the name-based scenario.

3   Database Design

3.1   Family Profile

The families were required to be composed of 2 parents and 2 children. The children are older than 10. They all live in the area of Lannion, where this work was conducted. 33 families were recruited: 19 with one son and one daughter, 10 with 2 sons and 4 with 2 daughters. They were asked to perform 10 calls from home, with their landline phone, during a period of one month. Hence, factors such as voice evolution over time or sensitivity to call conditions are not studied in this work.

3.2   Name-Based Scenario

In this scenario, the key point is the fact that there might be deliberate impostor attempts on a target speaker, as the user claims an identity to be recognised.

3.2.1   Training
For each member of a family, training is performed with 3 repetitions of his/her complete name (first + last name). This number of repetitions represents a good trade-off between performances and tediousness of the task.

3.2.2   Within Family Attempts
Each member of a family is asked to perform attempts on his own name, and also attempts on the name of each of the other members of his family.

3.2.3   External Impostor Attempts
A set of impostor attempts from people who do not belong to the family is collected. The external impostors are composed of members of other families who pronounced the name of the member of the target family.

3.2.4   Collected Database
As we focus on speaker recognition, we only retained the utterances where the complete name was correctly pronounced.

- 16 families completed their training phase.
- 13 families completed the testing phase also.
- 672 true speaker attempts collected for the 13 families, that makes an average of 52 true speaker attempts per family, thus an average of 13 true speaker attempts per user.
- 582 within family impostor attempts collected for the 13 families, that makes an average of 45 within family impostor attempts per family, thus an average of 11 within family impostor attempts per user.
- 2173 external impostor attempts (impostor attempts are performed on all the families who have completed the training phase)

3.3   Common Sentence-Based Scenario

In this scenario, the key point is the fact that there can not be deliberate impostor attempts on a target speaker, as the user does not claim identity to be recognised.

3.3.1   Training

For each member of a family, training is performed with 3 repetitions of the common sentence.

3.3.2   Within Family Attempts

Each member performs attempts by pronouncing the common sentence.

3.3.3   External Impostor Attempts

The attempts of other families are used to perform external impostor attempts.

3.3.4   Collected Database

As we focus on speaker recognition, we only retain the utterances where the sentence was correctly pronounced.

- 25 families completed their training phase.
- 17 families completed the testing phase also.
- 614 within family attempts collected for the 17 families, that makes an average of 36 attempts per family, thus an average of 9 attempts per user.
- 13549 external impostor attempts: all within family attempts are used to perform impostor attempts on the other families (impostor attempts are performed on all the families who have completed the training phase).

4   Experiments

4.1   Speaker Recognition System

For these experiments, the text-dependent speaker recognition system developed in France Telecom R&D is used. It basically relies on HMM modelling on cepstral features, with a special care on variances, with a speaker-independant contextual phone loop as reject model (Charlet et al., 1997). The task is open-set speaker identification. There was no particular tuning of the system to this new task. The rejection thresholds are set a posteriori, common to all families.

4.2   Typology of Errors

4.2.1   Name-Based Scenario

In this scenario, the identity claim is taken into account in the typology of errors. Within the family, when the speaker A claims to be speaker A (pronouncing the name of speaker A), the system can:

- accept the speaker as being speaker A: correct acceptance (CA)
- accept the speaker as being speaker B: false identification error (FI)
- reject the speaker: false rejection error (FR)

Moreover, in this scenario, within the family, a speaker can make deliberate impostor attempts on a target speaker. When the speaker A claims to be speaker B, the system can:

- reject the speaker: correct rejection on internal impersonation (CRII)
- accept the speaker as being speaker B: wanted false acceptance on claimed speaker (WFA)
- accept the speaker as being speaker A: unwanted correct acceptance (UCA)
- accept the speaker as being speaker C: unwanted false acceptance (UFA)
- Internal False Acceptance is defined as: IFA = WFA + UFA

Outside the family, when an impostor claims to be speaker A, the system can:

- reject the speaker: correct external rejection (CER)
- accept the speaker as being speaker A: external false acceptance on claimed speaker (EWFA)
- accept the speaker as being speaker B: external unwanted false acceptance (EUFA)
- External False Acceptance is defined as: EFA = EWFA + UFA

4.2.2   Common Sentence-Based Scenario

This is the classical typology of open-set speaker identification. Within the family, when the speaker A pronounces the common sentence, the system can:

- accept the speaker as being speaker A: correct acceptance (CA)
- accept the speaker as being speaker B: false identification error (FI)
- reject the speaker : false rejection error (FR)

Outside the family, when an impostor pronounces the common sentence, the system can:

- accept the speaker as being speaker A: external false acceptance error (EFA)
- reject the speaker: correct external rejection (CER)

5   Results

5.1   Name-Based Scenario

Figure 1 plots EFA, IFA and FI as a function of FR for the name-based system.

For the particular operating point where { FR=7.9%; FI=0.4%; IFA=21.1%; EFA= 8.1%}, let us see the details of errors:

- FI=0.4% is low and due to 2 types of surprising errors: a man identified as his wife and a 10-year-old girl identified as his father.
- UCA=20.6% : when a member within the family claims to be another member, he is "unmasked" (i.e. truly identified) in 20% of the cases. This is mainly due to the fact that, as the voiceprint of the members of the family shares important part of the phonetic content (same last name), an attempt with another first name may match reasonably well the voiceprint of the speaker if the first names are not too different.
- IFA=21.1% - EFA=8.1% : the rate of IFA (false acceptance from deliberate impostor attempts within the family) is more than 2.5 times as much as EFA (from deliberate impostor outside the family, with the same age/gender distribution as the impostors within the family). Although we cannot quantify what is due to line effects from what is due to physiological resemblance, we can note that the system is much more fragile to impostor within the same family than from outside the family.

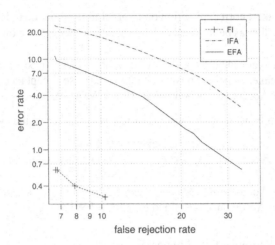

Fig. 1. Name-based speaker identification within the family

IFA is decomposed into WFA=18.0% and UFA=3.1%. Table 1 presents the false acceptance rate for deliberate impersonation (WFA : when speaker A claims the name of speaker B and is accepted as being speaker B) within the family, for the different types of speaker. "Son" can do impostor attempts on "son" when they are brothers. In the same way, "daughter" can do impostor attempts on "daughter" when they are sisters.

We analyze each type of speaker (father, mother, daughter, son) with respect to their ability to defeat the system and to their "fragility" to impostor attempts (Doddington et al., 1998). In the table, between brackets are given the numbers of tests of each type of imposture, in order to give an idea of the reliability of the results.

Table 1. False alarm rate according to the type of impostor and target speaker

Impostor speaker	target speaker			
	father	mother	son	daughter
father	–	11.8 [51]	12.3 [57]	2.2 [45]
mother	0 [52]	–	14.8 [54]	18.6 [43]
son	7.4 [54]	29.8 [47]	29.4 [17]	53.3 [30]
daughter	0 [45]	32.6 [43]	50 [36]	50 [8]

From the table, the following remarks can be done:

- the father, as an impostor, gets a moderate and equal success rate on his wife and his son, and a low success on his daughter. As a target, he is "fragile" against his son at a moderate level.

- the mother, as an impostor, gets a better success rate than her husband on her children, and a complete failure on her husband. The difference of success rate between the son target and the daughter target is not high. As a target, she is fragile against her husband at a moderate level, and she is equally fragile at a high level against her children.
- the son, as an impostor, has a low success rate on his father, a high level on his mother and brother and a very high level on his sister (the difference between brother and sister success rate might not be significant because of the small number of attempts in the case of 2 brothers attempts). As a target, he is moderately fragile against his parents and highly against his sister.
- the daughter, as an impostor, has a high success rate on her mother and a very high success on her sister or brother, and a complete failure on her father. As a target, she is not fragile against her father, moderately against her mother and very highly against her sister or brother.

5.2   Common Sentence-Based Scenario

Figure 2 shows the global performances of the common sentence-based system, for different operating points.

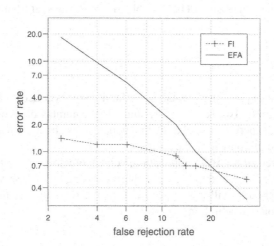

Fig. 2. Common sentence-based speaker identification within the family

For a particular operating point where globally {FR=6.1%; FI=1.2%; EFA=5.8%;}, analyzing the results family per family, we observe that over the 17 families who made identification attempts:

- 13 families have no false identification : FI=0%
- 3 families get a false identification rate : FI=2-2.5% (actually 1 observed error)
  - family #13: father identified as his 17-year-old son
  - family #16: 14-year-old girl identified as her mother

- family #20: mother identified as her 20-year-old girl
- 1 family get a false identification rate of FI=7% due to one unique cause of error: a 12-year-old girl was identified as her mother

Speaker identification within a family appears to be easily achievable for a majority of the families tested (13/17). For the remaining families, where errors were observed, the errors are not frequent and always concern a specific pair parent/same-sex teenager.

6 Discussion

In the name-based scenario, there is deliberate impersonation within the family. As the speech utterance to perform speaker authentication on is very short (on average 4 syllables) performances are very poor. However, the analysis of the differences of performances according to the type of impostor and target speaker is interesting. It shows that the most "fragile" to impersonation are the children, between them, and that they are also the most effective impostors.

In the common sentence-based scenario, there cannot be deliberate impersonation, as there is no identiy claim. Except for some rare cases where there is an identification error, it seems to be the most effective and ergonomic way to perform speaker recognition within the family. Considering the case of identification errors, as they always occured on the same pair, it should be possible to develop special training procedure to prevent them.

7 Conclusion

In this paper, we have presented a database of family voices collected for voice recognition within the family. Two scenarios are studied. The number of recorded attempts is enough to perform experiments and draw first conclusions about the particular difficulties of speaker recognition within the family.

Despite the novel nature of the application, voice biometrics seems the most natural way to manage the privacy and trust issues when accessing to voice services in a family context. Further research will attempt to improve the reliability of the system when dealing with the voices of children.

References

Charlet, D., Jouvet, D., Collin, O.: Speaker verification with user-selectable password. In: Proc. of the COST 250 Workshop, Rhodos, Greece (1997)

Doddington, G., Liggett, W., Martin, A., Przybocki, M., Reynolds, D.: Sheep, goats, lambs and wolves, a statistical analysis of speaker performance in the nist 1998 speaker recognition evaluation. In: Proc. of the ICSLP 1998, Sydney, Australia (1998)

van Leeuwen, D.: Speaker verification systems and security considerations. In: Proc. of Eurospeech 2003, pp. 1661–1664, Geneva, Switzerland (2003)

Wilpon, J., Jacobsen, C.: A study of speech recognition for children and the elderly. In: Proc. of the ICASSP 1996, pp. 349–352, Atlanta, USA (1996)

Secret Locking: Exploring New Approaches to Biometric Key Encapsulation

Seny Kamara[1], Breno de Medeiros[2], and Susanne Wetzel[3]

[1] Johns Hopkins University
Department of Computer Science
3400 N Charles Street, Baltimore, MD 21218, USA
seny@cs.jhu.edu
[2] Florida State University
Department of Computer Science
Tallahassee, FL 32306-4530, USA
breno@cs.fsu.edu
[3] Stevens Institute of Technology
Department of Computer Science
Castle Point on Hudson, Hoboken, NJ 07030, USA
swetzel@cs.stevens.edu

Abstract. Biometrics play an increasingly important role in the context of access control techniques as they promise to overcome the problems of forgotten passwords or passwords that can be guessed easily.

In this paper we introduce and provide a formal definition of the notion of *secret locking* which generalizes a previously introduced concept for cryptographic key extraction from biometrics. We give details on an optimized implementation of the scheme which show that its performance allows the system for use in practice. In addition, we introduce an extended framework to analyze the security of the scheme.

Keywords: Biometrics, secret sharing, secret locking, error-tolerance.

1 Introduction

Biometrics play an increasingly important role in a broad range of security applications. In particular, biometrics have manifold applications in the context of access control techniques which to date are largely based on the use of passwords. Biometrics promise to overcome the problems of forgotten passwords or passwords that can be guessed easily.

Most biometric systems used in practice to date store *profiles* of users. A user profile typically consists of a collection of measurements of the user's physical characteristics (e.g., the user's iris patterns or fingerprints) obtained during an initial enrollment phase. Later, when a user presents herself for identification, the system performs measurements and matches those against the database of stored user profiles. If a "good" match is found, the user is identified. While these systems protect against an *online* attacker, they however, pose a considerable risk for *offline* attacks in which an attacker may obtain and exploit the knowledge of the stored profiles.

J. Filipe et al. (Eds.): ICETE 2005, CCIS 3, pp. 101–112, 2007.

Recently, the alternative approach of *biometric key encapsulation* has been proposed: instead of replacing the use of passwords by means of biometrics, passwords are "hardened" by incorporating biometric features. No user profiles are stored in the system. Due to the inherent variability in biometric readings, the system, however, requires a *biometric feature extractor* in order to reliably recover the same (cryptographic) key from an imprecise input, i.e., to provide "error tolerance." In this context, a solution based on error-correcting codes and randomness extraction was developed (Juels and Wattenberg, 1999; Juels and Sudan, 2002; Dodis et al., 2004; Boyen, 2004). An alternative line of work based on secret sharing techniques was proposed in (Monrose et al., 2002; Monrose et al., 2001). While the former provides an information-theoretical optimal solution for error-tolerance, it at the same time requires a uniform level of error-tolerance for all users alike and as such poses significant challenges for use in practice. In contrast, the latter allows for an individual level of error-tolerance for each user.

In this paper we focus on extending the work in (Monrose et al., 2002). In particular, we introduce a formal definition of the notion of *secret locking* which generalizes the concept proposed previously. We furthermore provide an extended discussion on the determinant-based scheme. We give details on an optimized implementation of the scheme which show that its performance allows the system for use in practice. In addition, we introduce an extended framework to analyze the security of the scheme. In the original work, the security of the determinant-based construction was proved under an idealized attack model only. In this paper we consider arbitrary attacks. Finally, we discuss heuristic connections between the security of the scheme and well-known hard problems in computational mathematics and coding theory.

1.1   Motivation

Using biometrics in practice poses a number of challenges, in particular when used in applications to protect resource limited devices such as cell phones or PDAs. Ideally, these devices should obtain biometric measurements without requiring any additional dedicated hardware. Currently, most portable devices have built-in microphones, keyboards or writing pads. As such, systems using biometrics such as voice patterns, keystroke dynamics or stylus drawing patterns are more readily deployable than systems based on iris or retina scans. Furthermore, it should be difficult for an adversary to capture the user's biometric measurements, and in particular this counter-indicates fingerprint scans as a biometric in this regard, as fingerprint marks are quite easy to obtain.

Static vs. Non-static Biometrics. While *static* biometrics capture physiological characteristics of an individual (e.g., iris or retina patterns, and fingerprints), *non-static* biometrics (e.g., voice patterns, keystroke dynamics) relate to behavioral characteristics. In general, it is harder for an attacker to capture non-static than static biometrics, so they could prove useful for the type of application we consider. However, non-static biometrics have a high variability of robustness from user to user: Some users have more reliably reproducible feature readings than others. Consequently, less error-tolerance is required to support identification of users with more reliably reproducible feature readings (Doddington et al., 1998).

Biometric Key Encapsulation. requires the exact reconstruction of the underlying key, and some form of error-tolerance must therefore be employed in order to accommodate the variability in biometric readings. In order for a system to accommodate different levels of error-tolerance allowed to identify particular users, ideally it should allow for variable error-tolerance. Alternatively, the system-wide level could be adjusted to the worst case, i.e., the least robust user. In (Juels and Wattenberg, 1999; Juels and Sudan, 2002; Dodis et al., 2004; Boyen, 2004) error-tolerance is achieved by means of error-correcting codes and randomness extraction. In practice, this solution either requires uniformity, with the same error-correcting code employed for all users, or the codes need to be defined on a user-by-user basis. While the former solution suffers from the problem that the security of the system is reduced to the level of the least robust user, the latter reveals to an attacker the code used (and therefore the level of error-tolerance supported) upon inspection.

In contrast, the system introduced by Monrose et al. allows for non-uniformity of robustness of a user's biometric characteristics. In particular, the system hides the amount of error-tolerance required by a specific user. In other words, if the attacker has access to the key encapsulation value, his effort to decide how much error-tolerance the particular user required should be roughly equal to the effort of breaking the key encapsulation of that user.

2 Related Work

There are numerous approaches described in literature to use biometrics for authentication purposes or to extract cryptographic secrets from biometrics. There are various systems using biometric information during user login process (e.g., (Joyce and Gupta, 1990)). These schemes are characterized by the fact that a model is stored in the system (e.g., of user keystroke behavior). Upon login, the biometric measurements (e.g., user keystroke behavior upon password entry) are then compared to this model. Since these models can leak additional information, the major drawback of these systems is that they do not provide increased security against offline attackers.

In (Soutar and Tomko, 1996), a technique is proposed for the generation of a repeatable cryptographic key from a fingerprint using optical computing and image processing techniques. In (Ellison et al., 2000), cryptographic keys are generated based on users' answers to a set of questions; subsequently, this system was shown to be insecure (Bleichenbacher and Nguyen, 2000). Davida, Frankel, and Matt (Davida et al., 1998) propose a scheme which makes use of error-correction and one-way hash functions. The former allows the system to tolerate a limited number of errors in the biometric reading. This approach was generalized and improved in (Juels and Wattenberg, 1999) by modifying the use of error-correcting codes.

In (Monrose et al., 2002; Monrose et al., 2001), a new approach is proposed, focusing on using keystroke features and voice characteristics to *harden* the passwords themselves. The work improves on previous schemes in that it is the first to offer better security against a stronger attacker. Furthermore, this approach allows a user to reconstruct the key even if she is inconsistent on a majority of her features. The techniques introduced by (Ellison et al., 2000; Davida et al., 1998; Juels and Wattenberg, 1999) respectively, do not permit that.

Recently, a new theoretical model for extracting biometric secrets has been developed (Juels and Sudan, 2002; Dodis et al., 2004; Boyen, 2004), extending the work in (Juels and Wattenberg, 1999). The model is based on the use of population-wide metrics combined with (optimal) error-correction strategies. While the model is provably secure and allows for optimal constructions under certain assumptions, it has not been empirically validated that these constructions are applicable to biometrics of interest in practice.

3   Secret Locking and Secret Sharing Schemes

In the traditional setting, a *secret sharing scheme* consists of a dealer, a set of participants $P = \{P_1, \ldots, P_n\}$, an access structure $\Gamma \subseteq 2^P$ as well as algorithms Share and Recover. In order to share a secret K amongst the participants, the dealer uses the algorithm Share to compute each share s_i to send to user P_i. In order to reconstruct the shared secret using the algorithm Recover, only those shares are needed which correspond to authorized subsets of participants —i.e., shares corresponding to sets in the access structure Γ. The most well-known secret sharing schemes are threshold schemes. While these schemes have a simple access structure (which contains all user sets of cardinality larger than a threshold t, i.e., $S \in \Gamma \iff |S| > t$), for use with biometrics, we are interested in secret sharing schemes with different properties.

The concept of a compartmented access structure was introduced in (Simmons, 1990), and has received attention from a number of researchers (Brickell, 1989); (Ghodosi et al., 1998). In a compartmented secret sharing scheme, each user P_i is assigned a level $\ell(P_i)$. The same level may be assigned to different users. In order to reconstruct the secret, one share from each level is needed. More formally, the access structure of the compartmented secret sharing scheme is $\Gamma = \{A \in 2^P : A \cap P^i \neq \emptyset\}$, where $P^i = \{P_j \in P : \ell(P_j) = i\}$.

Compartmented access structures can be used to achieve error-tolerance in biometric key encapsulation: Let $\phi = (\phi_i)_{i=1,\ldots,m}$ be the set of discretized measurements[1] of biometric features (for instance timing intervals between different keystrokes). Each ϕ_i assumes a value in the same finite set D. For each user U, let $R_i(U) \subset D$ be the range of values that are likely[2] to be observed by measuring ϕ_i on user U. In order to encapsulate a key K for user U, where the key is a random value from a finite field $\mathbb{F}_q$, proceed as follows. First, define a virtual participant set $P = \{P_{i,j}\}_{\{i=1,\ldots,m; j \in D\}}$, and assign to $P_{i,j}$ a level $\ell(P_{i,j}) = i$. Next, use the Share algorithm for the compartmented access structure to compute initial shares $\hat{s}_i^j$. Finally, perturb this initial set of shares to obtain shares s_i^j which match the initial shares $\hat{s}_i^j$ whenever $j \in R_i(U)$, and are set to a newly chosen random share value otherwise. When the legitimate user U presents herself for authentication, it is sufficient to measure each value $\phi_i(U) \in D$ of the biometric feature ϕ_i on user U, then select the share $s_i^{\phi_i(U)}$ from level i and apply the

---

[1] Biometric measurements are continuous values. Measurements are discretized by breaking the range of the measurement into equal probability ranges.

[2] One needs repeated measurements of each biometric feature in order to arrive at the range of likely values. Particularly with non-static biometrics this range may vary over time. Refer to (Monrose et al., 2002) for details of a practical implementation of such a scheme.

Recover algorithm. By construction, the outcome is likely to be the encapsulated secret K. On the other hand, the same is not likely to be the case if a different user U' tries to impersonate U, as the feature values for U' are not likely to align (i.e., fall in the likely range at each level) with those of U.

The above idea can be readily applied with any efficient compartmented secret sharing scheme, such as that in (Ghodosi et al., 1998), if the target is simply user authentication. However, as we seek mechanisms to achieve secure key encapsulation, the scheme must moreover have the property that an attacker who has access to the set of all shares cannot determine which shares to pick at each level. It can be readily seen that the scheme in (Ghodosi et al., 1998) is not secure in this sense, and therefore is not sufficient for our purposes.

We can abstract the previously introduced concepts as follows: Let D be a finite set, and consider the product set D^m. We call an element $(\phi_i)_{i=1,\dots,m} \in D^m$ a *sequence of feature values*. Consider some universe $\mathcal{U}$, and for each element U of the universe, and for each feature value ϕ_i we associate the *likely range*, a subset $R_i(U) \subset D$. Let $\rho_i = R_i(U)/D$ be the relative size of the likely range $R_i(U)$. Let $\tau_i(U)$ be defined as $-\log(\rho_i)$, which equals the logarithm of the expected number of random trials before a value for $\phi_i(U)$ is chosen within U's likely range $R_i(U)$, among all values in D. Finally, let $\tau_U = \sum_i \tau_i(U)$. The value τ_U is the logarithm of the expected number of random trials before one produces a sequence of likely features (for U) by simply choosing random sequences in D^m. Clearly, τ_U is a natural parameter of the difficulty of guessing likely sequences for U.

Definition 1. *A secure secret locking scheme is a set of algorithms* Share *and* Recover *with the following properties:*

1. *Given a compartmented participant set $P = \{P_{i,j}\}_{\{i=1,\dots,m;j\in D\}}$, where D is a finite set, and given a secret K in $\mathbb{F}_q$,* Share *produces a collection s_i^j of shares (which are values in a set S) which implement the access structure $\Gamma = \{A \in 2^P : A \cap P^i \neq \emptyset, i = 1,\dots,m\}$, where $P^i = \{P_{i,j}\}_{j\in D}$. In other words,* Share *and* Recover *implement a compartmented secret sharing scheme with levels $i = 1,\dots,m$.*

2. *Assume that a set of shares s_i^j originally produced by* Share *has been perturbed by substituting for s_i^j a random element of S whenever j is not a likely value for $\phi_i(U)$. Then, each probabilistic algorithm $\mathcal{A}$, that receives as input the share set (partially randomized as above), and that terminates in polynomially many steps in τ_U has negligible probability of success in recovering the original shared secret.*

Binary Features: In the following we describe some general constructions of the secret locking concept introduced in (Monrose et al., 2002). For simplicity of argument, we assume that all features assume binary values, i.e., $D = \{0, 1\}$, even though all schemes described can be generalized to any finite D. In the binary case, the range of values $R_i(U)$ for a feature i and element U is one of three possibilities, namely $\{0\}$, $\{1\}$, or $\{0, 1\}$. In the latter we call the feature *non-distinguishing* for U, while in the former two cases the feature is *distinguishing*.

3.1 Secret Locking Constructions

For each construction, it is sufficient to provide the algorithms Share and Recover, as the security property is not constructive. Instead it must be verified for each construction. We first describe an implementation of secret locking introduced in (Monrose et al., 2002) which is based on the well-known Shamir secret sharing scheme:

Shamir Secret Sharing (SSS) is based on polynomial interpolation. In general, for a random polynomial $f(x)$ over $\mathbb{Z}_p$ of degree $d - 1$ and a secret $K = f(0) \in \mathbb{Z}_p$ to be shared, a share will be determined as a point on the polynomial, i.e., as the tuple $(x, f(x))$. Using Lagrange interpolation, the knowledge of at least d distinct shares will allow the reconstruction of the secret K (Shamir, 1979).

In order to construct a secret locking scheme based on SSS, it is sufficient to choose $f(x)$ as a polynomial of degree $m - 1$ with $f(0) = K$. The $2m$ shares $\{s_i^0, s_i^1\}_{1 \leq i \leq m}$ of secret K are determined as $s_i^0 = f(2i)$ and $s_i^1 = f(2i + 1)$. Consequently, any m shares will allow for the reconstruction of the secret K, and clearly one share per row will do. However, this scheme is not compartmented, but simply a threshold scheme. Furthermore, it does not provide security in the sense of our definition if the percentage of distinguishing features is small (i.e., less than 60% of the total number of features). This is due to the fact that it is then possible to treat the system as a Reed-Solomon list decoding problem, which can be solved by means of a polynomial time algorithms (Guruswami and Sudan, 1998).

A truly compartmented construction based on unimodular matrix constructions is also presented in (Monrose et al., 2002), and is the focus of our attention for the remaining part of the paper.

Determinant-based Secret Locking Construction. The determinant-based scheme introduced in (Monrose et al., 2002) encapsulates a secret by means of a set of vectors in a vector space. In general, for a secret $K \in \mathbb{Z}_p$ to be shared, the shares are determined as vectors in $\mathbb{Z}_p^m$. The secret can be reconstructed by arranging m of the shares in an $m \times m$-dimensional matrix and computing its determinant.

In order to construct the set of shares, initially m vectors s_i^0 in $\mathbb{Z}_p^m$ are chosen with the property that $\det(s_1^0, \ldots, s_m^0) \bmod p = K$, the secret to be encapsulated. The second set of shares is then determined by means of a unimodular transformation matrix $\Upsilon = (v_1, \ldots, v_m)$ where $v_i \in \mathbb{Z}_p^m$ ($1 \leq i \leq m$). The unimodular matrix can be efficiently generated by permuting the rows of a random, triangular unimodular matrix: $\Upsilon = \Pi \cdot \Upsilon' \cdot \Pi^{-1}$, where $\Pi = (\pi_1, \ldots, \pi_m)$ is any permutation matrix and $\Upsilon' = (v_1', \ldots, v_m')$ is an upper-triangular matrix that has 1 for each diagonal element and random elements of $\mathbb{Z}_q$ above the diagonal. Eventually, the second set of shares is computed as $s_i^1 = \Upsilon s_i^0$ for $1 \leq i \leq m$.

It can be easily seen from the way the shares are constructed, that this scheme indeed implements a compartmented access structure. In fact, if one share is picked from each one of the m levels (feature), the secret K can be reconstructed —due to the unimodular relation between the two shares at the same level. However, if the two shares from the same level are used, then the reconstructed secret is random, as the unimodular relationship between the two sets of shares is not preserved. In the following sections, we discuss the security characteristics of this scheme, and provide details on an optimized implementation of the scheme with good performance profile.

3.2   Security

In this section we explore some of the underlying hard problems that are related to the security of the determinant-based sharing scheme described above. Note that while the construction and its analysis are presented only for the case of binary features, similar arguments can be presented for the general case.

First, consider the case when all features are distinguishing, and thus only one sequence of feature values reveals the secret. By construction, all other shares are random and cannot be combined with the true shares to obtain any partial information about the secret. Moreover, without further information (such as cipher-text encrypted under the encapsulated key) the attacker cannot distinguish when the correct secret is reconstructed. The probability of success is therefore 2^{-m}, where m is the total number of features.

In the presence of non-distinguishing features the setting is different. For instance, consider the case where the first feature is non-distinguishing. Let ϕ^0 and ϕ^1 be two feature sequences that differ only in the first feature, with $\phi_1^0 = 0$ and $\phi_1^1 = 1$. Suppose further that both feature sequences are valid for U, i.e., lead to reconstruction of the correct secret. That means that the following matrices have the same determinant:
$$K = \det \left(s_1^0 \, s_2^{\phi_2} \, s_3^{\phi_3} \, \cdots \, s_m^{\phi_m} \right) = \det \left(s_1^1 \, s_2^{\phi_2} \, s_3^{\phi_3} \, \cdots \, s_m^{\phi_m} \right), \text{ where } \phi_i = \phi_i^0 = \phi_i^1,$$
for $i > 1$. It is well-known that the determinant is a multi-linear function of the matrix columns, which implies: $\det \left(s_1^0 - s_1^1 \, s_2^{\phi_2} \, s_3^{\phi_3} \, \cdots \, s_m^{\phi_m} \right) = 0 \mod p$. We conclude that if the first feature is non-distinguishing one finds a non-trivial algebraic relation on the sets of shares. The method is not constructive, however, because it requires previous knowledge of a valid sequence of values for all the other features. In order to search for such relations systematically, one represents the choice for the value of feature i as a function of a boolean variable:

$$\phi_i(x_i) = \texttt{if } x_i \texttt{ then } s_i^1 \texttt{ else } s_i^0.$$

The determinant computation may then be fully expanded as a boolean circuit, and the equation which expresses the determinant being equal to 0 mod p reduced to a single boolean formula. Any satisfying assignment to that formula corresponds to a sequence of feature values which may be a valid sequence for U, and conversely all valid sequences for U give rise to satisfying assignments.

Since SAT approximation algorithms can generally only handle relatively small boolean formulas (in the thousands of variables), the complexity of this approach can be estimated by studying a relaxation of the problem. In order to "linearize" the boolean formula, we allow feature choices in the whole field $\mathbb{F}_q$, by putting $\phi_i(x_i) = (1 - x_i)s_i^0 + x_i s_i^1$. Note that $\phi_i(0) = s_i^0$ and $\phi_i(1) = s_i^1$ correspond to legitimate shares, while for other values in $x_i \in \mathbb{F}_q$ there is no natural interpretation to the meaning of $\phi_i(x_i)$. Linearization enables the use of the rich machinery of computational algebra to attack the corresponding "relaxed" problem of finding zeros of the multilinear polynomial $\Delta(x_2, \ldots, x_m)$ which represents the determinant $\det(s_1^0 - s_1^1, (1 - x_2)s_2^0 + x_2 s_2^1, \cdots, (1 - x_m)s_m^0 + x_m s_m^1)$.

$m = 5$	6
$(2, 100, 25, 30.6)$	$(2, 60, 49, 60.25)$
7	8
$(2, 80, 97, 120.6)$	$(3, 60, 225, 252.3)$
9	10
$(3, 40, 449, 502.6)$	$(4, 10, 961, 1017.7)$

Fig. 1. m = # of features. The quadruplet under $m = 6$ indicates that the # of distinguishing features was 2, and Δ had a minimum of 49 and an average of 60.25 non-zero coefficients over 60 random trials.

The complexity of this zero-finding problem was assessed by means of experiments using the symbolic computation package MAPLE. In particular, the experiments determined the number of non-zero coefficients of $\Delta(x_2, \ldots, x_m)$, for $5 \leq m \leq 10$. It was assumed that only $\lfloor 0.4m \rfloor$ of the features were distinguishing —a conservative approach, since the fewer distinguishing features there are, the more symmetric the polynomial should be, and the greater the chances are that some of its coefficients evaluate to 0. The results or the experiments are shown in Fig. 1. These results support the security of the scheme, as the number of non-zero coefficients exhibits an exponential increase. As a consequence, this renders any algebraic attempts to attack the problem ineffective, and in fact, even the best approximation algorithms known to date to simply counting zeros (as opposed to finding them) on multilinear polynomials have linear cost with the number of non-zero coefficients (Karpinski and Lhotzky, 1991).

4 Implementation

In order to implement the scheme in practice, it is not sufficient to have error-tolerance purely from the secret sharing construction, as features ϕ_i will occasionally assume a value outside the likely range $R_i(U)$ even if evaluated on the legitimate user U. We call such errors "noisy errors." Unlike the natural variation of measurements within likely ranges, the variability introduced by noisy errors is not tolerated well by the secret locking construction. In practice, we can accommodate a few of these errors by simply executing an exhaustive search on a Hamming ball of small radius e centered on the measured input sequence $\phi = (\phi_i(U))_{i=1,\ldots,m}$. We show that with appropriate optimizations, this method is practical for small values of e, for instance $e \leq 3$, which seems more than sufficient to guarantee a reasonable false negative rate with keyboard typing patterns (Monrose et al., 2002).

The first optimization we made was to change the mechanism for reconstructing the secret from the selected matrix entries. Instead of insisting on sharing the determinant —which would require working with matrices over large finite fields $\mathbb{F}_q$, with $\log q \geq 80$ —we instead use a hash function such as SHA-1 to process the concatenation of all matrix entries from the distinguishing features. Recall from Section 3.2 that once a feature sequence is found with the correct values for all distinguishing features, the non-distinguishing positions can be detected by showing that the determinant remains unchanged if that feature value is flipped. Using this modified recovery algorithm we

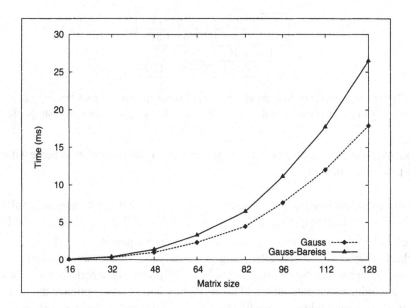

Fig. 2. Time to compute determinants as a function of the matrix size. The times are averaged over 10000 runs.

can allow the dimension of the base field to be made much smaller, without affecting the entropy of the keyspace. In our experiments we used $\mathbb{F}_q = \mathbb{Z}_{8191}$, which allows each matrix entry to fit in a 16-bit buffer. This also enables implementation of all modular and matrix operations using native 32-bit integer operations and optimized C code.

A second optimization is to save the (common value of the) determinant of a correct set of features to enable fast elimination of incorrect guesses during the exhaustive test of possible candidates in the Hamming ball. Note that saving the determinant does not present a security risk, since (1) the secret is no longer the determinant, but the entirely independent hash value of the concatenated matrix entries corresponding to distinguishing positions, and (2) identifying the determinant value reduces the degree of freedom in the possible choices by adding a single polynomial relation between these choices. Note that this extra information is comparable to that available to an adversary that is able to correctly guess the position of a non-distinguishing feature—when it may write a similar relation with determinant to equal zero (see Section 3.2).

Experimental Setup. All the experiments were conducted on a 64-bit dual 2 GHz PowerPC G5 running MacOS Server 10.3.5, with 3 GB main memory, and 4 KB virtual pages. Our implementation is in C and compiled with gcc 3.3 using the -O3, -ffast-math, -malign-natural and -fprefetch-loop-arrays optimization flags. (For more details on gcc optimizations see (The GNU Project, 2005).) We note that the Apple G5 provides native support for 32-bit applications and that all our code was compiled for a 32-bit architecture. All arithmetic is performed in $\mathbb{Z}_p^*$, where p is prime and equals $8191 = 2^{13} - 1$. Since we are working on a 32-bit architecture and $8191 < 2^{16}$, all elements in $\mathbb{Z}_{8191}^*$ can be stored in shorts. This means that multiplication in $\mathbb{Z}_{8191}^*$

	$m = 16$	32	48
$e = 2$	0.009	0.220	1.371
3	0.041	1.688	13.554
4	0.174	10.559	184.924

Fig. 3. Time (in seconds) to recover the key K from a feature sequence ϕ' such that $dist(\phi, \phi') = e$, where e = # of errors corrected and m = # of features. 80% of ϕ's features are distinguishing.

will not overflow the size of a regular `int` and that we can implement the scheme without multi-precision arithmetic.

Computing Determinants. Given feature sequence ϕ', we begin by generating all sequences within a hamming distance e of ϕ'. We call this set $\beta(\phi', e) = \{\phi^* \in \{0,1\}^m : dist(\phi^*, \phi') \leq e\}$. For each $\phi^* \in \beta(\phi', e)$, we then compute $\delta' = \det(s_1^{\phi_1^*} \cdots s_m^{\phi_m^*})$ and check whether $\delta' = \delta$, the latter being the stored determinant value of (any) correct choice of feature values. Since $|\beta(\phi', e)| = \sum_{i=0}^{e} \binom{m}{i}$, we have to perform a large number of determinant computations, and therefore it is important to optimize the running time of determinant evaluation. We first benchmarked the performance of various determinant algorithms and implementations, in particular Gaussian elimination and Gauss-Bareiss (both described in (Cohen, 1993)) and compared their performance (Fig. 2), concluding that plain Gaussian elimination performs better in this task. We found that a large part of the time spent was in the computation of modular inverses. Consequently, we precomputed all inverses in $\mathbb{Z}_{8191}^*$ and replaced our use of the extended Euclidean algorithm by simple table lookups. Since each element in $\mathbb{Z}_{8191}^*$ can be stored in two bytes, the entire table can fit in approximately 16 KB.

Reusing Computations. Apart from optimizing individual determinant computations we re-used intermediate elimination results to speed up Gaussian elimination when several determinants are computed in succession. Consider M_1 and M_2, two $m \times m$ matrices. During Gaussian elimination, elements in column i only affect elements in columns $j > i$. If the leftmost column where M_1 and M_2 differ is i, then the operations we perform on columns 0 through $i - 1$ when computing $\det(M_1)$ and $\det(M_2)$ will be the same, and we avoid repetition by storing the intermediate results. We take maximum advantage of this optimization by choosing an appropriate ordering when generating all the feature sequences within the Hamming ball. Figures 3 and 4 summarize the timings for recovering the correct key K. That is, these timings include determining the distinguishing features for those $\phi^* \in \beta(\phi', e)$ with $\delta = \det(s_1^{\phi_1^*} \cdots s_m^{\phi_m^*})$ and computing K as the respective hash value.

In the case of keyboard biometrics, the number of features is approximately 15 and one noisy error must be corrected with 12 distinguishing features (numbers from (Monrose et al., 2002)), which our implementation can compute in a fraction of a second. A measure with twice as much entropy, say 30 features and two noisy errors, would also take less than half a second. These results were obtained in a powerful machine by today's standards, however these times are sufficiently small that we feel confident the scheme can be practically implemented in most current 32-bit architectures.

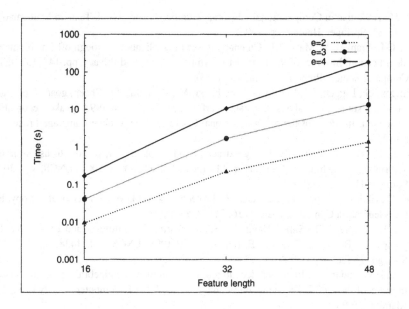

Fig. 4. Time to recover the key K from a feature sequence ϕ' such that $dist(\phi, \phi') = e$, where e is the # of errors corrected. 80% of ϕ's features are distinguishing.

5   Conclusions and Future Work

While the security analysis in this paper does not constitute a complete proof in the standard model, the outlined heuristic connections between the security of the scheme and well-known hard problems in computational mathematics show the difficulty of the underlying problem. The remaining open questions will be addressed by future research. In addition, future work includes testing of the implementation for use in the context of other non-static biometrics (e.g., voice patterns).

Acknowledgements

The authors would like to thank Fabian Monrose and Mike Reiter for helpful discussions and suggestions throughout this work. The first author is supported by a Bell Labs Graduate Research Fellowship.

References

Bleichenbacher, D., Nguyen, P.: Noisy polynomial interpolation and noisy chinese remaindering. In: Preneel, B. (ed.) EUROCRYPT 2000. LNCS, vol. 1807, pp. 53–69. Springer, Heidelberg (2000)

Boyen, X.: Reusable cryptographic fuzzy extractors. In: Proc. of the 11th ACM Conf. on Comp, ACM Press, New York (2004)

Brickell, E.F.: Some ideal secret sharing schemes. Journal of Combinatorial Mathematics and Combinatorial Computing 9, 105–113 (1989)

Cohen, H.: A Course in Computational Algebraic Number Theory. Grad. Texts in Mathematics, vol. 183. Springer, Heidelberg (1993)

Davida, G.I., Frankel, Y., Matt, B.J.: On enabling secure applications through off-line biometric identification. In: Proc. of the 1998 IEEE Symp. on Secur. and Privacy, pp. 148–157. IEEE Computer Society Press, Los Alamitos (1998)

Doddington, G., Liggett, W., Martin, A., Przybocki, M., Reynolds, D.: Sheep, goats, lambs and wolves. a statistical analysis of speaker performance in the nist 1998 speaker recognition evaluation. In: Proc. of the 5th International Conference on Spoken Language Processing (1998)

Dodis, Y., Reyzin, L., Smith, A.: Fuzzy extractors and cryptography, or how to use your fingerprints. In: Cachin, C., Camenisch, J.L. (eds.) EUROCRYPT 2004. LNCS, vol. 3027, Springer, Heidelberg (2004)

Ellison, C., Hall, C., Milbert, R., Schneier, B.: Protecting secret keys with personal entropy. Future Generation Computer Systems 16, 311–318 (2000)

Ghodosi, H., Pieprzyk, J., Safavi-Naini, R.: Secret sharing in multilevel and compartmented groups. In: Boyd, C., Dawson, E. (eds.) ACISP 1998. LNCS, vol. 1438, pp. 367–378. Springer, Heidelberg (1998)

Guruswami, V., Sudan, M.: Improved decoding of reed-solomon and algebraic-geometric codes. In: Proc. of the 39th IEEE Symp. on Found, pp. 28–37. IEEE Computer Society Press, Los Alamitos (1998)

Joyce, R., Gupta, G.: Identity authorization based on keystroke latencies. Comms. of the ACM 33(2), 168–176 (1990)

Juels, A., Sudan, M.: A fuzzy vault scheme. In: Proc. of the 2002 IEEE Internl, p. 480. IEEE Computer Society Press, Los Alamitos (2002)

Juels, A., Wattenberg, M.: A fuzzy commitment scheme. In: Proc. of the 6th ACM Conf. on Comp, pp. 28–36. ACM Press, New York (1999)

Karpinski, M., Lhotzky, B.: An (ϵ,δ)-approximation algorithm of the number of zeros of a multilinear polynomial over gf[q]. Technical Report 1991-8569, Uni. Bonn, Inst. für Informatik, Abteilung V (1991)

Monrose, F., Reiter, M.K., Li, Q., Wetzel, S.: Cryptographic key generation from voice (extend. abst.). In: Proc. of the 2001 IEEE Symp. on Secur. and Privacy, IEEE Computer Society Press, Los Alamitos (2001)

Monrose, F., Reiter, M.K., Wetzel, S.: Password hardening based on keystroke dynamics. Internl. J. of Info. Secur. 1(2), 69–83 (2002)

Shamir, A.: How to share a secret. Comms. of the ACM 22(11), 612–613 (1979)

Simmons, G.: How to (really) share a secret. In: Goldwasser, S. (ed.) CRYPTO 1988. LNCS, vol. 403, pp. 390–448. Springer, Heidelberg (1990)

Soutar, C., Tomko, G.J.: Secure private key generation using a fingerprint. In: Cardtech/Securetech Conf. Proc. vol. 1, pp. 245–252 (1996)

The GNU Project (1988–2005). The GNU compiler collection. http://gcc.gnu.org

Adaptive Real-Time Network Monitoring System: Detecting Anomalous Activity with Evolving Connectionist System

Muhammad Fermi Pasha[1], Rahmat Budiarto[1], Mohammad Syukur[2], and Masashi Yamada[3]

[1] School of Computer Sciences, University of Sains Malaysia, 11800 Minden,
Pulau Pinang, Malaysia
{fermi,rahmat}@cs.usm.my
[2] Faculty of Mathematics and Natural Sciences, University of Sumatera Utara, Medan 20155,
Sumut, Indonesia
mhdsyukur@usu.ac.id
[3] School of Computer and Cognitive Sciences, Chukyo University, 101 Tokodachi, Kaizu-cho,
Toyota, 470-0383, Japan
myamada@sccs.chukyo-u.ac.jp

Abstract. When diagnosing network problems, it is desirable to have a view of the traffic inside the network. This can be achieved by profiling the traffic. A fully profiled traffic can contain significant information of the network's current state, and can be further used to detect anomalous traffic and manage the network better. Many has addressed problems of profiling network traffic, but unfortunately there are no specific profiles could lasts forever for one particular network, since network traffic characteristic always changes over and over based on the sum of nodes, software that being used, type of access, etc. This paper introduces an online adaptive system using Evolving Connectionist Systems to profile network traffic in continuous manner while at the same time try to detect anomalous activity inside the network in real-time and adapt with changes if necessary. Different from an offline approach, which usually profile network traffic using previously captured data for a certain period of time, an online and adaptive approach can use a shorter period of data capturing and evolve its profile if the characteristic of the network traffic has changed.

Keywords: Adaptive System, Distributed Network Monitoring, Network Anomaly, Evolving Connectionist Systems.

1 Introduction

Over the past decades network technologies has grown considerably in size and complexity. More industries and organizations depend on the performance of its network to run their activities. Network problems mean less productivity and therefore it is necessary to manage and monitor the network so that it is consistently up and running. In managing a network, it is very crucial to control its performance, while the performance itself is dependent on traffic assessment, hence profiling the traffic would be one initial important aspect to be taken to secure the network.

J. Filipe et al. (Eds.): ICETE 2005, CCIS 3, pp. 113–125, 2007.

But simply profile the traffic only gives solutions for certain period of time, since as time goes the characteristic of the network traffic will change, and network administrator will need to re-profile the traffic to adapt with the changes. The main factors of these changes are nodes additions into the network, different types of software used, devices upgrades, topological changes, and different type of network access. Between these factors, nodes additions, types of access and types of software are causing the most significant changes to network traffic characteristic. For example, let say a corporate network has 100 computers connected on the first year, as the corporate grows, an additional of another 200 computers added into the network could definitely change the characteristic of the network traffic in the second year. These changes would invalidate the current profile and therefore it cannot be used to detect anomalous activity inside the network. Network administrator will need to either re-profile the traffic or manually edit the profile, which would be an arduous task to do.

We develop an adaptive and real-time network monitoring system with capabilities to profile the traffic in online lifelong mode and evolve the profile if significant traffic changes occurred. Furthermore, with the use of the profile, our system also try to detect anomalous activity inside the network in real-time.

With the ability to evolve, the system can be installed in any network without prior knowledge about the network traffic characteristics, just let the system grows as the network grows. This enabling the system to conduct distributed monitoring across different network (especially different network segment) without have to know the traffic's characteristic of each network segment in advance.

The rest of the paper is organized as follows. In section 2 we review some related work on network traffic profiling as well as network anomaly detection. Section 3 presents our connectionist engine architecture. Section 4 mentions about our system's scheme concept as a distributed application. Section 5 contains discussion on the obtained results and further analysis. Finally we summarize our conclusions and future work in section 6.

2 Related Work

Many research works have been devoted to automate the process of profiling network traffic and it was quite successful in general. The approaches taken are ranging from using statistical method with K-Means clustering and approximate distance clustering (Marchette, 1999), using data mining techniques to mine the network traffic and generate the profiles in terms of rules (Pasha et al., 2004), the use of three different approaches to specifically profile network application behaviour using rough sets, fuzzy C-Means clustering and Self Organizing Maps (Lampinen et al., 2002), etc. Some of it are already applied an artificial intelligence (AI) techniques and has shown a promising result. The drawbacks of these attempts are it is done in offline mode and pertinent to the network current behaviour.

An offline mode approach is usually composed of the following steps and each step is done separately:

1. Data Collection (for certain period of time).
2. Analyze the collected data.

3. Generate (automatically) or create (manually) the profile based on the analyzed data result.

This process is often time consuming and still requires a highly specialized network administrator on deciding when is the right time to conduct the data collection phase, analyzing the data and finally automatically using AI tools or manually extract the profile from the analyzed results. When the profiles outdated, the process will need to be repeated.

There is also Bro system developed primarily by Vern Paxson from University of California at Berkeley (Paxson, 1998), which focuses on intrusion detection on high stream bandwidth. It is a Linux/Unix based application that uses its own scripting language called Bro language to write the rule policy. Although Bro comes with predefined rules for detecting common anomalous activity, network administrator is still needed to write his own additional rule to cope with the network traffic characteristic in his network.

3 Connectionist Engine

An engine that facilitates learning in online mode is modelled in a connectionist way using Evolving Connectionist Systems (ECOS). ECOS are a connectionist architecture that enables us to model evolving processes and knowledge discovery. An evolving connectionist system can be a neural network or a collection of such networks that operate continuously in time and adapt their structure and functionality through a continuous interaction with the environment and with other systems (Kasabov, 2003).

The engine consists of two modules, and each is designed for a different purpose. The first module is the adaptive module for rule creation and adaptation, and the second one is the real-time detection module for online monitoring and anomaly detection.

Figure 1 depicts our ECOS based connectionist model architecture.

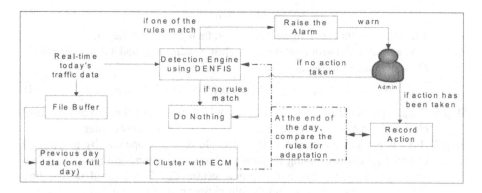

Fig. 1. ECOS based Connectionist Model Engine Architecture

3.1 Data Stream Online Clustering Using ECM

This is part of the first connectionist model module along with rule creation and adaptation functionality which are described in the next subsection. A packet capturing component is deployed to passively captured network traffic data stream in promiscuous mode. After being filtered, the data will be further clustered with one of the ECOS branches for online unsupervised clustering named Evolving Clustering Method (ECM). ECM is a fast one-pass algorithm for dynamic clustering of an input stream of data, where there is no predefined number of clusters. It is a distance-based clustering method where the cluster centres are presented by evolved nodes in an online mode (Song and Kasabov, 2001).

We had done a bit modification on the original ECM algorithm to fits our needs. Below is the algorithm:

Step 1. If it is not the first time, initialise the cluster centre C_{Cj}, $j = 1,2,...,n$, that already produced before, and then go straight to Step 3. Else, go to Step 2 to start creating clusters.

Step 2. Create the first cluster C_1 by simply taking the position of the first example from the input data stream as the first cluster centre C_{C1}, and setting a value 0 for its cluster radius R_{U1}

Step 3. If all examples from the data stream have been processed, the clustering processes finishes. Else, the current input example, x_i, is taken and the normalized Euclidean distance D_{ij}, between this example and all n already created cluster centres C_{Cj},

$$D_{ij} = \| x_i - C_{Cj} \| \tag{1}$$

where $j = 1,2,3,..., n$, is calculated.

Step 4. If there is a cluster C_m with a centre C_{Cm}, a cluster radius R_{Um} and distance value C_{C1} such that:

$$D_{im} = \| x_i - C_{Cm} \| = min \{D_{ij}\} = min \{ \| x_i - C_{Cj} \| \}$$

$$\text{for } j = 1,2,3,...,n; \tag{2}$$

and

$$D_{im} < R_{Um} \tag{3}$$

when the current x_i belong to this cluster, then go back to Step 3.

Step 5. Find a cluster C_a (with a centre C_{Ca} a cluster radius R_{Ua}, and a distance value D_{ia} which has a minimum value S_{ia}:

$$S_{ia} = D_{ia} + R_{Ua} = min\{S_{ij}\}, j = 1,2,3,..., n \tag{4}$$

Step 6. If S_{ia} is greater than 2 x $Dthr$, the example x_i does not belong to any existing cluster. Then repeat the process from Step 2 to create a new cluster.

Step 7. If S_{ia} is not greater than 2 x $Dthr$, the cluster C_a is updated by moving its centre, C_{Ca}, and increasing its radius value R_{Ua}. The updated radius R_{Ua}^{new} is set to be equal to $S_{ia}/2$ and the new centre C_{Ca}^{new} is located on the line connecting input vector x_i and the old cluster centre C_{Ca}, so that the distance from the new centre C_{Ca}^{new} to the point x_i is equal to R_{Ua}^{new}.then go back to Step 3.

A bit justification for terms "online" that we used in the clustering process, it is not like most online system terminology. In online video surveillance, for instance, every one/two second the captured image will be processed immediately to identify whether the image has something abnormal on it using some sort of image object recognition techniques. But for online network traffic clustering, the underlying data distributions in seconds or even in minutes count are not informative enough to be processed. Our system requires at least one day traffic data.

There are two types of traffic data model to be clustered. The first one is overall data (without filtering) and application based (http, ftp, icmp, ssh, NetBIOS, etc.) data. The clustering process will then performed on each model by using captured time, total packet and its size information.

3.2 Rule Creation and Evolving Procedure

Our system uses Takagi-Sugeno fuzzy rule type (Takagi and Sugeno, 1985) to forge the profile. There will be 7 resulted profiles (each profile was named the day to which the profile is referring) in the system on the first week running. These profiles are then evolved (following the procedure which will be described shortly after this) as the time goes to accurately describe each day's traffic behaviour in that particular network.

Number of rules in the profiles depends on number of clusters resulted from the clustering process. Two membership function (MF) of time (μt) and total packets (μs) are generated along with the rules. If in the future the rules were evolved, the MFs will also evolve. In creating the rule, the format is:

IF (A_{12} is T_1 OR A_{11} is T_2) AND (A_{21} is S_1) THEN status is C

where T_1 and T_2 defined by the fuzzy membership function μt, while S_1 defined by the fuzzy membership function μs.

The antecedents are the captured time position and the total packets obtained from the resulted cluster, while the consequent part is the state (normal, abnormal or uncertain). Figure 2 shows how the rules extracted along with both MFs (μt and μs) from the resulted clusters 2D space. Both the MFs are using triangular membership function.

The strategies for evolving procedures are quite straightforward. It consists of the following:

1. Compare the newly resulted profile with last week profile, and mark all the changes.
2. Check for generated Warning Alarm (WA) or Critical Alarm (CA) and recorded actions by the administrator and match every event with the previously marked profile changes (how this alarms created will be described in the next subsection).
3. If an action is taken by the administrator, keep the old rules unchanged. Else, evolve the rules by:

$$A_{VJn}^{new} = A_{VJn}^{old} \pm \| A_{VJn}^{current} - A_{VJn}^{old} \| \tag{5}$$

where n = sets of profile changes event without action, and each is calculated such that A_{VJ} are the first antecedent if $v = 1$ (in which $J = 1$ & 2) and the second antecedent if $v = 2$ (in which $J = 1$).

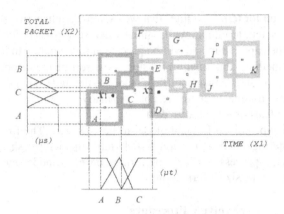

Fig. 2. Rule Extraction Scheme from 2D Space of the Resulted Clusters

Network administrator is also can evaluate and modify the resulted profiles if necessary. This would avoid black box symptoms like most connectionist system do (especially neural network based system) and network administrator can derive why such alarms was raised based on the profile on that day.

3.3 DENFIS for Detecting Anomalous Activity

The real-time detection module uses a modified Dynamic Evolving Neuro-Fuzzy Inference Systems (DENFIS) model engine for real-time anomalous activity detection. DENFIS uses Takagi-Sugeno inference method and utilises ECM in partitioning the input space (Kasabov and Song, 2002).

The engine will process every 5 minutes traffic data streaming in real-time to detect anomaly. Our modified DENFIS model engine was deployed using profiles created by the first connectionist module. It utilises alarm trigger mechanism specifically developed for the engine.

In process of adapting its structure, the profiles are inserted and adapted at the same time into the engine at the beginning of each day. If new rules were inserted or old rules were adapted, the MFs shape will also adjusted to evolve accordingly through gradient descent algorithm and a method given by (Purvis et al., 1999).

The system performs network-based anomaly detection. At presents, our system is not intended to detect signature based intrusion detection. We only focus on analyzing the traffic flows inside the network and detecting anomalous activity which was unusual. With this methodology, the system can detect Denial of Service (DoS) attack by analyzing the http traffic, detecting network device (such as router, hub, switch, etc.) failure by checking an extremely low traffic, detecting internet-worms which propagate through open file shares by analyzing NetBIOS packets statistics, detecting Novel NetWare server down (if applicable) by analyzing a low IPX type of packets, and a possibilities of other network traffic flows types of anomaly.

When the system is installed in new network, it will then assume the current traffic is normal and the engine will start to evolve under supervision of the network administrator. Basically there are two types of alarms that the system will generate.

The first one is the less important called Warning Alarm (WA) and the second one is Critical Alarm (CA) which requires an urgent immediate attention from network administrator.

The mechanisms for triggering the alarms are divided into two categories, alarms generation in peak time and in off-peak time. We are applying an extended standard working hours adopted by most companies and organizations (7 am to 9 pm) as the peak time and the rest are defined as off-peak time. The details are described as follows:

- Peak Time:

    We apply an extended period of commonly used working ours adopted by most companies and organization. This will enable categorizing an overtime shift as peak time when applicable. In this peak-time the alarms will be carefully triggered and mostly only WAs are raised. Events that fall under WA is unusual overall traffic flows which may come from node additions, different software types used other than its usual, plateau behaviour caused by traffic reaching environmental limits, etc. CA can also possible to be raised in this time period but only in extreme cases.

- Off-Peak Time:

    Most of CAs are generated under this category. CA is triggered for an event that is really needs an attention and the likeliness to be false is small. Events that fall under CA are network devices failure, Novel NetWare server down, internet worms, and some common DoS attack at night. A raised WA at this period will most likely not get an attention from network administrator. So even if WA is raised, the system then automatically adapts the profile with the changes.

The standard mechanism procedure in raising an alarm (both WA and CA) is expressed by $\forall$ Traffic $\exists$ x, where x is set of traffic which breaks the threshold. In this case, different events will have different threshold value. Following are more details mechanism for triggering alarms for based on the events (only some are presented):

- CA for network device failure:

    If incoming traffic at 5 minutes interval below 500 packets (all packets), Then there was a device failure either in the router if the system is monitoring the whole network, or in the switch or hub if the system is monitoring one network segment and a CA is raised.

- WA for unusual traffic flows caused by node additions:

    If incoming traffic at 3 pm is 3000 packets assuming according to the profile normally at that time only around 2000 packets, then a WA is raised.

- CA for an extreme unusual traffic flows:

    If incoming traffic at 3 pm is 12000 packets or 6 times bigger than normal traffic, then CA is raised.

Logs to record all the generated alarms are deployed to track the system's performance over time and help the administrator understand how and to what direction the system grows.

4 Distributed Application Scheme

Our system employs a distributed client-server application in monitoring the network. The idea of having the system works that way is to enable monitoring large network especially a large corporate network which is separated in two different buildings from one location. It also designed to enabling monitor multiple network segments in a switched network.

A managed and distributed network monitoring scheme employed by the system is enabling us to reduce the complexities of analyzing enormous amount of traffic at once to detect anomaly. Instead of having one profile for the whole network, it will create multiple profiles for each network segment and thus it would be easier to locate the source of problem. Figure 3 pictured the system's distributed architecture.

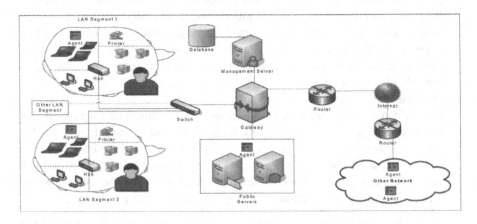

Fig. 3. Distributed Managed Client-Server Architecture

The system is not platform dependent since it is implemented using Java 2 Technologies and make it possible to have the server installed in a Windows based machine and have its agent resides on any Linux, Mac, or Sun Solaris based machine spreads in a different network segment.

Furthermore, the connectionist model of the system's engine are implemented using MATLAB and even though it is not using Java 2 Technology, it is fully integrated into the system.

4.1 Management Server

The management server can be installed in the gateway or resides in special machines dedicated for it. It has the abilities of performing the following task:

- Managing all the daily profiles from different network segment.
- Archiving all past traffic from different network segment in the databases.
- Authenticate an agent to use the profile for the segment where the agent was running.
- Add new agents including network segment information where the agent intends to monitor it.

- View all the logs for any alarmed events.
- Re-cluster specific traffic from the archived using its own ECOS module.
- View each profile if the network administrator wants to seek for explanation.

A comprehensive database is also deployed using MySQL to store all the system logs and archiving all past traffics.

When an alarm is triggered, the status of the agent will change to "Warning" for WA and "Urgent Attention" for CA. An email and sms will also be sent to the network administrator email and mobile phone respectively. Figure 4 is the running example of the Management Server.

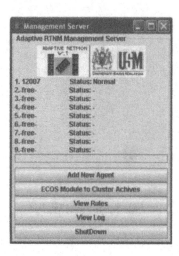

Fig. 4. Management Server GUI

4.2 Monitoring Agent

The Agent performs basic network monitoring functionality adopted by most network monitoring application available nowadays in addition to its ECOS based module which enables the Agent to detect anomalous activity and evolve its profile over time. It performs passive monitoring and a connectionless communication with the Management Server so that it is not adding more workload to the network.

Some of its cardinal functionalities among other functions are outlined as follows:

- It performs real-time traffic data stream capturing in a 10/100MB Ethernet network with promiscuous mode.
- Filter the data before further processed.
- Evolves its detection engine structure over time.
- Connect to the Management Server to adapt the profiles if necessary.
- Detects anomalous activity specifically in the network segments where the Agent was running.
- Generate WA and CA.

- Real-time statistical analyzer based on different perspective (application layer statistic, network layer statistic, and protocol based statistic).
- Basic packets decoding functionality.

A friendly graphical user interface is designed to help new user (especially network administrator).understand how to use the system better. Figure 5 is a running example of the Agent's GUI.

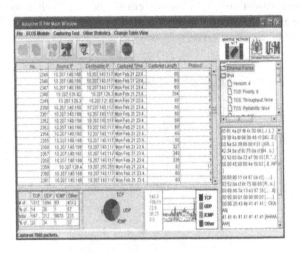

Fig. 5. An Agent GUI

5   Results and Analysis

The system was tested at our School of Computer Sciences' network for the duration of 2 months. The Monitoring Agent was installed on different network segments in our school's switched network. Our current preliminary results shows that the system is able to evolve as expected.

In Figure 6 we can see that the resulted profile has two clusters which differ significantly with others. At the time of running a WA is raised and as we (the network administrator) chooses not to take any action for that WA, the profile was adapted in next week at the same day as depicted in Figure 7.

Basically network administrator involvement in adapting the system is more as a guidance to which way the system should grow. Without the presence of network administrator the system is still able to evolve but if the attacker knows the behaviour and the evolving mechanism of the system, they can fool the system to adapt into the wrong way. This is where the hand of network administrator is needed.

Table 1 shows the simple statistic record on how many rules created in each day profile, counts for how many rules evolved in each day profile, and how many actions taken by the network administrator for any WA and CA events happened in the network for a two months period. It can be seen that working day profile (Monday-Friday) has more rules compare to off working day (Saturday and Sunday) since the network has more traffics at that days.

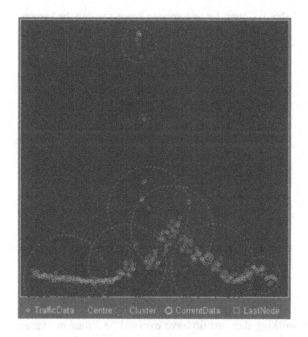

Fig. 6. Clusters Produced For Thursday, 27 January

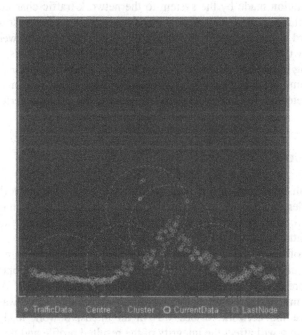

Fig. 7. Clusters Produced For Thursday, 03 February

Table 1. Counts for an Evolving Process within the System

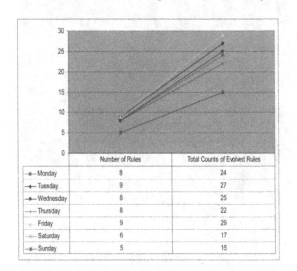

	Number of Rules	Total Counts of Evolved Rules
—●— Monday	8	24
—◆— Tuesday	9	27
—●— Wednesday	8	25
—+— Thursday	8	22
Friday	9	29
—✕— Saturday	6	17
—✳— Sunday	5	15

The rules on working day profile have evolved 58 times in average, or around 14 times each week. Actually more rules were evolved in the first week to adapt the initial profile with actual traffic in the particular network. The first week run was an important adaptation made by the system to the network traffic characteristic where the system is attached. This statistic was made based on a counter that we put on the system to record all the necessary events on the system. As such, no weekly statistic, which can show the number of times rules evolved after the initial rules, are recorded.

In this testing phase, the system detects some device failure (especially our switch) happened in some network segment. A simple DoS attack that we simulate was also successfully detected by the engine. As a whole, the system performance was satisfactory.

6   Conclusion

This work is an important step to build a complete evolvable network monitoring system. By understanding the network traffic characteristic, plenty can do to keep on eye on the network, these includes detecting more anomalous activity such as current worms, DDoS attack, and other advanced network intrusion.

Working in offline mode, the integrity of the data in the capturing process can be argued. While capturing the data for duration of (let say) two months, it cannot completely represent the normal traffic happened in the network. A case might happened for some heavy traffic captured in those two months period was because the corporate where the network resides was in an intensive work load to launch a product. This thing will affect the integrity of the resulted profile and might lead to be more burdens for network administrator to recapture the traffic, reevaluate the traffic, and finally re-profile the traffic.

Our system still needs improvements in many ways for future works. Currently we are improving the structure of the connectionist model by proposing new methods. By having these methods which specifically designed for network traffic data, the results can be more accurate and the system can grow from scratch. We also try to consider implementing a signature based intrusion detection engine to improve the detection engine's performance. Lastly, our future work will also to add in an intelligent module to automate an action as responses for such an alarmed event to prevent network down, which in turn will reduce the dependency of the network from network administrator's presence when an event which requires an immediate attention or response happened at late night.

References

Pasha, M.F., Budiarto, R.: Developing Online Adaptive Engine for Profiling Network Traffic using Evolving Connectionist Systems. In: NCEI'04, Conference on Neuro-Computing and Evolving Intelligence 2004. Auckland, New Zealand (2004)

Kasabov, N.: Evolving Connectionist System: Methods and Applications in Bioinformatics, Brain Study and Intelligent Machines, 1st edn. Springer-Verlag, London (2003)

Pasha, M.F., Budiarto, R., Sumari, P., Osman, A.: Data Mining and Rule Generation in Network Traffic using Fuzzy Clustering Techniques. In: M2USIC'04, MMU International Symposium on Information and Communications Technologies. Putrajaya, Malaysia (2004)

Lampinen, T., Koivisto, H., Honkanen, T.: Profiling Network Application with Fuzzy C-Means Clustering and Self Organizing Map. In: First International Conference on Fuzzy System and Knowledge Discovery: Computational Intelligence for the E-Age. Singapore (2002)

Song, Q., Kasabov, N.: ECM, A Novel On-line, Evolving Clustering Method and its Applications. In: ANNES'01, Fifth Biannual Conference on Artificial Neural Networks and Expert Systems (2001)

Marchette, D.: A Statistical Method for Profiling Network Traffic. In: Workshop on Intrusion Detection and Network Monitoring. USA (1999)

Paxson, V.: Bro: A System for Detecting Network Intruders in Real-Time. In: 7th USENIX Security Symposium. USA (1998)

Kasabov, N., Song, Q.: DENFIS: Dynamic Evolving Neuro-Fuzzy Inference System and its Application for time-series prediction. IEEE Trans. Fuzzy System 10(2), 144–154 (2002)

Purvis, D., Kasabov, N., Benwell, G., Zhou, Q., Zhang, F.: Neuro-Fuzzy methods for environmental modelling. System Research and Information Systems 8(4), 221–239 (1999)

Barford, P., Plonka, D.: Characteristics of Network Traffic Flow Anomalies. In: ACM Internet measurement Workshop ACM SIGCOMM'01. San Francisco, USA (2001)

Sureswaran, R.: Network Monitor. In: Conference of Asia Pasific Advance Network. Penang, Malaysia (2001)

Degioanni, L., Risso, F., Varenni, G., Viano, P.: WinPcap: The Free Packet Capture Architecture for Windows. (2003) In HYPERLINK http://winpcap.polito.it

Takagi, T., Sugeno, M.: Fuzzy Identification of Systems and its Application to Modeling and Control. IEEE Trans. System, Man. and Cybernetics 15(1), 116–132 (1985)

Host Identity Protocol Proxy

Patrik Salmela and Jan Melén

Ericsson Research NomadicLab, Hirsalantie 11, 02420 Jorvas, Finland
patrik.salmela@ericsson.com, jan.melen@ericsson.com

Abstract. The Host Identity Protocol (HIP) is one of the more recent designs that challenge the current Internet architecture. The main features of HIP are security and the identifier-locator split, which solves the problem of overloading the IP address with two separate tasks. This paper studies the possibility of providing HIP services to legacy hosts via a HIP proxy. Making a host HIP enabled requires that the IP-stack of the host is updated to support HIP. From a network administrator's perspective this can be a large obstacle. However, by providing HIP from a centralized point, a HIP proxy, the transition to begin using HIP can be made smoother. This and other arguments for a HIP proxy will be presented in this paper along with an analysis of a prototype HIP proxy and its performance.

Keywords: HIP, identifier-locator split, proxy.

1 Introduction

The current Internet is based on an over 20-year-old architecture. That architecture has flaws - some more serious than others. Many of these issues have been addressed by tools and methods designed to patch the flaws of the architecture. Examples of these new designs are e.g. IPv6 that provides a new larger addresses space in place of the one currently used, and IPsec (Kent (1), 1998) that provides security in the insecure network.

One of the more recent designs is the Host Identity Protocol (Moskowitz (1), 2004). HIP is still being researched and is not yet a complete product and thus not being used in a large scale. Considering that one of the main benefits of using HIP is secured communication, one can assume that HIP might appeal more to companies and organizations rather than the average home computer user. When HIP will begin to be utilized by a larger user group than just the developers and some other interested parties, as it is today, ease of use will be one factor that will affect how well and wide HIP will spread. Enabling HIP in a host requires that the host is updated with a HIP enabled IP-stack. This might be a disadvantage of HIP when a network administrator is considering different methods of protecting the communication to and from the network.

This paper studies the possibility of providing HIP services to hosts without having to modify them. Having legacy hosts communicating with HIP enabled hosts, using HIP, is possible with a HIP proxy. However, providing HIP to hosts via a proxy, with

J. Filipe et al. (Eds.): ICETE 2005, CCIS 3, pp. 126–138, 2007.

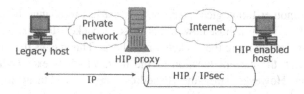

Fig. 1. HIP proxy scenario

the actual HIP implementation residing outside of the host, puts some restrictions on the network environment. A HIP proxy scenario is shown in Figure 1.

The paper is structured as follows; first some background information will be presented, with the focus on some of the problems of the current architecture. Different solutions for these problems will be presented, including HIP. Next follows a technical view of how HIP works and the reasoning for a HIP proxy. After that, the functionality of a HIP proxy is presented, followed by a look at the design and performance of a prototype HIP proxy. Then we look at how the prototype could be further developed, after which the conclusions are presented.

2   Background

Changing the current Internet architecture is a quite hot topic, and it has been that for some years already. The topic has been discussed in various papers, including the New Arch paper (Braden, 2000) and the Plutarch paper (Crowcroft, 2003). There are many issues with the current architecture that have helped to recognize the need for a change. Maybe the most recognized issues include the lack of support for security by the IP protocol, address space depletion, the heavy load on routers and the overloading of the IP address to serve as both identifier and locator. Additionally, mobile hosts are becoming more common which adds demand for an always better mobility solution.

To some of the aforementioned problems there are already working solutions; users who want security can utilize one of the many available security solutions e.g. IPsec, PGP, SSH or TLS. The utilization of the IPv4 address space has been improved with the help of Classless Inter-Domain Routing (CIDR). Also mobility is possible in the current Internet. Routers are heavily burdened because the size of the IPv4 address does not allow for much address aggregation. IPv6, with its four times bigger address size compared to IPv4, will improve the possibility for address aggregation. However, there is still no widely deployed method that provides an identifier-locator split.

2.1   Why Do We Need a Change

So what is the big deal with using the IP address both as an identifier and a locator? The problem can be spotted by examining how the IP address behaves when a host is changing its topological position in a network, while remembering what qualities are necessary for an identifier and a locator respectively. Consider a host with the IP address IP_A. The locator of the host, i.e. the information used to route packets to the host, is the IP address IP_A. The same information is used to identify the host. If the host moves to another topological position the host has to change its address to the new address IP$_A$'. When a host now wants to send packets to this host the new IP address, IP$_A$', is used to route the packets to the host. This means that the locator has changed to match the current location of the host, which is exactly how a locator should function. However, since the IP address serves as both an identifier and a locator the host has now been assigned a new identifier. This change is not welcome since having an identifier that can change frequently makes the identifier useless except for the short timeframe that it stays constant. A true identifier should stay constant, if not forever, at least for a very long time, in the range of years.

Because the notion of an identifier is used in the Internet, it should also fill the requirements set for an identifier. Namely that it is constant and uniquely identifies a host regardless of where in the network the host is located. This makes the IP address an unfit candidate for an identifier. What is needed is another coexistent address space, actually an ``identifier space'', from which hosts are assigned an identity. Another possibility could be something along the lines of what was suggested in the GSE proposal (Crawford, 1999); part of the IP address is used for identifying the host while the rest is used as a locator for the host. In this case the identifier part has to stay constant when the host moves in the network and updates the locator part to match the current location of the host.

2.2 The HIP Solution

The Host Identity Protocol is one of the new designs that, amongst other things, target the identifier-locator split. In addition, HIP also provides security, mobility and multi-homing. All the features provided by HIP are based on the solution for the identifier-locator split.

HIP separates the identifier from the locator by introducing a new name space for identifiers. The entities in that set are called Host Identities (HI) and are of variable length. A HI is the public key of an asymmetric key-pair, which is used to provide security in HIP. Because the HIs are of variable length it is difficult to use them as such in HIP, so instead a 128-bit hash over the HI, called a Host Identity Tag (HIT), is used. When operating in an IPv4 network a 32-bit hash over the HI, a Local Scope Identifier (LSI), is used. Because of its length, the LSI cannot be considered to be globally unique. When a HIP enabled host sends a packet to another HIP enabled host the packet is sent to a HIT, or an LSI respectively, but the packet is transported using the locator i.e. the IP address.

The use of HITs and LSIs is made possible by introducing a new layer to the IP-stack. The HIP-layer finds its place between the internetworking layer and the transport layer, and is sometimes referred to as layer 3,5. At the layers above the HIP-layer HITs, or LSIs, are used instead of IP addresses. At the HIP-layer a translation takes place; from HITs or LSIs to IPv6 or IPv4 addresses, or vice versa. In the remaining layers the IP addresses are used. Using HIP, the Host Identifier (HIT or LSI) of a host is always constant as it should be, and the locator can change when the peer moves to another position.

2.3 Other Similar Solutions

HIP is one of the more complete solutions that provide the identifier-locator split. However, there are also some other proposals that target the same problem. In this subsection three other solutions will be presented: the Forwarding directive, Association, and Rendezvous Architecture (FARA) (Clark, 2003), PeerNet (Eriksson, 2003) and the Internet Indirection Infrastructure (I^3) (Stoica, 2002).

FARA is a framework that can be used when designing a new architecture. The FARA model is divided into two layers; the upper layer contains the communicating entities and the communication endpoints, the lower layer handles the packet forwarding. The communication link between two entities is stateful and is called an Association. Each Association is identified by a locally unique Association ID (AId). When an entity moves its AIds stay constant while the information used to forward the packets to the entity changes. It is easy to draw some parallels between this and how HIP uses constant HIs while the IP address can change to reflect the current position. In the FARA paper (Clark, 2003) HIP is actually suggested as something that could be used in a FARA architecture.

PeerNet is based on peer-to-peer thinking. The hosts are located as leafs in a binary tree, with the path from the root presenting the address of the host. When a new host attaches to the network it asks one of the hosts in its vicinity for an address. The asked host splits its address space into two and assigns one of them to the new node and keeps the other for itself. The hosts also have an identity that stays constant regardless of node movements. PeerNet uses distributed peer-to-peer routing with each host storing some routing information, i.e. identity-to-address mappings. PeerNet is not a ready solution, it does have the identifier-locator split, but security issues have not been addressed.

The I^3 design introduces some new elements to the network, the I^3 servers. To be able to receive packets hosts have to register their identity and current locator into an I^3 server. This is called inserting a trigger. The trigger has a limited lifetime and thus it has to be updated periodically by the host if it wishes to continue to receive packets via it. In I^3 packets are sent to identities and the sent packet searches the I^3 servers for a trigger that matches the destination identity. Once a match is found the destination of the packet is changed for the IP address found in the trigger. By updating the trigger I^3 supports mobility, and by letting multiple hosts register with the same identity a multicast property is achieved. But just as PeerNet, I^3 is not a complete solution. The biggest concern of I^3 is the lack of security. To provide security for I^3 a combination of HIP and I^3, called Hi3, is being researched (Nikander, 2004).

2.4 Problems with Having a New Architecture

Even if these new designs might sound very good, creating them is only part of the job, getting the design deployed is also a big challenge. Deploying a new architecture is not the same as deploying a new standalone, e.g. security solution. Deploying the design in a small test network which one has full control over is easy, but when the target is a global public network, the Internet, there is not really any good way to get it done. The problem of deploying e.g. HIP is similar to getting IPv6 deployed globally. An ideal solution would be to get all of Internet updated by the flick of a switch, moving from an all IPv4 network to an all IPv6 network in a neglectable time interval. However, this is not possible, not for IPv6 nor HIP. An update of this proportion will proceed incrementally, requiring some sort of compatibility between the new and the old architecture. Deploying HIP is not as difficult as the IPv6 problem since HIP enabled hosts can still communicate with legacy hosts using regular IP. However, to truly benefit from all the features of HIP, it would be desirable that as many hosts as possible were HIP enabled.

3 HIP

To enable HIP in a host the IP-stack of the host has to be updated to a HIP modified one. An asymmetric key-pair has to be generated and the public key will serve as the identity of the host, with hashes of the key resulting in HITs and LSIs. To initiate a HIP connection with another HIP enabled host the HIT of the peer has to be obtained. This can be done from a HIP modified DNS or other similar lookup service.

The creation of a HIP connection between two HIP enabled hosts is called the HIP base exchange (Moskowitz (2), 2004) and it is depicted in Figure 2. When the Initiator wants to establish a connection it sends an I1 packet to the Responder. The packet contains the HIT of the Initiator (HIT_I), and if the HIT of the Responder (HIT_R) has been obtained it is also included in the message. If the Initiator does not know HIT_R it is set to NULL in the I1 packet. This is called opportunistic mode HIP. The I1 packet is actually just an initiation message for the connection.

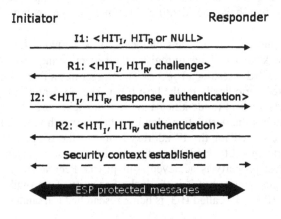

Fig. 2. The HIP base exchange

The Responder responds with an R1 packet which contains the HITs used in the I1 packet, the HI of the Responder and a challenge. If the Initiator is attempting opportunistic mode HIP the Responder has now added its HIT to the packet instead of the received NULL HIT. The R1 packet also initiates the Diffie-Hellman (Rescorla, 1999) exchange and gives the preferences of the Responder in respect of which IP Encapsulating Security Payload (ESP) (Kent (2), 1998) mode to use. The supported integrity and encryption algorithms are also presented. The challenge in the packet is a puzzle that the Initiator has to solve to prove that it is serious about creating a connection. The Responder can have in advance prepared R1 packets to ease its load, while the puzzle requires the Initiator to do heavy calculations. This makes connection initiation expensive and is thus a form of Denial of Service (DoS) protection.

When the Initiator has solved the puzzle it sends an I2 packet to the Responder. The packet again contains the two HITs and now also the solution to the puzzle. Also the HI of the Initiator is included, it is encrypted using the selected algorithms and generated keys. Based on the information that the Responder receives in the packet it can decrypt the HI. The Responder also receives the Security Parameter Index (SPI) to use when sending packets to the Initiator.

The last packet of the HIP base exchange, the R2 packet sent to the Initiator, contains the SPI that the Initiator should use along with the two HITs. Similar to all but the first packet of the base exchange, the R2 packet contains a digital signature, and in addition a HMAC (Krawczyk, 1997) calculated over the packet. Besides that, also other consistency checks are done on each packet, including checking that the received HITs are the correct ones. The result of the HIP base exchange is a pair of IPsec ESP security associations (SA). After the base exchange all traffic between the Initiator and the Responder is ESP protected.

The four packets used during the base exchange (I1, R1, I2, R2) are HIP specific packets. Apart from these packets there are also some other HIP specific packets of which the Update packet is the most important one. The Update packet is used for signaling rekeying when the old SA needs to be replaced, e.g. if the ESP sequence number is getting too big. The Update packet is also used for handling location updates by sending location update messages.

The security provided by HIP is basically very similar to IPsec without IKE. The HI of a host, and the corresponding private key, are used for authentication purposes and for negotiating security parameters and SAs. The SAs are established between two HITs, so when sending a packet the SA is located based on the HITs found in the outgoing packet. When receiving a packet the SA is located based on the SPI, and the HITs for the connection are found from the SA.

4 Why a HIP Proxy

The difficulty of deploying a new architecture was mentioned earlier; all hosts in a global network cannot simultaneously be update to support a new architecture, the migration to a new architecture will take time. HIP does not need to spread to all hosts in the Internet, and it probably never will, but the wider it spreads the more useful HIP is for its users. A HIP proxy that makes it possible for a HIP host to communicate with a legacy host, using HIP between the HIP host and the HIP proxy, could help to promote HIP. The more possibilities there are for using HIP the more appeal it will have. The problem with a HIP proxy is that if it is located in a public network the security features of HIP are rendered useless. The connection between the proxy and the legacy host is not protected in any way. If one would like, some other form of security could of course be applied between the HIP proxy and the legacy host.

To be able to benefit from the security functionality provided by HIP, when using a HIP proxy, the proxy would have to be situated in a secure network. One likely scenario might be a private network, e.g. the internal network of a company. By having a HIP proxy at the border between the private network and the Internet, the users of the private network could contact HIP enabled hosts in the Internet using HIP. Because the private network is considered to be secure the only difference of this scenario, compared to two HIP enabled hosts communicating with each other, is that the legacy host cannot take advantage of all the features provided by HIP, e.g. HIP mobility.

If the hosts of a private network do not need all the features provided by HIP, a HIP proxy might even be considered the preferred alternative compared to enabling HIP in all the hosts. Enabling HIP in all hosts might be considered to generate too much work compared to having a HIP proxy solution. With a static network configuration the work estimates might actually be correct. However, most networks are not static, and having a HIP proxy in a dynamic network will generate excess work in the form of keeping the proxy configurations up-to-date. A HIP proxy is not the preferred solution but it is well suited as a stepping-stone when going from an all legacy network to an all HIP network.

5 The HIP Proxy Prototype

As a proof of concept a HIP proxy prototype has been implemented. The implementation was done for FreeBSD 5.2, and tested with the HIP implementation developed at Ericsson Finland (http://hip4inter.net). Besides implementing the HIP proxy application also the kernel of FreeBSD had to be modified; a new feature, divert sockets for IPv6, had to be implemented. To perform its task the proxy utilizes divert sockets and the firewalls (ipfw and ip6fw) of FreeBSD. The network environment where the proxy operates is between two small LANs, one acting as a private network containing the legacy hosts and the other acting as the Internet containing the HIP enabled hosts. If the proxy was to function in one network in which there are both kinds of hosts the legacy hosts would have to be configured to route all their packets via the HIP proxy.

5.1 Functionality of a HIP Proxy

When looking at the HIP proxy as a host in the network its task is to serve as the endpoint for HIP associations between itself and HIP enabled hosts. HIP hosts connected via it believe that they are communicating with the legacy host using HIP while the legacy hosts believe that they are communicating with the HIP host using plain IP. For the communicating endpoints the HIP proxy is invisible. The proxy itself can be seen as a host that performs translation between the two communication formats; plain IP and HIP.

When a legacy host wishes to communicate with one of the HIP enabled hosts it queries DNS for the IP address of the peer. The query travels through the HIP proxy and on to a HIP modified DNS in the Internet. The reply contains the IP address and the HIT of the HIP host. When the reply passes the proxy it caches the IP-HIT mapping for future use when it possibly has to initiate a HIP base exchange with the host. The legacy host receives the IP address and can now use it to contact the HIP enabled host. HIP enabled hosts can contact legacy hosts via the proxy if the IP address of the proxy, and the HITs assigned to the legacy hosts, are registered into DNS. Thus a HIP enabled host will receive an IP address and a HIT, as expected, when querying the information about one of the legacy hosts.

When a packet passes through the HIP proxy host the packet must be diverted from its path and sent to the HIP proxy application. If the packet is on its way from a legacy host to a HIP enabled host the proxy checks if there is an SA available for the connection. If a matching SA is found the packet is sent out using the SA. Otherwise the proxy has to initiate the HIP base exchange to establish SAs for the connection. Using the IP-HIT mapping it has gotten from the DNS query, and the IP address of the legacy host along with the HIT assigned to the legacy host, the proxy can initiate the base exchange. When the HIP association has been established the packet sent by the legacy host can be sent to the HIP enabled host and the communication between the peers can begin. When a packet is received over an SA, from a HIP enabled host, the proxy decrypts the ESP packet and forwards it as a plain IP packet with the IP addresses of the peers. The packet is then sent to the legacy host whose IP address was found based on the destination HIT. The connection initiation is depicted in Figure 3.

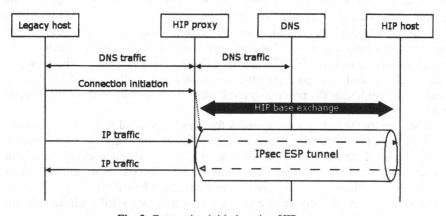

Fig. 3. Connection initiation via a HIP proxy

When a HIP enabled host initiates a connection to a legacy host it uses the information it has received from DNS. The HIP host believes that it is connecting to the legacy host, although the actual HIP connection is established to the HIP proxy. When the SAs have been established the HIP host begins sending packets over them. The HIP proxy converts the received packets to plain IP packets and forwards them to the correct legacy host.

5.2 The Prototype Design

The prototype HIP proxy does not function exactly as described in the previous section. We did not have a HIP enabled DNS so the IP-HIT mappings of both the legacy hosts and the HIP enabled hosts were added to a configuration file for the HIP proxy.

The proxy reads the configuration file and stores the HIT-IP mappings into two linked lists, one for legacy hosts and one for HIP enabled hosts. Apart from the DNS issue the HIP proxy works as described.

To get the received packets diverted to the proxy application we use the IPv4 and IPv6 divert sockets and the firewalls. Basically we tell the firewalls to divert all packets received from the private network except for broadcast packets and other packets that we intuitively know that are not meant for the proxy. This will result in that all connection initiations from the legacy hosts, and the subsequent packets of the connections, go through the proxy. To receive the ESP packets sent from the HIP enabled hosts we tell the proxy to divert all packets that have an address prefix of 01_{bin} for both source and destination addresses. This is a characteristic of HITs; a HIT always has the prefix 01_{bin} (there is also a secondary format for HITs with a 10_{bin} prefix). Even if the packets have IP addresses in the IP header while they travel the Internet, IPsec processing, where the IP addresses are replaced by HITs, happens before the firewall rules are checked. Finally, to allow HIP initiations from the HIP host, we tell the firewall to allow all traffic that uses the HIP protocol, i.e. the packets for the base exchange and the other HIP specific packets such as the Update packet.

The structure of the application is divided into two parts; in the first part the proxy is initialized, the second part consists of a read/write loop where the packets are processed. During the initialization part the configuration file is read and the mappings found in it are recorded. Before a HIP base exchange can begin the Initiator has to have a HIP context for that particular connection. A context consists of the Initiator HIT along with the HIT and IP address of the responder. The prototype creates the needed HIP contexts after the configuration file is read. Before the read/write loop begins the proxy also creates the divert sockets so that it can receive packets.

In the read/write loop the proxy waits for packets diverted to it. Once the proxy receives a packet it examines the source and destination addresses of the packet. Using the two linked lists with HIT-IP mappings the proxy can conclude where the packet is coming from and where it is going to, e.g. from the legacy network to the HIP network. If either of the addresses is not found in the linked lists the proxy cannot process the packet correctly, in that case the packet is forwarded unchanged by the proxy. If mappings for both addresses are found, and both addresses in the packet are found to be either HITs or IP addresses (a mix of one IP and one HIT is not accepted, it indicates an erroneous packet), the proxy changes the IPs for HITs or vice versa. After recalculating the checksums the packet is sent out again. If the packets are going to the legacy host they are forwarded via the output handling to the private network. If the packet is going to one of the HIP hosts it will have HITs as addresses in the IP header. In this case the packet will be sent to IPsec handling. If no SA is found for the specific connection the HIP daemon is signaled to perform the HIP base exchange after which the packet is sent out utilizing the newly created SAs.

Before the read/write loop starts over again the proxy checks if the configuration file should be re-read. This makes it possible to add information about new hosts without restarting the proxy. The prototype uses a very basic method for finding out if the file should be re-read; for each n packets the configuration file is re-read. When testing this feature, the value for n was set to 10. The value should be adjusted based on how heavy traffic there is through the proxy and the length of the list of hosts entered into the file. With heavy traffic n should be increased so that the re-read does not happen very frequently. Also with a long list of hosts n should be increased because with a longer list the updating of the linked lists takes longer. A more appropriate solution would be to check if the file has been updated, and only when an update has occurred should the file be re-read.

5.3 Performance

To measure how the HIP proxy prototype performs some tests were conducted. The first test was done to check how having the proxy in the path of the packets affects the round trip times (RTT). First the round trip times for ping6 were measured as an average over 20 packets with the packets going through the proxy but not being processed by it. To get values to compare against the average round trip times were also measured for the case when the packets did not have to go via the proxy, the host with the HIP proxy just forwarded the packets. Finally we measure how the use of the HIP proxy, and having it process packets affected the round trip times. The results from these measurements are presented in Table 1.

It can be concluded from the two first entries that introducing the proxy does add delay; with the proxy we get approximately 12% longer round-trip times. This is something that can be expected since having the packets go via the proxy adds processing on the path. Having to pass a packet to an application in user space, compared to only handling it in kernel space, adds delay.

Table 1. How the proxy affects round-trip times

Using proxy	Using HIP	Avg. RTT
No	No	0,624ms
Yes	No	0,698ms
Yes	Yes	0,851ms

The last entry in Table 1 concentrates on how applying IPsec ESP to the packets affect the delay. Based on the result we can see that when the HIT-IP mappings are found in the linked lists of the proxy the round-trip time increases approximately by 22% compared to having he proxy sending the packet to output handling without any processing. When we compare the delays of sending packets without using the proxy and the case when the proxy is used and it processes the packets we can see that the increase in delay is approximately 36%. This increase in delay includes both the added delay of having to send the packet to user space, approximately 0,070ms, and the delay that results from performing cryptographic functions, approximately 0,150ms. The by the HIP proxy added delay is mostly a result of doing the cryptographic functions on the data. This is something we cannot affect; if we want security it will cost us time. The total delay added by the proxy is not at an alarming level, and is as such acceptable.

Another interesting aspect of the performance of the proxy is how the amount of entries in the linked lists affects the delay. In the measurements presented in Table 1 there were a total of three entries, two in the HIP hosts list and one in the legacy hosts list. In the next set of measurements we had first 10 then 100 and finally 1000 entries per list. The correct information was situated last in the respective list so that the proxy would have to go through all of the lists. For each packet both the linked lists have to be examined. The results from these measurements are presented in Table 2.

From the measured values we can see that if we add enough entries to the lists it will show in the round-trip times. But since the prototype proxy is not meant for huge networks the delay added by looking up mappings from long lists should not be an issue. The values in Table 2 differ somewhat from the corresponding values in Table 1. The reason for the differing values is that the measurements were performed at different times, so the load on the network was different.

Table 2. The effects of serving many hosts

Hosts/list	Avg. RTT
10	0,676ms
100	0,705ms
1000	0,770ms

When the proxy reads the host information from a configuration file, as is the case with this prototype, the amount of hosts should be kept small to keep the configuration file manageable. If some automatic updating procedure is implemented it allows for more hosts. Still, the delay caused by having to look up host information from very long lists will sooner or later add too much delay. However, when the amount of hosts configured into the proxy reaches that level it will probably be the amount of traffic that the proxy has to handle that will be the performance bottleneck, not the delay from looking up the correct mappings.

6 Further Work

In the previous section we concluded that approximately a third of the added delay that results from using a HIP proxy compared to plain IP is a result of the proxy application. This is one aspect of the proxy that could be improved; by moving the application from user space to kernel space the delay induced by the proxy could probably be decreased. Overall the proxy still performs well and as expected. With a small set of hosts the delays are kept at an acceptable level, keeping the RTTs in roughly the same range as for legacy connections. However, one must remember that a HIP proxy is only a solution for a small set of nodes. When the amount of nodes configured into the proxy gets too big, either a second proxy should be introduced, and the load balanced between the proxies, or then the legacy hosts should be made HIP enabled. When a HIP modified DNS is available it will increase the limits of a HIP proxy by being able to dynamically add HIT-IP mappings when they are needed. Also old mappings that are considered obsolete can be deleted since they can be re-fetched from DNS if necessary. The amount of legacy hosts that the proxy can serve will still be a limiting factor.

If the HIP proxy is situated in a public network the security provided by HIP is in effect useless since all the information also travels unencrypted in the network, namely between the proxy and the legacy host. This is quite alright as long as both parties are aware of this. However, when using a HIP proxy the HIP enabled host does not know that it is communicating with a proxy but believes that it is actually communicating with another HIP enabled host. This puts the HIP enabled host at a disadvantage, and it is a problem that needs to be solved; the HIP enabled host must know when it is communicating via a HIP proxy so that it knows that the information it sends might not be secured all the way to the actual endpoint.

A last issue that will be mentioned regarding the HIP proxy is a problem that arises when the HIP host, that is using the services of the HIP proxy, is mobile. When a HIP host is mobile and moves to another location, and thus gets a new locator, it informs its communication parties of its new location. With two HIP enabled hosts this works well. However, when one of the endpoints is a HIP proxy the location update message sent to the proxy modifies established SAs as necessary, but the information does not reach the proxy. If a connection was established between a legacy host and the HIP host before the location change, the connection will continue to work even after the HIP host has moved. If another legacy host now tries to initiate a connection to the mobile host, using its new locator, the connection will not be established since the proxy has not gotten the new locator of the mobile HIP host. This can be solved by updating the proxy configuration file with the new information of the mobile HIP host. This works well if there are no connections established from legacy hosts to the old locator of the HIP host. However, if there still are connections to the old locator the result is that the legacy host using the old locator of the mobile HIP host will begin receiving packets from the HIP host's new locator without knowing that it actually is the same host. A solution for this problem could be that the HIP proxy would keep a record of previous locators of each HIP host, and state information for each connection. Using this information all connections could be maintained. All this of course adds delay to the system. The solution presented here is probably not the optimal one and some more research in this area is needed.

7 Conclusions

The HIP proxy prototype was constructed as a proof-of-concept for a HIP proxy. The proxy performs well and fills its tasks. However, as mentioned in the previous section there are still many areas in which the proxy may, and should, be improved. The preferred solution for using HIP is of course to have HIP enabled hosts. However, a HIP proxy might be a good tool to help HIP get spreading. The HIP proxy prototype described in this paper is probably not something that should be used as such for a HIP proxy. However, it might be a good starting point for developing a new and improved version that better fits the requirements of a HIP proxy.

References

Kent (1), Atkins. Security Architecture for the Internet Protocol. RFC 2401 (1998)
Moskowitz (1), Nikander, Host Identity Protocol Architecture. Internet-draft, draft-moskowitz-hip-arch-06 (work in progress) (2004)

Braden, Clark, Shenker, Wroclawski, Developing a Next-Generation Internet Architecture (2000)

Crowcroft, Hand, Mortier, Roscoe, Warfield, Plutarch: An Argument for Network Pluralism (2003)

Crawford, Mankin, Narten, Stewart, Zhang, Separating Identifiers and Locators in Addresses: An Analysis of the GSE Proposal for IPv6. Internet-draft (1999)

Clark, Braden, Falk, Pingali, FARA: Reorganizing the Addressing Architecture (2003)

Eriksson, Faloutsos, Krishnamurthy, PeerNet: Pushing Peer-to-Peer Down the Stack (2003)

Stoica, Adkins, Ratnasamy, Shenker, Surana, Zhuang, Internet Indirection Infrastructure (2002)

Nikander, Arkko, Ohlman, Host Identity Indirection Infrastructure (Hi3) (2004)

Moskowitz (2), Nikander, Jokela, Henderson, Host Identity Protocol. Internet-draft, draft-ietf-hip-base-00 (work in progress) (2004)

Rescorla, Diffie-Hellman Key Agreement Method. RFC 2631 (1999)

Krawczyk, Bellare, Canetti, HMAC: Keyed-Hashing for Message Authentication. RFC 2104 (1997)

Kent (2), Atkins. IP Encapsulating Security Payload (ESP). RFC 2406 (1998)

HIP for BSD project [Referenced 11.02.2005] http://hip4inter.net

Guaranteeing Security of Financial Transaction by Using Quantum Cryptography in Banking Environment

Solange Ghernaouti-Hélie and Mohamed Ali Sfaxi

HEC - University of Lausanne
1015 Switzerland
{sgh,mohamedali.sfaxi}@unil.ch

Abstract. Protocols and applications could profit of quantum cryptography to secure communications. The applications of quantum cryptography are linked to telecommunication services that require very high level of security such as bank transactions.

The aim of this paper is to present the possibility to use quantum cryptography in critical financial transactions, to analyse the use of quantum key distribution within IPSEC to secure these transactions and to present the estimated performances of this solution.

After having introduced basic concepts in quantum cryptography, we describe a scenario of using quantum key distribution in bank transactions in Switzerland. Then, we propose a solution that integrate quantum key distribution into IPSEC. A performance analysis is done to demonstrate the operational feasibility of this solution.

Keywords: Security guarantee, Quantum cryptography, Key management, secure financial transactions, IPSEC, performances.

1 Introduction

Banks and financial establishments need to secure transaction and communication between them and their clients. In fact, everyday thousand of million dollars transactions are performed between banks. This transmission must be secure and need to satisfy security requirement such as authentication, confidentiality and integrity. Quantum cryptography could be used, in this context, to offer unconditional secure communication.

The next section presents a scenario for quantum cryptography application to secure bank transaction over Internet and Intranet architectures. Then, we prove the feasibility of the use of quantum cryptography within the framework of IPsec.

Quantum cryptography could be applied to IP Security protocol (IPsec) [RFC 2401]. This protocol is related to a collection of standards that was designed specifically to create secure end-to-end secure connections. The standard was developed by the Internet Engineering Task Force (IETF) to secure communications over both public and private networks.

J. Filipe et al. (Eds.): ICETE 2005, CCIS 3, pp. 139–149, 2007.

2 Quantum Cryptography for Banks and Financial Establishments

Nowadays, Banks and financial institutions use either symmetric cryptography or asymmetric cryptography. Both techniques, as proved above, are not unconditionally secure. So transactions could be corrupted and altered without the awareness of the bank. This constitutes a serious danger because criminals and malicious organizations could profit of the breach to steal and highjack. Securing critical financial transaction is mandatory and will be more and more necessary to master economical crime.

2.1 Quantum Cryptography Solution

To ensure maximum security, we need to maximize the security in each field such as storage, generation, processing and transmission of data. In this paragraph, we will focus on securing transmissions. The transmissions are either from bank building to another bank building of the same company, from cash dispenser to bank and from a bank to another. The difference resides in the distance, the degree of security required and the duration and the quantity of information to send. Quantum cryptography ensures the unconditional security of transmission and the awareness if an eavesdropper tries to intercept or modify the content of the transmission. Quantum cryptography aims exploiting the laws of quantum physics in order to carry out a cryptographic task. The uncertainty relations of Heisenberg can in particular be exploited to implement communication channels that cannot be passively - i.e. without disturbance of the transmission - eavesdropped. Its legitimate users can detect eavesdropping, no matter what technology is available to the spy (Bennet1984; Gisin2002).

The power of quantum cryptography lies primarily in the fact that the keys distributed on the quantum channel are invulnerable to eavesdropping and can be guaranteed without assumptions on the computing power of an eavesdropper (Mayers1998; Lo1999). Banks can actually use quantum cryptography at least in two of the three types of transaction: bank building to another bank building of the same bank company or/and cash dispenser to the bank. In fact, we assume that the distance connecting two bank buildings in less than 100 km. So, the use of quantum cryptography based on optical fiber is possible (IdQuan2004). In this case, either a big amount of data could be exchange or a tiny amount of data that could be transmitted frequently between bank buildings. Transmission from cash dispenser to banks (if the cash dispenser is not in the bank) can also be done using quantum cryptography based on optical fiber. In fact, the danger is that a malicious person could intercept the communications between the bank and the cash dispenser and modify them like for instance credit some bank account or change the identification of debited account. Transaction, using quantum cryptography, would be at that moment unconditionally secure and no one can intercept them. Here we ensure the integrity and the confidentiality of the transmitted data.

2.2 Example of a Bank Scenario

In this paragraph, we present a scenario of quantum cryptography implementation in Switzerland (small country size). The bank company is called Swiss Bank (SB). We

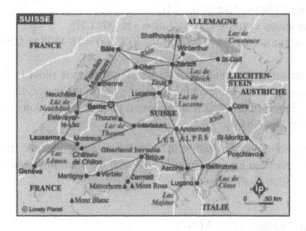

Fig. 1. Swiss bank - application of quantum cryptography

assume that each bank have a head quarter in every Canton. A main data base is located in Zurich and every head quarter bank has to communicate all transaction to the data base in Zurich. SB installs optic fiber between some head quarters in order to create a "private" quantum network (Figure 1). At least, each head quarter has a quantum cryptography receiver/sender. In order to reduce the volume of exchanged data every 6 hours all head quarters send data about transaction to Zurich (6h30, 12h30, 18h30 and 0h30).

The steps are the following:

All head quarters gather all transactions realized in the Canton. Bank head quarter located in the farthest Cantons from Zurich sends their adjacent canton. For instance, Lugano's SB head quarter sends data to Bellinzona, Poschiavo sends to Brigue... using quantum cryptography. These "nodes" has to wait until all adjacent cantons send have finished sending data (or time-out) then decrypt data and send them to the following BS head quarter according to a list. Finally, the nearest and direct linked to Zurich head quarters (Winterthur, Zoug, St-Gall, Coire...) exchange keys and communicate in a secure way using quantum cryptography.

Every head quarter (say H) has two different lists. Reception list: it is a list of all the head quarters that send data to H. Send List: usually it contains only one head quarter (the nearest to Zurich) but for availability purpose it contains 2 BS head quarters.

Example of such lists (for Bellinzona):

Reception list	Send list
Lugano	Coire
St-Moriz	
Ascona	

The possible cost of such scenario is:

The optical fiber total length: about 2000 Km

Number of quantum cryptography station: (twice the number of links) about 80

The cost of optical fiber per meter = 6 CHF
The cost of 2 quantum cryptography station = 150,000 CHF
The total cost of the scenario is 12000000 + 6000000 = 18 Million CHF   12 Million Euros.
So the price to ensure an unconditional secure transmission is about 12 Million Euros. This cost is huge but if we estimate the prestige gain (in the image, the reputation and in term of confidence) of the bank this expense is justifiable. This long term investment will be beneficial to the bank.

To apply this solution, we need to use algorithms and protocols. IPsec could support the use of quantum cryptography. We present the feasibility and the theoretical performances of such application.

3   SeQKEIP Operating Mode

As IPsec uses classical cryptography to secure communication, in this paragraph, we propose to use quantum cryptography to replace the classical cryptographic protocols used for symmetric distribution.

Using QKD in IPsec has already been proposed and implemented by Elliot of BBN technologies (Elliott2002). It proposes the idea of using QKD in IPsec as Key generator for AES. In 2003, BBN technologies describes the possibility of integrating QKD within the standard IKE (Elliott2003) and announces some concerns linked to the compatibility of QKD with IKE. In our paper, we propose a QKD solution for IPsec called SEQKEIP that is not based on IKE but on ISAKMP. Using this method, we avoid the problem of compatibility between IKE and QKD.

The idea is to stick to the traditional IPsec and the Internet Security Association and Key management Protocol (ISAKMP). In fact, ISAKMP does not impose any condition to is the negotiation mechanisms or to the SAs parameters. To use quantum cryptography with IPsec we have simply to define the two phases described above. We create a Secure Quantum Key Exchange Internet Protocol (SeQKEIP). The SeQKEIP like IKE uses ISAKMP mechanisms and takes advantage of quantum cryptography in order to build a practical protocol.

SeQKEIP runs nearly like the IKE. It includes 3 phases: the phase 1 for the negotiation of the ISAKMP SA, phase 2 for the negotiation of SA and we add a phase called "phase 0" in which Alice and Bob will share the first secret key. There are only three modes in SeQKEIP: Quantum Mode, Main Mode and Quick mode. Quantum mode is the quantum cryptography key exchange in the phase 0. Main Mode is used during the phase 1 and Quick Mode is an exchange in phase 2. Both the Main Mode and the Quick Mode are nearly the same of those in IKE.

Phase 0: Key exchange - Quantum Mode
This phase is the beginning of the secure exchange using quantum cryptography. After, these exchange both the sender and the receiver share a secret key. This key constitutes the pre-shared secret in IKE mechanism.

Phase 1: Negotiation of ISAKMP SA - Main Mode

During this phase, the cryptographic algorithm and the hash function are negotiated. Only the two parameters discussed in the phase 1 constitute the SeQKEIP attribute. The method to authenticate is the pre-shared secret (the secret key exchanged with Quantum Key Exchange method). Contrarily to IKE, SeQKEIP do not define DH groups and do not need to use digital signature nor digital certificates (Figure 2). No cryptographic key are generated in this phase. The first exchanged key is used to encipher packets and to authenticate users.

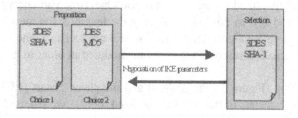

Fig. 2. Message exchanged during the first phase

After the phase 0 and the phase 1, both sender and receiver will have the following information:

Shared secret key	This key is generated during the phase 0 with Quantum Key exchange mechanism. The secret key is used to authenticate users and to encrypt packet.
Encryption algorithm	The encryption algorithm is applied to the phase 2 (negotiation of SA parameters). The algorithm could be 3DES, DES, AES. But, if we want to have the maximum security, we have to use One-Time-Pad function (OTP).
Hash function	The hash function will give the opportunity to the sender and the receiver to check the integrity of the message and the authentication of the correspondents.

Note that the phase 0 and the phase 1 are totally independent and could be done at the same time. We need the secret key only from the phase 2.

Phase 2: Negotiation of SA - Quick Mode
As in IKE, the exchanged messages in phase 2 are protected in authentication and confidentiality by the negotiated parameters of the phase 1 and phase 0. The authentication
is guaranteed by the addition of the HASH block after the ISAKMP header and the
confidentiality is ensured by the encryption of the whole message blocks. The aim of
this phase is to negotiate the SA. i.e. to negotiate the "IPsec" parameters. The SA parameters are (Mason2002): Destination address, Security Parameter Index (SPI), the
security mechanism (AH or ESP) and encryption & Hash function, the session key and
additional attribute like the lifetime of SA.

For SeQKEIP, to extend security, we can use One-Time-Pad encryption function.
The first exchanged key, in this case, will have the length of the message. We do not
need thus any encryption algorithm for SA. We still need a Hash function to verify the
integrity of the data. The run of IPsec could be modified in order to use one-time-pad
function.

In the beginning (Figure 3), the phase 0 and the phase 1 start (1&2). After these
two phases the parameters of the protocol are fixed. In (3), we will use key exchanged
thanks to quantum cryptography. This key will be used either as a session key (4) or in
the one-time-pad function (4').

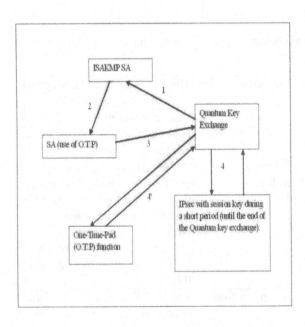

Fig. 3. Functioning of IPsec with Quantum Cryptography

In (4), we use traditional symmetric cryptography algorithms to exchange data. The
IPsec packets are the same as without the use of quantum cryptography. The session
key, therefore, is exchanged using quantum key exchange. The lifetime duration of the
session key is very short and it is equal to the time needed to exchange the secret key
using quantum cryptography. This solution is a transition solution to the (4')

In (4'), we use quantum cryptography concepts totally. The idea is to shift completely to the unconditional secure functions .i.e. quantum key exchange and one-time-pad function. After fixing the SA parameters, the "session" keys length will be of the size the data in the IPsec packet. Then, it is possible to use one-time-pad function (simply perform an XOR of the message and the key and then send the result). We need to exchange key for every packet. The weakness of this solution resides in the time needed to exchange the key. The total bit rate is highly affected due to this problem but as the quantum cryptography technology is progressing, this issue will soon be solved.

There are two possibilities. The first case is to exchange the key and distillation using the quantum channel (Time division multiplexing). The other is to exchange only the key over the quantum channel and all the other data over the public channel (Figure 4).

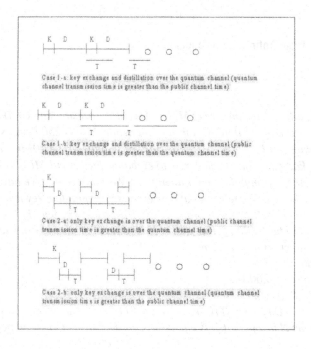

Fig. 4. The two cases of using totally quantum cryptography in IPsec

K: the duration to exchange the quantum key
D: the duration of key distillation
T: the duration of transmitting the message

1-first solution
In this case, we propose to use the quantum channel to exchange the key and for distillation. There are two possibilities: K+D is greater than T (K+D>T) and K+D is less or equal to T (K+D≤T).

The effectiveness (θ) of this solution is given by (θ represents the difference between the use of quantum cryptography and the use of unenciphered transmission):

a- K+D > T

If K+D>T then

$$\theta = \frac{T \times N}{(K + D) + T \times N + (N - 1) \times ((K + D) - T)} \qquad (1)$$

Where N is the number of packet.

$$\theta = \frac{T \times N}{(K + D) + T \times N - (N - 1) \times T + (K + D) \times (N - 1)} \qquad (2)$$

Finally, after simplification:

$$\theta = \frac{T \times N}{T + (K + D) \times N} \qquad (3)$$

If N is very large (infinite), θ is equal to:

$$\lim_{N \to \infty} \theta = \frac{T}{K + D} \qquad (4)$$

Example 1. *Traditionally, the size of MTU (Maximum Transmission Unit) is 1500 bytes (i.e. 12 Kbits); we suppose that the unprotected header size is 250 bytes, so we have to secure 1250 bytes i.e. 10 Kbits. Therefore, the key length will be 10Kbits if we want to use One-Time-Pad function. The flow rate to exchange the key is 1 MBit/s and about 100 MBit/s to exchange normal data on optical fiber. We suppose that we have an Internet connection of 1 Mbit/s. As the error rate for exchanging quantum key is normally 50%, we need to exchange 20 Kbits in order to get 10Kbits of key length. We estimate the distillation data to be 40 Kbits. The time to XOR data with the key is neglected.*

Having the previous assumption:
K = 20/1000 = 0.02 s
D = 40/100000 = 0.0004 s
And T = 12/1000 = 0.012 s
In this case, K+D (20.4 ms) is greater than T (12 ms). The effectiveness θ when the number of packet N is infinite (4) is equal to 120/204 ˜60 % of the total performance.

NB: if we have a faster Internet connection, say 10Mbit/s, the effectiveness θ given by (4) will be equal to 6 % of the total performance. In this case, the use of SeQKEIP is useless if we see only the performance. But, as the rate of quantum key exchange is progressing the effectiveness will increase.

b- K+D≤T

If K+D≤T then

$$\theta = \frac{T \times N}{(K + D) + T \times N} \qquad (5)$$

if N is very large (infinite), θ is equal to:

$$\lim_{N \to \infty} \theta = \frac{T}{T} = 1 \qquad (6)$$

So, in this case, there is no difference in the performance between using SeQKEIP and IP. The additional time cost induced by the use of quantum cryptography is negligible.

2-second solution
The quantum channel is used only to exchange the key. The distillation is done over the public channel. There are also two possibilities depending on the time needed to exchange the key and, on the other hand, the time to validate and send the message.

We take the same notation as previous:

K: the duration to exchange the quantum key

D: the duration of the key distillation

T: the duration of transmitting the message

So, we distinguish two scenarios: when $K > D+T$ and $K \leq T+D$.

a- $K > D+T$
If K>T+D then

$$\theta = \frac{T \times N}{K + (T + D) \times N + (N - 1) \times (K - (D + T))} \tag{7}$$

And, after simplification:

$$\theta = \frac{T \times N}{(T + D) + K \times N} \tag{8}$$

if N is very large (infinite), θ is equal to:

$$\lim_{N \to \infty} \theta = \frac{T}{K} \tag{9}$$

Example 2. *We take the same parameters as in the "NB" the previous example (10 Mbit/s for the Internet connection, 1Mbit/s to exchange the quantum key). Having the previous assumption:*

K = 20/1000 = 0.02 s

D = 40/10000 = 0.004 s

And T = 12/10000 = 0.0012 s

In this case, K (20 ms) is greater than T +V (42 ms). The effectiveness θ if the number of packet N is infinite (9) is equal to 12/200 = 6 % of the total performance.

The flow rate configuration is the both solutions gives the same performance rate (6 %) of the whole performance. To upgrade this rate, the only solution is to have the K $\leq$T+D in this case and K+D $\leq$T in the previous solution.

b- If $K \leq T+D$
If K$\leq$T+D then

$$\theta = \frac{T \times N}{K + (T + D) \times N} \tag{10}$$

if N is very large (infinite), θ is equal to:

$$\lim_{N \to \infty} \theta = \frac{T}{T + D} \tag{11}$$

If we take the following configuration: the rate of quantum key exchange is 1Mbit/s and the Internet connection is 1Mbit/s, then T= 0.012 s and D = 0.04s. T+V is greater than K (0.02 s). So, the effectiveness θ if the number of packet N is infinite (11) is equal to 12/52 = 23 % of the total performance.

4   Conclusion

Classical cryptography algorithms are based on mathematical functions. The robustness of a given cryptosystem is based essentially on the secrecy of its (private) key and the difficulty with which the inverse of its one-way function(s) can be calculated. Unfortunately, there is no mathematical proof that will establish whether it is not possible to find the inverse of a given one-way function. On the contrary, quantum cryptography is a method for sharing secret keys, whose security can be formally demonstrated.

As we have seen, using quantum cryptography in conjonction with IPsec to offer a better level of security for organisations is possible. If, we apply the quantum key exchange and one-time-pad function, we reach the unconditional security in communication. The distillation of the quantum key could be done in two different ways: over the optical channel or over the public channel. The cost of installing this solution stills expensive nowadays. The performance obtained when distilling the key over the optical channel is higher than when using public channel (up to 100% when using optical channel versus 23% when using public channel). Actually, we can reach 100Kbit/s when exchanging the quantum key and hope to reach 1Mbit/s next few years. The possible flow rate over an optical fiber is 100Mb/s. If, we use an Internet connection of 1Mbit/s, we get 60% of the total performance (solution1, a) i.e. a flow rate of 600Kbit/s if the distillation of the key is done over the optical channel and we get only 23% of the total performance if we validate the key over the public channel (solution 2, b) i.e. a flow rate of 230Kbit/s. If we could reach the rate of 10Mbit/s in quantum key exchange and we use the first solution, we will get a performance of 100% in the flow rate i.e. 1Mbit/s.

Acknowledgement

This work has been done within the framework of the European research project : SEC-OQC - www.secoqc.net. We would like to thank IDQuantique S.A (www.idquantique.com) and specially Gregoire Ribordy and Olivier Gay for their help and useful information.

References

Ghernaouti-Hélie, S., Sfaxi, M.A, Hauser, A., Riguidel, M., Alléaume, R.: Business model: advantages, scenarios, patents and laws related to quantum cryptography. Secoqc project deliverable (2004)

Alléaume, R.: Réalisation expérimentale de sources de photons uniques, caractérisation et application à la cryptographie quantique (Secoqc partner) (2004)

Bennet, C., Brassard, G.: IEEE International Conference on Computers, Systems, and Signal Processing. IEEE Press, Los Alamitos (1983)

Bennet, C.: Quantum Cryptography: Uncertainty in the Service of Privacy. Science 257 (1992)

Bethune, D.S., Risk, W.P.: AutoCompensating quantum cryptography. New journal of physics 4, 1–42 (2002),
http://www.iop.org/EJ/article/1367-2630/4/1/342/nj2142.html

Clark, C.W., Bienfang, J.C., Gross, A.J., Mink, A., Hershman, B.J., Nakassis, A., Tang, X., Lu, R., Su, D.H., Williams, C.J., Hagley, E.W., Wen, J.: Quantum key distribution with 1.25 Gbps clock synchronization, Optics Express (2000)

Ekert, A.: Quantum Cryptography based on Bell's Theorem. Physical Review Letters (1991),
http://prola.aps.org/abstract/PRL/v67/i6/p661_1

Elliott, C.: Building the quantum network. New Journal of Physics 4 46.1-46.12 (2002)

Elliott, C., Pearson, D., Troxel, G.: Quantum Cryptography in Practice (2003)

Freebsd people. IPsec outline. URL:
http://people.freebsd.org/~julian/IPsec_4_Dummies.html

freesoft,IPsec Overview. (2004). URL
http://www.freesoft.org/CIE/Topics/141.htm

Gisin, N., Ribordy, G., Tittel, W., Zbinden, H.: Quantum Cryptography. Reviews of Modern Physics 74 (2002),
http://arxiv.org/PS_cache/quant-ph/pdf/0101/0101098.pdf

Grosshans,Van Assche, Wenger, Brouri, Cerf, Grangier: Quantum key distribution using gaussian-modulated coherent states. Letter to nature (2003), http://www.mpq.mpg.de/Theorygroup/CIRAC-/people/grosshans/papers/Nat421_238.pdf

Hughes, R., Nordholt, J., Derkacs, D., Peterson, C.: Practical free-space quantum key distribution over 10km in daylight and at night. New journal of physics 4, 1–43 (2002),
http://www.iop.org/EJ/abstract/1367-2630/4/1/343/

Labouret, G.: IPsec: présentation technique. Hervé Schauer Consultants (HSC) (2000). URL
http://www.hsc.fr

Lo, H.K., Chau, H.F.: Unconditional security of quantum key distribution over arbitrarily long distances. Science 283 (1999),
http://arxiv.org/PS_cache/quant-ph/9803/9803006.pdf

Mason, A.: IPsec Overview Part Five: Security Associations. Cisco Press (2002), URL: http://www.ciscopress.com/articles/printerfriendly.asp?p=25443

Mayers, D.: Unconditionnal Security in Quantum Cryptography. J. Assoc. Comput. Math. 48, 351 (1998)

Paterson, K.G., Piper, F., Schack, R.: Why Quantum Cryptography? (2004),
http://eprint.iacr.org/2004/156.pdf

Riguidel, M., Dang-Minh, D., Le-Quoc, C., Nguyen-Toan, L., Nguyen-Thanh, M.: Quantum crypt- Work Package I. ENST/EEC/QC.04.06.WP1B (Secoqc partner) (2004)

Rivest, R.L., Shamir, A., Adleman, L.M.: A Method of Obtaining Digital Signature and Public-Key Cryptosystems. Communication of the ACM 21(2) (1978)

Wootters, W.K, Zurek, W.H.: A single quantum cannot be cloned. Nature 299, 802 (1982)

IdQuantique, A Quantum Leap for Cryptography (2004),
http://www.idquantique.com/files/introduction.pdf

Optimal Trade-Off for Merkle Tree Traversal

Piotr Berman[1,*], Marek Karpinski[2,**], and Yakov Nekrich[2,***]

[1] Dept.of Computer Science and Engineering
The Pennsylvania State University
berman@cse.psu.edu
[2] Dept. of Computer Science
University of Bonn
{marek,yasha}@cs.uni-bonn.de

Abstract. In this paper we describe optimal trade-offs between time and space complexity of Merkle tree traversals with their associated authentication paths, improving on the previous results of Jakobsson, Leighton, Micali, and Szydlo (Jakobsson et al., 03) and Szydlo (Szydlo, 04). In particular, we show that our algorithm requires $2 \log n / \log^{(3)} n$ hash function computations and storage for less than $(\log n / \log^{(3)} n + 1) \log \log n + 2 \log n$ hash values, where n is the number of leaves in the Merkle tree. We also prove that these trade-offs are optimal, i.e. there is no algorithm that requires less than $O(\log n / \log t)$ time and less than $O(t \log n / \log t)$ space for any choice of parameter $t \geq 2$.

Our algorithm could be of special use in the case when both time and space are limited.

Keywords: Identification and Authentication, Merkle Trees, Public Key Signatures, Authentication Path, Fractal Tree Traversal, Trade-off, Amortization.

1 Introduction

Merkle trees have found wide applications in cryptography mainly due to their conceptual simplicity and applicability. Merkle trees were first described by Merkle (Merkle, 82) in 1979 and studied intensively. In cryptographic applications, however, Merkle trees were not very useful for small computational devices, as the best known techniques for traversal required a relatively large amount of computation and storage. Several recent papers, e.g., (Jakobsson et al., 03) and (Szydlo, 04), improved the time and space complexity of Merkle trees. In this paper we address the issue of possible further improvements of Merkle tree traversals.

Merkle tree is a complete binary tree such that values of internal nodes are one-way functions of the values of their children. Every leaf value in a Merkle tree can be identified with respect to a publicly known root and the *authentication path* of that leaf.

---

* Research done in part while visiting Dept. of Computer Science , University of Bonn. Work partially supported by NSF grant CCR-9700053 and NIH grant 9R01HG02238-12.
** Work partially supported by DFG grants , Max-Planck Research Prize, DIMACS and IST grant 14036 (RAND-APX).
*** Work partially supported by IST grant 14036 (RAND-APX).

J. Filipe et al. (Eds.): ICETE 2005, CCIS 3, pp. 150–162, 2007.

An authentication path of a leaf consists of the siblings of all nodes on the path from this leaf to the root.

Merkle trees have many cryptographic applications, such as certification refreshal (Micali, 97), broadcast authentication protocols (Perrig et al., 02), third party data publishing (Devanbu et al., 01), zero-knowledge sets (Micali et al., 03) and micro-payments (Rivest, Shamir, 96). A frequent problem faced in such applications is the *Merkle tree traversal* problem, the problem of consecutively outputting the authentication data for every leaf. In (Merkle, 87) Merkle has proposed a technique for traversal of Merkle trees which requires $O(\log^2 n)$ space and $O(\log n)$ time per authentication path in the worst case. Recently, two results improving a technique of Merkle have appeared. In (Jakobsson et al., 03) the authors describe a Merkle tree traversal algorithm with $O(\log^2 n/\log \log n)$ space and $O(\log n/\log \log n)$ time per output. In (Szydlo, 04) Szydlo describes a method requiring $O(\log n)$ space and $O(\log n)$ time and provides a proof that this bound is optimal, i.e. he proves that there is no traversal algorithm that would require both $o(\log n)$ space and $o(\log n)$ time. Observe that we measure the time complexity of outputting the authentication path of a single leaf.

In this paper we investigate further the trade-off between time and space requirements of Merkle tree traversals.

First, we present an algorithm that works in $O(\log n/h)$ time and $O((\log n/h)2^h)$ space per round for arbitrary parameter $h \geq 1$. For $h = O(1)$ our result is equivalent to the result of Szydlo; however, we consider all operations (not just computations of one-way functions) in our analysis. Our result is also an extension of that of Jakobsson, Leighton, Micali and Szydlo (Jakobsson et al., 03); we prove that it can be extended for arbitrary values of h.

Secondly, we show that the results of Szydlo and Jakobsson, Leighton, Micali, Szydlo remain true, if we consider all operations and not just hash computations. (If h is not a constant, we ignore time that we need to output the values in the last case). In particular, we show that an algorithm with $2 \log n/\log \log \log n$ hash functions evaluations and storage requirement of $(\log n/\log \log \log n + 1) \log \log n + 2 \log n$ hash values per output can be constructed. This algorithm works with $O(\log n/\log^{(3)} n)$ operations per output.

At the end, we show that if a tree traversal algorithm works in time $O(\log n/h)$, then required space is $\Omega((\log n/h)2^h)$. Thus we show that our trade-off is optimal.

The presented results give a complete answer to the question of time and space complexity of the Merkle tree traversal problem. These results are also important for practical applications.

2 Preliminaries and Notation

Below we denote by a *hash* a one-way function, and hash computation will denote a computation of the value of a one-way function. In a Merkle tree leaf values are hash values of *leaf pre-images*. Leaf pre-images can be, for instance, generated with a pseudo-random generator. We will denote by *leaf-calc* a function that computes pre-images of the leaves. Let $\phi_1 = hash \circ leaf\text{-}calc$ be the function that computes value of the i-th leaf. Let $\phi_2(parent) = hash(left\text{-}child\|right\text{-}child)$ be the function that computes the value of the parent node from the values of its children. We will presume that we need one computation unit to compute ϕ_1 or ϕ_2.

We must generate n outputs, where n is the number of leaves. Every output consists of the leaf pre-image and its *authentication path*. An authentication path consists of the siblings of all nodes on the path to the root. Outputs for the leaves must be generated consecutively left-to-right. This makes our task easier, because outputs for consecutive leaves share many common node values.

In order to verify a leaf, one consecutively computes the values of its ancestors. Verification succeeds only if the computed root value equals to the known root value.

In this paper the following notation will be used. H will denote the Merkle tree height. We will say that a node is on level A, if its depth is $H - A$. The i-th node from the left on level A will be denoted by (A, i). A job, computing node (A, i) will also be denoted by (A, i). We will say that A is the job level and i is the index of the job. Sometimes we will identify a subtree of the Merkle tree by its root node (A, i). We will use a *subtree height* h as a parameter in our algorithm and L will be equal to H/h. We say that a node N is *needed* if it is a part of an authentication path.

3   Main Idea

We describe here the main idea of our algorithm and key observations on which the algorithm is based.

The well-known evaluation algorithm, shown on Fig. 1, is used to compute the value of the i-th node on level A and is an important part of all Merkle tree traversal algorithms.

```
Eval (A,i)
  if (A == 0)
     return φ₁(i);
  else
     minlev := A − 1
     V := Eval(A − 1, 2i)
     V := φ₂(V, Eval(A − 1, 2i + 1))
     minlev := A
     return V
```

Fig. 1. Evaluation of the i-th node on level A

This basic version of algorithm $Eval$ requires $O(2^A)$ computational units and A storage units. The last follows from the fact that at most one node value V for every height $i = 0, 1, \ldots, A$ has to be stored at every stage of the algorithm. These stored values will be further called *tail values*. Variable $minlev$ stores the value of the *minimal level* and equals to the minimum level for which the tail value of a job must be stored.

Our algorithm uses procedure $Eval$ to estimate the values of nodes that will be needed in the future authentication paths. The set of computations for finding the value of node (A, i) using procedure $Eval(A, i)$ will be further called a *job* (A, i).

Our algorithm combines two important observations that were also used in the papers of Jakobsson, Leighton, Micali and Szydlo (Jakobsson et al., 03), and Szydlo (Szydlo, 04). The first key observation on which our algorithm is based is that during the computation of node (A, i) its children $(A - 1, 2i)$, $(A - 1, 2i + 1)$ as well as all other descendants are computed. Therefore by storing intermediate results of evaluation some future computations can be saved. Actually, for every computed node N on level ih all its descendants on levels $ih - 1, \ldots, ih - h$ (i.e. a complete subtree of height h rooted in N) will be retained to be used in the future authentication paths. Thus only nodes at height ih, $i = 1, \ldots, L$ will be computed directly (see Fig 2).

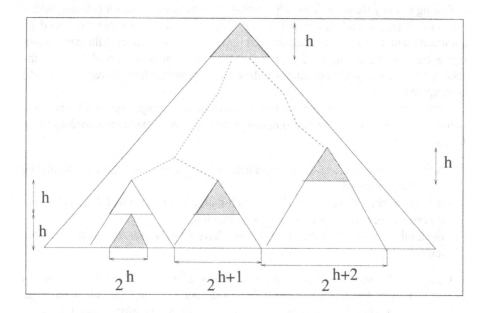

Fig. 2. Subtrees computed at a round of the algorithm

Another key observation is that we can schedule the computations of the nodes needed in the future in such a way that at most H storage units are necessary to store all tail values.

In section 6 a further constant improvement is described. We show that in a subtree only nodes with odd indices must be stored. We also show that the next subtree can be computed as the nodes of the current subtree are discarded so that the total number of nodes used by subtrees on a level is 2^h.

4   Algorithm Description

Our algorithm consists of three phases: **root generation, output,** and **verification**. During the first phase the root of the Merkle tree is generated. Additionally, the initial set of subtrees with roots at $(0, 2^{ih})$, $i = 1, \ldots, L$ is computed and stored. The verification phase is identical to the traditional verification phase (see, for instance, (Jakobsson et al., 03)). The output phase consists of 2^H rounds, and during round j an image of the j-th leaf and its authentication path are output. In the rest of this section we will describe an algorithm for the output phase and prove its correctness.

For convenience we will measure time in rounds. During each round $2L$ computation units are spent on computation of subtrees needed in the future authentication paths. Thus our algorithm starts at time 0 and ends at time $2^H - 1$, and the i-th round starts at time i. In the first part of the algorithm description we will ignore the costs of all operations, except of the computations of hash functions. Later we will show that the number of other operations performed during a round is $O(L)$.

During round j we store L already computed subtrees with roots at (sh, m_s) where $j \in [m_s 2^{sh}, (m_s + 1)2^{sh})$, $s = 0, 1, \ldots, L$. During the same round we also spend $2L$ computation units in order to compute jobs $(sh, m_s + 1)$ and construct the corresponding subtrees. At round $(m_s + 1)2^{sh}$ the subtree (sh, m_s) will be discarded, However the subtree $(sh, m_s + 1)$ will be retained for the next 2^{sh} rounds, while subtree $(sh, m_s + 2)$ is computed.

During each round there are at most L different jobs competing for $2L$ computation units. These jobs will be called *active*. Active jobs are scheduled according to the following rules:

1. A job (ih, k) $k = 1, \ldots, H/2^{ih}$ becomes active at time $(k - 1)2^{ih}$, i.e. during the $(k - 1)2^{ih}$-th round.
2. All active jobs $(s', k_{s'})$ with $s' > s$ such that minimal level of $(s', k_{s'})$ does not exceed s have priority over the job (s, k_s) on level s.
3. In all other cases jobs with the lower level have priority over jobs with the higher level.

Consider job (sh, i) that becomes active at time $2^{sh}(i - 1)$. Rule 2 guarantees us that all jobs with levels $s'h$ such that $s' > s$ do not store any tail values on levels $1, 2, \ldots, sh - 1$ when the computation of job (sh, i) starts. Therefore, when job (sh, i) is computed, only one tail node on each of the levels $(s - 1)h, (s - 1)h + 1, \ldots, sh - 1$ will be stored. Now consider a job $(s''h, is'')$ on level $s''h$, $s'' = 1, \ldots, s - 1$. If job (sh, i) stores a tail node on level $\tilde{s} < s''$, then $(s''h, is'')$ is either already completed (rule 3), or did not start yet (rule 2).

This scheduling guarantees us that at any time only one tail value for a level $i = 1, 2, \ldots, H$ will be stored by all jobs (sh, i). Only $2L$ subtrees (one currently used and one currently computed for each level ih) must be stored at each round, and subtrees require $(2H/h)(2^{h+1} - 1)$ space. Hence the memory requirement of our algorithm is $O((2H/h)2^h) + O(H) = O((H/h)2^h)$.

These considerations allow us to formulate the following trade-off between time and space complexity.

Theorem 1. *Merkle tree can be traversed in time $O(H/h)$ with $O((H/h)2^h)$ storage units for any $h \geq 1$.*

Corollary 1. *Merkle tree can be traversed in time $O(\log n / \log^{(3)} n)$ with $O(\log n \log \log n / \log^{(3)} n)$ storage units.*

In the next subsections we will prove the algorithm correctness by showing that all values are computed on time, and we prove the time bound stated in the theorem by analysis of the operations necessary for the job scheduling.

4.1 Correctness Proof

In this section we show that job (sh, k) will be completed at time $k2^{sh}$.

Lemma 1. *Suppose that at time* $(k-1)2^{sh}$ *for every level* $i = h, 2h, \ldots, (s-1)h, (s+1)h, \ldots Lh$ *there is at most one unfinished job on level* i. *Then job* (sh, k) *will be completed before* $k2^{sh}$.

Proof: Consider the time interval $[(k-1)2^{sh}, k2^{sh})$. There is at most one job $(s''h, k_{s''})$ with $s'' > s$, such that the minimal level of $(s''h, k_{s''})$ is smaller than s. After less than 2^{sh+1} hash computations minimal level of $(s''h, k_{s''})$ will be at least sh. Besides that, there are also jobs with lower indices that must be completed before (sh, k) can be completed. There are at most $2^{(s-s')h}$ such jobs for every $s' < s$. All jobs on level $s'h$ require less than $2^{(s-s')h}2^{s'h+1} = 2^{sh}$ computation units for every $s' < s$. Hence, the total number of computation units needed for these jobs is $(s - 1)2^{sh}$. Thus we have 2^{sh+1} computation units left to complete the job (sh, k).

Lemma 2. *At every moment of time there is only one running job on level* sh, $s = 1, 2, \ldots, L$.

Proof: At time 0 we start only one job on level sh. For every level sh and every index i, we can prove by induction using Lemma 1 that at time interval $[2^{sh}i, 2^{sh}(i + 1))$ there is only one running job with index i on level sh.

Lemma 3. *The computation of job* (sh, i) *will be finished before time* $i2^{sh}$

Proof: Easily follows from Lemma 1 and Lemma 2.

In our computation only every h-th node on the computation path is computed directly. Below we will show which nodes should be retained during the computation of (sh, i).

All nodes $(ih - m, s2^m + j)$, where $m = 1, \ldots, h$ and $j = 0, \ldots, m - 1$ must be retained. In other words, all descendants of (ih, s) at levels $ih - 1, \ldots, (i - 1)h$ must be retained.

Proposition 1. *Descendants of a node* (ih, m) *are needed during rounds* $[m2^{ih}, (m + 1)2^{ih})$.

Proof: Indeed, children of (ih, m) are needed during rounds $[m2^{ih}+2^{h-1}, (m+1)2^{ih})$ and $[m2^{ih}, m2^{ih} + 2^{h-1})$. For descendants on other levels this proposition is proved by the fact that when a node is needed, the sibling of its parent is also needed.

Combining Lemma 3 with Proposition 1, we see that every node will be computed before it is needed for the first time.

4.2 Time Analysis

We have shown above that our algorithm performs $2L$ hash function computations per round. Now we will show that all other operations will take $O(L)$ time per round.

Lemma 4. *Job scheduling, according to rules 1.-3. can be implemented in $O(L)$ time per round.*

For every level $s = ih$ we store a list Q_i of level s jobs that have to be performed. When a new job on level ih becomes active or when the minimal level of some job becomes smaller than ih, it is added to Q_i. Lists Q_i are implemented as queues (FIFO).

At round j our algorithm checks all queues Q_i in ascending order. If a non-empty Q_i is found, we spend $2L$ hash computations on computing the last job l in Q_i. If the job l is finished after $k < 2L$ hash computations, or if the minimal level of l becomes higher than $(i + 1)h - 1$ we remove l from Q_i and traverse queues $Q_i, Q_{i+1}, \ldots Q_L$ until another non-empty queue is found.

Procedure *Eval* can require up to $H - 1$ recursive calls in the worst case. However, an equivalent non-recursive implementation is possible (see procedure *EvalBottom* in Appendix).

5 The Lower Bound

In this section we prove the lower bound on space and time complexity of Merkle tree traversals and show that the algorithm described above is asymptotically optimal. We prove the following result:

Theorem 2. *Any Merkle tree traversal algorithm with average time per round $O(\log n/a)$ requires $\Omega((\log n/a)2^a)$ space for any $a > 1$.*

In order to prove this theorem, we will consider only time required for the hash computations.

First, we distinguish between nodes with even and odd indices, further called even and odd nodes respectively. Even internal nodes are needed after their children. In case of odd internal nodes the situation is opposite: they are needed before their children. Namely, $(s, 2i+1)$ is needed during the time interval $[2i2^s, (2i+1)2^s)$ and its children, $(s - 1, 4i + 3)$ and $(s - 1, 4i + 2)$, are needed during $[2^{s-1}(4i + 2), 2^{s-1}(4i + 3))$ and $[2^{s-1}(4i + 3), 2^{s-1}(4i + 4))$ respectively. We can generalize this observation: an odd node is needed before all its proper descendants. We have just proved it for children; to extend the proof by one more generation, observe that when a node is needed and it is not the root, then the sibling of its parent is needed.

During the computation, when we execute

$$v = Eval(s, i) = \phi_2(Eval(s - 1, 2i), Eval(s - 1, 2i + 1))$$

we can remove $v_0 = Eval(s - 1, 2i)$ and $v_1 = Eval(s - 1, 2i + 1)$ or not. Suppose that we are not removing value v_j, $j = 0, 1$, even though we will not keep v_j until it is needed . Then we can normalize our algorithm by removing v_j and keeping v instead:

computing v is the only use for v_j other than including it in a certificate. Clearly, this normalization increases neither memory nor time.

For every odd node in a Merkle tree we do three things: (a) we account for a certain number of steps – steps used to compute this node using other remembered values, (b) we account for a certain number of *memory units* (one memory unit allows to store one value through one round) and (c) we account for a certain number of *job units*; job units correspond to the steps that would be executed if this value were computed from scratch.

Computing $Eval(s, i)$ takes $2^{s+1} - 1$ computation units, and in our lower bound reasoning we can estimate this as 2^s steps. By adding s's over all needed odd nodes we obtain the total number of job units. The number of job units for odd nodes on level s is $2^s 2^{H-s-1} = 2^{H-1} = n/2$. Therefore the total number of job units for odd nodes of the Merkle tree is $Hn/2$. We do not count the costs of computing needed values of even nodes in our lower bound proof.

We account for the remembered values in order in which children precede the parents.

Suppose that we remember the value of node v_0 during the computation of node v, but do not remember the value of v_1, where v_1 is an ascendant of v_0. Then we can save more job units by remembering v_1 instead of v_0. Hence, if we remember the value of v_0 on level l_0 during computation of node v on level l, then values of all nodes on levels $l_0, l_0 + 1, \ldots, l$ are also remembered. Therefore when a node on level s is computed it is either computed "from scratch" with $2^{s+1} - 1$ steps or it is computed with 1 step because its children were already computed and remembered.

Suppose that we remember the result $Eval(s, 2i + 1)$ and we use this value a times for computation of node values (including node $(s, 2i + 1)$). The last use, when $Eval(s, 2i+1)$ is needed, requires 2^s memory units. If we want to use this value twice, we have to compute it before its parent (or other odd ancestor is needed), and since the parent (ancestor) is needed for 2^{s+1} rounds or more, we need at least 2^{s+1} memory units. By induction, if we want to use $Eval(s, 2i+1)$ for a node values, we need to use at least $2^{a-1}2^s$ memory units.

Consider a node $(s, 2i + 1)$. Suppose that its value was used in a computations. As shown above, we need either $2^{s+1} - 1$ steps or 1 step to compute it. If we need 1 step, then the total number of job values we accounted for is a, and the total number of memory units is $2^{a-1}2^s$. Suppose that we needed $2^{s+1} - 1$ steps to compute $(s, 2i+1)$. Then the total number of job units is $a(2^{s+1} - 1)$, and the number of memory units is $2^{a-1}2^s$. Now we can distribute the steps and memory units between the job units that we have accounted for. Each of them receives a^{-1} steps and at least $2^{a-1}/a$ memory units.

If we use z_k to express the amount of steps a job unit $k = 1, 2, \ldots, Hn/2$ obtains, then the minimal number of obtained memory units is $f(z_k) = \frac{1}{2}z_k 2^{1/z_k}$. Note that $f(z)$ is a convex function of z (the second derivative is positive for positive z). The total number of steps $\sum z_k = Hn/2a$. Since $f(z)$ is convex, $\frac{1}{Hn/2} \sum f(z_k) \geq f(\frac{\sum z_k}{Hn/2})$ and $\sum f(z_k) \geq (Hn/2)f(a) = 2^a/a \times Hn/4$

Thus we have shown that if the computation takes $Hn/2a$ steps, then it uses at least $2^a/a \times Hn/4$ memory units. Since the total number of rounds is n, during an average round we must remember at least $H2^a/4a$ values.

6 A Constant Improvement

In this section we describe an improved version of the algorithm from the section 4. In our improved version we do not compute all nodes in the subtrees. Instead of this, only the nodes with odd indices are computed. This is possible because even nodes will be needed after their children are needed. Therefore, if we store both children of an even node until their parent is needed, we can compute its value with one hash computation.

Thus, in a subtree (ih, k) we only compute nodes $(ih - 1, 2k + 1), (ih - 2, 4k + 1), (ih - 3, 8k + 1), \ldots$ and only the nodes $(ih - 1, 2k + 1), (ih - 2, 4k + 1), (ih - 2, 4k + 3), \ldots, (ih - h, k2^h + 1), \ldots, (ih - h, k2^h + 2^h - 1)$ must be stored. (see an example on Fig. 3)

Computation of all odd descendants of (ih, k) will take time $2^{ih-1+1} - 1 + 2^{ih-2+1} - 1 + \ldots + 2^{ih-h+1} - 1 = \sum_{k=0}^{h-1} 2^{ih-k} - h = 2^{ih+1} - 2^{(i-1)h+1} - h$. We will need h extra hash computations to compute the even nodes. Therefore the total number of computations for subtree (ih, k) is $2^{ih+1} - 2^{(i-1)h+1}$.

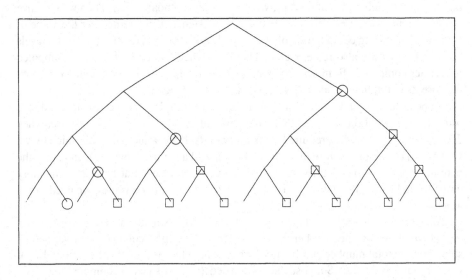

Fig. 3. Example of a subtree. Computed nodes are marked by circles. Nodes marked by circles or squares are stored.

It is easy to see that there is at most one "new" even node at every round. Therefore it takes at most one extra computation per round to deal with even nodes (if we compute even nodes just as they are needed).

To compute the node (s, j) with one hash computation we have to store its odd child $(s - 1, 2j + 1)$ during rounds $[(2j + 1)2^{s-1}, (2j + 2)2^{s-1})$. Thus there are at most h odd nodes that should be kept "extra time" and at most h nodes that are a part of an authentication path during each round. Therefore the total memory requirement is $(2^h - 1 + 2h)L$ per subtree. We need the first summand to store the odd nodes in the subtree and we need the second summand to store the even nodes from the current authentication path and odd nodes kept "extra time".

The nature of our trade-off depends on the subtree height h. For subtree height $h = 1$ this improvement results in speed-up of almost factor 2. This allows us to formulate the following result

Corollary 2. *A Merkle tree traversal algorithm can be implemented with* $\log n$ *hash function evaluations,* $3 \log n$ *memory locations for hash values and* $O(\log n)$ *time for other operations per round.*

For larger values of h the time improvement becomes very small but we have an almost two-fold decrease of the space used by hash values. In the last case we can also schedule our computation in such way that the values in the next subtree are computed almost exactly at the time when the corresponding values in the current subtree "expire" and can be discarded. In this case at most one extra value per subtree would have to be stored. In our modified procedure computation of odd nodes of subtree (ih, k), $i = 2, 3, , \ldots, L - 1$ is divided into two stages. In the first stage descendants of (ih, k) on level $(i - 1)h$ ("leaves" of the subtree) are computed. We will further call nodes $((i - 1)h, 2^h k + j)$, $j \in [0, 2^h)$ *bottom level* nodes of subtree (ih, k). In the second stage the odd nodes are computed from bottom level nodes. Observe that computation of the subtree (ih, k) takes place in the same time interval $[2^{ih}(k - 1), 2^{ih}k)$ as in our first algorithm. The idea of our modification is that nodes $((i - 1)h, 2^h k + j)$, $j \in [0, 2^h)$, i.e. bottom level nodes of (ih, k), are computed slower than odd nodes of subtree $(ih, k - 1)$ are discarded. Computation of the odd nodes from the bottom tree nodes is performed during the last 2^h rounds of the interval $[2^{ih}(k - 1), 2^{ih}k)$. We will further call the jobs computing the bottom level nodes *secondary jobs*, and the last job computing the remaining odd nodes of the subtree will be called a *primary job*. In order to reserve 2^h rounds for the primary job, we allocate $2^{(i-1)h} - 1$ rounds for computation of every secondary job. A pseudocode description of the modified procedure *Eval* is given in Appendix.

Now we prove the space bound of our modified algorithm. First we show that a secondary job of a node on ih can be completed in $2^{(i-1)h} - 1$ rounds.

Lemma 5. *Suppose that at time* $(k - 1)2^{ih} + m2^{(i-1)h} - m$, $m = 0, 1, \ldots, 2^h - 1$ *for every level* $l = h, 2h, \ldots, (i - 1)h, (i + 1)h, \ldots Lh$ *there is at most one unfinished secondary job of a job on level* l. *Then the* m-*th secondary job of* (ih, k) *will complete before* $(k - 1)2^{ih} + (m + 1)2^{(i-1)h} - m - 1$.

Proof: Consider the time interval $[(k - 1)2^{ih} + m2^{(i-1)h} - m, (k - 1)2^{ih} + (m + 1)2^{(i-1)h} - m - 1)$.

There is at most one job $(i''h, k_{i''})$ with $i'' > i$, such that the minimal level of $(i''h, k_{i''})$ is smaller than i. After at most $2^{ih+1} - 2$ hash computations minimal level of $(i''h, k_{i''})$ will be at least ih. Besides that, there are also jobs on lower levels that must complete before (sh, k) can be completed. There are at most $2^{(i-i')h}$ such jobs for every index $1 < i' < i$. Thus for any fixed $i' < i$ all jobs on level i' require $2^{(i-i')h}(2^{i'h+1} - 1) < 2^{ih+1} - 2$ job units. Another $(2^{h+1} - 1)2^{(i-1)h} < 2^{ih+1} - 2$ computation units are claimed by subtrees on level h. Hence the total number of computation units required by all other jobs is strictly less than $(L - 1)(2^{ih+1} - 2)$.

Thus we have at least $2^{ih+1} - 1$ computation units left to complete the m-th secondary job of (ih, k).

Lemma 6. *Computation of the m-th secondary job of (ih, k), $i = 2, 3, \ldots, L-1$ will be finished before time $(k-1)2^{ih} + (m+1)2^{(i-1)h} - m - 1$.*

Proof is analogous to the Proof of Lemma 3

It easily follows from Lemma 6 and the above discussion that the computation of the m-th bottom node of (sh, k) will be finished in interval $[2^{ih}(k-1) + m2^{(i-1)h} - m, 2^{ih}(k-1) + (m+1)2^{(i-1)h} - m - 1)$. It remains to compute how many odd nodes of $(ih, k-1)$ are discarded before $2^{ih}(k-1) + m2^{(i-1)h} - m$.

Let $w = 2^h$. After $2^{h(i-1)}m$ rounds the number of remaining nodes can be estimated as $(w-m)/2 + (w-m)/4 + \ldots + (w-m)/w \le (w-m)$. We did not count the nodes of the current authentication path in this estimation. Therefore the total number of stored nodes in subtrees (ih, k) and $(ih, k-1)$ in interval $[2^{ih}(k-1), 2^{ih}k - 2^h)$ is limited by 2^h.

The primary job for (sh, k) can be computed in 2^h rounds. This job can be performed in-place, because when a new node is computed its even child can be discarded.

In the modified algorithm we apply the job scheduling scheme only to subtrees on levels ih, $i = 2, \ldots, L-1$. Since there is only one subtree for $i = L$, it is not recomputed. Therefore the total number of tail nodes does not exceed $H - h$.

During each round we use two reserved computation units to compute the next level h subtree. By the same argument as above we can see that the number of remaining nodes in the current level h subtree after m rounds is limited by $2^h - m$. Therefore the total number of nodes in the current and future subtrees of level h is limited by 2^h. This computation would require up to h additional units for the tail values. Therefore the total number of tail values is $H - h + h = H$.

The above considerations allow us to formulate the following

Theorem 3. *A Merkle tree traversal can be implemented in $O(L)$ time with $2L$ hash operations. This algorithm requires $L2^h + 2H$ memory locations to store hash values.*

In the last Theorem we have ignored time necessary to output the $\log n$ values per round. The result described in the abstract follows if we choose $h = \log^{(3)} n$.

7 Conclusion

In this paper we describe the first optimal trade-off between time and space complexity of Merkle tree traversals.

We believe it is possible to improve further the constants in the described trade-off by differentiating between various types of nodes in our procedure.

Another interesting problem was described in (Szydlo, 04): given space to store only S hash nodes, what is the minimal number of hash computations per round? (Szydlo, 04) proposes it in a combination with (Jakobsson et al., 03) as a starting point of this investigation.

Yet another interesting problem is the complexity of the traversal of the so-called *skew (unbalanced) Merkle trees* (Karpinski, Nekrich, 04).

References

Coppersmith, D., Jakobsson, M.: Almost Optimal Hash Sequence Traversal. Financial Cryptography, 102–119 (2002)

Devanbu, P., Gertz, M., Martel, C., Stublebine, S.G.: Authentic Third Party Data Publication. In: 14th IFIP Workshop on Database Security (2000)

Jakobsson, M.: Fractal Hash Sequence Representation and Traversal. In: ISIT, p. 437 (2002)

Jakobsson, M., Leighton, T., Micali, S., Szydlo, M.: Fractal Merkle Tree Representation and Traversal. In: RSA Cryptographers Track, RSA Security Conference (2003)

Karpinski, M., Nekrich, Y.: A Note on Traversing Skew Merkle Trees, ECCC Report TR04-118

Lipmaa, H.: On Optimal Hash Tree Traversal for Optimal Time Stamping. In: Chan, A.H., Gligor, V.D. (eds.) ISC 2002. LNCS, vol. 2433, pp. 357–371. Springer, Heidelberg (2002)

Merkle, R.: Secrecy, Authentication and Public Key Systems. UMI Research Press (1982)

Merkle, R.: A Digital Signature Based on a Conventional Encryption Function. In: Pomerance, C. (ed.) CRYPTO 1987. LNCS, vol. 293, pp. 369–378. Springer, Heidelberg (1988)

Micali, S.: Efficient Certificate Revocation. Technical Report TM-542b, MIT Laboratory for Computer Science (March 22, 1996)

Micali, S., Rabin, M., Kilian, J.: Zero-Knowledge Sets. In: Proc. 44th FOCS, pp. 80–91 (2003)

Perrig, A., Canetti, R., Tygar, D., Song, D.: The TESLA Broadcast Authentication Protocol. Cryptobytes 5, 2–13

Rivest, R., Shamir, A.: PayWord and MicroMint - Two Simple Micropayment Schemes. Crypto-Bytes 1, 7–11

Szydlo, M.: Merkle Tree Traversal in Log Space and Time. In: Cachin, C., Camenisch, J.L. (eds.) EUROCRYPT 2004. LNCS, vol. 3027, pp. 541–554. Springer, Heidelberg (2004)

Appendix

In this Appendix we give a pseudocode description of the modified procedure **Eval(A,k)**, $A = ih$. Recall that first all descendants of (A, k) on level $(i - 1)h$ are computed and computation of the m-th descendant starts at time $2^{ih}(k - 1) + 2^{(i-1)h}m - m$.

```
Eval1 (A,k)
    i := A/h
    if ( round = 2^{ih}(k − 1) + 2^{(i−1)h}m − m)
        bottom[m] := \
            EvalBottom(2^{(i−1)h}, m + (k − 1)2^h)
    EvalTop(A, k)
```

Fig. 4. Procedure *Eval1*

Procedure *EvalBottom* is algorithmically identical to procedure Eval in section 3. That is, the same sequence of hash computations is performed. Therefore all proofs in section 4 remain valid if we use *EvalBottom* or *Eval1* instead of *Eval* . But the implementation presented here does not use recursion. Variables $Tail_{lev}$ are global, i.e. common for all procedures *EvalBottom*.

```
EvalBottom (A,k)
    ind := 2^A k
    minlev := lev := 0
    while (lev < A)
        V := φ_1(ind)
        while (ind mod 2 = 1)
            V := φ_2(Tail_lev, V)
            lev := lev + 1
            minlev := minlev + 1
            ind := ind/2
        Tail_lev := V
        ind := (ind + 1)2^lev
        minlev := lev := 0
```

```
EvalTop (A,k)
    ind := 2^A k
    minlev := lev := 0
    while (lev < A)
        V := bottom[ind]
        while (ind mod 2 = 1)
            leftind := 2^lev ind
            rightind := 2^lev (ind + 1)
            bottom[leftind] := \
                φ_2(bottom[leftind], bottom[rightind])
            lev := lev + 1
            minlev := minlev + 1
            ind := ind/2
        ind := (ind + 1)2^lev
        minlev := lev := 0
```

Fig. 5. Procedures *EvalBottom* and *EvalTop*

Procedure *EvalTop(A,k)* computes all odd nodes of the height h subtree rooted in (A, k) if all descendants of (A, k) on level $(i - 1)h$ are known. The pseudocode is very similar to *EvalBottom* but *EvalTop(A,k)* works in-place, i.e. with only a constant number of additional variables. When $(A, i) = φ_2((A - 1, 2i), (A - 1, 2i + 1))$ is computed, we store (A, i) in place of the node $((A - 1, 2i)$.

Supporting the Cybercrime Investigation Process: Effective Discrimination of Source Code Authors Based on Byte-Level Information

Georgia Frantzeskou, Efstathios Stamatatos, and Stefanos Gritzalis

Laboratory of Information and Communication Systems Security, Aegean University
Department of Information and Communication Systems Engineering, Karlovasi,
Samos, 83200, Greece
gfran@aegean.gr, stamatatos@aegean.gr, sgritz@aegean.gr

Abstract. Source code authorship analysis is the particular field that attempts to identify the author of a computer program by treating each program as a linguistically analyzable entity. This is usually based on other undisputed program samples from the same author. There are several cases where the application of such a method could be of a major benefit, such as tracing the source of code left in the system after a cyber attack, authorship disputes, proof of authorship in court, etc. In this paper, we present our approach which is based on byte-level n-gram profiles and is an extension of a method that has been successfully applied to natural language text authorship attribution. We propose a simplified profile and a new similarity measure which is less complicated than the algorithm followed in text authorship attribution and it seems more suitable for source code identification since is better able to deal with very small training sets. Experiments were performed on two different data sets, one with programs written in C++ and the second with programs written in Java. Unlike the traditional language-dependent metrics used by previous studies, our approach can be applied to any programming language with no additional cost. The presented accuracy rates are much better than the best reported results for the same data sets.

Keywords: Source Code Authorship Analysis, Software Forensics, Security.

1 Introduction

In a wide variety of cases it is important to identify the author of a piece of code. Such situations include cyber attacks in the form of viruses, trojan horses, logic bombs, fraud, and credit card cloning or authorship disputes or proof of authorship in court etc. But why do we believe it is possible to identify the author of a computer program? Humans are creatures of habit and habits tend to persist. That is why, for example, we have a handwriting style that is consistent during periods of our life, although the style may vary, as we grow older. Does the same apply to programming? Although source code is much more formal and restrictive than spoken or written languages, there is still a large degree of flexibility when writing a program (Krsul, and Spafford, 1996).

J. Filipe et al. (Eds.): ICETE 2005, CCIS 3, pp. 163–173, 2007.

Source code authorship analysis could be applied to the following application areas (Frantzeskou et al 2004):

1. *Author identification.* The aim here is to decide whether some piece of code was written by a certain author. This goal is accomplished by comparing this piece of code against other program samples written by that author. This type of application area has a lot of similarities with the corresponding literature where the task is to determine that a piece of work has been written by a certain author.
2. *Author characterisation.* This application area determines some characteristics of the author of a piece of code, such as cultural educational background and language familiarity, based on their programming style.
3. *Plagiarism detection.* This method attempts to find similarities among multiple sets of source code files. It is used to detect plagiarism, which can be defined as the use of another person's work without proper acknowledgement.
4. *Author discrimination.* This task is the opposite of the above and involves deciding whether some pieces of code were written by a single author or by some number of authors. An example of this would be showing that a program was probably written by three different authors, without actually identifying the authors in question.
5. *Author intent determination.* In some cases we need to know whether a piece of code, which caused a malfunction, was written having this as its goal or was the result of an accidental error. In many cases, an error during the software development process can cause serious problems.

The traditional methodology that has been followed in this area of research is divided into two main steps (Krsul, Spafford 1995; MacDonell et al. 2001; Ding 2004). The first step is the extraction of software metrics and the second step is using these metrics to develop models that are capable of discriminating between several authors, using a machine learning algorithm. In general, the software metrics used are programming - language dependent. Moreover, the metrics selection process is a non trivial task.

In this paper we present a new approach, which is an extension of a method that has been applied to natural language text authorship identification (Keselj et al., 2003). In our method, byte-level N-grams are utilised together with author profiles. We propose a new simplified profile and a new similarity measure which enables us to achieve a high degree of accuracy for authors for whom we have a very small training set. Our methodology is programming - language independent since it is based on low-level information and is tested to data sets from two different programming languages. The simplified profile and the new similarity measure we introduce provide a less complicated algorithm than the method used in text authorship attribution and in many cases they achieve higher prediction accuracy. Special attention is paid to the evaluation methodology. Disjoint training and test sets of equal size were used in all the experiments in order to ensure the reliability of the presented results. Note, that in many previous studies the evaluation of the proposed methodologies was performed on the training set. Our approach is able to deal effectively with cases where there are just a few available programs per author.

Moreover, the accuracy results are high even for cases where the available programs are of restricted length.

The rest of this paper is organized as follows. Section 2 contains a review on past research efforts in the area of source code authorship analysis. Section 3 describes our approach and section 4 includes the experiments we have performed. Finally, section 5 contains conclusions and future work.

2 Related Work

The most extensive and comprehensive application of authorship analysis is in literature. One famous authorship analysis study is related to Shakespeare's works and is dating back over several centuries. Elliot and Valenza (1991) compared the poems of Shakespeare and those of Edward de Vere, 7th Earl of Oxford, where attempts were made to show that Shakespeare was a hoax and that the real author was Edward de Vere, the Earl of Oxford. Recently, a number of authorship attribution approaches have been presented (Stamatatos et. al, 2000; Keselj, et al., 2003; Peng et al, 2004) proving that the author of a natural language text can be reliably identified.

Although source code is much more formal and restrictive than spoken or written languages, there is still a large degree of flexibility when writing a program (Krsul, and Spafford, 1996). Spafford and Weeber (1993) suggested that it might be feasible to analyze the remnants of software after a computer attack, such as viruses, worms or trojan horses, and identify its author. This technique, called software forensics, could be used to examine software in any form to obtain evidence about the factors involved. They investigated two different cases where code remnants might be analyzed: executable code and source code. Executable code, even if optimized, still contains many features that may be considered in the analysis such as data structures and algorithms, compiler and system information, programming skill and system knowledge, choice of system calls, errors, etc. Source code features include programming language, use of language features, comment style, variable names, spelling and grammar, etc.

Oman and Cook (1989) used "markers" based on typographic characteristics to test authorship on Pascal programs. The experiment was performed on 18 programs written by six authors. Each program was an implementation of a simple algorithm and it was obtained from computer science textbooks. They claimed that the results were surprisingly accurate.

Longstaff and Shultz (1993) studied the WANK and OILZ worms which in 1989 attacked NASA and DOE systems. They have manually analyzed code structures and features and have reached a conclusion that three distinct authors worked on the worms. In addition, they were able to infer certain characteristics of the authors, such as their educational backgrounds and programming levels. Sallis et al (1996) expanded the work of Spafford and Weeber by suggesting some additional features, such as cyclomatic complexity of the control flow and the use of layout conventions.

An automated approach was taken by Krsul and Spafford (1995) to identify the author of a program written in C. The study relied on the use of software metrics, collected from a variety of sources. They were divided into three categories: layout, style and structure metrics. These features were extracted using a software analyzer program from 88 programs belonging to 29 authors. A tool was developed to visualize the metrics collected and help select those metrics that exhibited little within-author variation, but large between-author variation. A statistical approach called discriminant analysis (SAS) was applied on the chosen subset of metrics to classify the programs by author. The experiment achieved 73% overall accuracy.

Other research groups have examined the authorship of computer programs written in C++ (Kilgour et al., 1997); (MacDonell et al. 2001), a dictionary based system called IDENTIFIED (integrated dictionary- based extraction of non-language-dependent token information for forensic identification, examination, and discrimination) was developed to extract source code metrics for authorship analysis (Gray et al., 1998). Satisfactory results were obtained for C++ programs using case-based reasoning, feed-forward neural network, and multiple discriminant analysis (MacDonell et al. 2001). The best prediction accuracy has been achieved by Case-Based Reasoning and it was 88% for 7 different authors.

Ding (2004), investigated the extraction of a set of software metrics of a given Java source code, that could be used as a fingerprint to identify the author of the Java code. The contributions of the selected metrics to authorship identification were measured by a statistical process, namely canonical discriminant analysis, using the statistical software package SAS. A set of 56 metrics of Java programs was proposed for authorship analysis. Forty-six groups of programs were diversely collected. Classification accuracies were 62.7% and 67.2% when the metrics were selected manually while those values were 62.6% and 66.6% when the metrics were chosen by SDA (stepwise discriminant analysis).

The main focus of the previous approaches was the definition of the most appropriate measures for representing the style of an author. Quantitative and qualitative measurements, referred to as metrics, are collected from a set of programs. Ideally, such metrics should have low within-author variability, and high between-author variability (Krsul and Spafford, 1996), (Kilgour et al., 1997). Such metrics include:

- Programming layout metrics: include those metrics that deal with the layout of the program. For example metrics that measure indentation, placement of comments, placement of braces etc.
- Programming style metrics: Such metrics include character preferences, construct preferences, statistical distribution of variable lengths and function name lengths etc.
- Programming structure metrics: include metrics that we hypothesize are dependent on the programming experience and ability of the author. For example such metrics include the statistical distribution of lines of code per function, ratio of keywords per lines of code etc.
- Fuzzy logic metrics: include variables that they allow the capture of concepts that authors can identify with, such deliberate versus non deliberate spelling errors, the degree to which code and comments match, and whether identifiers used are meaningful.

However, there are some disadvantages in this traditional approach. The first is that software metrics used are programming - language dependant. For example metrics used in Java cannot be used in C or Pascal. The second is that metrics selection is not a trivial process and usually involves setting thresholds to eliminate those metrics that contribute little to the classification model. As a result, the focus in a lot of the previous research efforts, such as (Ding 2004) and (Krsul, Spafford 1995) was into the metrics selection process rather than into improving the effectiveness and the efficiency of the proposed models.

3 Our Approach

In this paper, we present our approach, which is an extension of a method that has been successfully applied to text authorship identification (Keselj, et al 2003). It is based on byte level n-grams and the utilization of two different similarity measures used to classify a program to an author. Therefore, this method does not use any language-dependent information.

An n-gram is an n-contiguous sequence and can be defined on the byte, character, or word level. Byte, character and word n-grams have been used in a variety of applications such as text authorship attribution, speech recognition, language modelling, context sensitive spelling correction, optical character recognition etc. In our approach, the Perl package Text::N-grams (Keselj 2003) has been used to produce n-gram tables for each file or set of files that is required. An example of such a table is given in Table 1. The first column contains the n-grams found in a source code file and the second column the corresponding frequency of occurrence.

Table 1. n-gram frequencies extracted from a source code file

3-gram	Frequency
sio	28
_th	28
f_(	20
_=_	17
usi	16
_ms	16
out	15
ine	15
\n/*	15
on_	14
_in	14
fp_	14
the	14
sg_	14
_i_	14
in_	14

The algorithm used, computes n-gram based profiles that represent each of the author category. First, for each author the available training source code samples are concatenated to form a big file. Then, the set of the L most frequent n-grams of this file is extracted. The profile of an author is, then, the ordered set of pairs $\{(x_1; f_1); (x_2; f_2),\ldots,(x_L; f_L)\}$ of the L most frequent n-grams x_i and their normalized frequencies f_i. Similarly, a profile is constructed for each test case (a simple source code file). In order to classify a test case in to an author, the profile of the test file is compared with the profiles of all the candidate authors based on a similarity measure. The most likely author corresponds to the least dissimilar profile (in essence, a nearest-neighbour classification model).

The original similarity measure (i.e. dissimilarity more precisely) used by Keselj et al (2003) in text authorship attribution is a form of relative distance:

$$\sum_{n\in profile}\left(\frac{f1(n)-f2(n)}{\frac{f1(n)+f2(n)}{2}}\right)^2 = \sum_{n\in profile}\left(\frac{2(f1(n)-f2(n))}{f1(n)+f2(n)}\right)^2 \tag{1}$$

where $f_1(n)$ and $f_2(n)$ are the normalized frequencies of an n-gram n in the author and the program profile, respectively, or 0 if the n-gram does not exist in the profile. A program is classified to the author, whose profile has the minimal distance from the program profile, using this measure. Hereafter, this distance measure will be called Relative Distance (RD).

One of the inherent advantages of this approach is that it is language independent since it is based on low-level information. As a result, it can be applied with no additional cost to data sets where programs are written in C++, Java, perl etc. Moreover, it does not require multiple training examples from each author, since it is based on one profile per author. The more source code programs available for each author, the more reliable the author profile. On the other hand, this similarity measure is not suitable for cases where only a limited training set is available for each author. In that case, for low values of n, the possible profile length for some authors is also limited, and as a consequence, these authors have an advantage over the others. Note that this is especially the case in many source code author identification problems, where only a few short source code samples are available for each author.

In order to handle this situation, we propose a new similarity measure that does not use the normalized differences f_i of the n-grams. Hence the profile we propose is a Simplified Profile (SP) and is the set of the L most frequent n-grams $\{x_1, x_2,\ldots,x_L\}$. If SP_A and SP_P are the author and program simplified profiles, respectively, then the similarity distance is given by the size of the intersection of the two profiles:

$$\left|SP_A \cap SP_P\right| \tag{2}$$

where $|X|$ is the size of X. In other words, the similarity measure we propose is just the amount of common n-grams in the profiles of the test case and the author. The program is classified to the author with whom we achieved the biggest size of intersection. Hereafter, this similarity measure will be called Simplified Profile Intersection (SPI). We have developed a number of perl scripts in order to create the sets of n-gram tables for the different values of n (i.e., n-gram length), L (i.e., profile length) and for the classification of the program file to the author with the smallest distance.

4 Experiments

4.1 Comparison with a Previous Approach

Our purpose during this phase was to check that the presented approach works at least equally well as the previous methodologies for source code author identification. For this reason, we run this experiment with a data set that has been initially used by Mac Donell et al (2001) for evaluating a system for automatic discrimination of source code author based on more complicated, language-dependent measures. All programs were written in C++. The source code for the first three authors was taken from programming books while the last three authors were expert professional programmers. The data set was split (as equally as possible) into the training set 50% (134 programs) and the test set 50% (133 programs). The best result reported by Mac Donell et al (2001) on the test set was 88% using the case-based reasoning (that is, a memory-based learning) algorithm. Detailed information for the C++ data set is given in Table 2. Moreover, the distribution of the programs per author is given in Table 3.

Table 2. The data sets used in this study. 'Programs per author' is expressed by the minimum and maximum number of programs per author in the data set. Program length is expressed by means of Lines Of Code (LOC).

Data Set	C++	Java
Number of authors	6	8
Programs per author	5-114	5-8
Total number of programs	268	54
Training set programs	134	28
Testing set programs	133	26
Size of smallest program (LOC)	19	36
Size of biggest program (LOC)	1449	258
Mean LOC per program	210	129
Mean LOC in training set	206.4	131.7
Mean LOC in testing set	213	127.2

Table 3. Program distribution per author for the C++ data set

	Training Set	Test Set
Author 1	34	34
Author 2	57	57
Author 3	13	13
Author 4	6	6
Author 5	3	2
Author 6	21	21

We used byte-level n-grams extracted from the programs in order to create the author and program profiles as well as the author and program simplified profiles. Table 4 includes the classification accuracy results for various combinations of n (n-gram size) and L (profile size). In many cases, classification accuracy reaches 100%, much better than the best reported (MacDonell et al, 2001) accuracy for this data set (88% on the test set). This proves that the presented methodology can cope with effectively with the source code author identification problem. For n<4 and L<1000 accuracy drops. The same (although to a lower extent) stands for n>6.

More importantly, RD performs much worse than SPI in all cases where at least one author profile is shorter than L. For example for L=1000 and n=2, L is greater than the size of the profile of Author No5 (the maximum L of the profile of Author No 5 is 769) and the accuracy rate declines to 51%. This occurs because the RD similarity measure (1) that calculates similarity is affected by the size of the author profile. When the size of an author profile is lower than L, some programs are wrongly classified to that author. In summary, we can conclude that the RD similarity measure is not as accurate for those n, L combinations where L exceeds the size of even one author profile in the dataset. In all cases, the accuracy using the SPI similarity measure is better than (or equal to) that of RD. This proves that this new and simpler similarity measure is not affected by cases where L is greater than the smaller author profile.

4.2 Application to a Different Programming Language

The next experiment was performed on a different data set from a different programming language. In more detail the new data set consists of student programs (assignments from a programming language course) written in Java. Detailed information for this data set is given in Table 2. We used 8 authors. From each author 6-8 programs were chosen. Table 5 shows the distribution of programs per author. The size of programs was between 36 and 258 lines of code. The data set was split in training and test set of approximately equal size. This data set has been chosen in order to evaluate our approach when the available training data per author are limited

Table 4. Classification accuracy (%) on the C++ data set for different values of n-gram size and profile size using two similarity measures: Relative Distance and Simplified Profile Intersection

Profile Size L	n-gram Size													
	2		3		4		5		6		7		8	
	RD	SPI	RD	SPI	RD	SPI	RD	SPI	RD	SPI	RD	SPI	RD	SPI
200	98.4	98.4	97.7	97.7	97	97	95.5	95.5	94.7	95.5	92.5	92.5	92.5	94.7
500	100	100	100	100	100	100	99.2	100	98.4	98.4	97.7	97.7	97.7	97.7
1000	51	99.2	100	100	100	100	100	100	100	100	100	100	99.2	99.2
1500	5.3	98.4	100	100	100	100	100	100	100	100	99.2	99.2	99.2	100
2000	1.5	97.7	98.4	100	100	100	100	100	100	100	100	100	100	100
2500	1.5	95.5	99.2	100	100	100	100	100	100	100	100	100	100	100
3000	1.5	95.5	55.6	100	100	100	100	100	100	100	100	100	100	100

Table 5. Program distribution per author of the Java data set

	Training Set	Test Set
Author 1	3	3
Author 2	4	4
Author 3	3	2
Author 4	3	3
Author 5	4	4
Author 6	3	3
Author 7	4	3
Author 8	4	4

(6-7 short programs per author). Note that the programs written by students usually have no comments, their programming style is influenced by the instructor, they can be plagiarised, circumstances that create some extra difficulties in the analysis.

The results of the proposed method to this data set are given in Table 7. The best accuracy rate achieved with similarity measure RD was 84.6%. Again, when the profile size of at least one author is shorter than the selected profile size L, the accuracy of RD drops significantly. Using the similarity measure SPI, the best result was 88.5%. In generally SPI performed better than RD. Moreover, it seems that $4<n<7$ and $1000<L<3000$ provide the best accuracy results.

4.3 The Significance of Training Set Size

The purpose of this experiment was to examine the degree in which the training set size affects the classification accuracy. For this reason we used the C++ data set for which we reached classification accuracy of 100% for many n, L combinations with both similarity measures. This result has been achieved by using a training set of 134 programs in total. For the purposes of this experiment we used the same test set as in the experiment of section 4.1 but now we used training sets of different, smaller size. The smallest training set was comprised by only one program from each author and the biggest by 5 programs from each one (with the exception of one author for whom the available training programs were only 3). The presented source code author identification approach was applied to these new training sets using $n=6$ and $L=1500$ and similarity measure SPI. Note that the training size of authors was smaller than L in many of these experiments and as already explained, in such cases the classification accuracy decreases dramatically when using the similarity measure RD.

The accuracy results achieved are shown in Table 6. As can be seen, even with just one program per author available in the training set, high classification accuracy was achieved. By adding a second program per author the accuracy increased significantly above 96%. Note that the second programs added in the training set were in average longer than the first programs (see second column in table 7). We reached 100% of accuracy for training set based on five programs per author. This is a strong indication that our approach is quite effective even when very limited size of training set is available; a condition usually met in source code author identification problems.

Table 6. Classification Accuracy (%) on the C++ data set using different training set size (in programs per author)

Training Set Size	Mean LOC in Training Set	Accuracy (%)
1	52	63.9
2	212	96.2
3	171	97
4	170	99.2
5	197	100

Table 7. Classification accuracy (%) on the Java data set for different values of n-gram size and profile size using two similarity measures: Relative Distance and Simplified Profile Intersection

Profile Size L	n-gram Size											
	3		4		5		6		7		8	
	RD	SPI	RD	SPI	RD	SPI	RD	SPI	RD	SPI	RD	SPI
1000	80.8	80.8	84.6	84.6	84.6	84.6	80.8	80.8	80.8	80.8	84.6	84.6
1500	84.6	84.6	76.9	76.9	80.8	80.8	84.6	84.6	80.8	80.8	80.8	80.8
2000	53.8	80.8	65.4	80.8	76.9	80.8	84.6	88.5	84.6	84.6	84.6	84.6
2500	53.8	73.1	53.8	76.9	53,8	80.8	84.6	88.5	84.6	88.5	84.6	84.6
3000	53.8	73.1	53.8	80.8	50	76.9	53.8	84.6	69,2	84.6	84.6	84.6

5 Conclusions

In this paper, an approach to source code authorship analysis has been presented. It is based on byte-level n-gram profiles, a technique successfully applied to natural language author identification problems. The accuracy achieved for two data sets from different programming languages were 88.5% and 100% on test sets disjoint from training set, improving the best reported results for this task so far. Moreover the proposed method is able to deal with very limited training data, a condition usually met in source code authorship analysis problems (e.g., cyber attacks, source code authorship disputes, etc.) with no significant compromise in performance.

We introduced a new simplified profile and a new similarity measure. The advantage of the new measure over the original similarity measure is that it is not dramatically affected in cases where there is extremely limited training data for some authors. Moreover, the proposed method is less complicated than the original approach followed in text authorship attribution.

More experiments have to be performed on various data sets in order to be able to define the most appropriate combination of n-gram size and profile size for a given problem. The role of comments has also to be examined. In addition, cases where all the available source code programs are dealing with the same task should be tested as well. Another useful direction would be the discrimination of different programming styles in collaborative projects.

References

Ding, H., Samadzadeh, M.: Extraction of Java program fingerprints for software authorship identification. The Journal of Systems and Software 72(1), 49–57 (2004)

Elliot, W., Valenza, R.: Was the Earl of Oxford The True Shakespeare? Notes and Queries 38, 501–506 (1991)

Gray, A., Sallis, P., MacDonell, S.: Identified (integrated dictionary-based extraction of non-language-dependent token information for forensic identification, examination, and discrimination): A dictionary-based system for extracting source code metrics for software forensics. In: Proceedings of SE:E&P'98 (Software Engineering: Education and Practice Conference), pp. 252–259. IEEE Computer Society Press, Los Alamitos (1998)

Gray, A., Sallis, P., MacDonell, S.: Software forensics: Extending authorship analysis techniques to computer programs. In: Proc. 3rd Biannual Conf. Int. Assoc. of Forensic Linguists (IAFL'97), pp. 1–8 (1997)

Frantzeskou, G., Gritzalis, S., Mac Donell, S.: Source Code Authorship Analysis for supporting the cybercrime investigation process. In: Proc. 1st International Conference on e-business and Telecommunications Networks (ICETE04), vol. 2, pp. 85–92 (2004)

Keselj, V., Peng, F., Cercone, N., Thomas, C.: N-gram based author profiles for authorship attribution. In: Proc. Pacific Association for Computational Linguistics (2003)

Keselj, V.: Perl package Text:N-grams (2003), http://www.cs.dal.ca/ vlado/srcperl/N-grams, http://www.cs.dal.ca/ vlado/srcperl/N-grams

Kilgour, R.I., Gray, A.R., Sallis, P.J., MacDonell, S.G.: A Fuzzy Logic Approach to Computer Software Source Code Authorship Analysis. In: the Fourth International Conference on Neural Information Processing – The Annual Conference of the Asian Pacific Neural Network Assembly (ICONIP'97). Dunedin. New Zealand (1997)

Krsul, I., Spafford, E.H.: Authorship analysis: Identifying the author of a program. In: Proc. 8th National Information Systems Security Conference, pp. 514-524, National Institute of Standards and Technology (1995)

Krsul, I., Spafford, E.H.: 1996, Authorship analysis: Identifying the author of a program, Technical Report TR-96-052 (1996)

Longstaff, T.A., Schultz, E.E.: Beyond Preliminary Analysis of the WANK and OILZ Worms: A Case Study of Malicious Code. Computers and Security 12, 61–77 (1993)

MacDonell, S.G., Gray, A.R.: Software forensics applied to the task of discriminating between program authors. Journal of Systems Research and Information Systems 10, 113–127 (2001)

Oman, P., Cook, C.: Programming style authorship analysis. In: Seventeenth Annual ACM Science Conference Proceedings, pp. 320–326. ACM Press, New York (1989)

Peng, F., Shuurmans, D., Wang, S.: Augmenting naive bayes classifiers with statistical language models. Information Retrieval Journal 7(1), 317–345 (2004)

Sallis, P., Aakjaer, A., MacDonell, S.: Software Forensics: Old Methods for a New Science. In: Proceedings of SE:E&P'96 (Software Engineering: Education and Practice), Dunedin, New Zealand, pp. 367–371. IEEE Computer Society Press, Los Alamitos (1996)

Spafford, E.H.: The Internet Worm Program: An Analysis. Computer Communications Review 19(1), 17–49 (1989)

Spafford, E.H., Weeber, S.A.: Software forensics: tracking code to its authors. Computers and Security 12, 585–595 (1993)

Stamatatos, E., Fakotakis, N., Kokkinakis, G.: Automatic text categorisation in terms of genre and author. Computational Linguistics 26(4), 471–495 (2000)

Part III

Wireless Communication Systems and Networks

Iterative MMSE Detection for MIMO/BLAST DS-CDMA Systems in Frequency Selective Fading Channels – Achieving High Performance in Fully Loaded Systems

João Carlos Silva[1], Nuno Souto[1], Francisco Cercas[1], and Rui Dinis[2]

[1] Instituto Superior Técnico/IT, Torre Norte 11-11, Av. Rovisco Pais 1,
1049-001 Lisboa, Portugal
`joao.carlos.silva@lx.it.pt, nuno.souto@lx.it.pt,`
`francisco.cercas@lx.it.pt`
[2] CAPS, Av. Rovisco Pais 1,1049-001 Lisboa, Portugal
`rdinis@ist.utl.pt`

Abstract. A MMSE (Minimum Mean Square Error) DS-CDMA (Direct Sequence-Code Division Multiple Access) receiver coupled with a low-complexity iterative interference suppression algorithm was devised for a MIMO/BLAST (Multiple Input, Multiple Output / Bell Laboratories Layered Space Time) system in order to improve system performance, considering frequency selective fading channels. The scheme is compared against the simple MMSE receiver, for both QPSK and 16QAM modulations, under SISO (Single Input, Single Output) and MIMO systems, the latter with 2Tx by 2Rx and 4Tx by 4Rx (MIMO order 2 and 4 respectively) antennas. To assess its performance in an existing system, the uncoded UMTS HSDPA (High Speed Downlink Packet Access) standard was considered.

Keywords: MIMO-BLAST, Iterative Interference Canceller, W-CDMA.

1 Introduction

MIMO systems have been considered to be one of the most significant technical breakthroughs in modern communications, since they can augment significantly the system capacity, by increasing the number of both transmit and receive antennas (Foschini, 1998). Just a few years after its invention the technology is already part of the standards for wireless local area networks (WLAN), third-generation (3G) networks and beyond.

The receiver for such a scheme is obviously complex; due to the number of antennas, users and multipath components, the performance of a simple RAKE/ MF (Matched Filter) receiver (or enhanced schemes based on the MF) has a severe interference canceling limitation, that does not allow for the system to perform at full capacity. Therefore, a MMSE receiver (Latva-aho, 2000), adapted for multipath MIMO, was developed for such cases acting as an equalizer, yielding interesting results. In order to further augment the MMSE receiver's performance, an additional low complexity block performing interference suppression was added. Although the MMSE guarantees the minimum variance estimates, some estimates may exceed the

J. Filipe et al. (Eds.): ICETE 2005, CCIS 3, pp. 177–186, 2007.

threshold value in which they are supposed to be. The interference suppression block has a built-in SDD (Soft Decision Device), so that the initial estimates are adjusted in order to minimize their mean square error. The new estimates are then introduced in a iterative Parallel Interference Canceller (PIC) based solely on low complexity matched-filtering, so that a new solution is found within the imposed constraints. Such a scheme produces a performance improvement with little added complexity, when compared to the simple MMSE decoder.

The structure of the paper is as follows. In Section II, the MMSE receiver for MIMO with multipath is introduced. The simulation setup is detailed and results are discussed in Section III. The main conclusions are drawn in Section IV.

2 MMSE Receiver

A standard model for a DS-CDMA system with K users (assuming 1 user per physical channel) and L propagation paths is considered. The modulated symb ls are spread by a Walsh-Hadamard code with length equal to the Spreading Factor (SF). The signal on a MIMO-BLAST system with N_{TX} transmit and N_{RX} receive antennas, at one of the receiver's antennas, can be expressed as:

$$r_v(t)_{RX=1} = \sum_{n=1}^{N}\sum_{tx=1}^{N_{TX}}\sum_{k=1}^{K}\sum_{l=1}^{L} A_{k,tx} b_{k,tx}^{(n)} c_{k,tx,rx}(t) s_k(t-nT-\tau_{k,l}) + n(t)$$ where N is the number of

received symbols, $A_{k,tx} = \sqrt{E_k}$, E_k is the energy per symbol, K is the number of

users, $b_{k,tx}^{(n)}$ is the n-th transmitted data symbol of user k and transmit antenna tx,

$s_k(t)$ is the k-th user's signature signal (equal for all antennas), T denotes the symbol interval, $n(t)$ is a complex zero-mean AWGN (Additive White Gaussian Noise) with

variance σ^2, $c_{k,tx,rx}(t) = \sum_{l=1}^{L} c_{k,tx,rx,l}^{(n)} \delta(t-\tau_{k,l})$ is the impulse response of the k^-

th user's radio channel, $c_{k,tx,rx,l}$ is the complex attenuation factor of the k-ths user's l-th path of the link between the tx-th and rx-th antenna and $\tau_{k,l}$ is the propagation delay

(assumed equal for all antennas).

Using matrix algebra, the received signal can be represented as

$$r_v = S C A b + n,$$

where S, C and A are the spreading, channel and amplitude matrices respectively.

The spreading matrix S has dimensions $(SF \cdot N \cdot N_{RX} + \rho_{MAX} \cdot N_{RX}) \times (K \cdot L \cdot N \cdot N_{RX})$ (ρ_{max} is the maximum delay of the channel's impulse response, normalized to number of chips, and SF is the Spreading Factor), and is composed of sub-matrices S_{RX} in its diagonal for each receive antenna $S = \text{diag}(S_{RX,1},\dots,S_{RX,N_{RX}})$. Each of these sub-matrices has dimensions $(SF \cdot N + \rho_{MAX}) \times (K \cdot L \cdot N)$, and are further composed by smaller matrices S^L_n, one for each bit position, with size $(SF + \rho_{MAX}) \times (K \cdot L)$.

The S_{RX} matrix structure is made of $S_{RX} = \left[S_{SRX,1},\dots,S_{SRX,N} \right]$, with

$$S_{\text{SRX,n}} = \left[0_{(\text{SF}\cdot(n-1))\times(K\cdot L)} ; S_n^L ; 0_{(\text{SF}\cdot(N-n))\times(K\cdot L)} \right]$$

The S^L matrices are made of $K \cdot L$ columns; $S_n^L = \left[S_{\text{col}(k=1,l=1),n}, \cdots, S_{\text{col}(k=1,l=L),n}, \cdots, S_{\text{col}(k=K,l=L),n} \right]$. Each of these columns is composed of $S_{\text{col}(kl),n} = \left[0_{(1\times\text{delay}(l))}, sp_n(k)_{1\times SF}, 0_{(1\times(\rho_{MAX}-\text{delay}(l)))} \right]^T$, where $sp_n(k)$ is the combined spreading & scrambling for the bit n of user k.

These S^L matrices are either all alike if no long scrambling code is used, or different if the scrambling sequence is longer than the SF. The S^L matrices represent the combined spreading and scrambling sequences, conjugated with the channel delays. The shifted spreading vectors for the multipath components are all equal to the original sequence of the specific user.

$$S_n^L = \begin{bmatrix} S_{1,1,1,n} & \cdots & & \cdots & S_{K,1,1,n} & & \\ \vdots & \ddots & S_{1,1,L,n} & \cdots & \vdots & \ddots & S_{K,1,L,n} \\ S_{1,SF,1,n} & & \vdots & \cdots & S_{K,SF,1,n} & & \vdots \\ & \ddots & S_{1,SF,L,n} & \cdots & & \ddots & S_{K,SF,L,n} \end{bmatrix}$$

Note that, in order to correctly model the multipath interference between symbols, there is an overlap between the S^L matrices, of ρ_{MAX}.

The channel matrix C is a $(K \cdot L \cdot N \cdot N_{RX}) \times (K \cdot N_{TX} \cdot N)$ matrix, and is composed of N_{RX} sub-matrices, each one for a receive antenna $C = \left[C_{RX,1}^R ; \cdots ; C_{RX,N_{RX}}^R \right]$. Each C^R matrix is composed of N C^{KT} matrices alongside its diagonals.

$$C = \begin{bmatrix} C_{RX,1}^R = \begin{bmatrix} C_{1,1}^{KT} & & \\ & \ddots & \\ & & C_{N,1}^{KT} \end{bmatrix} & \\ \vdots & \\ C_{RX,N_{RX}}^R = \begin{bmatrix} C_{1,N_{RX}}^{KT} & & \\ & \ddots & \\ & & C_{N,N_{RX}}^{KT} \end{bmatrix} \end{bmatrix}$$

Each C^{KT} matrix is $(K \cdot L) \times (K \cdot N_{TX})$, and represents the fading coefficients for the current symbol of each path, user, transmit antenna and receive antenna. The matrix structure is made up of further smaller matrices alongside the diagonal of C^{KT}, $C^{KT} = \text{diag}\left(C_{K,1}^T, \cdots, C_{K,K}^T \right)$, with C^T of dimensions $L \times N_{TX}$, representing the fading coefficients for the user's multipath and tx-th antenna component.

$$C^{KT} = \begin{bmatrix} C_{1,1,1} & \cdots & C_{N_{TX},1,1} & & & \\ \vdots & & \vdots & & & \\ C_{1,L,1} & \cdots & C_{N_{TX},L,1} & & & \\ & & & \ddots & & \\ & & & & C_{1,1,K} & \cdots & C_{N_{TX},1,K} \\ & & & & \vdots & & \vdots \\ & & & & C_{1,L,K} & \cdots & C_{N_{TX},L,K} \end{bmatrix}$$

The A matrix is a diagonal matrix of dimension $(K \cdot N_{TX} \cdot N)$, and represents the amplitude of each user per transmission antenna and symbol, $A = \text{diag}\left(A_{1,1,1}, \ldots, A_{N_{TX},1,1}, \ldots, A_{N_{TX},K,1}, \ldots, A_{N_{TX},K,N}\right)$.

The matrix resultant from the *SCA* operation (henceforth known as *SCA* matrix) is depicted in Figure 1. It is a $N_{TX} \cdot K \cdot N \times N_{RX} \cdot (N \cdot SF + \rho_{MAX})$ matrix, and is the reference matrix for the decoding algorithms.

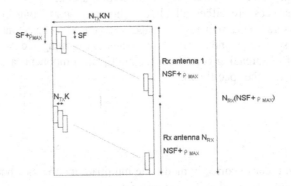

Fig. 1. Layout of the SCA matrix

Vector **b** represents the information symbols. It has length $\left(K \cdot N_{TX} \cdot N\right)$, and has the following structure $b = \left[b_{1,1,1}, \ldots, b_{N_{TX},1,1}, \ldots, b_{1,K,1}, \ldots, b_{N_{TX},K,1}, \ldots, b_{N_{TX},K,N}\right]^T$. Note that the bits of each transmit antenna are grouped together in the first level, and the bits of other interferers in the second level. This is to guarantee that the resulting matrix to be inverted has all its non-zeros values as close to the diagonal as possible. Also note that there is usually a higher correlation between bits from different antennas using the same spreading code, than between bits with different spreading codes.

Finally, the **n** vector is a $\left(N \cdot SF \cdot N_{RX} + N_{RX} \cdot \rho_{MAX}\right)$ vector with noise components to be added to the received vector r_v, which is partitioned by N_{RX} antennas, $r_v = \left[r_{1,1,1}, \ldots, r_{1,SF,1}, \ldots, r_{N,1,1}, \ldots, r_{N,SF+\rho_{MAX},1}, \ldots, r_{N,1,N_{RX}}, \ldots, r_{N,SF+\rho_{MAX},N_{RX}}\right]^T$ (note that the delay ρ_{MAX} is only contemplated in the final bit, though its effects are present throughout r_v).

The MMSE algorithm yields the symbol estimates,

$$y_{MMSE} = \left(E_M\right)^{-1} y_{MF}$$

Where y_{MF} is the (un-normalized) matched filter output

$$y_{MF} = \left(SCA\right)^H r_v$$

and the E_M is the Equalization Matrix (cross-correlation matrix of the users' signature sequences after matched filtering, at the receiver)

$$E_M = R + \sigma^2 I$$

with $R = A \times C^H \times S^H \times S \times C \times A$ and σ^2 as the noise variance of *n*.

The configuration is done in such a way that the E_M presents itself as if the Sparse Reverse Cuthill-McKee ordering algorithm (Liu, 1981) had been applied to it, and thus there is no fill-in when performing the E_M inverse using the Choleski algorithm. The expected main problem associated with such scheme is the size of the matrices, which assume huge proportions. This has been the main perceived drawback of such scheme, responsible for the reduced amount of work of MMSE-based schemes in MIMO and frequency selective channels. However, if the sparseness of the matrices is taken into account, only a fraction of the memory and computing power is required.

The Enhanced-MMSE (E-MMSE) receiver adds a PIC after the MMSE algorithm. The cancelling algorithm consists of removing the estimated interference from the matched filter result. The initial estimate is obtained from the MMSE result.

$$\hat{b}_1 = SDD\left(y_{MMSE}, \sigma^2_{estim}\right)$$

where σ^2_{MMSE} is the noise variance of y_{MMSE}. The cancellation operates on the MF result, and is simply the simultaneous removal of all influences that the symbols have on each other, throughout the transmission and receiver operations, in the absence of noise (accomplished with the removal of the main diagonal of R)

$$\hat{c}_{n+1} = y_{MF} - \left(R - diag\left(R\right)\right)\hat{b}_n$$

The result is then normalized and passed through the SDD, becoming the estimate for the next iteration

$$\hat{b}_{n+1} = SDD\left(\hat{c}_{n+1} \odot C_{NORM}, \sigma^2_{MMSE}\right)$$

where $\odot$ represents element-wise multiplication. The normalization consists simply of inverting the main diagonal of R, $c_{NORM} = diag\left(R\right)^{-1}$, so as to compensate for the spreading, amplitude, channel power and cross-correlation between symbols. The function $sdd()$ is the soft decision device function and $diag()$ refers to all the elements in the diagonal of a matrix. Note that the initial MMSE output does not need any normalization, since this is accomplished by the equalization from the E_M.

The SDD is based on the assumption that the remaining noise in the estimates is essentially AWGN (Divsalar, 1998), being taken as optimum under this assumption. Taking x as either the real or imaginary component of the symbol, and considering that the real and imaginary part of the QPSK constellation both consist of $\{-1,1\}$, the SDD for the QPSK modulation is given by $y = \tanh\left(\frac{x}{\sigma^2_x}\right)$.

Applying the same reasoning for the 16QAM case (assuming that the real/imaginary constellation components point have values of $\{-3,-1,1,3\}$), we get

$$y = \frac{3e^{-\frac{4}{\sigma^2_x}}\sinh\left(\frac{3x}{\sigma^2_x}\right) + \sinh\left(\frac{x}{\sigma^2_x}\right)}{e^{\frac{4}{\sigma^2_x}}\cosh\left(\frac{3x}{\sigma^2_x}\right) + \cosh\left(\frac{x}{\sigma^2_x}\right)}$$

where σ^2_x is the noise power of each real/imaginary component of the symbol prior to SDD.

Figure 2 illustrates the PIC. The added complexity to the MMSE algorithm is negligible since the main system matrices (S,C,A,R) required by the PIC have already been computed for the MMSE operation. The iterative algorithm only needs to multiply the current estimated symbol by pre-defined matrices, while performing the SDD. The main difference from the PIC structure shown to conventional PIC schemes is the fact that this new scheme makes use of the MMSE's structure and thus is able to correctly estimate the interference caused by ISI (Inter-Symbolic Interference) and MAI (Multiple Access Interference), aside the thermal noise component. The used normalization factor is also improved since, besides containing the effect of spreading and channel power, it contains the cross-correlation effects caused by multipath, which in conventional receivers isn't used.

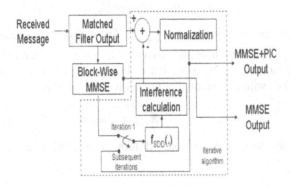

Fig. 2. PIC Structure

3 Simulation Setup and Results

This work was inspired on the uncoded 3G HSDPA standard, and thus considers a SF=16 using Hadamard codes, QPSK and 16QAM modulation, a chip rate of 3.84 Mcps and a Gold-sequence scrambling code. Each TX antenna can thus host a maximum of 16 physical channels. One user per physical channel is assumed. Simulations were run for SISO and MIMO orders 2 and 4, so that all the expected future UE types were covered. Minimum and full loading (0 and 15 interferers per transmit antenna respectively, assuming that the main user is using the first physical channel of each antenna) was considered. The E-MMSE scheme used cancellation of two iterations after the MMSE decoding. Blocks of 1024 bits per physical channel per antenna were used.

The main UMTS channels, namely Indoor A, Pedestrian A and Vehicular A (taken from (3GPP TR 25.943)) were simulated. Since only 1 sample per chip was used in the simulations, the channels were adjusted to the chip delay time of 260ns, using the constant mean delay spread method (Silva, 2003). For the particular case of Vehicular A, since the method yields 8 taps, with the last ones having low power levels, an adjustment was made so that only the main taps were considered. The resulting channels are depicted in Figure 3. The considered velocities were 50km/h for Vehicular A and 3km/h for the remaining channels.

IndA	delay (chips)	0	1		
	% received power	90,63%	9,37%		
PedA	delay (chips)	0	1		
	% received power	94,98%	5,02%		
VehA	delay (chips)	0	1	3	4
	% received power	49,50%	39,32%	6,23%	4,95%

Fig. 3. Resulting UMTS channels

The Monte Carlo method was employed for the simulations. All results were portrayed for received E_b/N_0 values *vs* BER (Bit Error Rate). For the sake of comparison, we also considered the simple MMSE receiver.

Based on the results of figure 4, only two PIC iterations are needed to achieve the best results; all results in the posterior figures thus consider only two iterations for the E-MMSE scheme.

In figures 5-8, the E-MMSE results for different MIMO orders, channels, modulations and loadings can be observed. The performance curves are parallel to the MMSE results, though a little deviated to the left; i.e. there is an offset of the curves corresponding to the performance gain over MMSE. Figures 9-11 compare some of the results of the E-MMSE to the simple MMSE algorithm.

For the SISO case without interference, there is a negligible difference between the E-MMSE and MMSE. This was expected, since the canceller is only rearranging the results so that the estimates symbols do not exceed their thresholds. For the MIMO 2x2 case without interference, differences between 1dB and 2dB can be found between channels and modulations, with the biggest differences being registered for QPSK modulations (due to smaller probabilities of bit errors, and thus having a very small error propagation in the canceling algorithm).

In the full loading scenario (15 interferers), differences over 5dB and 3dB can be found for QPSK and 16QAM respectively. The differences are greater than for the case of minimum loading, due to the PIC canceling interference from other users, thus being more effective.

3.1   E-MMSE Results

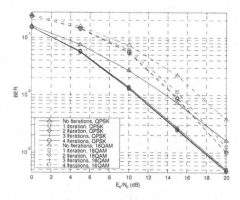

Fig. 4. BER performance for E-MMSE, Vehicular A channel, MIMO 2x2, 15 interferers - effect on number of cancelling stages.

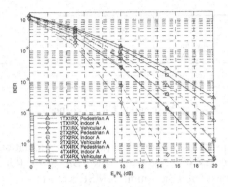

Fig. 5. E-MMSE scheme – QPSK modulation, 0 interferers

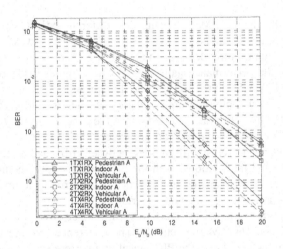

Fig. 6. E-MMSE scheme – QPSK modulation, 15 interferers

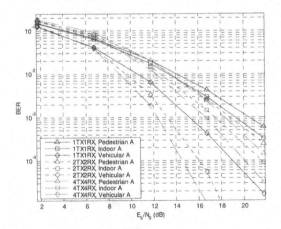

Fig. 7. E-MMSE scheme – 16QAM modulation, 0 interferers

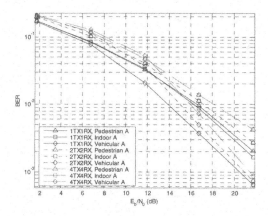

Fig. 8. E-MMSE scheme – 16QAM modulation, 15 interferers

3.2 E-MMSE vs. MMSE Comparison

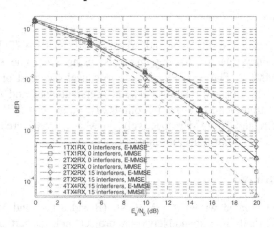

Fig. 9. E-MMSE vs MMSE scheme – QPSK modulation, Pedestrian A channel

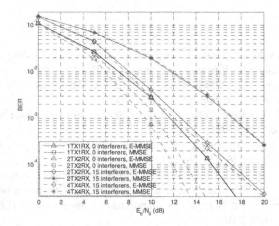

Fig. 10. E-MMSE vs MMSE scheme – QPSK modulation, Vehicular A channel

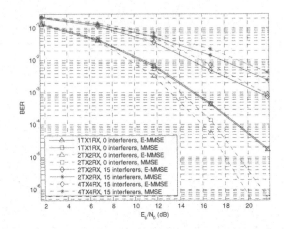

Fig. 11. E-MMSE vs MMSE scheme – 16QAM modulation, Vehicular A channel

4 Conclusions

In this work, an iterative PIC was added to a MIMO-BLAST MMSE receiver considering frequency-selective fading channels, using the same structure as that required by the MMSE. The used PIC is able to cancel out most of the interference caused by multipath, cross-correlation between users/antennas and thermal noise. It was shown that with a small increase in complexity, gains over 5dB and 3dB can be achieved for QPSK and 16QAM respectively, in what is considered one of the best joint-detection receiver algorithms presently.

Acknowledgements

This paper was elaborated within the B-BONE (Broadcasting and Multicasting over Enhanced UMTS Mobile Broadband Networks) project, and was partially funded by the Foundation of Science and Technology (FCT), of the Portuguese Ministry of Education.

References

Foschini, G.J., Gans, M.J.: On limits of wireless communications in a fading environment when using multiple antennas. Wireless Pers. Commun. 6, 311–335 (1998)

Latva-aho, M., Juntti, M.: LMMSE Detection for DS-CDMA Systems in Fading Channels. IEEE Transactions on Communications 48(2) (2000)

George, A., Liu, J.: Computer Solution of Large Sparse Positive Definite Systems. Prentice-Hall, Englewood Cliffs (1981)

Divsalar, D., Simon, M., Raphaeli, D.: Improved Parallel Interference Cancellation in CDMA. IEEE Trans. Commun. 46, 258–268 (1998)

3GPP, Deployment aspects, 3GPP TR 25.943 v5.1.0, Sophia Antipolis, France (2002)

Silva, J.C., Souto, N., Rodrigues, A., Cercas, F., Correia, A.: Conversion of reference tapped delay line channel models to discrete time channel models. In: VTC03 Fall, Orlando, Florida (October 6-9, 2003)

Flooding Attack on the Binding Cache in Mobile IPv6*

Christian Veigner and Chunming Rong

University of Stavanger, N-4036, Norway
christian.veigner@uis.no, chunming.rong@uis.no

Abstract. In the next generation Internet protocol (IPv6), mobility is supported by means of Mobile IPv6 (MIPv6). As a default part of the MIPv6 protocol, route optimization is used to route packets directly to a mobile node's currently used address at the mobile node's visited subnet. Return Routability is the protocol suggested by the IETF for managing this task. Route optimization is often carried out during handovers, where a mobile node changes network attachment from one subnet to another. To offer seamless handovers to the user it is important that route optimizations are carried out quickly. In this paper we will present an attack that was discovered during design of a new and more seamless protocol than the Return Routability. Our improved route optimization protocol for Mobile IPv6 suffers this attack; therefore we wanted to investigate if a similar attack was feasible on the Return Routability protocol. In this paper, we show that our new route optimization protocol offers no less security than the already standardized Return Routability protocol in this field.

Keywords: Binding Cache flooding attack, Mobile IPv6, Return Routability, ROM.

1 Introduction

Route optimization is introduced to the *Mobile IPv6* (MIPv6) protocol (Johnson, 2004). However, it is important that the new feature doesn't result in new vulnerabilities to the IPv6 protocol. If not properly designed, it is believed that certain attacks on this optimization protocol could cause serious problems to the stability of the entire Internet. Hence, it is most important to investigate different attacks and their countermeasures.

Authentication of *mobile nodes* (MNs) is one of the most important features of such a mobility protocol. Initially, strong authentication was thought to be the only solution, and IPsec was at some point of time believed to be the best fit for this purpose. Due to the fact that IPsec, in addition to other protocols that relies on additional infrastructure, is not very scalable, the strong authentication demand evolved into a weaker authentication demand. The lack of scalability when using IPsec, stem from the key exchange necessity of each pair of communicating nodes. The protocol finally suggested by the IETF was the *Return Routability* (RR) (Johnson, 2004).

---

* This work was supported by UiS 95310, Rogaland University Fund.

J. Filipe et al. (Eds.): ICETE 2005, CCIS 3, pp. 187–200, 2007.
© Springer-Verlag Berlin Heidelberg 2007

As an example, RR decreases an attacker's range of launching a redirecting attack (Deng, 2002) from the entire Internet, to the necessity of being on the route between MN's *home agent* (HA) and one of MN's *corresponding nodes* (CNs). The HA is a node at MN's home subnet that cooperates with MN when MN is visiting a foreign subnet. Any other node communicating with MN is referred to as a CN. The redirecting attack is possible due to weak authentication. However, this is a huge improvement, reducing an attacker's range from the entire Internet to the HA-CN route, without the need of any additional infrastructure.

Focusing on the main drawback of the RR protocol, the possibility of experiencing lack of seamless handovers, we designed *a new route optimization protocol for Mobile IPv6 (ROM)* (Veigner, 2004). This protocol intends to decrease the latency of route optimization when actually needed, that is, when the MN suddenly changes subnet.

We investigate (Veigner, 2004) to which extent the ROM protocol suffers from redirecting attacks (Deng, 2002), bombing attacks (Aura, 2002), amplification attacks (Aura, 2002) and flooding attacks. Flooding attacks on route optimization protocols in general are briefly described in (Nikander, 2005).

During analyses of the ROM protocol design, we discovered that flooding attacks on a corresponding node's (CN's) *binding cache* (BC) easily might be carried out. A BC is a cache allocated at CN's for storing bindings between home and foreign addresses of mobile nodes. A *flooding attack* aims to fill such BCs with spurious entries. A CN may thereby be unable to perform route optimization with new MNs.

In this paper we will further describe flooding attacks in detail, and also show to which extent such attacks are feasible on the Return Routability (RR) protocol as well as on our ROM protocol.

Even though the RR protocol does not store any state at a CN before the initiating MN's authenticity is verified, we will show that flooding attacks on a CN's BC are possible.

The rest of this paper is organized as follows. In Section 2, an introduction to route optimization and the binding cache (BC) is given. Section 3 introduces our ROM protocol design and exemplifies the BC flooding attack. Section 4 focuses on the RR protocol and elaborates the possibilities of similar BC flooding attacks on the RR protocol. Finally our paper is concluded in Section 5.

2   Route Optimization and the Binding Cache

The key advantage of *route optimization* is a corresponding node's (CN's) ability to continue its session with a MN over an optimal route, even when the MN changes its point of attachment to the Internet. Now the MN's home agent (HA) does not have to reroute all of MN's incoming packets to MN's dynamically changing location. Due to route optimization, latency of data transmissions and bandwidth misuse may be substantially reduced.

A MN having an ongoing session with a CN is shown in figure 1. If the MN moves to another subnet (figure 1), the packets should be routed directly from CN to MN as

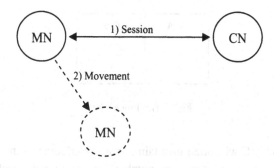

Fig. 1. Movement of a mobile node

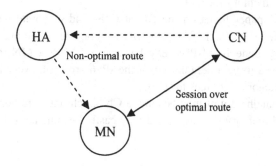

Fig. 2. Route optimization

shown in figure 2 (route optimization). The alternative suboptimal solution is seen as dotted lines in figure 2. The other way around however, sending packets directly from MN to CN (also shown in figure 2), is a problem solved long ago (Johnson, 2004), and will hence not be discussed in this paper.

By means of route optimization, only the initial packets from a CN may be routed through the MN's HA. This may occur if the CN has no entry of the receiving MN in its binding cache (BC). The CN thereby assumes that MN is situated at its home subnet. Whenever a packet forwarded by the HA arrives at the MN, MN initiates route optimization, informing the CN of its current location. The remaining packets from CN may from now on be routed directly to MN.

We will now give a brief introduction to the binding cache (BC) located at CNs. Mobile and fixed nodes are not differentiated in IPv6; thereby a packet-sending node always has to check its BC for an entry of the receiving node before a packet is transmitted. If an entry exists, the transmitting node must route its packets directly to the MN's care-of address (CoA).

Generally, a BC contains *home addresses* (HoAs) and *care-of addresses* (CoAs) of mobile nodes (MNs). This is shown in figure 3. A HoA is the address of a MN at its home subnet and a CoA is the address currently associated with the MN at its visited subnet. This information is contained in a CN's BC for each of the MNs that the CN has been in contact with recently.

HoA	CoA
⋮	⋮

Fig. 3. Binding cache

Additionally, the BC will often maintain remaining lifetime of these bindings, and maybe the highest received sequence number associated with each binding. The sequence numbers may be used for replay attack prevention. Both CNs and HAs must be able to allocate memory for a BC.

We will in this paper focus on the BC at CNs, and elaborate the possibility of launching a BC flooding attack, filling the BC with non-real bindings of non-existing MNs. Since every node in MIPv6 may become a CN to a MN, and the MIPv6 protocol is supposed to be a default part of the IPv6 protocol, every IPv6 node must able to allocate memory resources for a BC.

Even a small handheld unit may become a CN. Such units are normally equipped with quite limited memory resources, and may easily become targets of BC flooding attacks.

3   The ROM Protocol

In this section an overview of our ROM protocol is given. The protocol is described in more depth in (Veigner, 2004). The ROM protocol is supposed to be an alternative to, and a more seamless protocol than the IETF Return Routability (RR) protocol (Johnson, 2004). Hopefully, ROM offers security characteristics similar to the RR protocol.

A MN uses the ROM protocol to assign a unique hash value to its currently used CN. The hash value is sent via the HA. Simultaneously the home subnet of MN is authenticated by the CN by means of a three-way handshake. When moving into a new subnet, MN now only has to send a *binding update* (BU) message directly to the CN. The CN considers the BU message authentic due to MN's knowledge of the nonce value. The nonce value included in the BU message was previously used when generating CN's unique hash value. Routing packets over the optimal route may now begin.

The main part of the ROM protocol messages is shown in figure 4. These messages are sent in advance of MN's movement to a new subnet. The messages shown in figure 5 are sent as the final part of the handover procedure when MN arrives at its new subnet.

We will now introduce the messages of our ROM protocol. We'll start with the messages of figure 4. For more in depth explanation, see (Veigner, 2004).

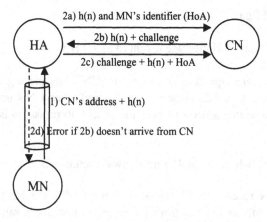

Fig. 4. The ROM protocol

Message 1: This message is sent by the MN to its HA. It contains the address of a CN and a unique hash value (h(n)). This message might of course contain a *list* of CNs and unique hash values for increased efficiency.

Message 2a: The received hash value is sent to the CN's address, along with MN's identifier (HoA). The source address of the 2a message is the address of the HA.

Message 2b: CN returns the hash value and includes a challenge for the HA.
Message 2c: HA returns the challenge, and once again the hash value is sent along with MN's HoA address. CN may thereby remain stateless until the MN's home subnet is authenticated by the 2a - 2c procedure.

Message 2d: If the HA doesn't receive a 2b message in reply of a 2a message, HA notifies MN of CN's absence. It is now in vain to proceed with the route optimization protocol with this CN.

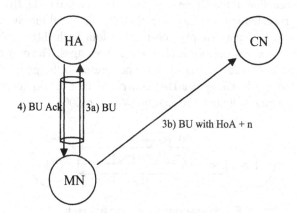

Fig. 5. BU messages sent from MN's new location

The messages of figure 5 are as follows.

Message 3a: An ordinary BU message is sent to MN's HA.

Message 3b: A BU message is also sent to the CN. This message contains MN's identifier (HoA) and the nonce value previously used when CN's unique hash value was generated. The source address of both the 3a and 3b messages is the MN's CoA address.

Message 4: As in the RR protocol, HA must always return a BUAck message.

Whenever a CN receives a BU message from a MN, the hash value used for authenticating the MN is deleted from its cache. A new hash value must now be assigned to the CN, otherwise CN will be unable to authenticate MN's next BU message, if one is ever to arrive.

We will in the following introduce a BC flooding attack on the ROM protocol.

3.1 BC Flooding Attack on the ROM Protocol

A BC flooding attack aims to flood a CN's BC with spurious bindings of non-existing nodes. A CN, which may be any node in an IPv6 network, must be able to allocate memory resources for this BC, mapping home addresses (HoAs) to care-of addresses (CoAs).

We will not go into all the details of our ROM protocol design in this paper, but rather focus on the possible binding cache (BC) flooding attack. Later on, in Section 4.1 and Section 4.2, we will show to which extent a similar attack may be launched on the RR protocol.

Due to the three-way handshake of the ROM protocol, an Eve may attack a CN from anywhere in the entire Internet.

As shown in figure 6, we may consider an Eve transmitting a 2a message to its victim CN. On reception of the 2b message from the attacked node, Eve replies with a 2c message. By repeatedly doing this, Eve may be able to fill the BC at the attacked CN. In this attack, Eve may simply generate random hash (h(n)) values and HoA addresses, and insert a new pair for each of her 2a messages. The only requirement is that the HoA addresses must be equal in subnet prefix to the prefix of the address used by Eve when Eve is acting as a HA. Otherwise the CN will not reply with a 2b message, and the attack will not be successful (Veigner, 2004).

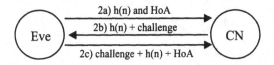

Fig. 6. Attacking a CN's binding cache

HoA	h(n)	CoA	Seq#	Lifetime

Fig. 7. The BC at CNs in the ROM protocol

Even though Eve has to send twice as many messages as the attacked node, Eve may easily carry out her BC flooding attack.

The BC at CNs when using the ROM protocol is shown in figure 7. For each of the MNs that carry out route optimization with the CN, a new row is added to the CN's BC. Each row consists of the following: The mapping from MN's home address (HoA) to its care-of address (CoA), a hash value (h(n)), a sequence number containing highest received sequence number from MN, and finally, remaining lifetime of MN's current binding.

The described BC flooding attack aims to flood the HoA, h(n) and Lifetime columns of the BC. The CoA and Seq# values are only added if a verifiable BU message is received later on (Veigner, 2004).

A MN's BC entry is deleted after 420 seconds if not updated (Veigner, 2004). By re-initiating the ROM protocol, a legitimate MN may update its entry in CN's BC. This solution was chosen for several reasons. The first reason was the fact that there are no known existing one-way hash functions yet. By restricting the valid time of an entry to 420 seconds, and at the same time using a fairly secure hash function, we obtain a one-way hash function for the duration of the 420 seconds. No adversary is able to divert a valid nonce value of an eavesdropped hash value, and is thereby unable to launch a redirecting attack (Veigner, 2004). Due to this 420 seconds validity, a MN must during this period send its BU message to authenticate its current location. Otherwise, a new protocol run is required to update the CN with a new hash value. Another reason for including this validity period in our protocol was to delete unused entries from a CN's BC. As mentioned, a CN may be any node, even a node with limited resources allocating memory for such a BC. Thereby, it is beneficial to delete entries that are not in use.

As a bonus, the described BC flooding attack on the ROM protocol suffers from the deletion of BC entries. An attacker must now be very efficient, or launch the attack in a distributed manner, to flood the attacked BC within 420 seconds.

When the BC flooding attack on the ROM protocol was discovered, it became in our interest to search for a similar attack feasible on the RR protocol. Studying (Hinden, 2003) gave us the idea of how this could be done. The attack is introduced in Section 4.1 and Section 4.2.

4   The Return Routability (RR) Protocol

In this section an overview of the RR protocol is given. RR is the route optimization protocol suggested by the IETF for authenticating a MN's binding update (BU) message sent to a CN. Whenever a MN moves from one subnet to another, it has to initiate route optimization with its CNs. When updating its binding at a CN, MN has to send and receive the messages of figure 8. The message exchange with the CN is carried out subsequent to the BU and BUAck message exchange with the HA. In RR, the message exchange of figure 8 is carried out when MN arrives at its new subnet.

In brief, the MN receives a key-generated token in the HoT message and another key-generated token in the CoT message. When a BU message is finally sent from MN to CN, MN must use its received tokens to make CN confident in MN's authenticity. MN has shown its ability to receive tokens at its two stated addresses (HoA and CoA) via two different routes, and is thereby authenticated by CN (weak authentication). The data from CN may now be routed directly to MN's new CoA address.

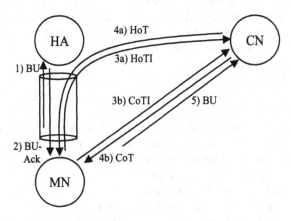

Fig. 8. The Return Routability protocol

We now introduce the RR protocol messages. Message 1 and message 2 are left out. The so-called home routability test and the care-of routability test are the two parts of the RR procedure.

The *home routability test* consists of the HoTI and HoT messages. The *care-of routability test* consists of the CoTI and CoT messages.

$$HoTI = \{HoA, CN, C_h\}$$

The HoTI message comprises the following. The home address (HoA) of the MN is the source address and the CN's address is the destination address. A home init cookie generated by MN is included. This cookie is returned in the response message from CN. MN is now able to match request with response. The HoTI message is reverse tunnelled through MN's HA.

$$CoTI = \{CoA, CN, C_c\}$$

The CoTI message consists of the following. The care-of address (CoA) of the MN appears as the source address. The care-of address is the address used by MN at its foreign subnet. The destination address of the message is the CN's address. A care-of init cookie generated by MN is also included. This cookie must be returned in the response message from CN.

$$HoT = \{CN, HoA, C_h, Token_h, i\}$$

CN generates the HoT message on reception of the HoTI message. This message is sent from CN to MN's HoA address. It is the HA at MN's home subnet that is responsible for redirecting the HoT message to MN when MN is away from its home subnet. On reception of the HoT message, MN uses the C_h cookie to match request with response. MN is now in possession of a key generated token called *home keygen token* ($Token_h$).

$$Token_h = First (64, HMAC\_SHA1 (K_{CN}, (HoA| nonce_i|0)))$$

The CN generates the home keygen token by using the first 64 output bits from a MAC function. Input to the MAC function is CN's secret key (K_{CN}) and the concatenation of MN's HoA address, a nonce value and a 0 octet.

The final parameter of the HoT message is the home nonce index (i). MN must later on return this index in its BU message. The CN may thereby remain stateless until the BU message is received. From a list at the CN, containing valid nonce values, the correct nonce value is easily recovered due to this index. The CN may then regenerate the home keygen token. Both the MN and CN use this token in the generation of their shared *binding management key* (K_{bm}). Another token is also needed in the binding management key generation. This token is sent to the MN in the CoT message.

$$CoT = \{CN, CoA, C_c, Token_c, j\}$$

CN generates a CoT message on reception of the CoTI message. The address of CN is source and the MN's CoA address as destination. This message is sent directly to MN at its current location. The cookie from the CoTI message is included, and a *care-of keygen token* ($Token_c$) is generated quite similar to the $Token_h$.

$$Token_c = First (64, HMAC\_SHA1 (K_{CN}, (CoA| nonce_j|1)))$$

Finally the care-of nonce index (j) is included in the CoT message. Later on this index is returned in the BU message from MN. Thereby helping the stateless CN identifying the nonce value used in the generation of the care-of keygen token ($Token_c$).

The MN is now in possession of both the keygen tokens and may generate a binding management key by hashing the tokens in the following way:

$$K_{bm} = SHA1 (Token_h|Token_c)$$

Finally the RR procedure is finished. The MN may now generate and send its BU message to the CN.

$$BU = \{CoA, CN, HoA, Seq\#, LT, i, j, MAC_{BU}\}$$

$$MAC_{BU} = First (96, HMAC\_SHA1 (K_{bm}, (CoA| CN|BU)))$$

In the BU message, MN's CoA address is source and the CN's address is destination. The MN's home address (HoA), a sequence number, proposed lifetime for the binding and the nonce indices are all part of the BU message. The HoA and indices are needed by the CN to be able to regenerate the keygen tokens. The CoA is also needed for this purpose. A MAC is finally appended to the BU message.

On reception of the BU message, the CN generates the K_{bm} from its regenerated keygen tokens. By use of the K_{bm}, CN is able to verify the MAC. Whenever a BU message is considered authentic, CN updates its binding cache (BC) with an entry of the MN.

4.1 BC Flooding Attack on the RR Protocol I

In this section we introduce our BC flooding attack on the RR protocol.

In general, whenever there is a cache or buffer that needs to be allocated memory resources, attackers might try to take advantage of it. An attacker may simply fill such storages with random data, resulting in others, non-fraudulent nodes, impossibility of updating the storages with usable information.

An attack with similar outcome as our proposed attack is briefly described in (Nikander, 2005). An attacker sends a spoofed packet to a MN. The packet appears to originate from a CN wanting to initiate communication with the MN. The CN is the attacked node in this scenario. The packet must be sent via the MN's home subnet, i.e. non-optimized routing. On reception of the packet, MN will initiate route optimization with the attacked CN. The protocol will be executed according to the specifications, and an entry of the MN will be added to the CN's BC. The proposed attack (Nikander, 2005) manage to flood the attacked CN's BC only if a sufficient number of entries are added to the BC before to many previously added entries starts expiring. In other words, the cache must be filled to maximum capacity, leaving the attacked node unable to perform route optimization with other MNs. To succeed in its attack, the attacking node must know the addresses of sufficiently many MNs. Unless such a MN is a MN away from its home subnet, the attacker will not succeed in getting the MN to initiate the Return Routability protocol with the attacked node.

However, the described attack is possible against any binding update authentication protocol, but finding sufficiently many MNs to succeed in the attack, might become challenging. Ingress filtering also renders the attack more difficult, since it makes it harder to forge the source address of the spoofed packets. We will therefore introduce a new way of launching BC flooding attacks on the RR protocol, showing that RR as well as our ROM protocol easily may become target of BC flooding attacks.

An IPv6 node may allocate several IPv6 addresses to a single interface (Hinden, 2003). This gave us the idea of how a CN may be victim to a similar BC flooding attack when using the RR protocol, as when using the ROM protocol.

Consider an Eve configuring lots of IPv6 addresses to a single interface. This may be done in an IPv6 stateless address autoconfiguration manner (Thomson, 1998). Eve is now associated with several IPv6 addresses, all with subnet prefixes equal to the prefix of the subnet where Eve is located.

Finally, by having two Eves at different subnets, both associated with lots of IPv6 addresses as shown in figure 9, the BC flooding attack is possible.

The attack may be launched in the following way. If Eve_1 initiates a home routability test with a victim node as shown in figure 10, i.e. sends a HoTI message to the victim, she will receive a HoT message in reply. The HoT message contains a home keygen token ($Token_h$). To the attacked CN, the source address of the HoTI

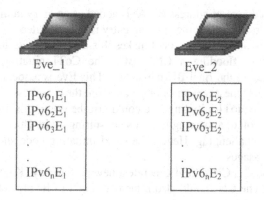

Fig. 9. Two Eves, both associated with numerous IPv6 addresses

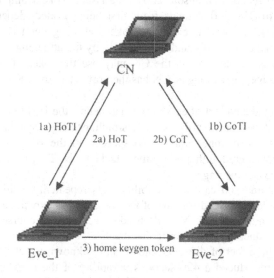

Fig. 10. Flooding attack on CN's BC

message seams to be the home address (HoA) of a legitimate MN. But in this attack, the address is actually one of Eve_1's previously configured addresses.

If Eve_2 initiates a care-of routability test she will receive a CoT message, and will thereby also be in possession of a keygen token, not a home keygen token ($Token_h$), but a care-of keygen token ($Token_c$).

Now, if Eve_1 forwards her $Token_h$ to Eve_2, Eve_2 will be capable of sending a verifiable BU message to the attacked CN. The BU message must be generated using the binding management key (K_{bm}). This key is generated by means of the received keygen tokens.

From the attacked CN's point of view, it seams as if a MN with HoA address equal to the address used by Eve_1 has moved to the address used by Eve_2. Whenever a verifiable BU message is received, a mapping from the MN's HoA address to the

MN's currently used care-of address (CoA) is added as an entry in the CN's BC. If an entry of this MN already exists, the existing entry is only updated.

The functionality of the RR protocol makes this a perfectly feasible attack, having *two* conspiring Eves flooding a CN's BC. The CoTI-initiating Eve should be responsible for sending the final BU messages. This Eve is associated with the CoA addresses, and the BU messages must originate from these addresses to succeed in the attack. However, the HoTI initiating Eve could also be doing this, but then its source address must be spoofed, appearing to be its conspiring node. Due to ingress filtering this might become challenging. Hence, the CoTI initiating node should generally be sending the BU messages.

In the RR protocol, a CN should generate a new private key (K_{CN}) and nonce value every 30 seconds. The CN should also remember eight of its previously used private keys and nonce values. A private key and nonce value pair is used as a part of the keygen token generation. If every K_{CN} and nonce value pair is employed by CN for the duration of 30 seconds (Johnson, 2004), the issued $Token_h$ and $Token_c$ are valid for the duration of 210–240 seconds from first being issued, depending on where within the 30 seconds time interval the tokens were generated by the CN. To summarize; the tokens are valid, and may be used by the attacking Eves to generate a verifiable BU message, as long as the CN may use the tokens to authenticate the received BU message, i.e. as long as CN has the previously used K_{CN} and nonce value in its memory.

The tokens are independent of each other, and hence, the HoTI and CoTI messages of figure 10 must not necessarily be sent simultaneously. Synchronization of the attacking Eves is hence unnecessary. To succeed in the BC flooding attack, the tokens must be considered authentic by the attacked CN. This is verified by the CN on reception of the BU message.

Initiating the home and care-of routability tests repeatedly, using the previously configured IPv6 addresses, and sending of BU messages as explained, may eventually fill the BC at the attacked CN. New IPv6 addresses may of course be dynamically configured by the attacking Eves during the attack.

To minimize the effect of different known and unknown attacks, the designers of the RR protocol introduced a 420 seconds durability of the mapping from a MN's HoA address to the MN's CoA address. If not updated, MN's entry in CN's BC is deleted. In addition to making different attacks more complicated, the deletion of BC entries is used as memory management. A CN may delete entries from its BC when not in use.

Due to the removal of BC entries, even an honest MN must initiate the RR procedure and send new BU messages to its CNs at least every 420 seconds. This feature was also used in the design of our ROM protocol. Attackers must now execute their BC flooding attacks within a 420 seconds time interval.

4.2 BC Flooding Attack on the RR Protocol II

IPv6 will continue to use the model from IPv4 (Hinden, 2003); a subnet prefix is associated with one link and multiple subnet prefixes may be assigned to the same link, e.g. an Ethernet. This will ease our flooding attack, reducing the need of two cooperating Eves to launch the attack, to only one Eve. If the subnet where an Eve is located is assigned multiple subnet prefixes, Eve may act as both Eve_1 and Eve_2. Eve may now configure lots of IPv6 addresses using two different subnet prefixes. Eve may then by herself launch the attack of Section 4.1. Of course Eve may have to be a more powerful node in this attack scenario than in the scenario of Section 4.1.

Since every node in MIPv6 may become a CN of a MN, and the MIPv6 protocol is supposed to be a default part of the IPv6 protocol, any IPv6 node may be victim to this BC flooding attack. However, attacking a node that is often used as a CN by other MNs, will be more harmful than attacking a node that is never used, and hence not in need of its BC.

5 Conclusion

Return Routability (RR) is the route optimization protocol suggested by the IETF (Johnson, 2004). RR is used to authenticate binding updates sent from mobile nodes (MNs) to corresponding nodes (CNs). Our ROM protocol (Veigner, 2004) intends to make MIPv6 route optimization more seamless than RR manage; in other words, to speed up the procedure and at the same time provide similar security characteristics. The importance of the protocol being seamless is the fact that route optimizations are often carried out during a MN's handover from one subnet to another.

This paper focuses on flooding attacks on the binding cache (BC) at CNs, and shows to which extent the RR protocol as well as our ROM protocol is vulnerable to such attacks.

Certain countermeasures have been suggested. The 420 seconds durability of BC entries is already included in both protocols. Nevertheless, the BC flooding attack discovered on the IETF suggested RR protocol is important to point out. Another countermeasure is to keep the number of entries allowed in a BC low. This is not necessarily a good solution, making DoS attacks easier to carry out by means of BC flooding attacks. Strong authentication was also considered, but the solution has a major disadvantage in scalability due to the lack of a global PKI. Use of asymmetric cryptography would also be a very CPU-consuming feature; resulting in increased DoS attack vulnerabilities.

As we all know, bandwidth in mobile and wireless networks is unpredictable and often low. In comparison to RR, the main benefit of the ROM protocol is the reduction of messaging when re-establishing route optimization from a new subnet.

It is important that we understand all the threats the new technology creates before a possible deployment.

References

Aura, T.: Mobile IPv6 Security. In: Christianson, B., Crispo, B., Malcolm, J.A., Roe, M. (eds.) Security Protocols. LNCS, vol. 2845, pp. 215–234. Springer, Heidelberg (2004)

Deng, R.H., Zhou, J., Bao, F.: Defending Against Redirect Attacks in Mobile IP. In: Proceedings of the 9th ACM conference on Computer and communications security, ACM Press, New York (2002)

Hinden, R., Deering, S.: Internet Protocol Version 6 (IPv6) Addressing Architecture, IETF RFC 3513 (2003)

Johnson, D., Percins, C., Arkko, J.: Mobility Support in IPv6, IETF RFC 3775 (2004)
Nikander, P., Arrko, J., Aura, T., Montenegro, G., Nordmark, E.: Mobile IP version 6 Route Optimization Security Design Background, IETF Internet-draft (2005)
Thomson, S., Narten, T.: IPv6 Stateless Address Autoconfiguration, IETF RFC 2462 (1998)
Veigner, C., Rong, C.: A new Route Optimization protocol for Mobile IPv6 (ROM). In: International Computer symposium 2004, Taipei (2004)

Performance of VoIP over IEEE 802.11G DSSS-OFDM Mode with IEEE 802.11E QOS Support

Gráinne Hanley, Seán Murphy, and Liam Murphy

Department of Computer Science
University College Dublin, Belfield, Dublin 4
hanleyg@gmail.com, sean.murphy@iname.com, liam.murphy@ucd.ie

Abstract. This paper examines, via simulation, the performance of an 802.11e MAC over an 802.11g PHY operating in DSSS-OFDM mode. The DSSS-OFDM scheme provides data rates of up to 54Mb/s as well as interoperability with 802.11b nodes. Due to the widespread use of 802.11b nodes, such interoperability is an important consideration. This paper involves a study of the number of simultaneous bidirectional G.711 VoIP calls that can be supported by such a WLAN. The results show that this mode of operation introduces a very significant overhead. The actual number of calls that can be carried is limited to 12 when using the 24Mb/s data rate and 13 when using either the 36Mb/s or 54Mb/s rates. These results demonstrate the well-known disparity between uplink and downlink performance, with the downlink imposing the limit on the number of calls that can be carried by the system in the cases studied. The results also show that when when a significant amount of lower priority traffic is introduced into the system, it can have a significant impact on VoIP call capacity despite the use of 802.11e.

Keywords: WLAN, IEEE 802.11e, QoS, Voice over IP, Medium Access Control.

1 Introduction

WLAN support for QoS is one issue that is receiving considerable interest at present. The IEEE 802.11e standard, which provides standardised QoS support, is in the final stages of development. Frustrated by the sluggish pace of development of the standard, the Wi-Fi Alliance, an industry forum, is attempting to promote development of WLAN QoS by offering certification for a subset of the standard's functionality which it calls *Wi-Fi Multimedia* (WMM). A significant number of vendors are already certified.

While vendors are beginning to ship systems with QoS support, there is still considerable debate within the community regarding how best to operate these systems. The standards have been written in such a way as to offer much flexibility to enable vendors to differentiate their product offerings. This flexibility, coupled with the complexity of the system, means that large differences in system performance are possible. At present, it is not clearly known how best to configure such systems. Hence, there is a need to understand how these systems behave for different parameter sets in different configurations.

One application driving the development of WLAN QoS support is *Voice over IP* (VoIP). Many enterprises and WLAN operators are very interested in providing *VoIP*

J. Filipe et al. (Eds.): ICETE 2005, CCIS 3, pp. 201–214, 2007.

over WLAN (VoIPoW) and indeed some vendors have product offerings which can address this need. However, such product offerings are typically proprietary. Standardised solutions offer many known benefits and for this reason, it is important to determine the performance of VoIPoW in a standardised 802.11e/802.11g setting.

As there are currently a very large number of 802.11b network interfaces in existence, it is interesting to see how backwards compatibility issues affect system performance for 802.11e/802.11g systems. 802.11g provides two modulation schemes with backwards compatibility mechanisms. The first is called ERP-OFDM, while the other is called DSSS-OFDM. ERP-OFDM is based on transmitting *Request To Send /Clear To Send* (RTS/CTS) signalling at a low rate such that legacy nodes know when the medium is unavailable. DSSS-OFDM is based on transmitting packet preamble and header information at an 802.11b compliant rate.

Some research has taken place to determine the performance of the ERP-OFDM scheme in certain circumstances. This paper aims to determine the performance of the latter – the DSSS-OFDM scheme – in a VoIP context.

This paper is structured as follows. Section II briefly outlines the operation of the 802.11e MAC and the 802.11g PHY, and Section III outlines some of the published work related to this study. In section IV, the simulation setup is described in detail. This is followed by a description of the simulations performed and a discussion of the results obtained in section V. The paper is concluded in section VI.

2   IEEE 802.11

The simulations studied here use an 802.11e MAC layer in association with an 802.11g PHY layer; the operation of these layers is briefly outlined below.

2.1   IEEE 802.11e

IEEE 802.11e (IEEE, 2005) provides for centralised and distributed QoS support at the *Medium Access Control*(MAC) layer. As there is considerably more complexity in the centralised scheme, the focus here is on the distributed approach, the *Enhanced Distributed Channel Access* (EDCA).

EDCA provides for 4 different so-called *Access Categories* (ACs). Different priorities for the 4 ACs are realised through 4 coupled *Carrier Sense Multiple Access with Collision Avoidance* (CSMA/CA) mechanisms. These mechanisms are coupled as they contend for access to the same medium, but they differ in that they are parameterised differently. More specifically, the parameters for the higher priority traffic are chosen to enable it to obtain access to the medium more quickly than the lower priority traffic. Contention between different priorities in a single station is resolved such that the higher priority traffic gains access to the medium, while the lower priority enters a backoff state.

Two of the key parameters which control how the different access categories obtain access to the medium are the *Contention Window* (CW) sizes and the *Arbitration Inter-Frame Space* (AIFS). The former controls how much random waiting, or backoff, delay should be introduced for each AC to avoid collision and the latter controls how long each AC waits after a transmission has terminated before attempting to access the medium.

The 4 ACs have been labelled *Voice* (VO), *Video* (VI), *Best Effort* (BE) and *Background* (BG). Parameter settings for each of the categories are shown in Table 1.

Table 1. Default IEEE 802.11e EDCA Parameter Set

AC	CWmin	CWmax	AIFSN
VO	(aCWmin+1)/4-1	(aCWmin+1)/2-1	2
VI	(aCWmin+1)/2-1	aCWmin	2
BE	aCWmin	aCWmax	3
BG	aCWmin	aCWmax	7

The values of the 802.11g parameters are shown to be relative to aCWmin and aCWmax. As stipulated in the standard, an aCWmin of 31 and an aCWmax of 1023 were used, to maintain compatibility with 802.11b systems carrying VoIP traffic.

2.2   IEEE 802.11g

The 802.11g *Physical layer* (PHY) (IEEE, 2003) enhancement outlines 4 modulation schemes. Two of which are mandatory – ERP-OFDM and ERP-CCK/DSSS – and two of which are optional – ERP-PBSS and DSSS-OFDM. Of the four schemes, only ERP-OFDM and DSSS-OFDM provide data rates of up to 54Mb/s using OFDM modulation schemes, while also providing explicit support for interoperating with 802.11b nodes. Such support is necessary as 802.11b nodes are not able to detect or understand OFDM modulated signals.

The ERP-OFDM scheme is a variant of the 802.11a PHY scheme modified for use in the 2.4 GHz band. The DSSS-OFDM scheme is a hybrid modulation scheme that combines a DSSS preamble and header with an OFDM payload transmission.

ERP-OFDM uses the RTS/CTS mechanism to provide 802.11b interoperability. This mechanism gives the 802.11g nodes time to freely transmit at the higher rates. In the DSSS-OFDM scheme, all packet headers and preambles are transmitted at the lower 1Mb/s rate using 802.11b compliant DSSS modulation. Thus, 802.11b nodes know how the medium is being used even if they cannot detect OFDM payload transmission.

3   Related Work

While WLAN performance analysis is currently a very active research area, little has been published on VoIP performance for 802.11e/802.11g systems.

Although Mangold et al. (Mangold et al., 2003) analysed the performance of the 802.11e standard, their study was performed in relation to 802.11e/802.11a. Therefore, backward compatibility with 802.11b was not a concern.

Choi and Pavon (Choi and Pavon, 2003) discussed backward compatibility of the 802.11g ERP-OFDM scheme with regards to the 802.11b standard. Their results showed that the ERP-OFDM RTS/CTS protection mechanism introduces a lot of overhead, thus greatly reducing the performance of the network when compared with a system containing only 802.11g nodes. Their results showed that the transmission time of a packet on 802.11g with a long preamble RTS/CTS exchange, was about double that of 802.11g with RTS/CTS disabled. However, Bianchi (Bianchi, 2000) showed that without the RTS/CTS mechanism, the performance of the 802.11b DCF scheme was highly dependent on the number of nodes in the system and the size of the minimum CW. Given that the DSSS-OFDM scheme does not require RTS/CTS signalling, it is interesting to see the performance levels that can be obtained using this scheme.

Garg and Kappes (Garg and Kappes, 2003) performed an analytical analysis of VoIP capacity for the 802.11b and 802.11a schemes. They developed a formula which can be used to calculate the VoIP call capacity of a WLAN network under certain assumptions. However, their paper did not discuss the use of the 802.11e QoS mechanism. In addition, although quite useful, their formula does not hold, unless there is only VoIP traffic on the system. Also, their formula is based on the assumption that there are only ever two active senders in the network, whereby the AP and one wireless node always have a packet to send. For these reasons, it was unclear that their work could accurately predict the levels of performance that can be attained by VoIP traffic on an 802.11e/g system.

An important phenomenon in these systems is the disparity between the system performance in the uplink and downlink; this has been reported in previous work by both Grilo and Nunes (Grilo and Nunes, 2002) and Casetti and Chiasserini (Casetti and Chiasserini, 2004). Both papers were however related to the 802.11e MAC layer over the 802.11b PHY layer. The same difference is apparent throughout the results in this paper but is further examined and discussed in relation to the 802.11g PHY scenario.

4   The Simulation Scenario

In order to determine the performance of VoIP in an 802.11e/802.11g system, a series of simulations were performed. In these simulations, the wireless nodes were arranged with an AP in the network which formed a connection between every 802.11e node in the wireless domain and a single node in the wired domain (see Fig.1). This AP was connected to the wired network by a high capacity link with negligible delay, which was dimensioned such that it could easily carry all the traffic and hence no loss occurred on this link. All wireless nodes were within radio range of each other, thus ensuring that no issues arose relating to hidden/exposed station problems. In addition, all nodes were situated sufficiently close together so that they were able to transmit at the highest data rate supported by 802.11g. Static routing [1] was used, so as to ensure realistic routing of the wireless traffic.

The simulations were configured such that each node used bidirectional CBR traffic sources, so as to model VoIP traffic. This was represented as *Constant Bit-Rate* (CBR)

---

[1] The *No Ad-Hoc Routing* (NOAH) patch for ns-2.26 was used - http://icapeople.epfl.ch/widmer/uwb/ns-2/noah.

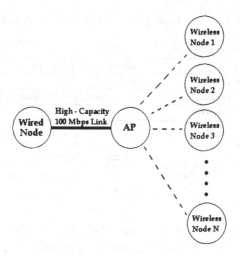

Fig. 1. Network Topology

traffic, transmitted using *User Datagram Protocol* (UDP). In a similar manner to that of Yu, Choi and Lee (Yu et al., 2004), these sources were parameterised to model G.711 voice at 64kb/s with 20ms payload. The G.711 scheme was chosen as it is still commonly used, due to its simplicity, despite the availability of schemes with better compression. As in (Yu et al., 2004) a VoIP data payload size of 160 bytes was generated every 20ms, to which the 20 byte IP header, the 12 byte RTP header and the 8 byte UDP header were added. In order to avoid issues with traffic synchronisation, a low level of random noise was introduced into the packet generation process. This resulted in a source which generated a 200 byte packet approximately every 20ms, resulting in 80kb/s of traffic in total per node. This VoIP traffic was always transmitted at the highest priority level of 802.11e in accordance with the standard.

In some of the later experiments, an additional bidirectional low priority, BE traffic source was introduced for each of the bidirectional VoIP sources in the simulation. Like the VoIP traffic, this was also parameterised as CBR traffic over UDP but at a rate of 250kb/s and with a 1500 byte data payload. The aim was to see how a VoIP application would perform if there was a heavy traffic load at the lower priority.

The IEEE 802.11g parameters (see Table 2) for the simulations using the DSSS-OFDM modulation scheme were chosen to allow backward compatibility with the IEEE 802.11b PHY. Hence, the long PLCP preamble, long slot time, and long *Clear Channel Assessment* (CCA) time were used. In accordance with the standard for DSSS-OFDM, the long PLCP preamble and long PLCP header were transmitted at 1Mb/s.

For this study, a simulation model of the IEEE 802.11e with the EDCA mechanism, developed by the TKN group in Berlin, for the Network Simulator package NS was used (Wietholter and Hoene, 2003).

Since the primary focus of this study was the VoIP traffic, a 50 packet queue limit was chosen for every node in the system, as there is no advantage in queuing VoIP packets for extended periods because they are delay limited. Furthermore, studies have indicated (Yu et al., 2004) that there is a minimal performance difference between a 50 and 100 packet queue.

Table 2. Extended Rate IEEE 802.11g PHY Characteristics

Characteristic	Value
SlotTime	$20\mu s$(long), $9\mu s$(short)
SIFSTime	$10\mu s$
CCATime	$<15\mu s$(long), $<4\mu s$(short)
aCWmin(0)	31
aCWmax	1023
Supported Rates	1, 2, 5.5, 6, 9, 11,12, 18, 24, 36, 48, and 54Mb/s
Mandatory Rates	1, 2, 5.5, 11, 6, 12, and 24Mb/s

Each simulation was run three times and the results were averaged over these three runs. All simulations were run for 250 seconds of simulation time, and the maximum mandatory 802.11g data rate of 24Mb/s as well as the optional higher 36Mb/s and 54Mb/s rates were studied.

5   Results

These results are an assessment of the performance of the DSSS-OFDM scheme with regards to VoIP capacity. This analysis is firstly performed at three different data rates but in the absence of any other traffic. Then the effect of the addition of a large amount of BE (see Table 1) traffic is examined at the same three data rates.

In these experiments, loss and delay measurements were taken at the UDP layer of the protocol stack. The downlink delays are the average packet delays from the originating wired node, to the receiving wireless node. Similarly, the uplink delays are the average packet delays from the originating wireless node, to the receiving wired node.

The loss examined here represents packets which were sent by the UDP transport layer of the transmitting node, but which were never received by the UDP transport layer of the receiving node. These loss rates therefore represent the percentage of packets which are dropped due to collisions on the medium or *Interface Queue* (IFQ) overflow.

There are MAC level retransmissions of all collided packets, but those packets which exceed the retransmission threshold without being successfully received are considered as lost. For these simulations, the Short Retry Limit was set to 7 in accordance with what is recommended by 802.11e.

VoIP requires certain quality levels: ETSI studies (ETSI, 2002) indicate that a packet loss rate of 5% is at the upper bound for acceptable voice quality. Also, for this study, WLAN delays of greater than 50ms were considered to be unacceptably high.

5.1   Analysis of VoIP Traffic in an 802.11e/802.11g Network with DSSS-OFDM Modulation

This set of simulations was performed using the DSSS-OFDM parameters, and in the absence of any traffic other than the VoIP traffic being analysed. The simulations were run at the maximum mandatory data rate of 24Mb/s, as well as at the optional higher rates of 36Mb/s and 54Mb/s. The results show a comparison of the uplink and downlink results for the end to end delays and loss rates, the average contention window sizes used for the backoff calculation and the percentage occupancy of the IFQ.

5.1.1 End-to-End Delay and Loss Rates

At first, the similarity in the results for each of the three data rates, 24, 36 and 54Mb/s, seems surprising. In fact, results show that increasing the rate at which the actual data is sent has quite a small impact on overall performance levels. This can be attributed to the fact that in the DSSS-OFDM scheme, the longer PLCP data is used and is sent at a slow 1Mb/s rate for backwards compatibility. Therefore a large overhead is introduced for each packet transmission. The negative performance effects of this large overhead dominate the overall system performance and to a great degree mask the positive impact of an increased data rate.

Results show that increasing the maximum data rate of the system from 24Mb/s, to 36Mb/s, and then to 54Mb/s, does lower the delay experienced by packets (see Fig.2). However, if the average delay for 15 bidirectional VoIP calls is examined for each of the three data rates, the average downlink end-to-end delay at 24Mb/s is 111ms, at 36Mb/s is 96ms, and at 54Mb/s is 86ms. Although notable, these improvements in delay at the higher data rates are quite low given the greatly increased data rates.

The known disparity between uplink and downlink performance is quite visible in these results: the delay difference between uplink and downlink is especially apparent when there are 13, 14 and 15 calls on the network. For this region there are quite large downlink delays in comparison to minimal uplink delays. This can be attributed to the saturation of the downlink occurring prior to that of the uplink. However, it can be seen that after 15 calls the uplink delays also begin to climb. By the 17 call point, there is more uniformity to the delays as both uplink and downlink are saturated and hence delay levels begin to converge.

It is clear from the results that in the 24Mb/s scenario a large increase in loss is experienced by the downlink when there are only 13 bidirectional calls on the system. In fact, at this stage loss rates are already in excess of the 5% threshold (see Fig.3). Results show that the 24Mb/s network can support only 12 bidirectional calls, and both

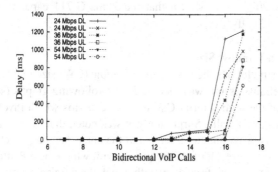

Fig. 2. End-to-End Delays With Only VoIP Traffic

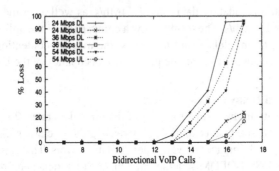

Fig. 3. Loss Rates With Only VoIP Traffic

the 36Mb/s and 54Mb/s systems can support only 13 bidirectional calls before loss rates on the downlink reach 6% or higher.

In this scenario, the majority of the downlink loss was due to queue overflow, whereas the majority of the uplink loss was caused by retransmission failure. Loss at the AP can be explained by noting that the AP has to handle downlink traffic for *all of the wireless nodes*; if the medium is congested, then it may not obtain sufficient access to the medium for all this downlink traffic, its queue builds up and it suffers packet loss. In contrast, the individual wireless stations have much lower traffic levels and so the queues at the wireless stations rarely contain many packets. Hence, wireless stations do not encounter IFQ overflow. However, it seems that the uplink does experience a higher probability of collision than the downlink. These higher levels of collisions and retransmissions on the uplink occasionally lead to a packet being dropped as it has exceeded its maximum number of retransmission attempts without being successfully received.

These results indicate that the use of parameters which enable backward compatibility lead to a serious reduction in the performance of VoIP applications. In previous experiments that were performed which focussed on the ERP-OFDM scheme without backward compatibility mechanisms, it was found that at 24Mb/s an ERP-OFDM 802.11g WLAN system could support approximately 48 bidirectional G.711 VoIP calls. In fact, in this scenario, the 802.11g DSSS-OFDM modulation scheme performs little better than a basic 802.11b in terms of VoIP call capacity: Garg and Kappes (Garg and Kappes, 2003) have shown that the 20ms G.711 capacity for an 11Mb/s 802.11b system is 12 calls.

5.1.2 Contention Window Size

For each of these simulations the *Contention Window* (CW) size that was used for any transmission or retransmission was recorded. The following graphs (see Fig.4) show the average size of the high priority CW for the scenarios which involved between 7 and 17 bidirectional VoIP calls. Surprisingly, it was noted that the average size of CW used by the AP was always smaller than that of the corresponding wireless node.

This difference is as a result of the frequency with which the AP attempts to access the medium as opposed to the frequency with which the wireless nodes attempt to gain access.

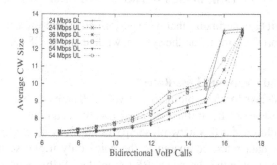

Fig. 4. Contention Window Sizes With Only VoIP Traffic

Due to the greater level of traffic at the AP, its IFQ fills much more quickly than that at any individual wireless node. This means that frequently when the AP is attempting to gain access it is not in direct contention with any of the wireless nodes. Due to this lower contention level, the AP has a lower probability of colliding with another packet and thus a lower probability of having to retransmit with an increased CW.

On the other hand, the wireless node will almost always be in direct contention with the AP when it is attempting to transmit, hence, it will have a higher potential for colliding with a packet sent by the AP.

5.1.3 IFQ Occupancy
The results show a breakdown of the IFQ occupancy for high priority traffic as a percentage of the simulation time. These statistics are very informative as to the point at which high priority traffic begins to encounter notable delays in accessing the medium (see Fig.5). If queue occupancy is at a high level for a large amount of the simulation time, it is an indication that there is a lot of congestion on the network, and hence packets are encountering difficulty in accessing the medium.

The results from the 24Mb/s simulations (see Fig.5 show that the queue occupancy rates of the wireless nodes are lower than that of the AP. This behaviour is not unexpected as the amount of traffic that a single wireless node has to handle is a lot lower than the traffic levels at the AP.

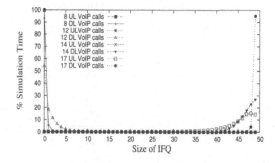

Fig. 5. 24Mb/s AP and Wireless Node IFQ Sizes With Only VoIP Traffic

5.2 Analysis of VoIP Traffic in the Presence of Best Effort Traffic

This section describes experiments that were performed to determine the impact of high levels of Best Effort CBR traffic on the system, while using DSSS-OFDM modulation.

5.2.1 End-to-End Delay and Loss Rates

If the end-to-end delays for these bidirectional VoIP calls are compared with the results obtained in the absence of BE traffic (see Fig.2 and 6), a significant increase in delay is observed. In addition, for this network setup, results show a definite increase in the losses at all three data rates, compared to the voice only traffic scenario (see Fig.3 and 7). It was found that in the absence of BE traffic, the 24Mb/s network could support 12 bidirectional calls, and that both the 36Mb/s and the 54Mb/s networks could support 13 bidirectional calls before delays and loss rates on the downlink reach unacceptable levels.

Based on the loss and delay results in the presence of BE traffic, it can be seen that the 24Mb/s network can support only 9 bidirectional calls, and both the 36Mb/s and 54Mb/s systems can support only 10 bidirectional calls. After this point, loss rates on the downlink become excessive and the VoIP traffic encounters a large increase in end-to-end delay. This indicates that with this amount of additional traffic in this network scenario, the number of supportable bidirectional VoIP calls is reduced by 3, which is a significant decrease in terms of VoIP call capacity.

Due to the nature of the 802.11e mechanism such a large increase in delay seems somewhat surprising as 802.11e was designed to facilitate medium access to higher priority traffic largely at the expense of lower priority traffic. However, here it is demonstrated that this is not always the case.

The influence of background traffic is dependent upon many factors. In general, extra traffic will increase the risk of collision, which will lead to an increased number of retransmissions as well as a greater number of lost packets.

In this case, the lower priority, BE traffic packets have a data payload of 1500 bytes as opposed to the 160 bytes in the VoIP packets, and hence will occupy the medium for longer periods. Such longer transmission times will further increase the risk of collision with VoIP traffic. In fact, the transmission of a BE packet at the 24Mb/s data rate will occupy the medium for approximately 1ms as opposed to only 590μs for a VoIP packet.

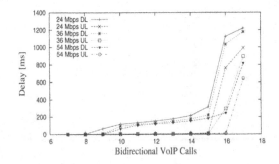

Fig. 6. End-to-End Delays With Best Effort Traffic

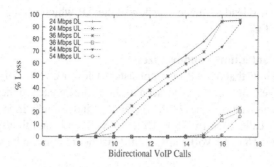

Fig. 7. Loss Rates With Best Effort Traffic

Therefore, during this additional $410\mu s$ delay more VoIP packets will have arrived in the AP queue. This will cause the queue at the AP to build much more quickly than when no BE traffic is present. This will lead to increased queuing delays, as well as an increase in back-off delays, for the VoIP traffic. Plus, as queue occupancy levels increase, it could eventually lead to packets being dropped due to queue overflow.

5.2.2 Packets Received After Retransmission
In order to further understand the increases in loss and delay, the levels of packets received after retransmission was examined.

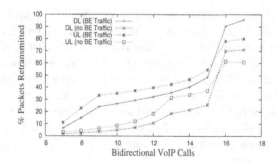

Fig. 8. VoIP Packets Received After Retransmission With Best Effort Traffic at 24Mb/s

In this scenario, results show that the additional BE traffic leads to a large increase in retransmissions at both the AP and at the wireless nodes. This can be clearly seen in Fig.8.

The medium capacity used when packets collide and are retransmitted is a highly inefficient use of resources. This inefficient use of resources leads to less available resources in the system, which results in lower system throughput and lower service rates on each queue in the system. This, in turn, causes queue occupancy to increase.

Due to the high traffic levels at the AP, an increase in retransmission levels has a large impact on the downlink delay in particular. Combined with its high packet arrival rate this can often also lead to queue overflow at the AP, which results in increased loss levels on the downlink.

5.2.3 Average Contention Window Sizes

The results again show that the AP has a consistently lower CW than the wireless nodes (see Fig.9). However, the results can be seen to show three phases in the relationship between the contention window sizes of the AP and the individual wireless nodes. Firstly, from 7 to 10 VoIP calls, then from the 10 to 15 VoIP calls and finally as the level of voice traffic reaches 16 to 17 VoIP calls, a third distinct region can be seen.

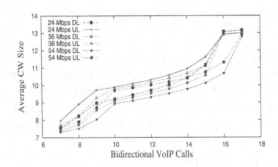

Fig. 9. Contention Window Sizes With Best Effort Traffic

If these results are considered in association with the IFQ occupancy rates then an association between both sets of results can be seen. In the first phase, both the AP and wireless nodes have an empty IFQ for the majority of the time, that is, at least more than 50% of the time the queues are empty. However in the second phase, it can be noted from the results that the AP IFQ has reached a point whereby the IFQ contains packets for most of the simulation time. Although at this stage the wireless node queues still remain empty for most of the time. The final section corresponds to a stage when both the AP and wireless nodes queues are full for the majority of the simulation time and the CW size can be seen to increase more rapidly until the CW size of the uplink and downlink ultimately converge.

The difference in the uplink and downlink CW sizes is a reflection of the differing levels of retransmissions on the uplink and downlink since retransmissions are sent with an increased CW; as the uplink has more retransmissions, its CW is higher. Also, in this scenario, there is correlation between the IFQ occupancy and the mean CW size. As the mean CW size increases (due to retransmissions on the medium), there are increased delays and lower medium throughput resulting in increasing occupancy levels at the IFQ.

6 Conclusion

The VoIP capacity of the DSSS-OFDM modulation scheme when using parameters which provided backward compatibility, showed that the 24Mb/s network can support only 12 bidirectional calls, and both the 36Mb/s and 54Mb/s systems can support only 13 bidirectional calls. Above these capacities, loss rates on the downlink reach an unacceptably high level. The results also clearly show that, as expected, the downlink quality begins to suffer long before the performance of the uplink begins to deteriorate.

Interestingly, the average size of CW used by the AP was generally smaller than that of the wireless nodes. This was due to the different medium access requirements of the AP and the individual wireless nodes. The AP almost always had a packet waiting in its IFQ for transmission and so due to the lower levels of traffic being sent by each wireless node often it was not in direct contention with another node. In contrast, the wireless nodes were frequently in direct contention with the AP, hence the wireless nodes often had a higher probability of collision. Since collided packets are retransmitted with an increased CW size, this led to a difference between the average CW size at the AP and at the wireless nodes.

Surprisingly, results also showed that the addition of BE traffic leads to an increase in end-to-end delay, loss rates and IFQ occupancy for the VoIP traffic. Additional traffic leads to an increased risk of collision for the VoIP packet, which was further increased by the large size of the BE load. It was found that the delays resulting from the additional collisions and retransmissions cause a large increase in queuing delay and so decreased the packet service rate, particularly at the AP.

In fact, it was found that, under such conditions, the 24Mb/s network can support only 9 bidirectional calls, and both the 36 and 54Mb/s systems can support only 10 bidirectional calls before loss rates on the downlink are in excess of 10%. These unanticipated results indicate that for this network scenario and with this amount of additional traffic, the number of supportable bidirectional VoIP calls is reduced by 3 calls.

Future work involves further investigation of backward compatibility mechanisms for 802.11g, further investigation into ways to equalise the division of resources between the uplink and the downlink and investigating the optimum transmission opportunity sizes for this scenario.

Acknowledgements

The support of the Informatics Research initiative of Enterprise Ireland is gratefully acknowledged.

References

Bianchi, G.: Performance Analysis Of The IEEE 802.11 Distributed Coordination Function. IEEE Journal on Selected Areas in Communications 18(3), 535–547 (2000)

Casetti, C., Chiasserini, C.F.: Improving Fairness And Throughput For Voice Traffic in 802.11e EDCA. In: Proc. IEEE PIMRC, Barcelona, Spain (2004)

Choi, S., Pavon, J.P.: 802.11g CP: A Solution For IEEE 802.11g And 802.11b Inter-Working. In: Proc. IEEE VTC, Jeju, Korea (2003)

ETSI, ETSI TR 101 329-6 V2.1.1, TIPHON Release 3; End-to-End Quality of Service in TIPHON Systems; Part 6 (2002)

Garg, S., Kappes, M.: Can I Add a VoIP Call?. In: Proc. IEEE ICC, Anchorage, Alaska, USA (2003)

Grilo, A., Nunes, M.: Performance Evaluation of IEEE 802.11e. In: Proc. IEEE PIMRC, Coimbra, Portugal (2002)

IEEE, Wireless LAN Medium Access Control and Physical Layer Specifications Amendment 4: Further Higher Data Rate Extension in the 2.4 GHz Band, IEEE Std 802.11g-2003 (2003)

IEEE, Local and Metropolitan Area Networks - Specific Requirements Part 11: Wireless LAN Medium Access Control and Physical Layer specifications: Amendment: Medium Access Control (MAC) Quality of Service Enhancements - P802.11e/D13.0 (2005)

Mangold, S., Choi, S., Hiertz, G., Klein, O., Walke, B.: Analysis of IEEE 802.11e for QoS Support in Wireless LANs. IEEE Wireless Communications 10(6), 40–50 (2003)

Wietholter, S., Hoene, C.: "Design And Verification of an IEEE 802.11e EDCF Simulation Model in ns-2.26: TKN-03-019". Technical report, TKN, Berlin (2003)

Yu, J., Choi, S., Lee, J.: Enhancement of VoIP Over IEEE 802.11 WLAN Via Dual Queue Strategy. In: Proc. IEEE ICC, Paris, France (2004)

The Robustness of Blocking Probability in a Loss System with Repeated Customers

Akira Takahashi[1], Yoshitaka Takahashi[1], Shigeru Kaneda[2], Yoshikazu Akinaga[2], and Noriteru Shinagawa[2]

[1] Graduate School of Commerce , Waseda University
Shinjuku, Tokyo 169-8050, Japan
`akira-takahashi@toki.waseda.jp`
[2] Network Laboratories , NTT DoCoMo,Inc.
3-5, Hikarinooka, Yokosuka, Kanagawa, 239-8536, Japan

Abstract. In this paper, we analyze and synthesize a multi-server loss system with repeated customers, arising out of NTT DoCoMo-developed telecommunication networks. We first provide the numerical solution for a Markovian model with exponential retrial intervals. Applying Little's formula, we derive the main system performance measures (blocking probability and mean waiting time) for general non-Markovian models. We compare the numerical and simulated results for the Markovian model, in order to check the accuracy of the simulations. Via performing extensive simulations for non-Markovian (non-exponential retrial intervals) models, we find *robustness* in the blocking probability and the mean waiting time, that is, the performance measures are shown to be insensitive to the retrial intervals distribution except for the mean.

Keywords: Teletraffic analysis, loss system, repeated customers, Little's formula.

1 Introduction

When the service system becomes extremely congested, a lot of customers cannot receive immediate service. Some of them may give up the service to leave the system, while others may stay in the system and retry their requests. This behavior of repeated customers leads to an additional load on the system and worsens its congestion. The importance of repeated requests on the performance of the service system was pointed out in the late 1940, and many researches have been performed since then. Pioneering studies on the multi-server loss system with repeated calls brought some kind of positive expressions of performance measures (See (Falin and Templeton, 1997), (Artalejo and Pozo, 2002), and (Udagawa and Miwa, 1965)). However, they are not necessarily convenient to calculate performance measures. Retrial queuing models including one discussed here are usually very complicated for queuing analysis and its results are not always suitable to numerical calculation. Many authors reported numerical approaches of approximation and truncation methods. For details on the numerical approaches, readers are referred to (Artalejo and Pozo, 2002) and (Stepanov, 1999).

J. Filipe et al. (Eds.): ICETE 2005, CCIS 3, pp. 215–225, 2007.

Most of them assume that the time intervals between repeated attempts are mutually independent and exponentially distributed. However, affected by many factors and circumstances, customers' behavior in repeating is so complex that these assumptions may lead to a risky assessment. There is necessity for generalization of the retrial interval distribution.

This assumption of exponential retrial intervals is a kind of simplification for queuing analysis. There is no guarantee that repeating customers behave in such a manner. Under this assumption, the number of repeated requests emerging in a unit time changes by the state of the retrial queue (See (Artalejo et al., 2001)). There is another type of retrial queuing model in which retrial rate is constant. In this type of model, blocked customers who want to repeat must wait in line and only the customer at the head of the line can retry to hunt, if any, an idle server. It has a wide range of applications like communication protocols. However, still there are systems more appropriately modeled by the classical type. On the constant retrial policy, there are fruitful investigations of models with single-server non-exponential retrial intervals like (Gómez-Correl and Ramalhoto, 1999). However, it remains open problem to investigate the effect of the retrial times distribution on the performance of the system. Customers' behavior in repeating is expected to be highly complex and it may be risky or inefficient to build and operate the system upon the results of exponential assumption. Thus, one finds it necessary to study sensitivity and robustness of the retrial time distribution

The main goal of this paper is to investigate the robustness (insensitivity) property between the performance measure and the retrial time distribution in a loss system with repeated customers seen in an NTT DoCoMo developed telecommunication network.

The rest of the paper is organized as follows. Section 2 gives teletraffic analysis of the retrial model. The main performance measures of practical interest are then derived. In Section 3, simulation results of non-exponential (deterministic/ two-stage Erlang/ two-stage hyper-exponential) retrial models are compared to find robustness of the system.

2 Numerical Results

2.1 Model Description

Consider the following loss system with repeated calls : (1) There are c servers in parallel; (2) Customers' service times, which are identical and independent from one another, are exponentially distributed with rate μ; (3) Customer arrivals follow a Poisson process of rate λ; (4) Customers who find all severs busy at their arrival epoch choose either to repeat their requests with probability p or to give up the service with probability $(1-p)$; (5) When they decide to repeat, customers wait in the retrial queue for a random time called "retrial interval", which is exponentially (generally) distributed with parameter γ in Section 2.2(Section 3) before making repeated requests; (6) Retrial customers who find again all servers busy choose either to waint in the retrial queue and repeat their requests with probability p or to stop repeating and leave the system with probability $(1-p)$; (7) Give-up customers leave the system immediately.

We introduce following notations. Suppose the existence of the stationary state, the state of the system is characterized by (1) the number of the busy servers and (2) the

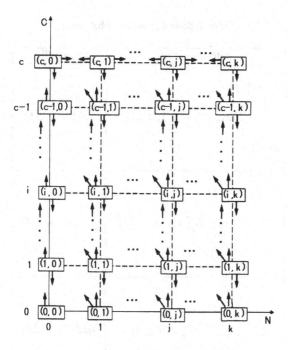

Fig. 1. State-transition diagram

number of the customers waiting to make a repeated attempt. The system will be said to be in state (i, j), if i servers busy and j customers waiting to repeat. If there are c servers in the system then the system is somewhere in the state space $\{0, 1, \cdots, c\} \times \{0, 1, \cdots\}$. Let $\pi_{i,j}$ denote the probability that the system is in state (i, j) from now on.

2.2 Calculation of the Stationary Distribution

By focusing on the possible state transition in a minute time Δt, we get the state-transition probabilities as shown in Table 1. Figure 1 illustrates the state-transition diagram of this model.

By Table 1, the state-equilibrium equations are expressed as below.

$$(\lambda + j\gamma)\pi_{0,j} = \mu\pi_{1,j}.$$
$$(\lambda + i\mu + j\gamma)\pi_{i,j} = \lambda\pi_{i-1,j} + (j+1)\gamma\pi_{i-1,j}$$
$$+ (i+1)\mu\pi_{i+1,j}$$
$$(1 \leqq i \leqq c - 1).$$
$$(\lambda\alpha + c\mu + j\gamma(1 - \alpha))\pi_{c,j}.$$
$$= \lambda\pi_{c-1,j} + \gamma\pi_{c-1,j} + \lambda\alpha\pi_{c,j-1}$$
$$+ (j+1)\gamma(1 - \alpha)\pi_{c,j+1}.$$

Our research purpose here is to study the effect of the retrial interval distribution and the existence of robustness. To this end, we adopt an simple approximation method of

Table 1. State-transition probabilities

state-transition	probability
$(i+1,j)$ $\uparrow \quad (0 \leqq i \leqq c-1, 0 \leqq j)$ (i,j)	$\lambda \Delta t + o(\Delta t)$
$(i+1,j-1)$ $\nwarrow \quad (0 \leqq i \leqq c-1, 1 \leqq j)$ (i,j)	$j\gamma \Delta t + o(\Delta t)$
(i,j) $\downarrow \quad (1 \leqq i \leqq c, 0 \leqq j)$ $(i-1,j)$	$i\mu \Delta t + o(\Delta t)$
$(c,j) \quad \rightarrow \quad (c,j+1)$ $(0 \leqq j)$	$\lambda \alpha \Delta t + o(\Delta t)$
$(c,j-1) \quad \leftarrow \quad (c,j)$ $(1 \leqq j)$	$j\gamma(1-\alpha)\Delta t$ $+o(\Delta t)$
$(c,j-1) \quad \leftarrow \quad (c,j)$ $(1 \leqq j)$	$j\gamma(1-\alpha)\Delta t$ $+o(\Delta t)$

replacing the infinite space for customers waiting to repeat requests by a finite number k. It is an extension of the way to calculate the steady-state probabilities introduced in (Hashida and Kawashima, 1979) and closely explained in (Falin and Templeton, 1997), so we only show the outline of the algorithm. Here, k is assumed to be a sufficiently large positive integer so that the overflow probability is small enough to be ignored. From a finite capacity argument,

$$\text{for } 1 \leqq j \leqq k-1, (\lambda + j\gamma)\pi_{0,j} = \mu\pi_{1,j}, \tag{1}$$

$$(\lambda + i\mu + j\gamma)\pi_{i,j} = \lambda\pi_{i-1,j} + (j+1)\gamma\pi_{i-1,j} + (i+1)\mu\pi_{i+1,j}(1 \leq i \leq c-1), \quad (2)$$

$$(\lambda\alpha + c\mu + j\gamma(1-\alpha))\pi_{c,j} = \lambda\pi_{c-1,j} + \gamma\pi_{c-1,j} + \lambda\alpha\pi_{c,j-1} + (j+1)\gamma(1-\alpha)\pi_{c,j+1}. \quad (3)$$

$$\text{For } j = k, (\lambda + k\gamma)\pi_{0,k} = \mu\pi_{1,k}, \quad (4)$$

$$(\lambda + i\mu + k\gamma)\pi_{i,k} = \lambda\pi_{i-1,k} + (i+1)\mu\pi_{i+1,k}(1 \leq i \leq c-1), \quad (5)$$

$$(c\mu + k\gamma(1-\alpha))\pi_{c,k} = \lambda\pi_{c-1,k} + \lambda\alpha\pi_{c,k-1}. \quad (6)$$

These recurrence equations enable us to compute the stationary distribution via the following steps.

(I) Take the appropriate k and introduce auxiliary variables $\phi_{i,j} \triangleq pi_{i,j}/\pi_{0,k}$.
(II) By definition , $\phi_{0,k} = 1$. From (4), $\phi_{1,k}$ can be determined. From (5), one can get $\phi_{i,k}(i = 2, 3, \cdots, c)$ sequentially.
(III) Equations (1) and (2) for $i = 1, \cdots, c - 1$ constitute a set of c equations with $c + 1$ unknown variables $\phi_{0,k}, \phi_{1,k}, \cdots, \phi_{c-1,k}, \phi_{c,k}$. Thus, with $\phi_{c,k}$ obtained by (6), one finds the set of equations become solvable . Hence, (3) gives $\phi_{c,k-2}$D
(IV) Operating steps $(I), (II)$, and (III) repeatedlyC we get all of the $\phi_{i,j}$. The normalization condition; $\sum_{i=0}^{c}\sum_{j=0}^{k}\phi_{i,j} = 1/\phi_{0,k}$ settles $\pi_{0,k}$ and $\phi_{i,j} \times \pi_{0,k}$ gives $\pi_{i,j}$.
(V) By repeating from (I) to (IV) with k plus 1 until the value of $\pi_{c,k}$ becomes less than 10^{-10}, $\pi_{i,j}$ can be calculated with an accuracy enough for our purpose.

2.3   Performance Measures

We are now in a position to derive the performance measures of the system.

Time congestion (B_T)

Letting B_T be the time congestion, so called, the probabilities that all the servers are busy, we have

$$B_T = \sum_{j=0}^{k}\pi_{c,j}.$$

Blocking probability (B)

When they blocked due to all servers busy, customers can wait for some random time and retry. After several retrials, some of them may give up the service demand, and leave the system. Here, we define the blocking probability B as the probability that customers finally leave without getting served due to successive blockings.

To the best of authors' knowledge, there are few investigations for a general retrial model. Here, applying Little's formula (Little, 1961) enables us to prove the following proposition.

Proposition 1. Consider a general retrial queuing system which has input with rate λ, service with rate μ and retrial with rate γ. Customers who try to receive a service and get blocked due to all servers busy, choose either to repeat their requests with probability p or to stop repeating and leave the system with probability $(1 - p)$. Blocking probability B, that is, the probability that arriving customers finally leave the system with not receiving the service, is expressed by

$$B = 1 - \frac{1}{\rho}\overline{C}.$$

Here, ρ denotes traffic intensity defined by λ/μ and $\overline{C}$ stands for the mean number of busy servers on the stationary condition. See Appendix 1 for the proof.

It should be noted that Proposition 1 has a different expression on the blocking probability from that in (Hashida and Kawashima, 1979), where the *PASTA* (*Poisson Arrivals See Time Averages*) property is heuristically used to provide an approximation. Our expression on the loss probability shown in Proposition 1 is exact (not approximate).

Mean waiting time (Wq)

Denote by Wq the mean waiting time, namely, the mean elapsed time from a customer's arrival epoch until the epoch where the customer gets served or stops repeating without receiving its service to leave the system.

Like B above, Wq is also derived from Little's formula and its relation to other parameters is preserved under more general situation. So we find the following proposition.

Proposition 2. Consider a general retrial queuing system which has input with rate λ, service with rate μ and retrial with rate γ. Customers who try to receive a service and get blocked due to all servers busy, choose either to repeat their requests with probability p or to stop repeating and leave the system with probability $(1 - p)$. The mean waiting time Wq, that is, the time that customers have to spend on average until they finally get served or decide to stop repeating and leave, is expressed by

$$Wq = \frac{\overline{K}}{\lambda}.$$

$\overline{K}$ is the mean number of customers in the retrial area in the steady state. See Appendix 2 for the proof.

3   Simulation Results

In the previous section, we get the numerical solution of the loss system with exponential retrial intervals. Next, we change the assumption about retrial. In this section we compare performance measures between the exponential retrial interval model and the models with non-exponential retrial intervals. Even under the exponential re-trial interval assumption, multi-server property involves great complicity and analytical solutions are obtained only a few special cases like (Falin and Templeton, 1997) and (Choi and Kim, 1998). So we employ computer simulation to estimate the performance measure of non-exponential retrial interval models. The assumptions for simulation are all the same with those for numerical calculation introduced in Section 2 except for the distribution of retrial intervals. It assumes a Poisson arrival of customers with rate λ and an identically independently distributed exponential service time with rate μ.

On the distribution of retrial intervals, in this paper we take four different models; the exponential retrial interval model (Exp model) the constant retrial interval model (D model), the 2-stage Erlang distribution model ($E2$ model), and the 2-stage hyper exponential distribution model ($H2$ model). Among $H2$ models, we also have three different types whose coefficient of variation (C_X) of the retrial interval distribution is lager than 1, equal to 1, or smaller than 1. In other words, the variance of the retrial interval distribution is large, equal or small in comparison to its mean. $H2(C_X = \sqrt{2})$, $H2(C_X = \sqrt{20})$ and $H2(C_X = \sqrt{200})$ denote the model with hyper-exponential retrial intervals whose C_X equals to $\sqrt{2}$, $\sqrt{20}$ and $\sqrt{200}$, respectively .

Through this section, $\tau \triangleq \mu/\gamma$ is used for the indicator of the mean retrial interval and $\rho \triangleq \lambda/\mu$ for the traffic offered to the whole system.

In simulation, c(= the number of servers) is set to 10, μ 0.01and p 5/6, which means the service time average is 100 and under the condition of successive blocking cus-tomers continue to repeat 5 times on average. An individual simulation results (ex-pressed as points in each figure) is based on 50 runs(approx. 5 hours on IBM Thnkpad PC).

First, the accuracy of the simulation should be investigated. Figure 2 shows the blocking probability B by numerical calculation and simulation with the mean retrial

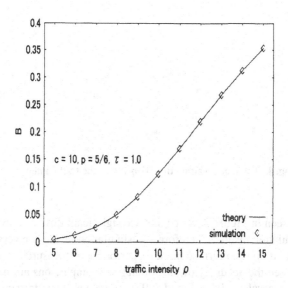

Fig. 2. The blocking probability B by numeric al calculation and simulation

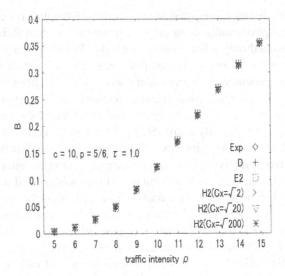

Fig. 3. The blocking probability B versus the traffic intensity ρ

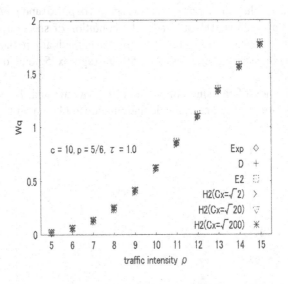

Fig. 4. The mean waiting time Wq versus the traffic intensity ρ

time $\tau = 1$. As seen in Figure 2, we cannot see significant difference between our numerical and simulation results. Therefore, our simulation results are very accurate. The accuracy of simulation is confirmed on other performance measures.

Now that we see the accuracy of the simulation, comparisons are performed when the mean retrial interval τ is 0.01, 1, and 100.0, which corresponds to the situations that repeated requests arises 100 times sooner than the service time on average, that they arise with the interval as long as the service time on average, and that they arise after a time 100 times longer than the service time on average.

Figures 3 and 4 show the relationship of the blocking probability B and the mean waiting time Wq to the traffic intensity ρ. One finds the retrial interval distribution makes little difference.

4 Conclusion

We have analyzed and synthesized a multi-server loss system with repeated customers, arising out of NTT DoCoMo-developed telecommunication networks. We have first provided the numerical solution for a Markovian model with exponential retrial intervals. Applying Little's formula, we have derived the main system performance measures (blocking probability and mean waiting time) for general non-Markovian models. We have compared the numerical and simulated results for the Markovian model, in order to check the accuracy of the simulations. Via performing extensive simulations for non-Markovian (non-exponential retrial intervals) models, we have found *robustness* in the blocking probability and the mean waiting time, that is, the performance measures have been shown to be insensitive to the retrial intervals distribution except for the mean.

It is left for future work to investigate the robustness for a more general (e.g., a general service time distribution) model.

Acknowledgements

The present research was partially supported by a Grant-in-Aid for Scientific Research (C) from Japan Society for the Promotion of Science under Grant No. 1458049.

References

Artalejo, J., Gómez-Correl, A., Neuts, M.: Analysis of multiserver queues with constant retrial rate. European Journal of Operational Research 135, 569–581 (2001)

Artalejo, J., Pozo, M.: Numerical calculation of the stationary distribution of the main multiserver retrial queue. Annals of Operations Research 116, 41–56 (2002)

Choi, B., Kim, Y.: The M/M/c retrial queue with geometric loss and feedback. Computers and Mathematics with Applications 36, 41–52 (1998)

Falin, G., Templeton, J.: Retrial Queues, 1st edn. Chapman and Hall, London (1997)

Gómez-Correl, A., Ramalhoto, M.: The stationary distribution of a markovian process arising in the theory of multiserver retrial queueing systems. Mathematical and Computer Modelling 30, 141–158 (1999)

Hashida, O., Kawashima, K.: Buffer behavior with repeated calls. The IECE Transactions J-62B, 222–228 (1979)

Little, J.D.C.: A proof for the queuing formula: L = λ W. The Journal of the Operations Research Society of America 9, 383–387 (1961)

Stepanov, S.: Markov model with retrials:the calculation of stationary performance measures based on the concept of truncation. Mathematical and Computer Modelling 30, 207–228 (1999)

Udagawa, K., Miwa, E.: A complete group of trunks and poisson-type repeated calls which influence it. The IECE Transactions 48, 1666–1675 (1965)

Appendices

Appendix 1

Proof of Proposition 1
We restrict ourselves to the sub-system only composed of c servers. We apply Little's formula [$L = \lambda W$] (Little, 1961) to this sub-system.

Let λ' and $\overline{C}$ respectively denote the sub-system throughput and the mean number of busy servers. By Little's formula, we have

$$\overline{C} = \lambda' \frac{1}{\mu}, \tag{A.1}$$

now that $\overline{C}$ [the mean number of customers in the sub-sytem] corresponds to L, λ' [the effective arrival rate of the sub-system] corresponds to λ, and $1/\mu$ [the mean sojourn time in the sub-system] corresponds to W.

The blocking probability B is defined as the probability that an arriving customer cannot finally receive its service, however often it may repeat the retrial process [being blocked, waiting, and retrying].

Since on average λ customers arrive at the system in unit time, the mean number of customers who leave the system without being served is given by λB. The mean number of customers who receive their services is obtained as

$$\lambda(1 - B) = \lambda'. \tag{A.2}$$

Substituting (A.2) into (A.1), and solving for B we finally get

$$B = 1 - \frac{1}{\rho}\overline{C}. \qquad \square$$

Appendix 2

Proof of Proposition 2
We restrict ourselves to the sub-system only composed of the retrail queue (with a finite capacity of k customers). We apply Little's formula [$L = \lambda W$] to this sub-system.

Let S and $\overline{K}$ denote the mean number of retrials and the mean number of customers in the retrial queue, respectively. Since on average λ customers arrive at the system in time unit, then each one of them go through the retrial queue S times on average. That is, the mean number of customers who go to the retrial queue in time unit equals to $S\lambda$. By Little's formula, we have

$$\overline{K} = S\lambda \frac{1}{\mu} \tag{A.3}$$

now that $\overline{K}$ [the mean number of customers in the sub-sytem] corresponds to L, $S\lambda$ [the effective arrival rate of the sub-system] corresponds to λ, and $1/\mu$ [the mean sojourn time in the sub-system] corresponds to W. From (A.3), we have

$$S = \frac{\overline{K}\gamma}{\lambda} \tag{A.4}$$

Since the mean retrial interval is $1/\mu$ and customers repeat their requests S times on average, then the mean wainting time Wq is

$$Wq = S\frac{1}{\gamma} \tag{A.5}$$

Substituting (A.4) to (A.5), we get

$$Wq = \frac{\overline{K}}{\lambda}. \qquad \qquad \square$$

On the Evaluation of a Secure Solution to Access 802.11 Networks

Fernando da Costa Jr.[1], Luciano Gaspary[1], Jorge Barbosa[1],
Gerson Cavalheiro[1], Luciano Pfitscher[1], and José Dirceu G. Ramos[2]

[1] Universidade do Vale do Rio dos Sinos
Programa Interdisciplinar de Pós-Graduação em Computação Aplicada
Av. Unisinos, 950 – 93.022-000 – São Leopoldo, Brazil
fcaprio@exatas.unisinos.br
[2] Hewlett Packard do Brasil

Abstract. Despite offering the possibility to develop and distribute a new set of applications to its users, the widespread and unrestricted use of mobile computing depends on the provisioning of a secure network environment. Regarding the communication established from mobile devices such as PDAs (Personal Digital Assistants), one of the most currently used standards is the IEEE 802.11b, which presents known security flaws. To overcome them, some alternative setups are commonly deployed, based on link, network, transport or application-layer. In this paper we evaluate the impact on data reception rate and energy consumption of IPSec-based PDAs access to 802.11b (WiFi) wireless LANs. As a result of this work we identify the overhead imposed by the security mechanisms and the capacity of the device to run CPU and network-intensive applications.

Keywords: WiFi networks, data reception rate, PDA energy consumption, IPSec.

1 Introduction[1]

The miniaturization of electronic components and the growing offer of wireless communication technologies have stimulated the development of small and high capacity computational devices, which enable the concrete implementation of the *mobile computing* concept. In a mobile context it is common to have portable devices such as PDAs interconnected to the wired network infrastructure through wireless links. The easiness of connection and physical mobility of these devices leads to the possibility of providing the users of this technology with a new set of applications (e.g. location-aware and video on demand). However, in order to execute these applications in a production environment some security issues need to be addressed.

One of the most currently used standards to allow network connectivity from mobile devices is the IEEE 802.11b, which has several security flaws (Cam-Winget et al., 2003). In order to overcome them, some alternative security setups, ranging from link to application layer, have been widely deployed in production environments (e.g. IPSec and SSL).

---

[1] This work was partially developed in collaboration with HP Brazil R&D.

J. Filipe et al. (Eds.): ICETE 2005, CCIS 3, pp. 226–235, 2007.

These additional components are essential to enable the secure communication of millions of devices using IEEE 802.11b that have already been sold, and cannot be replaced by other equipment without extra investments.

Regardless of the security mechanism used, it leads to an overhead in terms of both the data sent/reception rates achieved by the mobile device and its energy consumption. Identifying this overhead and determining which applications can be executed by mobile devices such as PDAs (keeping their autonomy) is valuable, because one can adjust security mechanisms to achieve the best tradeoff between security and consumption.

In this paper we evaluate the impact on data reception rate and energy consumption of IPSec-based PDAs access to 802.11b wireless LANs. We have chosen IPSec because it is the most current, widely adopted setup. Furthermore, since it is a network-layer technology, all applications can take advantage of the security mechanisms that it provides: authentication, privacy, and integrity.

The paper is organized as follows: section 2 describes some related work. Section 3 presents the setup configured to achieve a secure wireless network environment. In sections 4 and 5 we detail the experiments carried out. Section 6 presents some final considerations.

2 Related Work

Measuring and characterizing the current limits of portable devices in terms of both communication capabilities and energy consumption, to mention just a few aspects, are issues that have been gaining attention recently. This topic grows in importance when secure wireless communications are demanded. Since a lot of extra computation is required to guarantee properties such as authentication, privacy, and integrity, the feasibility to run a variety of applications is directly affected.

Potlapally, Ravi, Raghunathan, and Jha present in (Potlapally et al., 2003) an analysis of the energy consumed by mobile devices when using several combinations of security mechanisms in SSL-based applications. Various cryptography (RSA, DSA, and ECDSA) and hashing (MD2, MD4, MD5, SHA, SHA1, and HMAC) algorithms have been used in the experiments.

Other work related to PDA energy consumption was published by Karri and Mishra in (Karri and Mishra, 2003). The authors measure the energy consumed by the device (i) when secure WAP (Wireless Application Protocol) sessions are established and (ii) during secured data transfer. An additional contribution of the paper is the proposal of techniques to reduce energy consumption. By applying techniques based on information compression, session negotiation protocol optimization, and hardware acceleration of crypto-mechanisms, the energy consumed for session establishment has been reduced by more than 6.5 times, when compared to the normal power consumption. Similarly, the energy for data transmission has diminished more than 1.5 times.

The overhead introduced by WEP (Wireless Equivalent Privacy) and IPSec protocols in IEEE 802.11b wireless networks has been measured by Maciel et al. in (Maciel et al., 2003). The data throughput achieved by desktop computers (with wireless cards attached to them) has been calculated under two different configurations: employing (i) solely WEP and (ii) both WEP and IPSec. This comparison is of little practical utility, however. WEP becomes unnecessary when IPSec is used, because besides being vulnerable, the first leads to an undesired additional overhead.

In this paper we measure the data reception rate and the energy consumed by a Personal Digital Assistant with and without the employment of IPSec protocol. We identify the type of applications that can be efficiently executed by the portable device even when security mechanisms are employed. We also characterize how much these mechanisms impact the autonomy of the PDA.

3   A Secure Wireless Local Area Network Setup

There are several approaches that can be applied to secure current IEEE 802.11b wireless networks with no extra investments in hardware: IPSec (IP Security) (Kent and Atkinson, 2004), CIPE (Crypto IP Encapsulation) (cip, 2004), and VTUN (Virtual Tunnel) (vtu, 2004) at the network-layer; SSL (Secure Socket Layer) (Freier et al., 1996) at the transport-layer; SET (Secure Electronic Transaction) (set, 2004), and OpenVPN (ope, 2004) at the application layer.

CIPE, VTUN, and OpenVPN are not supported by mobile device operating systems such as PalmOS and PocketPC 2003. SSL and IPSec are by far the most deployed schemes. The former is used to provide application-specific end-to-end encrypted transfers. The latter, on the other hand, offers a general purpose cryptographic tunnel capable of providing secured communication to any application running on the PDA. Due to this generality, we have chosen to use IPSec in our experiments.

The setup is composed of a L2TP (Layer 2 Tunneling Protocol) (Townsley et al., 1999) and an IPSec server (FreeS/WAN (fre, 2004)) running on the gateway (figure 1). L2TP/ IPsec is one the mechanisms that can be used by Pocket PC 2003 to acquire a virtual IP address from the internal network. This scheme has been chosen because (i) it is used by Pocket PC 2003's built-in VPN client (which is free!) and (ii) it is an official IETF standard.

We have configured the IPSec server to run in tunnel mode, i.e. both the header and the payload of packets sent/received by the PDA to/from the gateway are encrypted. Although this is a very conservative setup, it has been used so that worst case measurements could be made.

The authentication process used was PSK (Pre-shared Key). A Pre-shared Key is a secret password that is shared by both sides of the IPSec tunnel. Preferably, the PSK is distributed through "out-of-band" medium, such as phone call, paper, face to face, and should not be transmitted over public networks.

4   Experimental Setup

Mobile devices face problems on battery working time and packet processing, which get critical when CPU and network-intensive applications are executed. Due to these restrictions, it is important to figure out the impact of the security mechanisms intended to be used in the wireless network infrastructure (the idea is to avoid imposing many extra limitations to the use of the device). To better understand the relation between data reception rate and energy consumption under different scenarios, we have carried out some experiments (described henceforth).

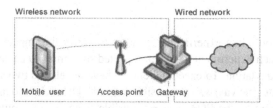

Fig. 1. IPSec-based PDAs access to 802.11b wireless LANs

4.1 Testing Environment

The setup of the experiments was composed of a client and a server (gateway). The client was an iPAQ 5550 with a 400MHz Xscale processor 128MB RAM, running Pocket PC 2003 operating system. The gateway was an Intel Celeron 500MHz 128MB RAM. In order to provide support for IPSec in the gateway, we have installed the following software: Debian Linux, kernel 2.6 (ker, 2004) (with native support for IPSec), FreeS/WAN[2], and L2TP. The communication between the client and the gateway was done through a Linksys WAP11 access point (IEEE 802.11b), located around 15 meters far from the client.

The energy consumed by the mobile device during the data transmissions has been measured through the battery output voltage and the electric current data, which were acquired with an oscilloscope. The circuit implemented for acquiring these signals is showed in figure 2. The oscilloscope used was an Agilent 54622D MegaZoom, 100MHz, 200MSa/s. To monitor the electric current, a shunt resistor of $0.1\,\Omega$ has been applied.

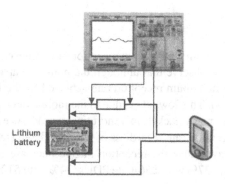

Fig. 2. Circuit for measuring the energy consumed by the mobile device

The determination of the energy consumed (W) has been obtained by the integration of the voltage x electric current, and can be expressed by the following equation: $W = \int v.i.dt(Joule)$.

---

[2] FreeS/WAN had to be patched to support NAT-T (Traversal NAT for UDP packets).

4.2   Experiments

We have carried out three experiments in order to verify the impact of IPSec on the mobile device. Each experiment has been repeated five times to calculate the average and the standard deviation. To execute them we have developed two applications. The first, running on the gateway, was responsible to send UDP packets to the mobile device. The second, running on the PDA, was responsible to analyze the number of received UDP packets so that we could measure the reception rate in Mbps.

The first experiment assessed the maximum reception rate achieved by the mobile device (using IPSec). In this test we analyzed the data flow with no speed control during a 180-second period. We have used different PDU sizes: 256, 512, and 1024 bytes. 3DES and SHA1 algorithms have been applied, respectively, for encryption and integrity checking.

The second experiment aimed at measuring energy consumption and packet reception rate in controlled speed UDP stream transmissions. We have divided it in two groups: low speed (56, 128, and 256Kbps) and high speed stream transmissions (1, 2, 4, and 8Mbps). In low speed tests each transmission lasted 8 minutes (for better accuracy), while in high speed tests they ran for 3 minutes. For all these tests 1024-byte PDUs have been used. Again, IPSec traffic has been encrypted using 3DES and SHA1.

In order to get a more refined view on energy consumption and packet reception rate we have repeated the previous UDP stream transmission at 2Mbps using several PDU sizes (256, 512, 1024, and 2048 bytes).

In the third experiment we have evaluated the impact of using some combinations of encryption and hashing algorithms on the PDA energy consumption. We transmitted 1024-byte UDP packets at 2Mbps from the gateway to the PDA, using DES and 3DES cryptographic algorithms combined with SHA1 and MD5 integrity algorithms.

5   Results

Figure 3 shows the maximum UDP stream reception rate achieved by the mobile device. From the graph one can observe that although the nominal capacity of WiFi wireless LANs is 11Mbps, the maximum reception rate achieved by the PDA was 3,109Mbps (using 1024-byte PDUs). This low rate is due to the mobile device limited CPU, which is not able to process so many packets in a short time period. As expected, the PDU size affects directly the reception rate regardless of whether IPSec is used or not. However, the use of IPSec always cause the reception rate to decrease compared to the non-encrypted transmission: 27% with 256-byte PDUs, 34% with 512-byte PDUs, and 33% with 1024-byte PDUs.

In the second experiment two aspects have been analyzed: successful packet reception rate and energy consumption overhead[3]. As already mentioned in section 4.2, this experiment has been divided in two groups: high speed and low speed stream transmissions. The packet reception rate for the low speed data stream transmissions was almost

---

[3] The overhead has been calculated by decreasing the PDA absolute energy consumption value after a fixed period data transmission from the energy consumed by the device during an equivalent time period when it was idle.

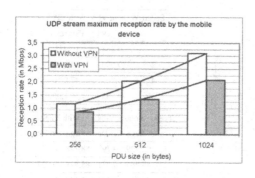

PDU	Without VPN	With VPN
	Pkts rcvd	Pkts rcvd
256	107.644	78.762
512	93.756	61.820
1024	71.633	47890

PDU	Without VPN		With VPN	
	Avg	Std Dev	Avg	Std Dev
256	1,168	0,039	0,855	0,004
512	2,035	0,013	1,342	0,048
1024	3,109	0,066	2,079	0,012

Fig. 3. Maximum reception rate achieved by the mobile device

100%. This was expected, since in the previous experiment we have shown the PDA is able to cope with the 3,109Mbps reception rate.

Figure 4 shows the energy overhead consumed by the mobile device to receive low speed UDP streams. The consumption is directly affected by the transmission speed (the higher the speed, the higher the number of packets to be processed). It is worth observing in the graph how much the use of IPSec affects energy consumption in each transmission rate. The overhead of using IPSec at 56kbps is 18%. This difference gets bigger as the transmission rate increases, achieving 47% for 256kbps. Taking into account the total battery energy is 13.72KJ (measured prior to the experiments), the consumption of 25J to receive a 8-minute UDP stream at 128Kbps using 1024-byte packets corresponds to 0,001% of the battery capacity.

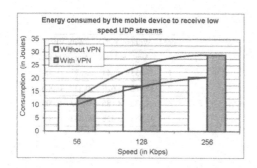

Speed	Without VPN		With VPN	
	Avg	Std Dev	Avg	Std Dev
56	10,200	23,091	12,500	12,261
128	17,000	2,646	25,000	9,899
256	20,500	2,121	29,000	11,314

Fig. 4. Mobile device energy consumption overhead to receive low speed UDP streams

For the high speed data stream transmissions it is valuable to illustrate two graphs: successful packet reception rate (figure 5) and energy consumption overhead (figure 6). The first shows the number of UDP packets received and processed by the mobile device in relation to the number of packets transmitted by the gateway under different speeds (from 1 to 8Mbps). From the graph one can infer that 2Mbps is the maximum reception rate the PDA using IPSec is able to handle with less than 20% of packet loss. When VPN is not used this rate grows up to 4Mbps. Above these rates the PDA receives less than 60% of the packets, which is not acceptable for applications such as video streaming.

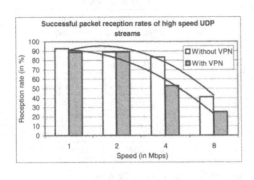

Speed	Without VPN	With VPN
	Pkts rcvd	Pkts rcvd
1	20.864	19.975
2	39.990	39.995
4	75.203	47.834
8	73.885	45.125

Speed	Without VPN		With VPN	
	Avg	Std Dev	Avg	Std Dev
1	92,729	9,793	88,778	0,050
2	88,867	0,031	88,878	0,003
4	83,558	0,034	53,148	0,276
8	41,047	0,192	25,069	0,004

Fig. 5. Mobile device successful packet reception rates of high speed UDP streams

The second graph (figure 6) shows the energy overhead consumed by the mobile device to receive high speed data stream transmissions. Since its maximum reception rate is 3.109Mbps (figure 3), the energy consumption reaches the maximum value between 2 and 4Mbps (around 90J). The PDA consumes 37% more energy when IPSec is used to transmit/receive streams at 1Mbps, and 64% at 2Mbps. At 4Mbps and 8Mbps the energy consumed does not grow proportionally, because the number of packets received and processed is similar to what happens at 2 Mbps (figure 5); most of the packets are lost in these rates.

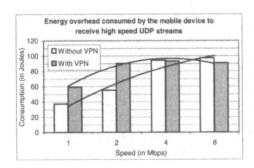

Speed	Without VPN		With VPN	
	Avg	Std Dev	Avg	Std Dev
1	37,333	4,243	59,333	0,000
2	55,083	5,620	90,333	0,000
4	94,333	8,185	93,333	0,000
8	97,333	2,828	90,833	0,707

Fig. 6. Mobile device energy consumption overhead to receive high speed UDP streams

Figures 7 and 8 illustrate a zoomed view of the mobile device successful packet reception rate and energy consumption overhead when UDP streams at 2Mbps are transmitted to it. As one can notice in figure 7, the reception rate increases as larger packets are used (up to 1024 bytes). When 2048-byte long packets are transmitted by the gateway, they are fragmented and the mobile device reception rate drops unexpectedly to less than 10%. This is a good indicative that network intensive applications such as streaming video should be tuned to use the largest packet size that can be sent without fragmentation.

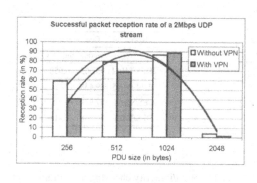

PDU	Without VPN	With VPN
	Pkts rcvd	Pkts rcvd
256	106.273	72.514
512	71.167	61.748
1024	39.058	39.983
2048	867	324

PDU	Without VPN		With VPN	
	Avg	Std Dev	Avg	Std Dev
256	59,041	8,630	40,285	5,452
512	79,074	1,758	68,609	2,377
1024	86,796	0,566	88,850	0,024
2048	3,851	0,651	1,440	0,314

Fig. 7. Packet reception rate of a 2Mbps UDP stream using different PDU sizes

The energy overhead consumed by the mobile device to receive a 2Mbps UDP stream is shown in figure 8. The use of IPSec imposes a considerable overhead in the energy consumption compared to the non-encrypted transmissions: 3,72% for 256 byte packets, 27,67% for 512 byte packets, 50,22% for 1024 byte packets, and 53,12% for 2048 byte packets. Regarding the consumption associated with the first three transmissions, they are almost equivalent. This is explained in figure 7, where one may notice the packet reception rates increase as less, larger packets are transmitted by the gateway. When 256 byte PDUs were used, 72.514 packets have been received and processed by the PDA. On the other hand, only 39.983 packets have been received when 1024 byte PDU were transmitted. A lot of the consumption in the first case is related to header protection. Therefore, the best tradeoff between successful reception rate and energy consumption is reached when 1024-byte long packets are used.

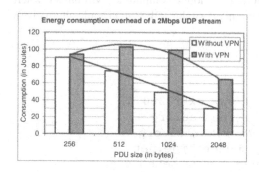

PDU	Without VPN		With VPN	
	Avg	Std Dev	Avg	Std Dev
256	90,494	12,021	93,994	8,485
512	74,494	0,707	102,994	1,414
1024	49,494	0,707	99,438	0,707
2048	30,438	2,121	64,938	1,414

Fig. 8. Energy consumption overhead to receive a 2Mbps UDP stream

Figure 9 shows the results of the third experiment, where we have assessed the impact of using different encryption (DES and 3DES) and integrity checking (MD5 and SHA1) algorithms on the PDA energy consumption. As depicted in the graph, the combination 3DES/SHA1 is the most computational intensive. It is explained by the higher complexity of both algorithms compared to DES/MD5 (Stallings, 2002).

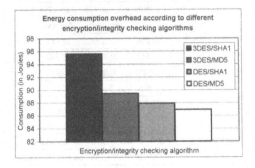

Algorithms	Consumption	
	Average	Std Dev
3DES/SHA1	95,605	6,658
3DES/MD5	89,438	2,121
DES/SHA1	87,938	0,000
DES/MD5	86,938	1,414

Fig. 9. Energy consumption using different encryption/integrity checking algorithms

6   Conclusions

In this paper several approaches to solve some of the existing flaws in 802.11b networks have been commented. Then we have described the IPSec-based setup and the testing environment. The experiments carried out aimed at assessing the impact on data reception rate and energy consumption of IPSec-based PDAs access to 802.11b wireless LANs.

From the results obtained, it is important to highlight the maximum reception rate achieved by the mobile device is less than 50% of the nominal capacity (it gets worse when IPSec is used). The PDA energy consumption increases considerably when the security mechanisms are employed. It is also worth mentioning that the mobile device does not cope well with fragmentation. Depending on the number and size of the UDP packets it is not able to process more than 50% of them. Finally, we found out 3DES/SHA1, which are the the the most common used encryption/integrity checking algorithms, are the ones that consume more. In a mobile computing environment, where maximizing the battery working time is highly desirable, DES/MD5 could alternatively be used.

References

Crypto ip encapsulation (2004), http://www.extra300.nl
Linux frees/wan (2004), http://www.freeswan.org
Linux kernel archives (2004), http://www.kernel.org/
Openvpn (2004), http://openvpn.sourceforge.net
Secure electronic transaction (2004), http://www.setco.org
Virtual tunnels over tcp/ip networks (2004), http://vtun.sourceforge.net
Cam-Winget, N., Housley, R., Wagner, D., Walker, J.: Security flaws in 802.11 data link protocols. Communications of the ACM (2003)
Freier, A.O., Karlton, P., Kocher, P.C.: The ssl protocol version 3.0. In: IETF Internet Draft (1996)
Karri, R., Mishra, P.: Optimizing the energy consumed by secure wireless sessions: Wireless transport layer security case study. In: Mobile Networks and Applications (2003)

Kent, S., Atkinson, R.: Security architecture for the internet protocol. In: IETF RFC 2401 (2004)

Maciel, P., Nunes, B., Campos, C., Moraes, L.: Sobrecarga introduzida nas redes 802.11 pelos mecanismos de segurana wep e vpn/ipsec. In: 3rd Brazilian Workshop on Security of Computing Systems (2003)

Potlapally, N., Ravi, S., Raghunathan, A., Jha, N.: Analyzing the energy consumption of security protocols. In: Dept. of Electrical Engineering, Princeton University (2003)

Stallings, W.: Network Security Essentials. Prentice Hall, Englewood Cliffs (2002)

Townsley, W., Valencia, A., Rubens, A., Pall, G., Zorn, G., Palter, B.: Layer two tunneling protocol l2tp. In: IETF RFC 2661 (1999)

Searching for Resources in MANETs – A Cluster Based Flooding Approach

Rodolfo Oliveira, Luis Bernardo, and Paulo Pinto

Faculdade de Ciências e Tecnologia, Universidade Nova de Lisboa,
P-2829-516 Caparica, Portugal
{rado,lflb,pfp}@uninova.pt

Abstract. In this paper, we propose a searching service optimized for highly dynamic mobile ad-hoc networks based on a flooding approach. MANETs unreliability and routing costs prevent the use of central servers or global infra-structured services on top of a priori defined virtual overlay networks. A flooding approach over a virtual overlay network created on-demand performs better. Flooding is supported by a light-weight clustering algorithm. The paper compares the relative efficiency of two clustering approaches using 1.5-hop and 2.5-hop neighborhood information, and of a non-clustered approach. It presents a set of simulation results on the clustering efficiency and on searching efficiency for low and high mobility patterns, showing that the 1.5-hop algorithm is more resilient to load and to node movement than the 2.5-hop algorithm.

Keywords: Performance analysis of wireless ad hoc networks, searching service, clustering protocol.

1 Introduction

The problem of looking for resources on 802.11 Mobile Ad hoc NETworks (MANETs) is complex due to the networks unstable nature. Nodes move around independently creating a very dynamic network topology. It is assumed that no geographic position information is available, which is most of the time true, mainly in indoor scenarios. MANET routing protocols can be seen as resource lookup service that look for IP addresses.

Experience with fast moving nodes (Tsumochi, 03) showed that standard proactive, table-driven, routing protocols perform worst than on-demand routing protocols, which flood the network looking for an address only when it is needed. It also shows that both approaches fail to handle extreme mobility conditions. The problem is that routing information becomes outdated too fast, especially for lengthy paths. Due to bandwidth restrictions, it is not feasible to maintain proactively the tables always updated. On-demand approaches fail due to packet collisions and due to the breaking of the return path in result of intermediate node movement. These conclusions are extensible to generic searching services implemented at application layers. Structured peer-to-peer p2p (services) and directory services have much higher update costs than flooding based services (Bernardo, 04). A flooding approach is more adapted to

J. Filipe et al. (Eds.): ICETE 2005, CCIS 3, pp. 236–245, 2007.
© Springer-Verlag Berlin Heidelberg 2007

unstable MANETs due to the null registration costs. All efforts are concentrated during the search phase.

The searching protocol performance depends strongly on the lower layers of the protocol stack, responsible for routing IP packets, and for handling the Medium Access Control (MAC). Traditional flooding peer-to-peer (p2p) services create virtual overlay networks. They are formed by several nodes connected using static TCP links. Their performance drops sharply on a MANET if the virtual overlay topology is not similar to the network physical topology, due to the routing protocol overhead. Crossing a virtual link may lead to a route recovery procedure (usually a network flood) if the MANET topology changes.

The MANET routing protocol overhead can be avoided if the searching protocol's query message is broadcasted, hop by hop, during the searching flood (e.g. ad hoc mode of the JXTA rendezvous protocol (JXTA, 04)). However, two problems may occur: the 802.11 MAC layer is more error prone for multicast/broadcast packets than for unicast packets, and dense networks may suffer from the broadcast storm problem (Tseng, 02). This latter problem can be minimized organizing nodes into clusters, and reducing the number of nodes sending messages to the network.

This paper presents a new searching algorithm, optimized for very dynamic continuous MANETs. It focuses mainly on the clustering algorithm. Section two overviews existing cluster based searching algorithms. The proposed clustering and searching protocols are presented on sections three and four. Section five presents the ns-2 simulation setup, and several performance measurements. Finally, section six draws some conclusions and presents future work directions.

2 Cluster Based Searching

Cluster based searching approaches group nodes into broadcast groups (BGs), and using a set of heuristics select BG leaders (BGLs), responsible for forwarding packets for their BG. Nodes periodically broadcast a beacon packet, that may carry (Wu, 03): local information (1-hop); its BGL (1.5-hop); a neighbor node (within radio range) list (2-hop); the neighbor's list with the BGLs information (2.5-hop); etc. Most MANET protocols adopt a 2-hop or above approach (e.g. OLSR (Jacquet, 01)). 2-hop is the minimum information required to define a set of active nodes that cover all nodes, usually called a Connected Dominant Set (CDS). Although, on an unstable MANET, it is possible that 2-hop and further distant neighbors information is out-of-date, introducing errors on the CDS construction that result in failure to cover all nodes. Additional errors may result from the impossibility of revoking explicit state configurations created using signaling (e.g. OLSR BGL election).

Another approach is to adopt 1-hop strategies (e.g. SBA (Peng, 00)), just for maintaining the list of neighbors, and to use an external searching protocol for restraining the number of active nodes. In SBA, nodes delay the sending of query messages for a random time waiting for its possible transmission by other neighbors. Nodes include their neighbor list (Nq) on the query message before sending it. Receivers store the union of Nq lists received (Nu) and compare it with their list of neighbors (Nr), canceling the transmission when Nu is equal to Nr. ABC-QS (Choi, 02) modifies the forwarding rule proposed by SBA reducing searching delay: nodes do not delay the query message sending if the number of neighbors in Nr and not in Nq is above the number of neighbors common to Nr and Nq. Otherwise, they delay an average time proportional to the number of nodes in Nr and not in Nq. ABC-QS may fail for dense MANETs where overlapped nodes may send packets without waiting.

MANETs are not homogeneous. Some nodes stay together during a large period of time (e.g. students on a bus tour) while others move independently. Beacons can also be used to detect relative stability relationships. Toh introduced the concept in ABR (Toh, 97), measuring the number of beacons received. ABC-QS extended the metric to cope with asynchronous piggybacked beacons. Other authors introduced link stability measurements based on packet probability failure (McDonald, 99). Nevertheless, most clustering approaches do not take link stability into consideration (OLSR, etc.), producing unstable clusters for unstable MANETs.

ABC-QS and (McDonald, 99) create proactive routing information within islands of stable connected nodes, to speed up searches. However, they ignore the stability information for thorough flooding network searches that cover several stable islands. This paper proposes a new solution, which improves flooding using stability information.

3 Clustering Algorithm

The proposed clustering algorithm groups "stable" nodes into 1-hop radius clusters. Each node selects a BGL periodically using a local soft-state protocol. The resulting network simplified view is used to reduce the flooding search overhead.

Each node periodically broadcasts a beacon message. All nodes that receive a beacon from a node n_y are defined as n_y neighbor nodes. Nodes keep a table of neighbors' link stability η (called the beacon table). Following ABR, link stability for n_y is defined as the sum of consecutive beacons received from n_y. If more than one beacon is lost, then link stability is set to null. The stability measurement trades-off a faster link failure detection (compared to packet loss rate measurements) for a higher probability of false link loss detection due to two successive beacon collisions. High stability values represent low nodes relative mobility and vice-versa.

In each beacon message, a node sends its node identification, its BGL node address, and the higher link stability value contained in its beacon table, which is represented by μ. The beacon table includes the neighbor's address, their link stability (η); their BGL address; and the μ value received in the last beacon. Every beacon table entry is automatically destroyed if a beacon is not received during two beaconing time periods. Table 1 is a hypothetical beacon table of node 3 illustrated in figure 1. Node 3 received 43 beacons from neighbor node 1.

Table 1. Beacon table of node 3 on figure 1

Neighb.	Stability (η)	BGL	Neighb. Stability (μ)
1	43	1	43
2	8	6	64
4	2	5	33

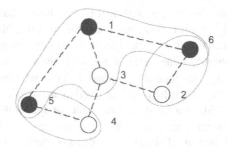

Fig. 1. Illustration of a MANET with 3 BGs. Nodes 1, 5 and 6 are BGLs.

```
1.   (η_max)=find_maximum_η_value_in_table()
2.   last_addr = MAX_INT
3.   pre_selected = -1
4.   if is_stable(n_a)    // stable node
5.      //insert all known BGL's stable neighbor
        //nodes in BGL_list
6.      for each neighborhood_node n_x
7.         insert_in_sort_list(BGL(n_x),BGL_list)
8.      if is_BGL(n_a) // if this node is BGL
9.         insert_in_sort_list(n_a,BGL_list)
10.     // Choose BGL based on stability and
        // lowest address criteria
11.     for each bgl_x contained in BGL_list
12.        for each neighborhood_node n_x
13.           if ((n_x=bgl_x)and(is_stable(n_x)))
14.              pre_selected = n_x
15.        if (pre_selected ≠-1) break;
16.        if (n_a=bgl_x) // self-selection
17.           pre_selected = n_a
18.           break
19.     //select new BGL
20.     if (pre_selected=-1)//BGL is not selected
21.        for each neighborhood_node n_x
22.           if (η_max-η(n_x)-transient_threshold ≤ 0)
                        ∧ (addr(n_x)<last_addr)
23.              last_addr = addr(n_x)
24.              pre_selected = n_x
25. BGL_SELECTED = pre_selected
```

Fig. 2. BGL node selection algorithm applied in node n_a

A node is stable if there is at least one η value in its beacon table that is higher than a defined `stability_threshold`. BGL selection algorithm is run on each node before sending a beacon. The selection algorithm for node n_a is summarized in figure 2.

A stable node first computes a sort list of all available neighbor's BGL (lines 5 to 7), that includes the node in case of being BGL (lines 8 to 9). This list is sorted from the smallest to the largest BGL address. If there are BGLs selected in the neighborhood, the node chooses the BGL that has the lowest address (lines 11 to 15), which can be the node itself if it was chosen as BGL by a neighbor (lines 16 to 18). If there are no BGLs selected in its neighborhood, a node simply selects as BGL its neighbor with the highest η value (lines 20 to 24). If there is more than one neighbor owning the maximum η value then it is selected the node with lowest address.

During system startup, transitory cluster overlap may appear, because the initial criteria for selecting BGL is a local measurement for link stability (lines 21 to 23), which may differ from node to node. The `transient_threshold` was set to one, to compensate different beacon delivery time drifts (jitter). The initial BGL is the neighbor with the lowest address that could get the maximum stability value during the present beaconing period. Yet, when several BGLs exist within radio range connected by stable links, they are merged into a single cluster (lines 10 to 18) after one beacon period. Two nodes from overlapped clusters sort neighbor's BGLs independently into the same order (only node address is considered) and converge to the same BGL.

Cluster overlapping also occurs for continuous groups of stable nodes wider than one hop. The algorithm leads to the construction of multiple tree structures of BGLs, called cluster-trees, centered on BGLs with local minimum addresses. Each branch has a sequence of BGLs (n_i) with increasing addresses, whose BGL is the branch predecessor ($BGL(n_i) = n_{i-1}$). The exception is the periphery of the cluster-tree, where nodes with lower addresses can exist. Due to line 16, a node can only self-select as BGL if another node previously selects him. This avoids the existence of single node clusters on the periphery of a cluster-tree.

Within a connected stable group (a group of cluster-trees connected by stable links), the border between cluster-trees' BGLs is composed by one or two non-BGL nodes. It cannot be zero because lines 12-15 would merge the BGLs. Also, it cannot be more than two because that would mean that a node would not have a BGL in the neighborhood, and lines 20-24 would select a new BGL.

Figure 1 presents a cluster-tree with a root BGL (node 1) and two branch BGLs (nodes 5 and 6). Node's 6 BGL is node 1, but node 6 is also a BGL selected by node 2. Node 2 will only form an independent cluster-tree if a new node creates a stable link and selects him as BGL.

The clustering algorithms' performance depends on the network stability. If a large percentage of the nodes are stable, the algorithm is able to detect them, and reduce their load by grouping them in clusters. If all nodes are unstable, beaconing only introduces overhead. A lower beacon period value tolerates higher nodes velocity. However, it increases the bandwidth overhead and the network collisions. It is better to reduce the clustering overhead and increase the flooding algorithm redundancy, to tolerate clustering inaccuracies. If conventional criteria were used, the clustering algorithm would create highly unstable clusters, which would include passing-by moving nodes, and would route query packets based on this error prone information.

4 Searching Algorithms

The searching algorithms were developed as an evolution of the basic source routing flooding algorithm (SR). In SR the lookup operation is started with a query message originated by a source node, which carries a unique identification (Q_{id}), the source node address (n_{source}), a resource identification pattern to locate (R_{id}), and the path (P). This message is successively resent by each node, as long as it has not been received before and the hop limit is not reached. Each sender appends its identification to P. Nodes maintain a local table indexed by source node id, with last query' ids received. A hit message is sent to the source node when any local information satisfies the query. Hits are routed to the query's node source using the path included in the query message.

This paper proposes 1.5-hop and 2.5-hop algorithms that enhance SR flooding phase, reducing its overhead, and the hit message routing, improving its resilience to node movement and failure. SR is modified in three ways:

(a) The number of active nodes is reduced using the clustering node information. A node can be: a BGL if it receives a beacon selecting it; a non-BGL if it selects a BGL but is not selected a BGL; or isolated if it does not select a BGL. An unstable node with one or more stable nodes in its neighborhood selects for BGL the node with the highest μ value, strictly for flooding purposes. Two approaches are presented above;

(b) Query message size is reduced by removing all non-BGLs and isolated nodes' ids before the last BGL from the path field (P). The partial path is stored and pruned, each time the message passes on a BGL. In case of node failure, the node can always use the BGL list (stored in the query message) to recover the route to the source node;

(c) When hit messages follow the query reverse path, unicast is used and their sending is confirmed. When a link fails, the node looks at its neighbor list, and neighbor's BGL list, looking for any node on the reverse path. As a last resort, when no information is available, the node that detects the failure starts a hit message flooding. The hit message is treated as a special query packet, looking for a node id within the remaining query path list, which does not receive any reply. Hit flooding stops when the message reaches a node whose neighbor's (or the node itself) are part of the remaining path. Therefore, contrary to SR, the proposed algorithm is able to survive to extreme mobility, and is able to route hit messages over failed or moving nodes.

A. 1.5-hop searching algorithm

BGL and isolated nodes always broadcast queries one time (though isolated delay message transmission). A non-BGL delays the query sending for a fixed delay plus a jitter interval, and lists the visited BGL on a local variable. While the timer is active, the node continues to receive replicas of the query message resent by neighbors. It just extracts the query path list (P), and updates the visited BGL list with the node's address and the nodes's BGL address. When the timer goes off, the node checks to see if all its neighbors' BGLs and his own BGL are already listed. If they are not, then it resends the message to cover the missing BGLs. Otherwise, it drops the message.

Since BGLs do not delay the message and isolated nodes do, search path goes preferentially over BGL nodes. For cluster-tree borders defined by non-BGLs, the timer's jitter limits the number of retransmissions that occur on dense networks. The faster non-BGL on an area transmits the query to the destination BGL (or non-BGL for BGLs separated by two non-BGLs), which retransmits it. The BGL is added to the visited BGL list of other non-BGLs on the same area suspending their transmissions.

The algorithm improves SBA (Peng, 00) and ABC-QS (Choi, 02): It reduces the searching delay while crossing a connected set of stable nodes because BGLs never delay a query message; it reduces the message size (the number of BGL is lower than the number of nodes); it bases search paths preferentially over stable nodes, less likely to disappear; and it degrades more gracefully in the presence of transmission errors. It handles transmission errors similarly to SBA and ABC-QS: nodes keep sending a query message as long as a BGL does not appear on the path. Therefore, it only fails to reduce the load if none of the neighbor members of a BGL cluster retransmit the query message. This behavior improves the algorithm effectiveness for high network loads (due to the higher collision rate) and for high mobility conditions.

The algorithm does not guarantee total coverage on unstable networks, because it does not take into account unstable nodes in the neighborhood that did not yet transmit a beacon.

B. 2.5-hop searching algorithm

A second searching algorithm was developed as an extension of the 2.5-hop algorithm proposed in (Wu, 03).

A clustering algorithm modification is needed to support 2.5-hop searching algorithms: the neighbor's BGL list is added to the beacon message. The original 2.5-hop clustering algorithms (Wu, 03) sent the entire list of neighbors on the beacon producing more overhead.

On this algorithm, a node has information about all BGLs and isolated nodes within 2-hop distance. In order to reduce bandwidth usage, each sending node puts in the query message the list of non-BGL nodes at 1-hop distance (v) that must resend the message. The message is sent by the query starting node; by each BGL visited and isolated nodes; and by the non-BGL nodes that are in list v. List v is constructed from the set of 1 hop neighbors, and includes the non-BGLs required to cover all 2-hop distance BGLs. The algorithm: 1) first adds the neighbor nodes with unique paths to a BGL; 2) then, adds the neighbors that cover the maximum number of BGLs not yet in the list. A minimum node identification criterion was used to select from nodes with similar number of BGLs accessible.

The algorithm is more sensible to errors in the clustering information than the 1.5-hop version, since it uses topology information received one beacon period ago to select on-demand the next hop for the query message flooding. It also has less redundancy to tolerate transmission and topology errors, because it floods queries on a minimum CDS.

5 Simulations

The proposed algorithms and the source routing algorithm were implemented on version 2.27 of ns-2 platform (ns-2). The presented simulations compare the algorithms performance, using the same query generation and node movement patterns. In each simulation scenario 200 nodes are moving during 1000 seconds on a

1000m x 1000m area according to the Generalized Random Waypoint mobility model. Five different mobility scenarios were defined to study the mobility behavior of each flooding technique. Node's average speeds of 0m/s, 1 m/s, 10m/s, 30 m/s and 40m/s were obtained using constant pause times of 1000, 150, 10, 9 and 5 seconds, respectively. Each node has approximately 100 meters of communication range using IEEE 802.11b over the two-ray ground propagation model. The beaconing frequency of each node is 1 Hz. The clustering algorithm parameters `transient_threshold` and `stability_threshold` are one and five seconds, respectively.

Ten thousands of different resources are randomly distributed on the network nodes. Three different behavior patterns were defined using the model presented in (Ge, 03). High, medium and low network load correspond, to 10927, 1125 and 267 generated queries, respectively. Finally, all broadcasts are sent with a jitter value of 100 ms, and the 1.5-hop algorithm uses a delay of 700 ms for non-BGLs and isolated nodes.

Figure 3 presents experimental results for the average BGL selection time for the fifteen combinations of speed and load, and for 1.5-hops and 2.5-hops neighborhood information. The selection time values not shown on the graph, for low and medium load and mobility zero were respectively 195 and 78 seconds for 1.5-hop and 118 and 61 seconds for 2.5-hop algorithm. These results show that the BGL selection time is negatively influenced by the beacon size and the load, but the average speed is the dominant parameter.

For zero mobility, all BGL changes resulted from having two successive beacon losses, producing a significant churn on the BG composition for heavy loads. Beacons are sent using multicast, and these results show how sensible multicast traffic is to collisions. The clustering algorithm stability could be improved for low mobility scenarios by tolerating more beacons losses. However, the algorithm's performance would degrade significantly for high average speed values. Notice that the algorithm also degrades for the 2.5-hops algorithm, due to the largest beacon length.

Node movement introduces extra BGL re-selections due to topology changes, which become the dominant factor for the two highest speeds. For node average speeds of 30 and 40 m/s the BGL persistent time converges for the minimum possible value (5 minus the selection tolerance of one). The percentage of nodes without a

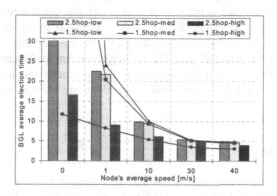

Fig. 3. Average BGL selection time *versus* node average speed for 1.5-hop and 2.5-hop algorithm

BGL also increased significantly, which means that on these scenarios the clustering is almost turned off.

Figure 4 presents the percentage of successful queries for two extreme mobility scenarios of 1 m/s and 40 m/s, where 1.5-hop, 2.5-hop and source routing algorithms are compared using the medium load. It shows that the 1.5-hop searching algorithm outperforms the other two algorithms on both scenarios. It also shows that the pure source routing algorithm performance is poor for both scenarios. The main factor that penalizes source routing algorithm is the dependence on a single reverse path to route the hit packet. Source routing performance for 1 m/s is conditioned by the higher number of nodes disseminating query messages and the longest query message (it carries the complete path), which lead to more packet collisions, destroying query messages and hit messages. For the highest speed, the success probability drops to 2% is result of a high probability of return path failure.

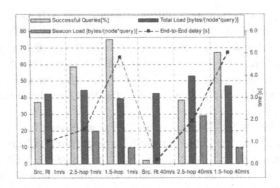

Fig. 4. % Successful queries, load and end-to-end delay *versus* algorithm and node speed for medium load

2.5-algorithm has a higher beacon overhead, which penalizes the bandwidth load. It is also sensible to packet loss during the query message dissemination due to using a minimum CDS. A node movement or a packet loss may produce a query coverage shedding, reducing the successes rate for higher speeds.

The 1.5-hop algorithm has the lowest load levels and is more tolerant to network changes, presenting a low degradation on the successful query rate. On the other hand, it increases the end-to-end search delay. Notice that due to the clustering reduced efficiency for high mobility, the 1.5-hop algorithm load increases, tending for SBA model for extreme mobility scenarios. This characteristic limits the network scale and to the network load supported by the algorithm for very high node average speeds.

6   Conclusions

The results presented in this paper show that the proposed 1.5-hop searching protocol has a strong resilience to network load and node movement, constituting a good choice for extreme mobility scenarios with low load levels. Its adaptability results from an adaptive clustering protocol, based on link stability, which adapts the controls the clustering granularity based on the network conditions. It reduces the cluster size and duration for extreme mobility scenarios increasing searching redundancy; it reduces redundancy for low mobility nodes, reducing the searching overhead.

The obtained results show that for high mobility scenarios, performance improves for the algorithms that use the least possible network information (1.5-hop). It is concluded that source routing approach fails for high mobility scenarios. Since most MANET routing protocols are based on source routing, this can present an important problem for common applications, not prepared to handle this kind of instability.

This paper presents on-going work. Further study is being made on beacon overhead reduction and beacon self-stabilization algorithms, which reduce beacon collision effects.

References

Bernardo, L., Pinto, P.: A Scalable Location Service with Fast Update Responses. In: Proc. ICETE'04, vol. 1, pp. 39–47 (2004)

Choi, Y., Park, D.: Associativity based clustering and query stride for on-demand routing protocol. Journal of Communications and Networks 4(1), 4–13 (2002) Korean Institute of Communications Sciences (KICS)

JXTA Project, 2004. JXTA v2.0 Protocols Specification. Retrieved September 2004 from http://spec.jxta.org/nonav/ v1.0/docbook/JXTAProtocols.html

Ge, Z., Figueiredo, D., Jaiswal, S., Kurose, J., Towsley, B.: Modeling Peer-Peer File Systems. In: IEEE INFOCOM'2003 (2003)

Jacquet, P., Mülethaler, P., Clausen, T., Laouitit, A., Qayyum, A., Viennot, L.: Optimized Link State Routing Protocol for Ad Hoc Networks. In: IEEE INMIC'01, pp. 63–68. IEEE Press, Los Alamitos (2001)

Klingber, T., Manfredi, R.: RFC Draft of Gnutella v0.6. (2002) Retreived from http://rfc-gnutella.sourceforge.net/src/rfc-0_6-draft.html

McDonald, A.B., Znati, T.F.: A Mobility-Based Framework for Adaptive Clustering in Wireless Ad Hoc Networks. IEEE Journal on Selected Areas in Communications 17(8), 1466–1487 (1999)

Network simulator - ns-2. Retrieved from http://www.isi.edu/nsnam/ns/

Peng, W., Lu, X.: On the Reduction of Broadcast Redundancy in Mobile Ad Hoc Networks. In: MobiHoc'00, pp. 129–130. ACM Press, New York (2000)

Toh, C.-K.: Associativity-Based Routing for Ad-hoc Mobile Networks. Journal of Wireless Personal Communications 4, 103–139 (1997)

Tseng, Y.-C., Ni, S.-Y., Chen, Y.-S., Sheu, J.-P.: The Broadcast Storm Problem in a Mobile Ad Hoc Network. Wireless Networks 8(2/3), 153–167 (2002)

Tsumochi, J., Masayama, K., Uehara, H., Yokoyama, M.: Impact of Mobility Metric on Routing Protocols for Mobile Ad Hoc Networks. In: IEEE Pacific Rim Conf. on Communications, Computers and Signal Processing (PACRIM03), pp. 322–325. IEEE Press, Los Alamitos (2003)

Wu, J., Lou, W.: Forward-node-set-based broadcast in clustered mobile ad hoc networks. Wireless Communications and Mobile Computing 3, 155–173 (2003)

A Comparative Study of IEEE 802.11 MAC Access Mechanisms for Different Traffic Types

Mohammad Saraireh, Reza Saatchi, Samir Al-khayatt, and Rebecca Strachan

Sheffield Hallam University, Pond Street, Sheffield, UK
mohammad.saraireh@student.shu.ac.uk,
{r.saatchi,s.alkhayatt,r.strachan}@shu.ac.uk

Abstract. The fast growth and development of wireless computer networks and multimedia applications make the Quality of Service (QoS) provided to their transmission an important issue. This paper aims to investigate the impact of varying the number of active stations on the network performance. This was carried out using different data rates. The investigations also considered both MAC protocol access mechanisms, i.e. the basic access and the Request To Send / Clear To Send (RTS/CTS). The effect of traffic type i.e. Constant Bit Rate (CBR) and Variable Bit Rate (VBR) traffics was also examined. The findings revealed that in large networks (larger than 15 stations), the RTS/CTS access mechanism outperformed the basic access mechanism since the performance of the latter was more sensitive to the increase and decrease of the number of active stations. Increasing the data rate improved the network performance in term of delay and jitter but it degraded the network performance in term of channel utilisation and packet loss ratio.

Keywords: Quality of Service (QoS), IEEE 802.11 Medium Access Control (MAC) Protocol, Network Performance.

1 Introduction

Wireless systems are increasingly used for transmitting different type of applications such as voice, video and data. Wireless transmission requires a controller to manage accessing the medium in a fair and suitable manner and to share the resources. Random transmission may lead to incomprehensible or unpredictable results. Therefore, a controller for accessing and sharing the resources is an essential tool for achieving a successful transmission process between the communication parties.

The Medium Access Control (MAC) protocol in wireless networks controls access to the shared medium by applying rules and procedures that permit the communication pairs to communicate with each other in an efficient and fair manner.

The IEEE 802.11 standard defines two coordination functions (IEEE, 1999). They are Distributed Coordination Function (DCF) and Point Coordination Function (PCF). The focus of this study is the DCF that is part of the Carrier Sense Multiple Access with Collision Avoidance (CSMA/CA).

Under DCF protocol, data packets are transferred using two mechanisms. The main mechanism is a two-way handshaking process which is called basic access mechanism.

J. Filipe et al. (Eds.): ICETE 2005, CCIS 3, pp. 246–256, 2007.

The optional or alternative mechanism is called RTS/CTS access mechanism that based on the exchange of RTS and CTS messages before data packets transmission.

RTS/CTS access mechanism is used to reserve the channel before data transmission. Under DCF, all stations in the same Basic Service Set (BSS) have to compete between each other to gain access to the medium. The competition between stations is controlled by different parameters of the physical layer (PHY) and the MAC sub-layer. The parameters include the Inter Frame Space (IFS) i.e. time period between the transmission of frames, Contention Window (CW), and backoff mechanism that randomises instants at which stations are attempting to access the channel.

All these parameters play important roles on the network performance through their effect on the degree of competition between the active stations within the same BSS. Consequently, an increase in the number of active stations in the BSS increases the degree of competition which in turn increases the probability of collisions. As a result of that, an increase in the number of stations has an obvious impact on the network performance.

2 Related Work

The variation of the number of active stations in IEEE 802.11 DCF protocol has been investigated in several studies by both simulation tools and mathematical models. An analytical model was proposed to analyse DCF operation and compute the saturated throughput performance through employing Markov chain models (Bianchi, 2000). This proposed model considered a finite number of stations with ideal channel conditions. The results obtained in this paper showed that the performance of the basic access mechanism depends on the MAC parameters mainly contention window minimum and number of wireless stations in the wireless networks. On the other hand, the results showed that the RTS/CTS access mechanism is marginally dependent on the system parameters. In another study the capacity of the medium was investigated by developing a mathematical model that calculates the DCF throughput and the packet virtual transmission time (Cali, 2000).

IEEE 802.11 CSMA/CA protocol over wireless channel was investigated in (Kleinrock, 1975). They provide an analysis for the channel performance during the up-time of unstable channel. They showed that CSMA theoretically exhibits behaviour similar to ALOHA. In (Haitao, 2002) a scheme named DCF+, which is compatible with DCF; to enhance the performance of reliable transport protocol over WLAN was proposed. Moreover, the impact of increasing the number of stations on the saturated throughput and delay in DCF and in the proposed scheme DCF+ was investigated. Their results revealed that increasing number of stations has an obvious impact on the network performance.

In (Sweet, 1999), throughput performance measures for varying number of stations in CSMA/CA were presented. They showed that the RTS/CTS access mechanism achieved higher throughput for CBR traffic when the number of stations increased above 10 stations. Their results also showed that higher transmission speeds yielded lower average throughput results.

Changing the number of active stations has an obvious impact on achieving QoS over wireless ad-hoc networks. This is due to the increase of collision probability over the medium. Also varying the data rate has a considerable impact on the average end-to-end delay and jitter. These parameters have critical impact on the transmission of multimedia applications.

An aim of this study is to investigate the impact of increasing the number of active stations and data rate on the network parameters. In particular, on the QoS parameters, throughput, end-to-end delay, jitter, and data packets drop. The performance of MAC protocol access mechanisms for CBR and VBR traffics was analysed.

This paper is organised into five sections. In the next section, the basics of the IEEE 802.11 MAC protocol are introduced. The experimental procedure is introduced in section 4. The findings and discussions are presented in section 5. The conclusion and future work is presented in section 6.

3   IEEE 802.11 MAC Protocol

The IEEE 802.11 standard (IEEE, 1997) specifies a CSMA/CA protocol. In CSMA/CA, when a station has a packet to send, it first listens to the medium to ensure no other transmission is currently taking place. If the channel is idle, it then transmits the packet. Otherwise, it picks a random "backoff interval" which determines the period of time the station has to wait until it is allowed to transmit its packet. The selection of the random number of the backoff time is based on a binary exponential backoff algorithm. The competing stations select a random number between 0 and CW-1 with equal probability. If the data packet is successfully transmitted, the backoff counter of the transmitted station will reset and then the station starts to compete with the other stations for accessing the medium. During the idle period of the channel, the transmitting station decrements its backoff counter. When the backoff counter reaches zero, the station transmits the packet as shown in Figure 1. During the busy period the station suspends its backoff counter. After successful receiving a packet, the receiving station replies with a positive acknowledgement (ACK) after waiting for a Short Inter Frame Space (SIFS) period. If an ACK is not detected within a SIFS period after the packet transmission, the transmission is assumed to be unsuccessful, and a retransmission is scheduled according to the specified backoff rules. The unsuccessful transmission is due to collision over the link. If a collision occurs CW will be doubled until reaching the maximum value $CW_{max} = 2^m(CW_{min} + 1) - 1$, where m is the number of retransmission attempts.

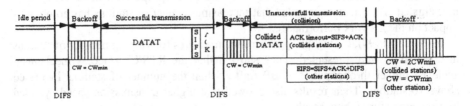

Fig. 1. Timeline of Basic access mechanism in DCF

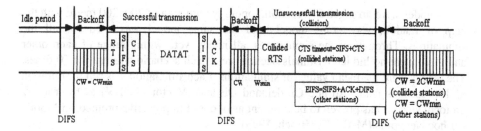

Fig. 2. Timeline of RTS/CTS access mechanism in DCF

The RTS/CTS access mechanism is mainly used to minimize the amount of time spent when a collision occurs since collision occurs in these short messages.

Before commencing the transmission of a data packet, the source station sends a short control frame, called RTS, declaring the duration of the forthcoming transmission. When the destination station receives the RTS frame, it replies with a CTS frame after SIFS interval, with the duration of the future transmission. Upon hearing RTS and CTS, all other stations in the vicinity of the sender and the receiver update their Network Allocation Vectors (NAV). This process reserves the medium for the sending station. Thus, all stations in the neighbourhood of the sender and receiver defer their transmissions and receptions to avoid collisions. After the successful RTS/CTS exchange, the source station transmits the data packet then the receiver responds with an ACK frame. Figure 2 depicts the time line of the RTS/CTS access mechanism.

4   Experimental Procedure

To analyse the impact of varying the number of active stations and data rate on the network performance for both the MAC protocol access mechanisms and the two different traffic types a number of simulation studies were carried out using the network simulator package (ns2) version 2.27 (ns2). The studies were carried out under different scenarios and they were based on the QoS parameters; throughput, delay, delay variation, and packet loss.

The performance of the IEEE 802.11 MAC protocol was investigated when the number of active stations in the same BSS was increased. Two different channel data rates were chosen for data packet transmission; low data rate equal to 2Mbps and high data rate equal to 11Mbps. While the control frames were transmitted at data rate equal to 1Mbps. IEEE 802.11b standard was used since it offers multi data rates. The protocol parameter settings were as shown in Table 1. A random topology with 20 stations was adopted when all stations were located in the same BSS. The network was offered by 100% of offered load every time the simulation run. Each connection was specified as a source - destination pair in which the number of connections was varied each time the network simulation was run. The simulation was carried out for CBR and VBR traffic at both MAC protocol access mechanisms. The CBR traffic had fixed packet size (1280-byte) while the VBR traffic had variable packet size and variable interval (mean packet size 3993 bytes and 2541 bytes standard deviation).

All nodes were arranged in a random topology with area of 200x200 metre with the help of random way point model, and the same model was used for all the simulations. Throughout the simulations, all nodes were within range of each other and there were no hidden terminals occurrences. Each scenario was run for 10 times. The results were the mean value for simulations. Each simulation was run for duration of 100 seconds using Ad-hoc On-demand Distance Vector (AODV) as the routing protocol since it has proven to be efficient as opposed to proactive protocol in Mobile Ad-hoc Networks (MANET) (Broch, 1998).

Table 1. IEEE 802.11b Parameter (ORiNOCO) settings

Parameter	Value
Data Rate	2, 5.5, 11 Mbps
Basic Rate for broadcast	1 Mbps
DIFS	50 µsecs
SIFS	10 µsecs
CWmin	31
CW max	1023
Slot time	20 µsec
Short Retry Limit	7
Long Retry Limit	4

5 Results and Discussions

This section outlines performance evaluation of the Distributed Coordination Function (DCF) that is a part of the IEEE 802.11 standard. It demonstrates through simulations the performance of the IEEE 802.11 MAC protocol when the number of stations is varied. Further, the impact of this variation on the QoS parameters is analysed. A comparison of the access methods provided by the IEEE 802.11 MAC protocol is carried out and comments are made as to when each should be employed.

5.1 Average Throughput

An increase in the number of contending stations in the same BSS causes more collisions and as a result more channel bandwidth is wasted. This wastage of bandwidth causes a reduction in the achieved throughput for both MAC protocol access mechanisms.

Figures 3a and 3b show the relationship between the active stations and the channel utilisation (channel utilisation is the ratio of the received bits to the channel data rate). When the number of active stations was increased, the channel utilisation slightly declined when the RTS/CTS access mechanism was used compared to the basic access mechanism. In RTS/CTS mechanism, collisions only involve control frames which are relatively small in size compared to data packet sizes, hence the bandwidth wasted in collisions is less than the basic access mechanism. This explains

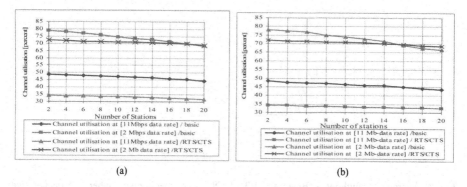

(a)   (b)

Fig. 3. Channel utilisation for CBR and VBR traffic at two different data rates and at two MAC protocol access mechanisms. (a) Channel utilisation for CBR. (b) Channel utilisation for VBR.

the slight rate of decrease in the channel utilisation curve when the RTS/CTS access mechanism was used.

If there are few stations in the network, (i.e. less than 10 stations), the RTS/CTS access mechanism provided a lower channel utilisation and lower average throughput. This was due to the overhead introduced by the control frames RTS and CTS. The impact of this overhead on the average throughput became very small when data packet sizes was very large (above 2000 bytes) as shown Figure 4. At small packet sizes, the basic access mechanism outperformed the RTS/CTS access mechanism due to the impact of the overhead, while at large packet sizes, the RTS/CTS access mechanism outperformed the basic access mechanism since the size of RTS and CTS is very small compared to data packet sizes.

With regard to channel data rate, low data rate (2Mbps) achieved better channel utilisation than high data rate (11 Mbps). This is because in low data rate the data packets were sent at 2 Mbps while the headers and control frames were sent at basic rate (1 Mbps). The two data rates (low data rate and basic rate) are relatively close to each other which resulted in better channel utilisation. At high data rate, the data packets were sent at 11 Mbps while the headers and control frames were sent at 1 Mbps, the difference here was relatively high compared to low data rate which resulted in a high rate of reduction in the channel utilisation. In this case, the transmission of headers and control frames caused a bottleneck when data packets were sent at high data rate.

The channel utilisation was degraded for CBR and VBR traffics. For CBR traffic, the reduction over an increase from 1 to 20 stations was 4.3% at 11 Mbps and 10.5% at 2 Mbps when the basic access mechanism was used. When the RTS/CTS access mechanism was used the reduction was slightly smaller, it was 2.4% at 11 Mbps and 3.5% at 2 Mbps. For VBR traffic, the channel utilisation degraded by 4.8% at 11 Mbps data rate and by 11.5% at 2 Mbps data rate when the basic access mechanism was used. When the RTS/CTS access mechanism was used the reduction in the channel utilisation was 1.8% at 11 Mbps and 3.5% at 2 Mbps. The results obtained indicate that the channel utilisation was degraded for CBR and VBR traffic in both; the RTS/CTS and the basic access mechanisms, but the RTS/CTS access mechanism

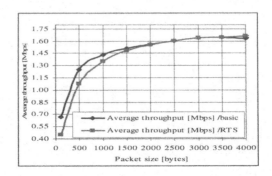

Fig. 4. Average throughput at Basic and RTS/CTS access mechanisms when the packet size increased

provided a smaller rate of decrease in the channel utilisation when the number of stations was increased. Also high data rate (11 Mbps) provided a slight decrease in the channel utilisation compared to the low data rate (2 Mbps).

5.2 Average Delay

The packet delay from and end-to-end should not exceed 400 ms for time sensitive applications in order to achieve the required QoS (Coverdate, 2000). As shown in Figures 5a, 5b, 5c and 5d, low data rate (2Mbps) in both MAC access mechanisms does not meet this QoS requirement if the number of active station was increased to more than 4 stations. A high data rate (11 Mbps) achieved better performance (small values of average delay). The average delay was slightly increased which met the QoS requirements up to 10 stations and then started to exceed the limit as the number of active stations was increased.

Because of the strict delay and jitter requirements for multimedia applications (CBR and VBR traffics), the time interval between the packet transmissions has to be within a given period. This can be obtained by assigning small values of CW_{min} and CW_{max} for these applications. In this study The IEEE 802.11 and IEEE 802.11b protocols were used, and their CW_{min} and CW_{max} were kept at the default values (31 and 1023 respectively) for the pairs of communication, therefore, their delay and jitter values were increased at low data rates and slightly increased at high data rates.

At high data rate (11 Mbps) with the basic access mechanism, the average delay was reduced by 69% and 66% compared with low data rate for CBR and VBR traffics, respectively. When the RTS/CTS access mechanism was used, the average delay at high data rate was also reduced by 58% and 63% for CBR and VBR traffics respectively.

The values of average delay in both MAC access mechanisms were located outside the desired range of QoS (150 ms for high QoS and 400 ms the minimum limit) when low data rate (2 Mbps) was used (Coverdate, 2000). Conversely, high data rate (11 Mbps) can provide acceptable QoS requirements in term of average delay.

5.3 Average Jitter

One of the major roles of QoS is to keep delay, jitter and packet loss for the transmitted applications within the acceptable range (Coverdate, 2000). For instance, to achieve high QoS for multimedia applications, the average jitter should not exceed 20 ms.

The average jitter increased as the number of active stations was increased. In other words, as the number of stations was increased; the probability of collisions increased due to a high degree of competition between stations. This in turn forced the MAC protocol to retransmit the collided packets. If the collided packets were successfully received at the destinations, they experienced delay variation, and this variation depended on the number of packet retransmissions.

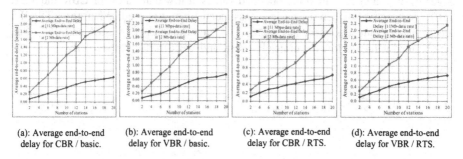

(a): Average end-to-end delay for CBR / basic.

(b): Average end-to-end delay for VBR / basic.

(c): Average end-to-end delay for CBR / RTS.

(d): Average end-to-end delay for VBR / RTS.

Fig. 5. Average end-to-end delay vs. number of stations

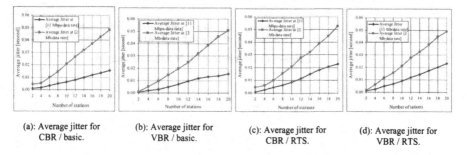

(a): Average jitter for CBR / basic.

(b): Average jitter for VBR / basic.

(c): Average jitter for CBR / RTS.

(d): Average jitter for VBR / RTS.

Fig. 6. Average jitter vs. number of stations

As shown in Figures 6a, 6b, 6c and 6d, the transmission of data packets with high data rate (11Mbps) had a noticeable positive impact on the achieved value of average jitter. High data rate resulted in small values of average jitter. This was because the transmission time of data packets at high data rate was smaller.

The results obtained at 11 Mbps indicated that the values of average jitter for CBR and VBR traffic in both MAC access mechanisms were kept within the acceptable range of QoS (less than 20 ms), where as low data rate resulted in large values of average jitter (more than 20 ms).

5.4 Packet Loss

In this study the packet loss was due to collisions, especially when the MAC retry limit exceeded and buffer overflow. Figures 7 and 8 show that the performance was downgraded with the increase in the number of stations in the same BSS.

It is well-known that high transmission rates have a lower Signal to Noise Ratio (SNR) than low data rates (Thruong, 2003). Therefore, at high data rates, the probability that a packet can not be received correctly by the destination is high.

The results obtained showed that the drop due to buffer overflow is relevant in the total loss ratio only with low data rate if the number of active stations was increased, while with high data rate the main cause of packet loss was the collisions (MAC retry limit) as shown in Figures 7 and 8

As shown in Figures 8a, 8b, 8c, and 8d, at high data rates the packet loss ratio was larger by 30% and 23% than the obtained values at low data rates for CBR and VBR traffics, respectively when the basic access mechanism was used. When the RTS/CTS access mechanism was used, the packet loss ratio was larger by 36% and 35% than the obtained values at low data rates for CBR and VBR traffic, respectively.

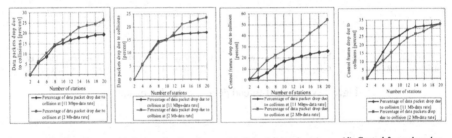

(a): Data packet drop due to collision for CBR/basic.

(b): Data packet drop due to collision for VBR/basic.

(c): Control frame drop due to collision for CBR/RTS.

(d): Control frame drop due to collision for VBR/RTS.

Fig. 7. Percentage of Collision drop vs. Number of stations

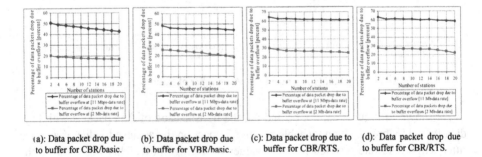

(a): Data packet drop due to buffer for CBR/basic.

(b): Data packet drop due to buffer for VBR/basic.

(c): Data packet drop due to buffer for CBR/RTS.

(d): Data packet drop due to buffer for CBR/RTS.

Fig. 8. Percentage of buffer drop vs. Number of stations

In this scenario, the basic mechanism outperformed the RTS/CTS mechanism in term of packet loss when the number of stations was small. For large networks, the RTS/CTS access mechanism outperformed the basic access mechanism because of collisions. In RTS/CTS access mechanism, collisions occurred for control frames while in the basic access collisions occurred for data packets as well as control frames.

6 Conclusion

In this study extensive experiments were carried out using ns2 simulation software to investigate the performance of the IEEE 802.11 MAC protocol by varying the number of active stations and varying the channel data rate.

Both MAC protocol mechanisms, i.e. the basic access and RTS/CTS access mechanisms were employed. The effect of traffic types (i.e. CBR and VBR) on the performance of the access mechanisms was also analysed.

The study indicated that increasing the number of active stations had an impact on the average throughput when the basic access mechanism was used.

High data rates improved the average throughput, but degraded the channel utilisation. This was because the control frames were sent at low data rate (1 Mbps).

The basic access mechanism outperformed the RTS/CTS access mechanism when the number of active stations was small. For a large network size, greater than 15 stations, the RTS/CTS access mechanism outperformed the basic access mechanism.

In the future a detailed evaluation of QoS parameters for various applications such as audio, video, file transfer and data will be carried out for small and large networks. Furthermore, the network parameters will be used for predicting the QoS and other network conditions as an approach for improving the protocol performance.

References

Bianchi, G.: Performance Analysis of the IEEE 802.11 Distributed Coordination Function. IEEE journal on selected Areas in Communication 18(3), 535–547 (2000)

Broch, J., Maltz, D., Johnson, D., Hu, Y-C.: A performance Comparison of Multi-hop Wireless Ad-hoc Network Routing Protocol. In: proceedings of IEEE/ACM MobiCom, pp. 85–97. ACM Press, New York (1998)

Cali, F., Conti, M., Gregori, E.: Dynamic Tuning of the IEEE 802.11 Protocol to Achieve a Theoretical Throughput Limit. IEEE/ACM Transactions on Networking 8(6), 785–799 (2000)

Coverdate, P.: ITU-T study group 12: Multimedia QoS requirements from a user perspective. In: Workshop on QoS and user perceived Transmission Quality in Evolving Networks (2000)

Haitao, W., Yong, P., Keping, L., Shiduan, C., Jian, M.: Performance of reliable transport protocol over IEEE 802.11 wireless LAN: analysis and enhancement. In: Proceedings IEEE INFOCOM 2002 Conference on Computer Communications. Twenty-First Annual Joint Conference of the IEEE Computer and Communications Societies, vol. 2, pp. 599–607. IEEE Computer Society Press, Los Alamitos (2002)

IEEE standard 802.11, Wireless LAN Medium Access Control (MAC) and Physical Layer (PHY) Specifications (1997)

IEEE standard 802.11, Wireless LAN Medium Access Control (MAC) and Physical Layer (PHY) Specifications (1999)

Kleinrock, L., Tobagi, F.: Packet Switching in Radio Channels: Part 2: The Hidden Terminal Problem in Carrier Sense Multiple-Access and the Busy-Tone Solution. IEEE Transactions on Communications COM 23, 1417–1433 (1975)

ns2, The network simulator-ns-2. [Online]. Last accessed on April 5, 2005 at URL http://www.isi.edu/nsnam/ns/

Sweet, C., Sidhu, D.: Performance Analysis of the IEEE 802.11 Wireless LAN Standard (1999) [Online]. Last accessed on August 30, 2004 at URL, http://www.csee.umbc.edu/ sweet/papers/

Thruong, H., Vannuccini, G.: Performance Evaluation of the QoS Enhanced IEEE 802.11e MAC Layer. Vehicular Technology Conference, 2003. VTC 2003-Spring. In: The 57th IEEE Semiannual, vol. 2, pp. 940–944 (2003)

An Automatic Blind Modulation Recognition Algorithm for M-PSK Signals Based on MSE Criterion

M. Vastram Naik, A. Mahanta, R. Bhattacharjee, and H.B. Nemade

Department of Electronics and Communication Engineering, Indian Institute of Technology,
Guwahati, Assam , 781039, India
{vastram,anilm,ratnajit harshal}@iitg.ernet.in

Abstract. This paper addresses Automatic Blind Modulation Recognition (ABMR)problem, utilizing a Mean Square Error (MSE) decision rule to recognize and differentiate M-ary PSK modulated signals in presence of noise and fading. The performance of the modulation recognition scheme has been evaluated by simulating different types of PSK signals. By putting appropriate Mean Square Error Difference Threshold (MSEDT) on Mean Square Error (MSE), the proposed scheme has been found to recognize the different modulated signals with 100% recognition accuracy at Signal to Noise Ratio (SNR) as low as 1 dB in AWGN channels. The data samples required to be used for performing recognition is very small, thereby greatly reducing the time complexity of the recognizer. For fading signal Constant Modulus (CM) equalization has been applied prior to performing recognition. It has been observed that when CM equalization is used, 100 % recognition can be achieved at SNR as low as 6 dB.

Keywords: Automatic Blind Modulation Recognition (ABMR), Mean Square Error power (MSE), Mean Square Error Difference (MSED), Threshold On Moment (TOM), Constant Modulus Algorithm (CMA), Tapped Delay Line filter (TDL).

1 Introduction

Automatic blind modulation recognition has its roots in military communication intelligence applications. In literature, most recognition method proposed initially were designed for recognizing analog modulations. The recent contributions in this area deal with recognition of digitally modulated signals as now a days digital modulation schemes are employed in almost all form of communication systems. With the rising development in software defined radio (SDR) systems, automatic modulation recognition has gained more attention than ever. Automatic recognizer units can act as front-end to SDR systems before demodulation takes place. Thus a single SDR system can robustly handle multiple modulations, therefore modulation recognition is an important issue for SDR systems. Many techniques have been reported in literature for AMR. Early works on modulation recognition can be found in a report by Weaver, Cole, Krumland and Miller (Weaver et al., 1969) where the authors use frequency domain parameters to distinguish between analog modulation types. In the area of recognition of digitally modulated signal, the paper

J. Filipe et al. (Eds.): ICETE 2005, CCIS 3, pp. 257–266, 2007.
© Springer-Verlag Berlin Heidelberg 2007

by Liedtke (Liedtke, 1984) is a well-known early work. The author presented results based on a statistical analysis of various signal parameters to discriminate between amplitude shift keying (ASK), Frequency Shift Keying (FSK), and Phase Shift Keying (PSK) signals. A variety of techniques such as Artificial Neural Network (ANN) (Wong and Nandi, 2004), (Halmi and Abdalla, 2003), constellation shape (Mobasseri, 2000), Statistical moment matrix method (Azzouz and Nandi, 1996b), maximum likelihood (Wei and Mendel, 1999), (Boiteau and Martret, 1998), zero crossing detection (Hsue and Soliman, 1990), pattern recognition (Weaver et al., 1969), (Halmi and Abdalla, 2003) and their combinations have been used for AMR. Especially, there are few threshold-based techniques (Wong and Nandi, 2004), (Azzouz and Nandi, 1996b), (Soliman and Hsue, 1992) to estimate modulation schemes. For such schemes, the threshold level becomes SNR dependant and hence threshold setting is difficult under variable SNR scenario.

In this paper, we have proposed a method based on MSE decision rule to recognize received M-PSK modulated signals. In this method we compute MSE between the prototype message points stored in the receiver library and the received signal points. Classification is made by computing the differences in MSE of different PSK signals against specified threshold values obtained through extensive simulation. The performance of the proposed algorithm has been evaluated for digitally modulated M-PSK signals. As in (Wei and Mendel, 1999), (Halmi and Abdalla, 2003) and (Umebayashi et al., 2000), we have assumed perfect symbol and carrier synchronization while evaluating the performance of the scheme. The rest of the paper is organized as follows, Section-2 describes the effect of channel on constellation points. The proposed blind modulation recognition algorithm is presented in section-3. Simulation results are presented in section-4. Conclusions are drawn in section-5.

2   Effect of AWGN and Fading Channel on Constellation Points

In AWGN channel, the received bandpass signal in the k-th signaling interval may be written as

$$r(t, k) = s_m(t, k) + n(t, k), \ k \, T_s \leq t \leq (k+1) \, T_s$$

where T_s : symbol duration, $s_m(t)$ is the message waveform corresponding to the M-PSK symbol s_m, m = 1, 2, 3,.....M . Assuming perfect carrier synchronization and timing recovery as in [8, 12, 14] and employing I-Q demodulation we get

$$\mathbf{r}(k) = [r_I(k), \ r_Q(k)]$$
$$= [s_{mI} + n_I(k), \ s_{mQ} + n_Q(k)]$$

Thus in the signal space the received signal points wander around signal points in a completely random fashion, in the sense it may lie anywhere inside a Gaussian distributed noise cloud centered on the message point. The effect of Additive White Gaussian Noise on signal points for MPSK signals at the receiver is shown in Figure 1(B). For wireless communication scenarios, in addition to AWGN, there will be the effect of multipath fading. Multipath fading channel can be modelled by a Tapped Delay Line(TDL) (Proakis, 2001): the test signal is convolved with the impulse response

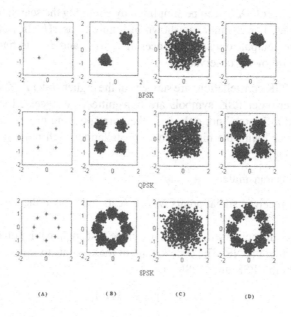

Fig. 1. Effect of Noise and Fading on MPSK constellation at SNR=15 dB, (A) Prototype signal points, (B) Received noisy signal constellation, (C) Received noisy and faded signal constellation (D) Equalized constellation

of the TDL to account for the effect of fading that is induced by the channel. The TDL parameters are chosen corresponding to power delay profile of physical channels (Chen and Chng, 2004). Figure 1(C) and Figure 1(D) respectively shows the faded received signal constellation and equalized signal constellation after CM equalization.

3   Proposed Method for Automatic Blind Modulation Recognition

A sequence of N received signal samples $\{\mathbf{r}(k)\}$, k = 1, 2, ...N, are collected at demodulator output. Using this sequence, we check how closely the received signal samples "match" with each of the prototype constellations available at the receiver library. The degree of "closeness" or "match" is measured in terms of a Mean Square Error power defined as

$$MSE(M) = \frac{1}{N} \sum_{k=1}^{N} D_{k,\,M}^2, \ M = 2^q, \ q = 1, 2, ...$$

where

$$D_{k,\,M} = \min_{m}\{|\,\mathbf{r}(k) - \mathbf{s}_m\,|\}, \quad m = 1, 2, ...M$$
$$= \min_{m}\{|\,d_{k,\,m}\,|\}$$

The computation of $D_{k,M}$ can be simplified by confining the search to that quadrant in which $\mathbf{r}(k)$ lies. For example, as shown in Figure 2, as $\mathbf{r}(k)$ lies in first quadrant (Q_1), we need to compute only the distances $d_{k,\,1}, d_{k,\,2}$ and $d_{k,\,3}$ to find $D_{k,\,8}$.

We make the following observations:

Lower-order PSK constellations are sub-sets of the higher-order PSK schemes; therefore, when lower-order PSK symbols are transmitted, the received signal sequence $\{\mathbf{r}(k)\}$ will find a "match" not only with the corresponding prototype constellation, it will also "match" with the higher-order constellation(with more or less the same degree of accuracy).

Case 1. BPSK is transmitted

In this case, the received signal points will be scattered around the symbols s_2 and s_6 shown in Figure1.

(a) Majority of the points will be confined in the first and the third quadrants (Q_1 and Q_3) especially at high SNR. The contribution of these points towards MSE power will be the same in both BPSK and QPSK , i.e.

$$MSE(2) = MSE(4),$$

$$\forall\,\mathbf{r}(k) \in Q_1 \cup Q_3$$

However, this same set of points will result in a slightly lower MSE when matched to 8-PSK as some of these points will have closer match to 8-PSK symbols s_1 or s_3 and s_5 or s_7 shown in Figure 2. Thus,

$$MSE(8) < MSE(2), MSE(4),$$

$$\forall\,\mathbf{r}(k) \in Q_1 \cup Q_3$$

(b) For a small fraction of the received points which lie in Q_2 and Q_4, their 'match' with the BPSK prototype will be proper (the nearest symbols being s_2 and s_6) as compared to QPSK prototype (nearest symbols s_4 and s_8) and 8-PSK (nearest symbols s_3, s_4, s_5 and s_7, s_8, s_1). Thus,

$$MSE(8) < MSE(4) < MSE(2),$$

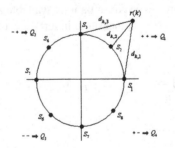

Fig. 2. Distance vector calculation for M-PSK signals

$$\forall \, \mathbf{r}(k) \in Q_2 \cup Q_4$$

Conclusions:

(i) when BPSK is transmitted, at any SNR , we shall find $MSE(8) < MSE(4) < MSE(2)$

(ii) at high SNR , the differences in MSE are negligibly small; only at low SNR , the differences are distinguishable, it is shown in Figure 3.

Case 2. QPSK is transmitted

Now $\{\mathbf{r}(k)\}'s$ are scattered around the four symbols s_2, s_4, s_6, s_8. It follows that $\{\mathbf{r}(k)\}$ will match well with QPSK and 8-PSK prototypes while there will be large mismatch with BPSK prototype. Thus,

$MSE(2) > MSE(4), MSE(8)$ at all SNR
$MSE(8) \approx MSE(4)$ at high SNR
$MSE(8) < MSE(4)$ at low SNR

This is shown in Figure 4.

Case 3. 8-PSK is transmitted

Following similar reasonings we conclude

$MSE(2) \gg MSE(4) \gg MSE(8)$ at all SNR.

The three curves are now well-separated, it is shown in Figure 5.

Proposed Algorithm

Step 1

Check for constant envelope property by computing fourth order moment of the received signal over a few samples, and compare with a Threshold On Moment(TOM), denoted by λ_M to distinguish between M-PSK and M-QAM signals.

$$m = \frac{1}{N} \sum_{k=1}^{N} \mid \mathbf{r}(k) \mid^4$$

where N is number of received signal samples considered.

Step 2

Observation space is partitioned into four quadrants, named as Q_1, Q_2, Q_3, Q_4. Check signs of received signal points $[r_I(k), r_Q(k)]$ to know to which quadrant it belongs:

If signs of real and imaginary part are $+, + \Rightarrow Q_1$
If signs of real and imaginary part are $-, + \Rightarrow Q_2$
If signs of real and imaginary part are $-, - \Rightarrow Q_3$
If signs of real and imaginary part are $+, - \Rightarrow Q_4$

Step 3

(a) Compute

$$D_{k,\,2} = |\, \mathbf{r}(k) - \mathbf{s}_m \,|,$$
$$m = 2 \; if \; \mathbf{r}(k) \in Q_1$$
$$m = 6 \; if \; \mathbf{r}(k) \in Q_3$$
$$D_{k,\,2} = \min_m \{ |\, \mathbf{r}(k) - \mathbf{s}_m \,| \},$$
$$m = 2, 6 \; if \; \mathbf{r}(k) \in Q_2 \; or \; Q_4$$
$$D_{k,\,4} = |\, \mathbf{r}(k) - \mathbf{s}_m \,|,$$
$$m = 2 \; if \; \mathbf{r}(k) \in Q_1$$
$$m = 4 \; if \; \mathbf{r}(k) \in Q_2$$
$$m = 6 \; if \; \mathbf{r}(k) \in Q_3$$
$$m = 8 \; if \; \mathbf{r}(k) \in Q_4$$
$$D_{k,\,8} = \min_m \{ |\, \mathbf{r}(k) - \mathbf{s}_m \,| \},$$
$$m = 1, 2, 3 \; if \; \mathbf{r}(k) \in Q_1$$
$$m = 3, 4, 5 \; if \; \mathbf{r}(k) \in Q_2$$
$$m = 5, 6, 7 \; if \; \mathbf{r}(k) \in Q_3$$
$$m = 7, 8, 1 \; if \; \mathbf{r}(k) \in Q_4$$

(b). Compute

$$MSE(M) = \frac{1}{N} \sum_{k=1}^{N} D_{k,\,M}^2, \; M = 2, 4, 8$$

Step 4

Compute Mean Square Error Difference(MSED)

$$MSED_{2-4} = MSE(2) - MSE(4)$$
$$MSED_{4-8} = MSE(4) - MSE(8)$$

Step 5

Decision rule (compare with thresholds determined through simulation):

(i) If $MSED_{2-4} < \lambda_{2-4}$, declare BPSK is transmitted

(ii) If $MSED_{2-4} > \lambda_{2-4}$, then check if $MSED_{4-8} < \lambda_{4-8}$. If $MSED_{4-8} < \lambda_{4-8}$, declare QPSK is transmitted.

(iii) If $MSED_{4-8} > \lambda_{4-8}$, declare 8-PSK is transmitted.

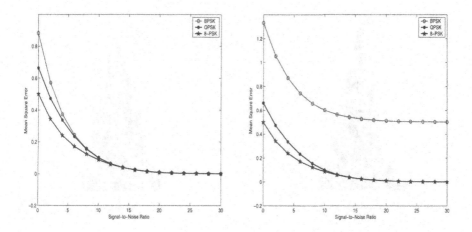

Fig. 3. Characteristics of BPSK signal in an AWGN channel

Fig. 4. Characteristics of QPSK signal in an AWGN channel

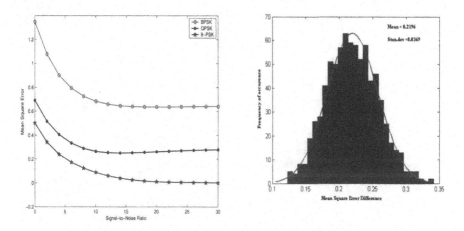

Fig. 5. Characteristics of 8-PSK signal in an AWGN channel

Fig. 6. Distribution of $MSED_{2-4}$ at SNR = 0 dB in an AWGN channel

4 Simulation Results

Manto-carlo simulation runs were carried out with N = 250 samples at SNR ranging from 0 dB to 30 dB. Average values of MSEs obtained from 800 such runs at each SNR are plotted in Figures 3-5 (in AWGN channel) and Figures 10-12 (in fading channels) for the three cases (e.g BPSK, QPSK and 8-PSK).

Determination of the thresholds λ_{2-4}^{a} , λ_{4-8}^{a}, λ_{2-4}^{f} **and** λ_{4-8}^{f}**.**

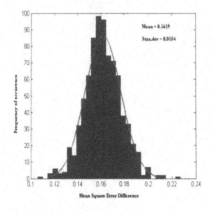

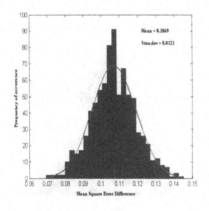

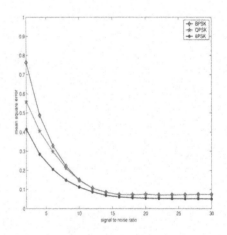

Fig. 7. Distribution of $MSED_{4-8}$ at SNR = 0 dB in an AWGN channel

Fig. 8. Distribution of $MSED_{2-4}$ at SNR = 3 dB in multipath fading channel

Fig. 9. Distribution of $MSED_{4-8}$ at SNR = 5 dB in multipath fading channel

Fig. 10. Characteristics of BPSK signal in multipath fading channel

For AWGN channel:

Figure 6 shows the distribution of $MSED_{2-4}$ at SNR = 0 dB. The distribution is approximately Gaussian. We set $\lambda_{2-4}^{a} = \mu_{2-4} + \sigma_{2-4} = 0.2196 + 0.0369 = 0.2565$. The distribution of $MSED_{4-8}$ is shown in Figure 7, from where we obtain $\lambda_{4-8}^{a} = \mu_{4-8} + \sigma_{4-8} = 0.1619 + 0.0154 = 0.1773$. With these thresholds we have observed 100% recognition in all three cases at SNR $\geq$ 1 dB in AWGN channel.

For fading channel:

Figure 8 and Figure 9 show the distribution of $MSED_{2-4}$ at SNR = 3 dB and $MSED_{4-8}$ at SNR = 5 dB respectively. Following the same procedure, the thresholds obtained for fading channel are $\lambda^f_{2-4} = \mu_{2-4} + \sigma_{2-4} = 0.1378 + 0.0327 = 0.1705$ and $\lambda^f_{4-8} = \mu_{4-8} + \sigma_{4-8} = 0.1069 + 0.0121 = 0.1190$ respectively. With these thresholds, 100% recognition is achieved in fading channel at SNR $\geq$ 6 dB.

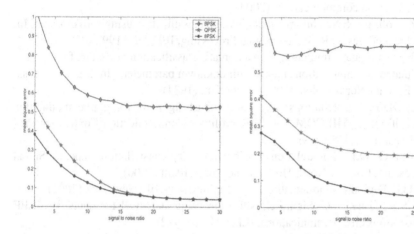

Fig. 11. Characteristics of QPSK signal in multipath fading channel

Fig. 12. Characteristics of 8-PSK signal in multipath fading channel

5   Conclusion

In this paper we have presented a novel approach to automatic digital modulation recognition of M-PSK signals. The performance of the proposed scheme has been tested in AWGN and fading channels. Simulation results show that the proposed scheme gives a much higher recognition performance for MPSK signals compared to the methods reported in literature (Wong and Nandi, 2004), (Azzouz and Nandi, 1996a), (Mobasseri, 1999), (Umebayashi et al., 2000) at low SNR in fading channel. Moreover, the number of samples required by the recognizer for performing recognition task is much smaller compared to the earlier reported methods (Wong and Nandi, 2004), (Azzouz and Nandi, 1996a), (Mobasseri, 1999) and (Umebayashi et al., 2000).

References

Azzouz, E.E., Nandi, A.K.: Automatic modulation recognition of communication signals. Kluwer Academic Publishers, Dordrecht (1996a)

Azzouz, E.E., Nandi, A.K.: Procedure for automatic recognition of analog and digital modulations. In: IEE Proceedings on Communication, IEE, UK (1996b)

Boiteau, D., Martret, C.L.: A generalized maximum likelihood framework for modulation classification. In: ICASSP'98, IEEE International conference on Acoustics, Speech, and Signal Processing, IEEE, USA (1998)

Chen, S., Chng, E.S.: Concurrent constant modulus algorithm and soft decision directed scheme for fractionally-spaced blind equalization. In: ICC '04, IEEE international conference on Communication, IEEE, USA (2004)

Halmi, M.H., Abdalla, A.G.E.: Detection of modulation scheme for software defined radio systems in 4th generation mobile network. In: APCC'03, The 9th Asia-Pacific conference on communications (2003)

Hsue, S.Z., Soliman, S.S.: Automatic modulation classification using zero crossing. In: IEE Proceedings on Radar and Signal Processing, IEE, UK (1990)

Liedtke, F.F.: Computer simulation of an automatic classification procedure for digitally modulated communication signals with unknown parameters. In: Signal Processing, Elsevier North-Holland, Inc. Amsterdam (1984)

Mobasseri, B.G.: Constellations shape as a robust signature for digital modulation recognition. In: MILCOM '99, IEEE Military Communication Conference Proceedings, IEEE, USA (1999)

Mobasseri, B.G.: Digital modulation classification using constellation shape. In: Signal Processing, Elsevier North-Holland, Inc. Amsterdam (2000)

Proakis, J.G.: Digital Communication, 4th edn. McGraw-Hill, New York (2001)

Soliman, S.S., Hsue, S.Z.: Signal classification using statistical moments. In: IEEE Transactions on Communications, IEEE, USA (1992)

Umebayashi, K., et al.: Blind adaptive estimation of modulation scheme for software defined radio. In: PIMRC'00, The 11th IEEE International symposium on Personal, Indoor and Mobile Radio Communication, IEEE, USA (2000)

Weaver, C.S., et al.: The automatic classification of modulation types by pattern recognition. In: Standford electronics laboratories Technical report No.1829-2. Standford electronics laboratories (1969)

Wei, W., Mendel, J.M.: A fuzzy logic method for modulation classification in non-idle envornoment. In: IEEE Transaction on Fussy Syatems, IEEE, USA (1999)

Wong, M.L.D., Nandi, A.K.: Automatic digital modulation recognition using artificial neural network and genetic algorithm. In: Signal Processing, Elsevier North-Holland, Inc. Amsterdam (2004)

Part IV

Multimedia Signal Processing

Properties of Dominant Color Temperature Descriptor

Karol Wnukowicz and Wladyslaw Skarbek

Faculty of Electronics and Information Technology,Warsaw University of Technology
Nowowiejska 15/19, 00-665 Warsaw, Poland
{K.Wnukowicz,W.Skarbek}@ire.pw.edu.pl

Abstract. The concept of color temperature is derived from an innate characteristics of the human visual system. It is formulated as a visual feature referring to a kind of perceptual feeling about perceived light. Color temperature has also a physical-based definition, and hence, color temperature of observed scenes and visual objects can be modelled in a mathematical way as a one-parameter characteristics of perceived light. In the Amendment to the Visual Part of the MPEG-7 Standard the Color Temperature descriptor for image browsing has been proposed. To extend the functionality of content-based image search by color temperature we proposed the Dominant Color Temperatures descriptor, which allows a user to perform query by example and query by value searches. The extraction algorithm was originally adopted from dominant color's one, which utilizes vector quantization in 3D color space. We also proposed a second, much faster algorithm based on scalar quantization in one-dimensional color temperature space. In this paper we present a comparison of the two extraction algorithms. We also compare the querying results of the Dominant Color Temperature descriptor and two conceptually related descriptors: Dominant Color and Color Temperature.

Keywords: Image indexing, Image databasess, Color temperature.

1 Introduction

Color temperature is a feature of light, associated with color (Wyszecki, Stils, 1982), and is derived from light perception of the human visual system. Color temperature is a promising feature in content-based image indexing, because viewers can easily judge perceptual image similarity using color temperature. The Amendment to the Visual Part of the MPEG-7 Standard (ISO/IEC, 2004) specifies the Color Temperature descriptor, which refers to the color temperature of image scene illumination (Kim, Park, 2001a). It is extracted by an iterative procedure, in which the average color of pixels having significant influence on color temperature perception is estimated. This descriptor is mainly intended for image browsing by classification of images into one of the four given subjective color temperature categories: hot, warm, moderate, cool. Its usefulness in search tasks of other kinds, such as query by example or query by color temperature value is rather poor. Another limitation of this descriptor is that images may contain a few regions of different color temperatures, in such a case the average color only roughly estimates the perceived color temperature

J. Filipe et al. (Eds.): ICETE 2005, CCIS 3, pp. 269–278, 2007.

of images, and a significant piece of information about color temperature content might be lost.

In some applications the user may want to have the possibility for a more powerful searching, and for a more precise ranking of query results than it is possible using the simple Color Temperature descriptor. Moreover, two other kinds of queries for color temperature-based search, in addition to the subjective categorization, may be of the user interest. The first is a query by value, in which the user simply inputs the required color temperature in Kelvin degrees, and the system retrieves images having the perceived color temperature closest to the user input. The second type of query is a query by example, in which the user chooses an example image, and the system retrieves the most similar ones. The example image may be a real image or an image drawn by the user as a colored sketch. This type of query is possible for other color descriptors contained in the MPEG-7 Standard (ISO/IEC, 2002b): Color Histogram (Scalable Color), Dominant Color, Color Structure, Color Layout, but is not available for the Color Temperature descriptor. These two search functionalities can be achieved using Dominant Color Temperatures descriptor, which describes a few representative color temperatures in an image. We proposed two algorithms for extraction of the descriptor. One of them is similar to the extraction method of the MPEG-7 Dominant Color descriptor (Wnukowicz, 2004). But that method is not optimally suited for dominant color temperatures extraction, and is also computationally costly (vector quantization of pixel values in 3D color space). To avoid these drawbacks, we proposed a new extraction algorithm (Wnukowicz, 2005) based on scalar quantization in one-dimensional color temperature domain. The syntax of the Dominant Color Temperatures descriptor remains the same as the originally proposed one. Section 2 outlines the extraction methods, and section 3 presents experiments for comparison of the methods.

Although Dominant Color Temperature descriptor relates conceptually to two other descriptors: Dominant Color and Color Temperature, there are significant differences between them. We carried out some experiments for comparing the results obtained by those descriptors and Dominant Color Temperatures descriptor for a test dataset of images. They are presented in sections 4 and 5.

2 Extracting Dominant Color Temperatures

The general idea of the Dominant Color Temperatures descriptor is to describe images by color temperatures of their representative colors. This will result in more precise description of images regarding color temperature feature in comparison with the one-parameter Color Temperature descriptor. The Dominant Color Temperature descriptor extends the functionality of image searching using color temperature by enabling two additional types of queries: query by color temperature value and query by example. Other types of queries are also possible, of which examples are the following:

- find images that contain at least 80% of dominant colors with warm color temperature category;
- find images that contain regions of different color temperature categories (for example warm>20% and moderate>40%);

– rank query result according to the relevance to the user query.

The originally proposed method for dominant color temperatures extraction is based on the extraction algorithm for dominant colors (ISO/IEC, 2002a). This solution is justified by the fact that perceptually distinct dominant colors are obtained by averaging color values of similar group of pixels in an image. The averaging of color values for pixels which influence color temperature perception is also used in extraction of the Color Temperature descriptor (Kim, Park, 2001b).

The overall scheme of the dominant-color-based extraction method can be outlined in the following steps:

1. Extract the dominant colors of an image using the GLA color quantization algorithm;
2. Compute the chromaticity coordinates on uv plane for each dominant color;
3. Compute the color temperatures from the chromaticity coordinates for each dominant color;
4. Construct the descriptor as an array of elements that hold values and percentages of the color temperatures in the image. The "black" colors are not included into the descriptor.

To extract the descriptor, first, up to eight dominant colors of the image are obtained, and next, color temperatures for the dominant colors are estimated. As a result K pairs of values $[t_i, p_i]$ are obtained, where t_i denotes color temperature value, p_i denotes percentage of pixels with color temperature t_i, $0 \le i \le K-1$, and $K \le 8$.

The dominant color based approach for dominant color temperatures extraction has two significant drawbacks. The first is a high computational cost caused by the vector quantization of pixel values in 3D color space. The second drawback is that dominant colors do not always correspond to distinct color temperature values. For example, two distinct dominant colors, light-red and dark-red, may have undistinguishable color temperatures. The better solution would be if the dominant color temperatures were well distinguishable. Such solution is the extraction method proposed in the second algorithm (Wnukowicz, 2005).

The new extraction algorithm is based on scalar quantization in one-dimensional color temperature domain. The algorithm can be outlined in the following steps:

1. Compute color temperature values, in reciprocal megakelvin scale, for all pixels in the image;
2. Mark pixels without significant color temperature values, that should be omitted (e.g. black colors);
3. Compute a histogram of color temperature for the remaining pixels;
4. Perform scalar quantization of the histogram bins to obtain dominant color temperatures;
5. Merge similar dominant color temperature bins (by using a merging threshold).

The histogram is computed from pixel samples represented by color temperature values. The values of color temperature are converted to reciprocal megakelvin scale (mired, $1MK^{-1}=1000000/K$), which is usually used in color temperature calculations instead of Kelvin scale. Values of the samples are clipped to the range from 40 MK^{-1} (25000K) to 600 MK^{-1} (1667K), and quantized with step q. The resulting histogram has $(600-40)/q$ bins. We used $q=1$, what gives 560 bins in the histogram. Scalar quantization is performed by modified Lloyd algorithm (Lloyd, 1982) in color temperature histogram domain. The range of color temperature values is being split into K subranges, the mass centers of the histogram subranges are considered to be the representative points of the relevant subranges. The algorithm calculates (locally) optimal division of the color temperature range into K subranges having minimum distortion. The distortion is calculated as a sum of distances from the representative points of each subrange to the color temperature values represented by positions of histogram bins contained within this subrange, weighted by values of the relevant histogram bins. K obtained representative points are candidates for the dominant color temperatures. In the next step, the color temperature representative points which are closer to each other than a given merging threshold T_{merg} are merged to obtain perceptually distinct dominant color temperatures.

3 Comparison of the Extraction Methods

The experiments for comparison of the two extraction methods were performed using a test dataset from core experiments of the MPEG-7 Color Temperature descriptor (Kim et al., 2001c). In those experiments 3056 test images were classified into four color temperature categories according to subjective user's voting. The subjective categories were: hot (reddish colors dominate), warm (orange and yellowish colors), moderate (white, grey, green colors) and cool (bluish colors).

Figure 1 and 2 show graphs which depict ranking of query result of the test images for moderate color temperature category. The graphs depict relationships between the viewer's subjective assessment of images and the ranking of query results for the two extraction methods of Dominant Color Temperatures descriptor. The vertical axes in both graphs represent percentage of viewer's votes assigning images to moderate color temperature category. The horizontal axes represent image positions on the ranked result lists for moderate category. Figure 1 shows the result for the new extraction method (scalar quantization), and figure 2 shows the result for the original extraction method. The ranking of query result were done according to the distance to reference color temperature of a chosen subjective category as explained in (Wnukowicz, 2004), and the reference color temperature $RT_{REF}=181,92$ MK^{-1} was taken for the experiments (the middle of the moderate category subrange in reciprocal scale). The user votes (given in %) were smoothed in the graphs by averaging in a shifted window of 50 consecutive images. As it can be intuitively assumed, it is desirable that images positioned at the beginning of the result list had the percentages of viewer's votes close to 100%.

Additionally, the graphs contain lines which best fit the smoothed relationships for the two descriptions. The line parameters were obtained by linear regression of the data. The equation of the approximated line is $y=a*x+b$, where x is the image position (horizontal axis of the graph), y is the smoothed percentage of votes value, a is the slope of the line, and b is the intersection of the line with the vertical axis of the graph (intercept, percentage of votes for the first positioned image on the retrieved list). Table 1 shows start points (b parameter values) of the lines for all of the four

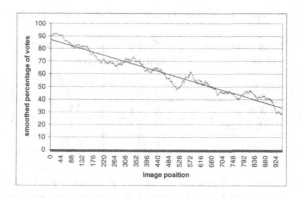

Fig. 1. Ranking of query result for the scalar- quantization-based extraction algorithm

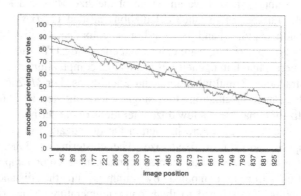

Fig. 2. Ranking of query result for the dominant-color-based extraction algorithm

Table 1. The first point of the regression line (b parameter)

Color temperature category	Scalar quantization	Dominant color quantization
Hot	91.69	92.26
Warm	75.23	73.76
Moderate	87.12	86.5
Cool	87.91	87.46

subjective color temperature categories, table 2 shows average deviations of the data points from the approximated lines. In table 1 the bigger value is the better. In table 2 the smaller value is the better.

The main advantage of the new extraction method is a significant decrease of the computational complexity, as it utilizes scalar quantization of 1D color temperature histogram with fixed size instead of vector quantization in 3D color space with complexity depending on image size. In the case of vector quantization, the most time

Table 2. Average squared deviation of percentage of votes (regarding regression line).

Color temperature category	Scalar quantization	Dominant color quantization
Hot	5.36	5.47
Warm	13.03	15.7
Moderate	13.13	11.42
Cool	6.98	6.22

consuming task is an iterative process of clustering, which is performed by finding the nearest representative point for each pixel of the indexed image, until the change of quantization error in two consecutive iterations comes down below an established threshold. For example, if we have an image of the size MxN and K representative color points, the number of distance calculations needed is $MxNxK$, The distance between two colors $[l_1, u_1, v_1]$ and $[l_2, u_2, v_2]$ in 3D color space is given by: $(l_1 - l_2)^2 + (u_1 - u_2)^2 + (v_1 - v_2)^2$, where l, u, v are color components in LUV color space, which is used due to its perceptual homogeneity. It means that computation of a single distance requires 3 subtractions, 3 multiplications and 2 additions. For M=256, N=256, K=8, the number of distance calculations in a single clustering step is: 256 x 256 x 8 = 524288. Quantization may need a few dozen iterations of clustering.

In the case of color temperature histogram the quantization is performed in one dimensional space for data of fixed size. The clustering is done, by assigning subrange's cut points between neighboring representative color temperature values. The quantization error is computed by summing up the distances from the representative points to assigned to them color temperature values represented by histogram bins, weighted by histogram bin values. This task needs B distance calculations, involving two basic operations: subtraction and multiplication, where B is the number of histogram bins (e.g. B=560). Experiments showed that even for small images (384x256) the generation of indexes is more than two times faster when the new algorithm is used. For bigger images the difference in computation time could be even greater.

4   Comparison of Dominant Color Temperatures and Color Temperatures

To compare the Dominant Color Temperature descriptor and the Color Temperature descriptor, experiments of ranking the search results were carried out, where matching according to human perception was evaluated. It was assumed that the order of retrieved images should match the user perception. The measure of matching to subjective tests was performed by evaluation of smoothed vote percentage graphs in image rank domain, which was obtained as specified in the previous section.

Experiments were performed for all of the four color temperature categories, for the Dominant Color Temperature descriptor, and for the Color Temperature descriptor. In the case of Color Temperature descriptor the query results were ranked according to the distance from color temperature of image to the reference color temperature value of relevant subjective category. The graph of the query result ranking for the moderate color temperature category is depicted in figure 3. Tables 3 and 4 contain the parameters of estimated regression lines for all categories.

The results of the experiments show that searching by the Dominant Color Temperature descriptor matches the subjective assessment of color temperature. This matching is generally better than in the case of the Color Temperature descriptor, but the largest improvement is achieved for moderate category, as it can be easy seen when comparing the graph in figure 3 with the ranking of the Dominant Color Temperature descriptor depicted in figures 1 and 2. This is due to the fact that images which belong to the moderate category have the largest variation of dominant colors, and the varied dominant color temperatures could not be well discriminated by one-parameter descriptor.

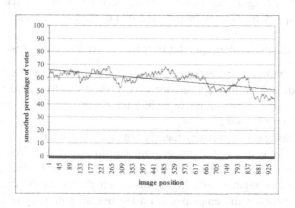

Fig. 3. Ranking of query result for Color Temperature descriptor (moderate category)

Table 3. The first point of the regression line (b parameter)

Color temperature category	Dominant color temperatures	Color temperature
Hot	91.69	90.83
Warm	75.23	74.12
Moderate	87.12	66.14
Cool	87.91	84.91

Table 4. Average squared deviation of percentage of votes (regarding regression line).

Color temperature category	Dominant color temperatures	Color temperature
Hot	24.96	5.47
Warm	7.039	15.7
Moderate	20.34	11.42
Cool	12.58	6.22

The experiments show that in the case of the Dominant Color Temperatures descriptor the user perception corresponds better to search results obtained for all of the four subjective color temperature categories with the following reference values: 1667K (hot), 2924K (warm), 5497K (moderate), 25000K (cool). However, this justifies the suitability of this descriptor to be used for any other color temperature value that a user may want to query for in a search application.

5 Comparison of Dominant Color Temperatures and Dominant Color

Although the Dominant Color Temperature descriptor is based on the Dominant Color descriptor, there are significant differences between them. We carried out some tests comparing the query results obtained by the two descriptors for test images from the dataset.

There are at least three conceptual differences between the two descriptors:

- differences between concepts of color and color temperature. Dominant colors in an image of a dissimilar appearance may at the same time make an impression about the image to be similar regarding their dominant color temperatures, e.g. gray/green, orange/pink;
- different concepts of similarity measure for query by example. In the case of the Dominant Color descriptor, images are considered to be similar if they have regions with very close colors and similar percentages (ISO/IEC, 2002a). Images can have minor regions with highly dissimilar colors. In the case of Dominant Color Temperature the emphasis is on the overall similarity of dominant color temperatures and their percentages, so single regions which have dissimilar color temperatures make images be more dissimilar;
- the Dominant Color Temperature descriptor is intended to be an enhancement of the Color Temperature descriptor by functionalities such as query by example, query by value, image ranking, and searching for images with multiple color temperatures.

To compare the Dominant Color descriptor and the Dominant Color Temperature descriptor a set of queries has been performed for the test dataset (3056 images) and image positions on the retrieved lists were registered.

The result of experiments for comparing the ranking of query results for the two descriptors is presented in the graph in figure 4. The graph shows histogram of correlation of ranked query results for the two descriptors: Dominant Colors and Dominant Color Temperatures. The variables used for computing the correlations were image positions on two ranked result lists obtained for the two descriptors (image positions were in the range from 1 to 3056). For each image from the test dataset two queries using the two descriptors were performed, the results were ranked and the positions of retrieved images were registered, which were used as input variables to compute the correlation of image positions.

Correlations were computed for 3056 queries (each image in the dataset was a query), and the histogram presents the results (correlation values are smoothed with

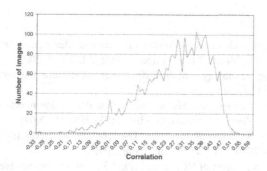

Fig. 4. Correlation of query results for Dominant Color Temperatures and Dominant Color descriptors

step 0.01). Pearson formula was used to compute the correlation, where 0 means no correlation between variables, 1 indicates maximum correlation (the datasets are the same), -1 means that variables are inversely correlated.

As it can be seen in the diagram, the correlations span values from -0.32 to 0.53, but the average value is about 0.26, so the correlation between results obtained by dominant colors and dominant color temperatures is not very high. This confirms that the two descriptors give different search functionalities.

6 Conclusions

We have presented some experiments demonstrating the properties of the Dominant Color Temperatures descriptor, which was designed for content-based image searching. First, two available extraction algorithms have been compared. The originally proposed algorithm makes it possible to extract the Dominant Color Temperatures descriptor directly from the Dominant Color descriptor, what may be an advantage in same cases. But generally the new algorithm, which uses fast scalar quantization in color temperature domain, is a better solution for extraction of the Dominant Color Temperatures description.

We also compared this descriptor with two conceptually related visual descriptors: Color Temperature and Dominant Color. On the one hand the Dominant Color Temperatures descriptor can be regarded as an enhancement to the Color Temperature descriptor – it support new functionalities of searching by color temperature. On the other hand it have significantly different properties than the Dominant Color descriptor.

Acknowledgments

The work presented was developed within VISNET, a European Network of Excellence (http://www.visnet-noe.org), funded under the European Commission IST FP6 programme.

References

ISO/IEC, Information technology - Multimedia content description interface – Part 8: Extraction and Use of MPEG-7 Descriptions, ISO/IEC 15938-8 (2002a)

ISO/IEC, Information technology – Multimedia content description interface – Part 3: Visual, ISO/IEC 15938 3 (2002b)

ISO/IEC, Information technology – Multimedia content description interface – Part 3: Visual, AMENDMENT 1: Visual extensions, ISO/IEC 15938 3/AM 1 (2004)

Kim, S.-K., Park, D.-S.: Proposal for Color Temperature Descriptor for image description, ISO/IEC JTC1/SC29 WG11 M6966, Singapore (2001a)

Kim, S.-K., Park, D.-S.: Report of VCE-6 on MPEG-7 color temperature browsing descriptors, ISO/IEC JTC1/SC29/WG11 M7265, Sydney (2001b)

Kim, S.-K., Park, D.-S., Choi, Y.: The Ground Truth Set of VCE-6 on MPEG-7 color temperature browsing descriptors, ISO/IEC JTC1/SC29/WG11, Pattaya (2001c)

Lloyd, S.P.: Least Squares Quantization in PCM. In: IEEE Transactions on Information Theory, IEEE Press, Los Alamitos (1982)

Wnukowicz, K.: Image Indexing by Distributed Color Temperature Descriptions. Fundamenta Informaticae 61(3-4) (2004)

Wnukowicz, K., Skarbek, W.: Extracting dominant color temperatures. In: WIAMIS'05, International Workshop on Image Analysis for Multimedia Interactive Services (2005)

Wyszecki, G., Stiles, W.S.: Color Science Concepts and Methods, Quantitative Data and Formulae, 2nd edn. A Wiley-Interscience Publication, New York (1982)

Test Environment for Performance Evaluation of an Internet Radio

David Melendi, Manuel Vilas, Xabiel G. Pañeda, Roberto García,
and Víctor G. García

Computer Science Department, University of Oviedo
Campus Universitario de Viesques. Sede Departamental Oeste, 33204 Xixón-Gijón, Asturies
{melendi,mvilas,xabiel,victor,roberto}@correo.uniovi.es

Abstract. This paper presents a test environment designed to improve Internet radio services through the evaluation of different service features. The environment comprises the generation of audio streams, the delivery of those streams through different communication networks, and the access of final users to those contents. A broad set of service architectures can be emulated, and several network configurations can be deployed using the available communication devices. It is also possible to simulate users' behaviour thanks to a workload generator that can be configured using statistical information obtained from real service access data. A case study is also presented, where a glimpse of the possibilities of the environment can be caught. This test environment will allow service administrators or research teams to predict what will happen in a real service if its configuration is modified, or if user behaviour changes. Furthermore, managers will be capable of knowing whether an Internet radio service can be improved or not.

Keywords: Audio, Evaluation, Internet, Live, Multimedia, Radio, Streaming.

1 Introduction

The emergence of the World Wide Web has changed the Internet world. This service has become a powerful medium. Daily, millions of users in the world browse the web, produce an important number of accesses, and a huge volume of information is delivered to them. Like other communication enterprises, traditional Radio companies have discovered the Internet to be an important tool to reach millions of users in the world without any constraint related to commercial licenses, limited frequency spectrums, high infrastructure costs, etc. Now technology is not an issue for these companies. The bandwidth increase in subscribers' access capabilities, and the development of the streaming technology have given rise to the appearance of a new complementary service: the Internet Radio.

There are two types of audio services on the Internet: live-audio and jukebox (audio-on-demand). In jukebox services, the user requests the information at any time and the server delivers it exclusively. This system allows users to interact with information: Pauses, backward and forward jumps are allowed. Its behaviour is similar to a CD player, and it is the user who controls what to listen to in every

J. Filipe et al. (Eds.): ICETE 2005, CCIS 3, pp. 279–292, 2007.

moment: these are *user driven* services (Veloso, 2002). On the other hand, live-audio is more similar to a traditional radio service. Contents are received directly by a multimedia server, which broadcasts them straight out to the audience. In these services users cannot choose what to listen to, as there is a previously established programme. These are *object driven* services (Veloso, 2002).

Most radio services on the Internet are based on streaming technology. The advantages of audio streaming and the subscribers' expectations are important. However, this technology presents some problems. Although audio delivering is not so resource-consuming as video, it also requires a constant quality of service. What is more, live-audio services require greater transmission capabilities than jukebox services, due to the fact that they tend to suffer stress periods depending on programme evolution, known as *prime-time* periods. In these stress periods a wide range of users connect at the same time to the same source of contents. To maintain service quality under control, it is important to select the best configuration parameters possible. These parameters include, among others, the quality of the produced contents, the architecture of the service, the configuration of the network, etc.

Nowadays, all these parameters are usually established by service managers based on their own experience. These managers usually know what the most appropriate configuration is, what qualities must be generated, or where to place each service device. Nevertheless, each service is usually different to the rest: there are problems which can be found in one service that would never affect others. Furthermore, experience is knowledge based on the past, but technology is constantly evolving and producing solutions to solve old problems or to improve previous solutions. Now the problem is to answer the following question: how can managers test these technology evolutions knowing what will happen in a real service? It is very risky to make changes in a working environment, as it can lead to unexpected situations.

A solution for this issue may be to have a reduced copy of the real service under a controlled environment. This copy could be used to carry out small tests. But some questions go beyond the possibilities of such a copy: How does the service behave under extreme conditions? How can real users affect service performance? How do network devices affect this type of services? What impact do routing protocols have in heavy loaded radio services? If a radical change is carried out in the service, how will it behave? All these questions can only be answered if a complete and flexible test environment is available to service managers.

In this paper, a test environment for performance evaluation of Internet radio services is presented. The main aim of the presented environment is to help service managers in planning, deploying, configuring and improving live-audio services. Furthermore, the paper has followed an interesting practical approach, based on the evaluation and improvement of a real Internet Radio service.

The problem of delivering live streams to end-users with a certain degree of quality has long been studied. There are abundant papers focused on improving service architectures for live streaming, such as (Jonas, 1998), (Dutta, 1999), (Chawathe, 2000), (Deshpande, 2001), (Padmanabhan, 2002), (Dutta, 2001) or (Melendi, 2004). Other papers, such as (Holbrook, 1999) or (Banerjee, 2002), try to improve these services taking advantage of technologies such as multicast. Others, such as (Bolot, 1993), (Jian, 2000), or (Mena, 2000) study the effects of network conditions in streaming services and other types of applications. Users' behaviour in streaming services has also been studied in papers like (Chesire, 2001) or (Veloso, 2002). A flexible test environment could help service managers to test the conclusions offered by all these papers for a given service.

The rest of the paper is organized as follows: Section 2 provides a detailed description of an Internet radio service. The presented test environment is set out in section 3. Section 4 offers a practical case study in the proposed environment, where the impact of a network configuration option on radio services is analyzed. Finally, conclusions are presented in section 5.

2   Service Description

There are mainly two possibilities while developing an Internet radio service: to capture and distribute live audio streams, or simulate live contents using stored information.

Usually, when a live audio stream is captured to be distributed over the Internet, the service provider has an already existing transmission or the necessary resources to generate one. This type of Internet radio service is the most suitable for traditional radio companies. These companies have an available audio stream and require a secondary distribution channel to reach a wider audience. As shown in Figure 1, in this type of services two main software components are used: a production tool and a multimedia server. The production tool, also known as *producer*, must capture live contents, probably using the sound card of the machine where it is being executed. While it is capturing those contents, the *producer* applies the proper data conversions using a specific codec and a pre-established set of quality parameters. Once the conversions have been made, the *producer* delivers the obtained audio packets to the multimedia server. This server is in charge of processing customers' requests and delivering them the audio stream generated by the *producer*.

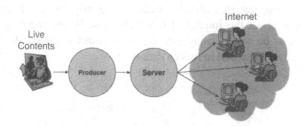

Fig. 1. Radio Service with Live-Contents

On the other hand, if stored information is used, the service provider only needs a set of stored files coded with the necessary quality. These files are later sequenced to form a continuous audio stream. This type of services is based on the use of two software modules: a *simulated live transfer agent*, or *slta*, and a multimedia server. The *slta* generates a continuous audio stream by sequencing several stored multimedia files. This stream is then sent to the multimedia server that will deliver the generated contents to final users. In order to know which files must be sequenced, the *slta* uses a text file as input data. This file, also called *playlist*, has the path and the names of the files that must be used, alongside the meta-data that will be provided with the audio stream to final users. Figure 2 shows the main components in an Internet radio service with stored contents.

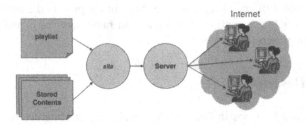

Fig. 2. Radio Service with Stored-Contents

It must be taken into account that these service architectures are deployed on a communication network. While installing an Internet radio on a network, several alternatives are possible. All the needed software components can run on a single machine, or can be installed in dedicated computers. If dedicated computers are used, these computers can be in the same network, or in different networks interconnected by several devices. Furthermore, depending on the number of connected customers, advanced architectures can be used. These architectures are mainly based in the use of redundant systems, and intermediate devices such as multimedia *proxies*.

3 Environment Design

The test environment has been designed to emulate the behaviour of a broad set of service architectures. It allows service administrators or research teams to deploy a simple radio service, test that service, modify its configuration or architecture, and draw conclusions about the impact of those changes. Furthermore, several network configurations can be tested using the available communication devices. Figure 3 shows the equipment installed in this environment.

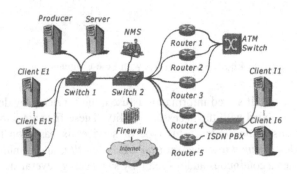

Fig. 3. Environment Physical Architecture

Providing a real service, using this test environment will allow service administrators to predict what will happen if a certain change is applied, and whether the service can be improved or not. In order to meet these expectations, the test environment provides mechanisms to emulate the main steps on every Internet radio: content generation, content delivery and content access.

3.1 Content Generation

In a real service, two possible sources can be used to deploy an Internet radio: an existing radio transmission, or a set of stored files sequenced to obtain a continuous audio stream. Given the fact that the source of audio may be irrelevant –it is not affected by computing or networking issues-, the test environment uses stored files to generate the contents that will be broadcast.

Although it is possible to use a common production tool, in its default configuration, this test environment uses a *simulated live transfer agent* or *slta*. This agent generates a continuous audio stream by sequencing several multimedia files. The audio stream is then sent to a multimedia server that will deliver the generated contents to final users.

Service administrators will code the multimedia files using the quality parameters they want to test. Once the final files have been generated, the administrators will only need to edit the *playlist* and write the names of the files on it. If new quality parameters are required, the contents must be recoded and the old files need to be replaced.

The environment, shown in Figure 3, has a machine running Linux called *Producer*, where the *slta* is being executed and the multimedia files must be stored. This *slta* produces an audio stream and sends it to the multimedia server executed in the machine named *Server*.

Moreover, the environment allows service administrators to test advanced configurations in this stage: redundancy and file sharing. Redundant data sources can be used installing more *Producer* machines with their correspondent *slta* application. These machines could use their own audio files –stored locally-, or could use a common file-system through *NFS*. So it is possible to test just software redundancy – using file sharing– or a complete redundancy duplicating everything: files and programmes.

3.2 Content Delivery

Once we have generated the necessary contents, it is time to deliver those contents to final users.

The *slta* generates an audio stream that is sent to a multimedia server. In the test environment shown in Figure 3 a streaming server has been installed on a machine running Linux called *Server*. The task of this server is to attend users' requests and to redistribute the audio stream under their commands.

Furthermore, the environment permits the testing of advanced configurations in this stage such as redundancy and intermediate devices. Redundant servers can be installed in order to attend users' requests. This is possible by adding new *Server* machines to the environment. In the simplest case, servers will inform users about other servers that manage the same audio stream. If a problem is detected in the main server, users will try to plug into the redundant server.

A more complex scenario uses several intermediate devices or *proxies*. Combining proxies with redundant servers, users will first go to the proxy and it will redirect their requests to the proper server. If poor performance periods are detected in one of the servers, the proxy can redirect users to a more efficient server. This proxy configuration is called *pass-through* mode: proxies are only redirecting devices. Another way of using proxies is a *splitting* mode, where proxies act as servers for final users. The original servers send the audio streams to proxies, and the proxies redistribute those contents among users. Again, this service configuration can be tested: new machines can be added to act as redundant servers or as proxies.

Apart from servers and proxies, another important element in any distributed service is the communication network. Here we can find two different scenarios for delivering audio streams to users: an Intranet Scenario and an Internet Scenario.

In an Intranet Scenario, the audience connects to the service using the same network where all the devices are installed. The size of this network varies from an office LAN to a network operator's WAN. Nevertheless, the owner of the network can usually control three critical points: available resources –for users and service devices-, service architecture, and network configuration.

On the other hand, in an Internet Scenario, the audience connects to the service using different networks and technologies. The owner of the network where service devices are installed does not control everything that happens in the service, so he would have difficulty in solving the problems that may arise while delivering the contents to final users.

To emulate these two scenarios, several network devices have been installed in the test environment shown in Figure 3. The installed equipment is broadly used in IP networks and allows service administrators to test radio services using different backbone and access technologies, where different routing protocols can be found. Almost every network device is from Cisco, mainly due to its position in the market and to the flexibility of its operating system *CISCO IOS*, which provides a broad range of communications techniques and standard protocols.

Two switches have been installed to give network access to every device in the test environment. These switches have 24 ports each and are interconnected using a *trunking* protocol, acting as one switch of 48 ports of 10/100 Mbps. Several *VLANs* can be created in these switches. Each *VLAN* has a set of ports assigned to the switches, so the devices plugged into those ports are working as if they were in different networks.

In order to interconnect the *VLANs*, several routers are available in the test environment. Furthermore, different models have been installed. Simpler routers can emulate small office connections, with firewall capabilities, QoS policies based in *WFQ* or *RSVP*, *NAT* and *PAT* translation, etc. Others are appropriate for larger companies or small network operators, supporting up to 70 heterogeneous network modules and up to 225 Kpps. All these routers have been equipped with different modules including *Fast Ethernet*, *ISDN*, *ATM* and serial communications.

The test environment also includes an *ATM* switch. This equipment simulates the behaviour of a network backbone that uses this technology. Several routers have been connected to this switch, emulating the connections that large enterprises contract to network operators under guaranteed bandwidth policies, connections between different network operators, or connections between network segments of the same operator.

An *ISDN* and *PSTN PBX* device has also been installed in the test environment. It allows routers to receive connections from users that access through *ISDN* or *PSTN* connections. Depending on the phone number provided by those users, the *PBX* redirects their calls to the proper router, simulating the behaviour of different *ISPs*.

A firewall has been installed in the system. In Figure 3 this firewall is restricting the access to the test environment from an external network. Nevertheless, if different networks are configured in the test environment, this firewall can be moved to apply restrictions in any of the existing connections. Furthermore, the chosen device can apply advanced firewall techniques working with *statefull filtering*. It is able to support 128,000 concurrent connections with a maximum throughput of 188 Mbps, and it can apply *NAT* and *PAT* conversions.

3.3   Content Access

The last phase in every test environment is that of content access. In some way, customers' accesses must be simulated in order to produce requests in the system. The proposed environment uses a workload generation tool, designed to request the available radio contents in the service.

This workload generation tool has been designed with three main goals: to simulate a high number of simultaneous accesses, to behave as real users do, and to work in a distributed fashion. With these goals in mind, the workload generator has been structured in three different modules: a coordinator module, a user module, and a player module. The structure of the generator is shown in Figure 4.

The coordinator module is in charge of generating a unique time line for a group of users involved in the emulation, and launching all the instances for those users. Several coordinator modules can be executed simultaneously, in order to control the workload process in different computers. Thanks to an initial interchange of control messages, the different coordinator modules are able to establish the reference start time of the emulation. After this initial coordination, these modules create one independent thread for each simulated user. Once the threads have been launched, the coordinators only have to wait until these threads reach their end. The number of users involved in the emulation, and the duration of the workload generation are the main parameters used in the configuration of coordinator modules.

The user module emulates the behaviour of a single user. Using a pseudorandom process generation mechanism configured with information obtained from real services, the user module decides when to make a request to the server, the length of the request, and finally, the number, length and start time of the pauses to be carried out. All these parameters are taken from an input *XML* file where service managers can adjust the behaviour of the users using information obtained from their actual services. If this information is not available, works like (Chesire, 2001) or (Veloso, 2002) propose interesting characterization profiles which can be utilized to fulfil this configuration task. In this *XML* file several statistical distributions are configured with their main parameters. The duration distribution sets the length of the requests, while

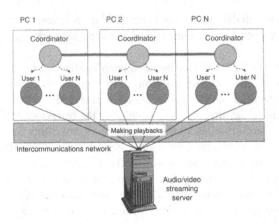

Fig. 4. Workload Generator Structure

the inter-request time distribution sets the time between requests generated by the same user. Interaction distributions permit the generation of pauses in certain points of the reproductions. Also, if several audio channels are available, the popularity distribution sets which channels are most suitable to be chosen by this user. Although other distributions can be used, the loader calculates popularity using a zipf-like distribution; managers only need to set the proper θ parameter in this configuration file.

Once the user module has calculated all the necessary values, it passes all this information to the player module. The player module is in charge of establishing the connections with the streaming server. It is triggered by the user module, and it connects to the streaming server, requests a resource, negotiates session parameters, and receives the audio stream sent by the server. This module is based on the *HelixDNA* (RealNetworks, n.d.). This technology is the result of the collaborative effort of RealNetworks, independent developers and other leading companies, and offers the first open multi-format platform for digital creation, media delivery and playback. The developed player module acts as if it were the player of a real user. It does the same operations, apart from the audio and video rendering, which are not relevant for this environment and can limit the number of concurrent users per computer that can be emulated. Once the player has received a data packet from the server, it collects the necessary information and throws the packet away.

As shown in Figure 4, one exact replica of the workload generator runs on each of the computers used in the tests.

3.4 Test Evaluation

Once the tests have been executed, it is time to analyze the obtained data and draw the proper conclusions. There are several data sources that can be used in order to extract detailed information of the executions.

Every service device has a log utility that can be used to retrieve information. Log files in multimedia services usually provide detailed information about users, resources, requests, and data packet transmission (RealNetworks, 2002). Users' information includes their identification –IP address and player ID– and their environment specification –e.g. type, release, language, and id of the player, type and version of the operating system, etc.–. Resource information includes the URI of the stream, CPU throughput, memory consumption, license utilization, etc. Requests information comprises start and end dates and times, protocol, the amount of delivered data –in seconds and bytes–, the average bitrate, interactions made by the user, etc. Data packet transmission information includes number of data packets, disordered and lost packets, early and late packets, resent packets, failed resends, etc. An analysis tool such as our *Fesoria* (Pañeda, 2003) can be installed in the environment in order to analyze the log files provided by the multimedia server or any other service device.

It is also possible to retrieve information from the network devices installed in the environment. In Figure 3 a machine called *NMS* or *Network Management Station* collects information from network devices thanks to the *SNMP* protocol. While the tests are running, this computer polls routers, switches and firewalls to obtain traffic statistics and performance information. It is possible to track network latency, packet loss, traffic, bandwidth, CPU loads, etc.

The workload generator also provides detailed information about the incidents that occurred during the executions. Its user module generates a trace file with relevant information. This trace file holds information about significant events that have happened during the playbacks, and final statistics of the reproductions. An example of trace file follows:

```
<trace id_user="0" delay="32">
  <playback num="0">
    <url time="1104915121">
       rtsp://192.168.100.3/radio.rm
    </url>
    <begin>1104915122</begin>
    <playing>1104915122</playing>
    <buffering>1104915122</buffering>
    <playing>1104915125</playing>
    <stop>1104915132</stop>
    <statistics>
       <normal>277</normal>
       <recovered>8</recovered>
       <received>285</received>
       <lost>0</lost>
       <late>0</late>
       <bw>225000</bw>
    </statistics>
    <end>1104915132</end>
  </playback>
</trace>
```

Trace files are *XML* documents, and include the types of events and the times when they occur. Taking into account that the end of a given event corresponds to the beginning of the following one, the duration of those events can also be known. E.g. when the buffering process ends, the playback process starts, and when the latter ends, the stop event happens. These files are easily readable and can be used by analysis tools in order to generate detailed reports of the emulations. These trace files can also be installed on a web server in order to publish the results and see them on-line. An *XSL* template has been designed to generate *SVG* graphs with the results of the simulations. Figure 5 shows an example, where packet statistics are exposed.

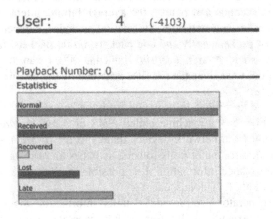

Fig. 5. *SVG* graph with packet statistics

Service managers can analyse the obtained results through these graphs in a more intuitive way.

4 Case Study

The digital news service **Asturies.Com** available from the domain www.asturies.com offers an Internet Radio service with considerable success. This service has been operating since April 2004 and offers a 24 hour channel of contents closely linked with Asturian culture: traditional and modern music, special programmes, news, jingles, etc.

By installing the Asturies.Com service in the test environment, we are able to estimate the maximum amount of users with a certain behaviour that can be supported by its current configuration and the increase in the number of users if configuration changes are applied to the service.

4.1 Service Description

The Asturies.Com radio service is based on the distribution of stored contents. This service has an architecture similar to that shown in Figure 2. Several files are stored daily in the main server. In this machine, both an *slta* module and a multimedia server have been installed. The *slta* generates a continuous stream of audio using the available files, and sends that stream to the multimedia server, in charge of distributing the contents among service users. The *Helix Universal Server* has been installed as multimedia server, and a license that allows up to 10 Mbps of transmission rate has been acquired. No intermediate devices have been installed.

The server machine has been installed in the network of the cable operator **Telecable**, under a *housing* contract. A service level agreement of 5 guaranteed Mbps has been established with this operator, in order to attend users' requests.

The utilized contents are coded using RealNetworks' *surestream* technology, which allows service manages to include several qualities in the same audio file. The responsibility of choosing the correct quality from the file is delegated to the multimedia server, which selects the most suitable depending on the quality of the connection with each client. Asturies.Com uses 11 kbps, 16 kbps and 20 kbps as reference qualities to produce the audio contents.

After almost one year of life, the service has registered thousands of users' accesses. During this period of time, we have been analyzing all these accesses, and have extracted several conclusions about the behaviour of the users of the service. Although the main goal of this paper is not to offer an extensive study on users' behaviour it is important for the case study to know certain details of this behaviour.

The Asturies.Com radio service presents the interesting characteristic that the length of the requests can be represented using an exponential distribution with parameter $\mu=1,470.15$ seconds. This feature is shown in Figure 6 and it will be used to configure the workload generator during the tests.

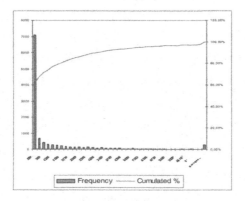

Fig. 6. Length of reproductions

4.2 Case Study Description

Given the Asturies.Com service description and its users' behaviour, we would like to know the maximum amount of users that could be supported by its current service configuration.

There are principally two limits in the current configuration that can influence the number of accepted users: the contracted bandwidth and the license of the *Helix* server. Depending on the number of users, more bandwidth can be requested from the network operator, and a higher license can be acquired in order to increase the server limit. Nevertheless, all these changes in the service are expensive and must be studied in detail. In order to know what changes should be carried out, it is important to estimate the number of users that will be supported by the service. An accurate estimation is essential to calculate the investment profitability.

The service configuration of Asturies.Com Radio has been deployed in the test environment, and the workload generator has been configured for six different workloads. Each workload simulates a different amount of users behaving as shown in Figure 6 during a period of one hour. These users can make successive requests depending on the inter-request time obtained from an exponential distribution with parameter $\mu=600$ seconds.

4.3 Results

The results obtained after running the tests are shown in Table 1 and the evolution in the bit-rate consumed in the server is shown in Figure 7.

Table 1. Maximum bit-rate values (Mbps)

Users	Max. Bitrate	Users	Max. Bitrate
100	1.71	500	8.37
200	3.18	600	9.75
300	4.87	700	11.4
400	6.62		

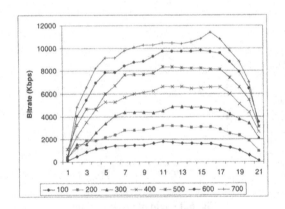

Fig. 7. Bit-rate evolution

With the current limit of 5 Mbps of contracted upload capacity, 300 users can be processed by the service. On the other hand, if more bandwidth is contracted and the current server license is kept, a maximum of 600 users can be accepted by the service.

During the tests no performance issues were detected in the main server, reaching a maximum value of 5 % of CPU load.

5 Conclusion

The configuration and deployment of an Internet radio is a complex process, due to the high resource consumption of these services, the difficulty of transmitting continuous information over a shared data network, and the heterogeneity of cases that can be found in users' access connections. Nowadays, the configuration of one of these services is mainly based on managers' experience. However, a test environment flexible enough to predict what will happen if changes are applied to actual services, is a powerful tool for these administrators.

The presented test environment allows administrators to emulate the behaviour of almost any real radio service: different network configurations can be tested, different service architectures can be used, it is possible to work with the quality of contents, etc. This test environment can help managers to attain a service of quality, increasing its performance and profitability, at the same time as customers' satisfaction.

6 Future Work

Now that a test environment has been designed, it is time to analyse the behaviour of service users. This analysis will permit the configuration of the workload generator in order to behave as users do.

Once the behaviour of users has been analyzed, several studies will be undertaken in order to estimate the impact of network configurations on multimedia services: transport and routing protocols, network address translations, proxies, firewalls, etc.

Acknowledgements

This research has been financed by the operator **Telecable de Asturias S.A.U.** and the newspaper **La Nueva España** within the *Media XXI II* project, and the **Spanish National Research Program** within *INTEGRAMEDIA* project (TSI2004-00979). This research has also received the cooperation of **Asturies.Com** and its Internet radio service.

References

Banerjee, S., et al.: Scalable Application Layer Multicast. In: Proceedings of ACM SIGCOMM 2002, ACM Press, New York (2002)

Bolot, J.: Characterizing End-to-End Packet Delay and Loss in the Internet. In: Proceedings of ACM SIGCOMM Conference 1993, ACM Press, New York (1993)

Chawathe, Y.: Scattercast: An Architecture for Internet Broadcast Distribution as an Infrastructure Service, Ph.D. Dissertation, UC at Berkley, U.S.A (2000)

Chesire, M., et al.: Measurement and Analysis of a Streaming-Media Workload. In: Proceedings of USITS'01 (2001)

Deshpande, H., et al.: Streaming Live Media over a Peer-To-Peer Network, Standford University, U.S.A (2001)

Dutta, A., et al.: MarconiNet - An Architecture for Internet Radio and TV Networks. In: Proceedings of NOSSDAV99 Conference (1999)

Dutta, A., et al.: Streaming Architecture for Next Generation Internet. In: Proceedings of ICC (2001)

Holbrook, M., et al.: IP Multicast Channels: EXPRESS support for large-scale single source applications. In: Proceedings of ACM SIGCOMM'99 Conference, ACM Press, New York (1999)

Melendi, D., et al.: Deployment of Live-Video Services Based on Streaming Technology over an HFC Network. In: Proceedings of ICETE 2004 Conference (2004)

Mena, A., et al.: An empirical study of real audio traffic. In: Proceedings of Infocom (2000)

Jian, W., et al.: Modeling of Packet Loss and Delay and Their Effect on Real-Time Multimedia Service Quality. In: Proceedings of NOSSDAV 2000 (2000)

Jonas, K., et al.: Get a KISS - Communication Infrastructure for Streaming Services in a Heterogeneous Environment. In: Proceedings of ACM Multimedia 98, ACM, New York (1998)

Padmanabhan, V.N., et al.: Distributing Streaming Media Content Using Cooperative Networking. In: Proceedings of ACM NOSSDAV 2002, ACM Press, New York (2002)

Pañeda, X.G., et al.: Analysis Tool for a Video-on-Demand Service based on Streaming Technology. In: Freire, M.M., Lorenz, P., Lee, M.M.-O. (eds.) HSNMC 2003. LNCS, vol. 2720, pp. 375–384. Springer, Heidelberg (2003)

RealNetworks, The Helix™ DNA Client. Retrieved from https://helixcommunity.org/2002/intro/client

RealNetworks, Helix Universal Server Administration Guide, RealNetworks, Inc. (2002)

Veloso, E., et al.: A Hierarchical Characterization of a Live Streaming Media Workload

Author Index